All Things Lincolnshire

good wishes

David Robinson

11.2.07

DAVID N ROBINSON OBE MSc

expertise is frequently sought by researchers. His support and encouragement for other researchers is appreciated by many, particularly his generosity with information and sources.

He moved to Louth in 1965 where he has worked tirelessly for the Louth 'Ants & Nats' and has served as their president since 1989. He has been the driving force behind the redevelopment of Louth Museum which was extended and refurbished in 2005. In addition to his academic achievements he has a lifelong commitment to the Methodist Church where he has served as a local preacher and on many committees including as a Council Member on 'Churches Together in Louth and District', a principle which is most important to him.

A great many people have been inspired by David's knowledge of, and enthusiasm for, Lincolnshire. This book is a festschrift in his honour to mark his 80th birthday in August 2007. The contributors to this book bring together a very wide range of subject matter from folklore to geology and from literature to archaeology. This is not a disparate selection, but an acknowledgement of the wide diversity of David's interests and expertise: most of all they represent his passion for *All Things Lincolnshire*.

David Norman Robinson OBE MSc was born in Croft Street, Horncastle in August 1927. He was educated at Queen Elizabeth's Grammar School and went on to graduate from Nottingham University with an honours degree in geography. He gained his MSc with a thesis on the coastal evolution of north-east Lincolnshire. David taught geography in schools in Immingham and Grimsby and, in 1965, became Tutor Organiser for the WEA in South Lindsey. Ten years later he joined the staff of the University of Nottingham and became resident tutor for North Lincolnshire.

He has become a household name in this county through writing and editing, notably for the county magazine, Lincolnshire Life. Others have met him through his long association with the Lincolnshire Wildlife Trust where he has served as Hon. Secretary since 1969. His wide interests and influence spread into heritage and history and his

All Things Lincolnshire

A collection of papers and tributes
to celebrate the 80th birthday of
David N Robinson OBE MSc

Edited by

Jean Howard and David Start

The Society for Lincolnshire History and Archaeology
2007

First published by the Society for Lincolnshire History and Archaeology 2007

ISBN 978 0 903582 27 8

British Library Cataloguing in Publication Data
A CIP catalogue record for this book is available from the British Library

Front Cover: The illustration on the front cover is a painting especially commissioned
from artist Tom Brooker. It shows a view from Scamblesby Top towards Lincoln Edge.

Designed by Susan Unsworth
Printed in the UK by J W Ruddock and Sons Ltd, Lincoln

Foreword

by Sir Patrick Cormack, FSA MP

I have known David Robinson for over fifty years. I first met him in the summer of 1955. He had just been appointed Head of Geography at the Havelock School in Grimsby. I was about to enter the sixth form, and contemplating Geography as one of my chosen subjects. In the event I opted for English, History and French but during that long summer holiday I came to know my potential Geography Master very well. He was completing an MSc on Coastal Evolution and this involved his going to the Lincolnshire coast every day and taking various measurements. He needed an assistant and I readily volunteered.

Morning after morning during what, in retrospect, was a summer of bright sunshine and cloudless skies, he would collect me in his motorbike and sidecar. We would go to such places as Somercotes or Saltfleetby or Donna Nook. We were out from early morning to early evening and worked at a fairly leisurely, though very organised, pace covering miles and eating what seemed like an endless supply of sandwiches washed down with ginger beer. Occasionally, another school friend would come and I would then forsake the comfort of the sidecar and ride pillion. It was a memorable summer and they were happy days.

Although I was never taught by him I saw a great deal of David Robinson over the next couple of years and I have kept in touch with him from time to time ever since. I became an avid reader of his contributions to the *Lincolnshire Poacher* and later, to *Lincolnshire Life*. I moved away from Grimsby in 1966, just after fighting the General Election that year and by June 1970 I was in the House of Commons.

Throughout, I have kept in touch with my native county, paying very frequent visits to my mother until she died in 2000, and reading *Lincolnshire Life* almost every month. A few years ago David asked me to be one of the Patrons of the Louth Museum Project and I spent a happy day in his company looking at plans and admiring the magnificent Louth Panorama, about which he wrote such a splendid book. I am more than aware, therefore, of the incalculable debt Lincolnshire owes to David Robinson – Geographer, Naturalist, Historian, upholder of so many good causes and repository of so much Lincolnshire wit, wisdom and folklore.

I was very honoured to be asked to write the foreword to this book, to be published for his eightieth birthday, as a tribute to his many contributions to Lincolnshire and a record of his encyclopaedic knowledge of, and interest in, all things pertaining to our county. That so many distinguished people have willingly contributed is a testament to the high regard, affection and esteem in which he is held and I am particularly glad to see that my parliamentary colleague, Lord Norton of Louth, has contributed such a fascinating piece on Lincolnshire Members of Parliament and glad too to see the fine article, by Julia Bruce, on Sir Joseph Banks, one of Lincolnshire's greatest sons. I know the book will be widely read and greatly enjoyed and I am sure, too, that it will serve to remind a younger generation of how wonderful our county is and how much it has depended through the centuries on men like David Robinson who have appreciated and recorded its beauties and its history and have striven to maintain and conserve them.

I am very glad too to see that the book includes a piece by Joyce. I remember her from all those years ago as the maker of excellent sandwiches and, the provider of the family pet. Our much-loved dog had just died when I met David for the first time and Joyce gave us one of her puppies.

Contents

List of Contributors

John Aram BEd FRGS has followed careers in civil engineering and further education and continues to tutor geology and environmental courses for the Open University. He runs a geological consultancy service, is a warden of the LWT reserve at Welton le Wold and is a member of the Lincolnshire RIGS committee.

Eleanor Bennett is a former Primary School teacher. A perpetual student of poetry, history, music, theology, natural history, and of Brackenborough, its land and people, past and present.

Clive Birch MBE FSA FRSA founded Barracuda Books in 1974 and currently publishes under the Baron imprint. He founded, chaired and was president of the Buckingham Heritage Trust. He is a visiting tutor at the Royal College of Art.

Anne Boyle BA PhD is medieval pottery specialist for Archaeological Project Services. She conducted research into Cistercian ware pottery for her thesis and is currently secretary of the Medieval Pottery Research Group.

Tom Brooker, a Louth born artist, has worked in Planning and Conservation. He lives and loves Lincolnshire Landscapes, the mood and atmosphere of which is reflected in his work.

Julia Bruce MSc FLS is a freelance writer and editor based in Oxford. David Robinson introduced her to Sir Joseph Banks back in 1975, and inspired a lifelong interest. She became the first Project Editor of the Banks Archive Project at the Natural History Museum in London.

Jean Burton is a local historian whose interest in Henry Winn goes back over 30 years. She has written a booklet, mounted an exhibition and lectured on Winn's life and works. More recently, she has initiated the establishment of the Sir Joseph Banks Study Centre in premises in Horncastle.

Ray Carroll BA FCILIP was County Librarian for Lincolnshire. He has published a bibliography of Lincolnshire maps (Lincoln Record Society, 1996), edits book reviews for the SLHA and has been active with the Tennyson Society for 27 years.

Peter Chapman was the first editor of Lincolnshire Life magazine. He has written several books concerning Lincolnshire and continues to write a weekly column in the Grimsby Telegraph.

Glyn Coppack BA PhD FSA is a senior Inspector of Ancient Monuments with English Heritage. He is an acknowledged specialist in monastic archaeology with particular interest in the Cistercians, the Carthusians and Lincolnshire.

Rodney Cousins, local historian and retired curator of the Museum of Lincolnshire Life. Author of *Lincolnshire Buildings in the Mud and Stud Tradition* (2000) and *'A Basketful' Willow growing and Basket making in Nottinghamshire and Lincolnshire* (2007).

Rex Critchlow Dip Arch RIBA graduated in Architecture at Sheffield and, together with his wife Jenifer, has been in practice in Lincolnshire since the 1960s. He is an active supporter of many county and national, heritage and arts organisations.

Stuart Crooks is the Director of the Lincolnshire Wildlife Trust. Originally from the London area, he spent four years with the Cheshire Wildlife Trust before moving to Lincolnshire in the late 1970s, becoming Director of the Trust in 1992.

Linda Crust BA was born in Goxhill, the daughter of a Methodist minister. She is well known as a writer of children's books, for her many features in Lincolnshire Life magazine and as the author of several books on historical aspects of Lincolnshire.

Brian Dawson is the county's leading collector and performer of Lincolnshire folk songs and a recognised expert on the song collector, Percy Grainger.

Roger Evans, who did his doctoral dissertation on Charles Turner of Grasby, pays regular visits to Lincolnshire where he is on the publications board of the Tennyson Society.

John Haden MA BPhil has twenty years experience as a secondary school Head. He now works as an independent adviser to schools and runs the American Roots In English Soil (ARIES) Project helping schools and communities to celebrate their heritage links with early English speaking North America.

Hilary Healey NDD MPhil FSA is an independent artist, archaeologist and local historian. She has a particular interest in medieval pottery, gravestones, vernacular building and all aspects of the Lincolnshire landscape.

Jean Howard spent ten years enjoying the views from the county's mobile libraries before training as a Blue Badge Guide for Lincolnshire. She is Hon. Curator of Louth Museum, a member of SLHA Local History Team and was a founder member of the Lincolnshire Heritage Open Days Steering Group.

Tom Lane FSA MIFA is the Senior Archaeologist at the Heritage Trust of Lincolnshire. He is a specialist in the archaeology of the Lincolnshire Fens in general and of the archaeology of saltmaking in particular.

Kevin Leahy BA PhD FSA MIFA has just retired after more than 28 years at the North Lincolnshire Museum in Scunthorpe. During this time he has carried out major excavations and been active both in community archaeology and as a pioneer in the recording of metal detector finds.

John Lill TD is a lifelong Ludensian, sometime farmer, soldier, thespian and natural historian with a love of and admiration for all that is good in the county and the people who live in it.

Frank W Marston NDD ATD MA is a Yorkshire born artist who has lived in Lincolnshire for the past 50 years. He has spent many years teaching art and as a therapist in psychiatric hospitals, helping all to develop and enjoy their full artistic potential.

Bill Meek and **Keith Parkinson** were both teachers at Havelock School, Grimsby, in the late 1950s and early 1960s in the Geography Department run by David Robinson. Bill and Keith were both honours graduates from Birmingham and Liverpool Universities respectively and, after leaving Havelock School, remained in secondary and higher education for the rest of their careers.

Dennis R Mills MA PhD is a specialist in the rural social structure of Victorian England and author of *Lord and Peasant in Nineteenth Century Britain* (1980).

Roger Norburn MA is a retired WEA tutor organiser. In 2004 he published *A James Joyce Chronology* (Palgrave) and has just completed a book on Katherine Mansfield.

Philip Norton PhD (Lord Norton of Louth) is Professor of Government at the University of Hull. He has written extensively on politics, government and parliaments.

P K Parkinson – See under Bill Meek.

Roger Parsons BSc MSc CBiol MIBiol is a zoologist and freelance consultant. He is a member of the Lincolnshire Naturalists' Union and has served on their Executive Committee. He edits a weekly email bulletin to support LNU biological recording in the county.

Valerie Purton MA (Cantab) PhD (University of East Anglia) is a Senior Lecturer in English at Anglia Ruskin University and the author (with Christopher Sturman) of *Poems by Two Brothers*: the Poetry of Tennyson's Father and Uncle (1993).

Ken Redmore worked successively as a teacher, lecturer and local education authority administrator before retirement. He is an active member of the SLHA and the British Brick Society. He has a wide interest in the buildings and machinery of Lincolnshire's industrial heritage.

Chris Robinson MA is technical specialist and part-time tutor at the Conservation Unit of the University of Lincoln. He owes his lifelong interest in history to his parents Joyce and David. The origins of his article date from his introduction, well over 40 years ago, to Gibraltar Point – a place he has visited regularly ever since.

Joyce Robinson BSc studied the same university geology course as David Robinson. Their combined interests, geography with geology (David) and zoology with geology (Joyce), have worked together very well; they have been married for over fifty years.

Ted Smith CBE is the President of Lincolnshire Wildlife Trust (since 2000) was Chairman of the Trust from 1969 and was its founding Hon. Secretary in 1948. He received an honorary doctorate from Hull University in 1998 and was awarded the CBE in 1999 for services to nature conservation.

Stewart Squires is a Chartered Town Planner and has worked as a conservation planner in many part of the county. He has written a number of books and articles about the industrial history of the county and is Chairman of the SLHA Industrial Archaeology Team.

David Start BSc MIFA FSA is the Director of the Heritage Trust of Lincolnshire and Vice Chairman of the Society for Lincolnshire History and Archaeology.

Judy Theobald, until recently editor of Lincolnshire Life magazine, worked with David for eight years, and has benefited greatly from his knowledge of the county.

Pearl Wheatley MBE BSc is a geographer who has followed her interest in archaeology for over 50 years. She has held numerous offices related to that interest in Lincolnshire and the East Midlands. She is presently Chairman of the SLHA and a Lincolnshire Blue Badge Tourist Guide.

Catherine Wilson OBE FSA FMA FRGS is a retired museum professional with a broad interest in and knowledge of the archaeology and history of Lincolnshire. She succeeded David Robinson as President of SLHA in 2005.

Peter Wilson MA ARPS is a retired Health Service professional who has had a second career as a wildlife photographer, author and tour guide. He has an extensive knowledge of Lincolnshire's natural history, with a particular interest in birds and bugs.

Kate Witney BEd (Hons) Cantab was born in Louth and studied at Homerton College, Cambridge and The Royal Northern College of Music, Manchester. She is Vocal Co-ordinator for Lincolnshire Music Service and, as a singer in both the folk and the classical fields, is a busy performer.

Jane Young is an independent medieval pottery specialist. She has worked extensively in the East Midlands, though her main area of expertise is Lincolnshire. Her work on the pottery of Lincoln culminated in a corpus, which was published in 2005.

Bibliography

There are possibly some students of Lincolnshire who have never visited David in his study. The first visit is awe-inspiring: the high ceilinged Edwardian room is lined floor to ceiling with bookshelves, almost every one full to capacity; a map chest occupies the bay window; an enormous map of Lincolnshire papers the far wall, and your host is seated at a large desk behind a low wall of filing trays. In response to your questions he propels himself by means of a wheeled chair between catalogue drawers and filing cabinets, occasionally reaching for a book. Your precious audience time is constantly interrupted by the phone bell as other researchers ring, assured that David will know the answer to their question, or, at least, where to find it. Infrequently a call will be for Joyce, that serene lady whose skills of friendship, hospitality and Lincolnshire botany underpin the powerhouse in the study; Joyce will take the call on 'the other phone' so that David will always have within reach the phone, the address book, pipe and tobacco.

The list of David's published work is impressive, but it belies the extent of his publishing endeavours. Because he has always been so helpful to others there are any number of Lincolnshire books, articles, theses and papers that may never have come to fruition without him. He has inspired, encouraged, cajoled and supported many other writers.

Most of the contributors to this volume, on being approached, immediately acknowledged their indebtedness to David's Lincolnshire knowledge from matters archaeological to zoological. Without David our county would be much less well recorded.

This bibliography lists David's main published works – it does not include a full listing of his articles in Lincolnshire Life nor his correspondence to journals and periodicals nor his reviews of other people's work. We have been assisted in this compilation by Roger Parsons, Dennis Mills and David Robinson and we gratefully acknowledge their input.

Published Books

The Book of Louth: The Story of a Market Town, Barracuda (Buckingham 1979 & 1981), 2nd impression, Baron Books (Buckingham, 1992).
A History of Methodism in Louth, (with W Leary) Louth Methodist Church (1981).
The Book of the Lincolnshire Seaside: The Story of the Coastline from the Humber to the Wash, Barracuda, (Buckingham, 1981) reprinted 1983 & 1989 & 4th edition Baron Books, (Buckingham, 2001) with additional chapter.
The Book of Horncastle and Woodhall Spa, Barracuda (Buckingham, 1983).
Lincolnshire Railways in Camera, Vol. 1, (with W B Herbert) Quotes (Buckingham, 1986).
Lincolnshire Railways in Camera, Vol. 2, Quotes (Buckingham, 1988).
Horncastle and its Inns, Taverns and Pubs in Camera, Quotes (Buckingham, 1988).
Lincolnshire Boats and Bridges in Camera, Quotes (Buckingham, 1989).
Skegness to Horncastle Walk in Camera, (with Len and Pat Blades) Quotes (Buckingham, 1989).
Lincolnshire Tramways in Camera, Quotes (Buckingham, 1991).
Beside the Seaside - Lincolnshire in Camera, Quotes (Buckingham, 1991).
Fowler of Louth, (with David Kaye and Sam Scorer), L N A L Soc., (Louth, 1992).
The Great Storm Flood of 1953, (illustrated by Ray Chapman), Mablethorpe Press (1993).
The Louth Flood - The Story of the Events of Saturday 29th May 1920, L N A L Soc. (Louth 1995 – reprinted 2000 with supplement).
Lincolnshire Wolds (Wish You Were Here), Quotes (Buckingham 1997).
The Kidgate Story, L N A L Soc., (Louth 1997).
Lincolnshire Bricks, History and Gazetteer, Heritage Lincolnshire (Sleaford, 1999).
William Brown and the Louth Panorama, (with C J Sturman) L N A L Soc., (Louth, 2001).
Willoughby, A Village with a Remarkable History, edited by David Robinson, W. Vill. Hist. Gp. (2003).

Papers on Geography, Geology and Geomorphology

1953 The Failure of the Coastal Defences of Lincolnshire Survey 3, 2, pp.37-44.
The Sea Defences of Lincolnshire, *Lincolnshire Poacher* 1, 4, pp.29-32.

1954 Beach Excavations at Ingoldmells Point Survey. 5, 1, pp.42-45.

1960 Sea Surge Brought Disaster to Lincolnshire Coast, *Grimsby Evening Telegraph* (29 January).

1961 Horncastle and the Bain Valley Floods (with F A Barnes), *East Midland Geographer* 2, 15, pp.52-55.

1965 Sites of Geological Interest in Lincolnshire, *Newsletter Lincs & South Humberside Trust for Nature Conservation* 2, 9, pp.6-10.

1966 Landscapes round Old Bolingbroke, *Bolingbroke Festival booklet.*

1967 *The Lymn Valley* (Tennyson Society leaflet).
Regional Economic Development in Lincolnshire and the Countryside (et al) Lincolnshire Branch CPRE.
An Exposure of the Red Chalk at Ings Farm, Belchford, *Trans Lincs Nats Union* XIV,4, pp.222-224.

1968 Describing the Weather in Lincolnshire Dialect, *Weather* XXIII, 2, pp.72-74.
'Soil Erision by Wind in Lincolnshire' in *East Midlands Geographer*, vol. 4, part 6, pp.351-362.

1969 The Rivers of Lincolnshire, *Newsletter Lincs & South Humberside Trust for Nature Conservation* 35, pp.6-9.

1970 'Coastal Evolution in North East Lincolnshire' in *Geographical Essays in Honour of K C Edwards*, edited by R H Osborne et al, Nottingham Univ Geog Dept, (1970) pp.62-70; also in *East Midlands Geographer*, vol. 5 1/2, pp.62-70.

1971 East Lincolnshire (pp.119-124) and South Humberside (pp.178-181), in *Field Excursions in the East Midlands* Ed J B Neilson (London).
Geology and Scenery of the Lincolnshire Wolds - Excursion Report, *Mercian Geologist* 4, 1, pp.63-68.

1972 Geology Report *Trans Lincs Nats Union* XVIII, 1, pp.6-7.

1974 Weather and Country Lore, *Journal Northampton Natural History Society & Field Club* XXXVIII, 257, pp.7-11.

1975 Pleistocene Deposits in Lincolnshire - Excursion Report, *Mercian Geologist* 5, 4, pp.337-339.
Geology and Scenery (pp.9-16) in *The Flora of Lincolnshire* - E J Gibbons (Lincoln).

1976 Geological Conservation (pp.117-119) in *The Geology of Lincolnshire*, 2nd ed - H H Swinnerton & P E Kent (Lincoln).

1977 Gibraltar Point Lincolnshire and the Northern Fen Edge - Excursion Report *Mercian Geologist* 6, 2, pp.133-135.
Geology Report, *Trans Lincs Nats Union* XVIII, 1, pp.6-7.

1979 Some Features of the Heath and Fen of South Lincolnshire - Excursion Report *Mercian Geologist* 7, 3, pp.235-238.
Wilsford Heath Quarry, *Newsletter Lincs & South Humberside Trust for Nature Conservation* 51, pp.20-21.

1981 Geology Report, *Trans Lincs Nats Union* XIX, 2, pp.56-57.

1982 Geology Report, *Trans Lincs Nats Union* XX, 3, p.102.

1983 Geology Report, *Trans Lincs Nats Union* XX, 4, pp.137-138.
Glebe Quarry, Colsterworth, *Trans Lincs Nats Union* XX, 4, pp.163-166.
Geology and Scenery of Lincolnshire (pp.22-25) in *The Butterflies and Larger Moths of Lincolnshire & South Humberside* - J H Duddington & R Johnson (Lincoln).

1984 'The Buried Forest of Lincolnshire' in *A Prospect of Lincolnshire*, edited by N Field and A White (Lincoln) pp.6-10.
The Saltfleet Theddlethorpe Coastline (Presidential address) *Trans Lincs Nats Union* XXI, 1, pp.1-12.

1987 The Wash: Geographical and Historical Perspectives (11pp) in *Research and Survey in Nature Conservation No 7: The Wash and its Environment*, Nature Conservancy Council.

1988 Geology Report, *Trans Lincs Nats Union* XXII, 1, pp.40-41.
Geology and Scenery Traverse of North Lincolnshire (South Humberside) - Excursion Report *Mercian Geologist* 11, 3, pp.195-198.

1989   'Geology and Building Materials' (with Terence Miller) in *The Buildings of England: Lincolnshire* edited by N Pevsner and J Harris, Penguin (1989 - 2nd edn revised by N Antram).
'The Changing Coastline' in *Twentieth Century Lincolnshire*, edited by D R Mills, History of Lincolnshire Committee Vol XII (Lincoln, 1989) Ch 7, 26pp.

1990   The Shifting Shoreline (8pp) in *Sea and Tidal Defences - Canute v Neptune* National Rivers Authority.

1991   RIGS for Rocks *Natural World* 31, p.7.

1992   Geological Conservation, *Conservation Management* 14, pp.9-12 (Lincolnshire Trust for Nature Conservation).

1993   Sea Defences and Nature Conservation, *Lapwings* 80, pp.10-11.
Every Rock Tells a Story, *Natural World* 39, pp.16-18.

1995   Beach Nourishment, *Conservation Management* 17, pp.9-13.

1996   'The Lincolnshire Coast in 1860' in *Lincolnshire Past and Present,* No.24, pp.17-19.

1998   Beach Nourishment, *Lapwings* 95, p.13.

1999   Beach Nourishment and Gibraltar Point, *Gibraltar Point NNR Wildlife Report 1998*, pp.85-87.

2000   Geomorphology of the Lincolnshire Wolds: an excursion guide, *Mercian Geologist* 15, 1, pp.41-48.

2001   Climate Change, *Lapwings* 105, pp.4-5.

2003   50 Years On (from 1953 Storm Surge), *Lapwings* 110, p.23.
The Lincolnshire Wolds, *Lapwings* 112, p.11.

2004   Blow Wells of North-East Lincolnshire, *Lapwings* 115, pp.12-13.

2005   Canute v Neptune, *Lapwings* 119, pp.4-5.

Other Articles And Papers

1956   *The North East Coast of Lincolnshire: A Study in Coastal Evolution*, unpub MSc thesis (Univ of Nottingham).

1961   'Poachings' in *Lincolnshire Life*, Country Life Ltd, (Lincoln 1961 to date).

1966   *Report on Humberston Fitties*, Lincs Branch of CPRE.

1981   *Double Century: Eve and Ranshaw Ltd 1781-1981*, (Louth).

1993   'Natural Regions' pp.8-9, 'Drainage and Reclamation' pp.72-73, 'Brick and Tile Making' pp.116-117, 'Seaside Resorts and Spas' pp.122-123, in *An Historical Atlas of Lincolnshire*, edited by Stewart Bennett and Nicholas Bennett, Univ of Hull Press, reprinted Phillimore & Co, (Chichester, 2001).

1994   The Battle of Winceby, in *Lincolnshire Past and Present* No. 15.
Thunderstorm in Horncastle and Neighbourhood, in *Lincolnshire Past and Present* No. 16, pp.26-27.

1996   'Eastgate Revolutionised', in *Lincolnshire Past and Present* No. 26.

1996   Sir Joseph Banks and the East Fen in *People and Places: Essays in Memory of Terence Leach (1937-1994)* edited by C Sturman, Soc for Lincs Hist and Archaeol (Lincoln), pp.97-105.

1998   *Double Century: The Story of William Crowder & Sons, Nurserymen*, (Horncastle).

2001   Bartholomew Howlett and his Views: An introductory essay to the reprinted edition, in, *Bartholomew Howlett, A Selection of Views in the County of Lincoln*, reprinted edition, Heritage Lincolnshire (Sleaford).

2001   'The Changing Landscape' in *Twentieth Century – What Heritage?* edited by P Judson and C Lester, Heritage Lincolnshire (Sleaford) pp.6-12.

2005   'Putting into Port' in *Lincolnshire on the Move* edited by J. Howard and C. Lester, Soc for Lincs Hist and Archaeol (Lincoln) pp.31-41.

passim *The Poacher: An Annual Companion to 'Lincolnshire Life'*. Country Life Ltd, Lincoln.

Journals and Magazines edited

1952-1953   *Survey* (University of Nottingham scientific magazine)

1954-1955   *The Lincolnshire Poacher*

1966-1976   *Transactions Lincolnshire Naturalists' Union*

1967-1971   *Signpost* (Louth Methodist Circuit magazine)

1971-1976   *Focus* (Louth Council of Churches newspaper)

1970-   *Lapwings* (Lincolnshire Wildlife Trust)

1976-1989   *Lincolnshire Life*

1988-1989   *Bulletin of Local History: East Midland Region*

1995-2003   *The Poacher/Lincolnshire Poacher*

Editors' Notes and Acknowledgements

Neither of the editors can claim the credit for conceiving the idea of a festschrift for David: that goes to Roger Norburn who had contacted only a handful of people when he realised his commitments exceeded his time available. Being one of the handful and recognising the worth of the concept I was anxious to pursue it. However, aware that my enthusiasm can exceed my ability I knew I must find a co-editor whose expertise would save me from failure. I had no doubt that should be Dave Start and was relieved when he immediately consented. He above everyone deserves my thanks, and for the impact that this has had on his 'holidays' I apologise not only to him but also to his family. I offer grateful thanks to the Society for Lincolnshire History and Archaeology for agreeing to publish a book in honour of their former president. My only regret has been to see the frustration of the 'Birthday Boy' at not knowing quite what was going on, and being unable to take control of it!

Jean Howard

This volume contains a great many photographs and drawings to illustrate its very wide range of subjects. Most authors who have provided illustrations have acknowledged their sources, either within the illustration caption or in an 'Acknowledgement' at the end of their article. Illustrations not thus acknowledged are presumed to be the property of the author. However, some specific comments are relevant: the illustrations that accompany Eleanor Bennett's poem (The Land) are by kind permission of Josephine Pearse, Ken Jones and the Lincolnshire Film Archive. Some photographs supplied by authors have found their way into slightly different applications than those perhaps intended and I am grateful to those contributors. Absent and/or inadequate photographs and drawings have been speedily and ingeniously furnished by Jean Howard and David Hopkins respectively and Hilary Healey supplied the drawings which appear at the end of the articles. I must thank Patrick Cormack for his 'Foreword' which was delivered on time despite an absurdly tight deadline. Thanks also to Susan Unsworth at Heritage Lincolnshire for the typesetting and design, to Steve Adamson for the musical typesetting (a 'first' for me!), to Kate Mitchell for assistance with the indexing and to Rodney Callow and the team at SLHA/Jews' Court who have handled the sponsorship administration. Most of all my thanks to our authors who have created a volume which I am sure David will be proud of, and which we hope will take its place among the significant publications about Lincolnshire.

David Start

REFLECTIONS

The Land 2007

Eleanor Bennett

'For now the year draws on towards its ending...
The steepled ricks with frost are hoar
In silent yard.' Thus Vita Sackville-West.
Indeed it is not so. The times are changed.
Where once the binder swished its gentle way,
And stooks stood graciously in golden fields,
That monstrous brute, the combine harvester,
Advances, seeing all before it fall,
And loaded corn-cart trundles to the yard.
No more we picnic in the half-reaped field,
Sitting on piles of straw or bench of bales.
Those giant rolls of straw in plastic coats
Seem to have strayed from factory to farm,
No human needed in the countryside?
The 'steepled ricks' have given way to space.
The empty yard is car-park, tractor-way.
No gentle breezes dry the harvest yield.
The farmyard, silent once, is quiet no more.
Tall metal corn-bins hum through night and day.
A button pressed, cascades of shimmering grain
Pile up in lorries, ready for the road.
No autumn rest now. Still the work goes on,
And drilling starts as soon as harvest's in.
The landscape, golden once, is richly brown,
Smoothed over, waiting for the winter frosts.
And yet, however man and methods change,
The seasons still hold sway. Man is not master.
The weather rules. Come snow, wind, rain,
Sun, drought, despair, still germinates
The dormant seed. Green shoots appear,
And the whole cycle, faithful as before,
Matures to autumn, and the harvest comes.

A Man for all Reasons

Clive Birch

'The pursuit of perfection, then, is the pursuit of sweetness and light…He who works for sweetness and light united, works to make reason and the will of God prevail.'
(*Literature and Dogma,* 1883, Matthew Arnold)

You know when you walk in the room. Here is someone you'll like, someone you can trust, and to whom you can relate. As soon as I clapped eyes on Robinson, I knew. Whenever we met - whenever we meet - it's always the same. There isn't enough time for all we want to say, not enough windows through which we can fly, to create opportunities, arrest stupidities, plan books and change the world. As David would say, 'we'll give it the treatment'.

It was 1978 and I'd started a new genre in local studies – town books, founded in academe, in popular prose

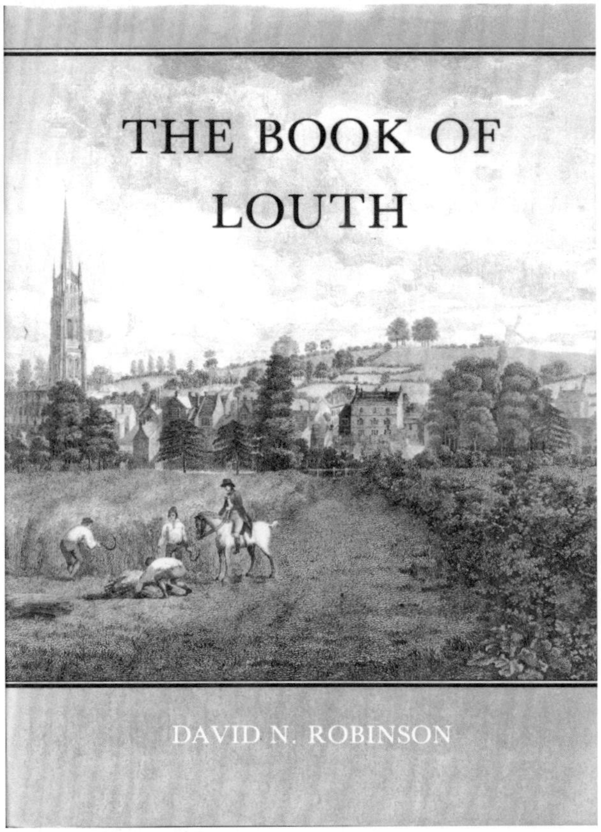

Fig. 1: The Book of Louth was the first of the Lincolnshire town books, published in 1979 – now in its third edition

with a wide-angle approach to illustration. I looked at Lincolnshire and I wanted *The Book of Louth*. I wrote to the local paper and the library and they told me about David, so I went to call at 160 Eastgate. He loved the idea.

I do not know how many hours we spent together, but it set the pattern. He showed me Louth, for David has a passion for the place and knows it like no other. And then he introduced me to the mysteries of 'Robinsonia' – drawer upon drawer of postcards, shelf upon shelf of books, tray upon tray of maps. Outside my own home, I have never seen anything like it, and his Lincolnshire collection far exceeds mine on Buckinghamshire. It climbed the stairs, it served as stools on landings, it enclosed the bedroom where I sometimes slept. It still does.

For David, make no mistake, is a collector. When John Bourne died and his Louth Manor House was on the market in 1981, David called me. Auction time! Together we roamed the rooms and passages, and I still have the stagecoach print we bought together, but more significantly, the Staffordshire Wesley I secured reminds me of David's practical, no-nonsense Christianity. Wesley stands guard and guardian to this day as you enter my home: Robinson's messenger.

In all our years of writing, planning, designing, publishing, making museums and promoting conservation, not once has David imposed his faith on me, yet it undoubtedly informs his life. And, of course, at The Manor House, it was David who spotted the coal-store, found the collection of glass plates, and brought them back into the fold. But then, he would, wouldn't he?

He has this encyclopaedic memory for who and what and where, and a dedication to discovery and communication. Now the Museum is up and running again, those glass plates will emerge from the garage, or wherever else he has them stored, and find themselves back on record with the Ants and Nats.

We published David's *Louth,* and *Horncastle,* and *Lincolnshire Seaside,* and many more besides, and how they illuminate our world, for David is a historian who understands the geography of the past, and finds the right words to blend the two: 'Bright is the ring of words, When the right man rings them'(R L Stevenson). Then one day

Fig. 2: This Staffordshire Wesley group from the Manor House, Louth, now guardian to my home, reminds me of David's no-nonsense Christianity

naturalist Rennie Bere, who helped Dudley Stamp's son record 'our' Bude, introduced the famous Blameys. They envisaged a paperback on Cornwall's wildlife. I consulted David. We decided on a new approach - by habitat, with maps, photographs and drawings, separate fauna and flora listings – and we persuaded the Prince of Wales to give it his forewordly imprimatur. Thus the comprehensive, Audubonesque hardback *Nature of Cornwall*.

The upshot of that in turn was The Nature of Britain series, which we fashioned together, but which I could never have attempted without David's knowledge and insights and contacts, and which won us a European Conservation Foundation award. As he would say, 'we gave it the treatment'.

David asked me to join the RSNC, and then him, on its education committee, and we served together – I learnt to change my views and, while he did not ask me to change my shooting habits, he gave me a new insight into the wildlife all around me and, with Shakespeare, 'to hold, as 'twere, the mirror up to nature'. David wanted me to join *Natural World's* board, but the publisher, a man I once appointed as my successor at *Illustrated London News,* would have none of it, so I simply sat on the sidelines instead.

Journeys to David established a pattern. I would drive to Louth – three hours plus, take lunch, make visits, meet people, and then we would settle down in the study. Whether it was *Lincolnshire Life* or David's latest book, a project with Kaye or Ekberg or Honeybone or Rogers, *Natural World*, the latest wildlife volume, the Ants and Nats, or our respective Museum plans, we would fire up, build up, exchange, spark idea after idea after idea.

That is how it has always been. We have an idea, we start to think, express our thoughts and inevitably, we move each other faster and faster down a thoroughfare of shared objectives and shared means. We out-think each other. Like minds? Sometimes I think we've one mind in two men, though his is by far the better trained, and the more knowledgeable.

We are both dedicated to discovery, the accurate record, the right words. We share an ability to visualise, often stumbling over one another as we unfold a panorama of text and type and map and illustration. We share an understanding of what can and cannot be done in print and on the page and, dare I say it, we have ever lacked patience with shoddy work, the unaffordable and the impractical, despairing of those who simply don't do their homework, or know their onions, and especially, those not prepared to learn.

Perhaps there is a certain arrogance in that, for which I take sole responsibility, for we did not suffer fools gladly in our private counsels. I cannot number the times we sat and looked at one another and David peered over his specs and pronounced sentence – with that favourite epithet – the accused was clearly 'daft', with a short 'a'. And then, we would 'find a solution', and back in the mouth would go the ubiquitous pipe. We coined a name for those unfortunates – The Bogles of Dingle Dell.

Usually nearing midnight, we would realise the time, and I would start the drive back home. When we had Board meetings, it happened in reverse; David would drive to Radclive, and then make the long, late haul home again. As we get older, one of our few gestures to advancing

Fig. 3: David signing Lincolnshire Seaside – 'a bracing experience' – on publication day at the Lincolnshire Wildlife Trust's coastal sanctuary in 1981.
(4th edition 2001)

Fig. 4: Presenting The Book of Horncastle and Woodhall Spa on publication, 1983

years is to drive to Stamford from time to time, to break bread and chew the fat. Halving the journey doesn't halve the pleasure.

For David became more than an author. He joined my Board, and together we drove 49 books to 750+. We remained partners in publishing until my so-called retirement which, like David's, was more in name than nature. Looking back on some thirty years of collective effort, I think we might both agree with Carlyle that 'The true University of these days is a collection of books'.

When I added a second publishing house, David helped, and contributed ideas, books and authors. After my faux retirement, David's *Lincolnshire Seaside* was an early reprint. Throughout, we have always sought perfection, and striven for 'as good a quality product as we can possibly do', though we know that there is no such thing as a perfect book.

In Buckingham in 1984, I formed a charitable trust, acquired a landmark building, and created a museum and information centre. From the beginning, I turned to David for advice and ideas, for he was my university. When David in turn sought funding for Louth's museum, I shared my experience with him. Not that he needed it. His network, knowledge and nous ensured success.

Whatever his books, magazine, church, museum, RSNC, Ants and Nats, wildlife trust, county arch and hist, or day job, David's overarching priority was always quite clear – home, wife and family. For Carolyn and I, Joyce's kindness and forbearance speak volumes for their enduring life together, and I doubt he and I would have made so many books, or with such satisfaction, had it not been for Joyce's benign presence, often just beyond that study door, or in their delicious garden of so many different delights.

Joyce infused renewed vigour into our deliberations with her caring ministrations and her occasional reminders that there was in fact another world out there, occasionally needing David's attention, and that I too had a wife, who might like me back home sometime soon!

Highlights? Ekberg's 1985 book about the Grimsby fishing industry. Charlie was a 'journo' of the old school – he gathered the facts, he knew the folk, and he spilt it all out quickly. But a book – that was different, for Charlie had accumulated a lot of material and it was like its subject – flipping and flapping about all over the place. David and I had several major sessions fighting it, and then David took control. He was a surgeon, slicing, suturing, selecting,

Fig. 5: David's presentation of Lincolnshire Methodism by William Leary to the President of the Methodist Conference, May 1988: 'another one for the record, and one with which I was particularly pleased to be associated'

sewing, stapling until we had a splendid specimen. In David's words 'Seven days and two bottles of Tippex later', we had a publishable text for *Grimsby Fish*.

Lincolnshire Seaside – that was a tour de force fashioned from David's original vision and material until he had created a model of its kind, and a book which I believe will endure.

The Book of Horncastle and Woodhall Spa gave David the chance to put his home town on record, and this was arguably the only time we faced a fleeting difference – David wanted a lot more space than usual, and space costs money. Oddly, it was I who suggested the book, yet David who 'didn't know how much material I had accumulated'. This is the only time I recall David admitting that!

And of course, *The Book of Louth*: without doubt, it is a classic. It is not only one of the best Town Books we produced in an oeuvre of some 500, it comprises

and compresses Louth's life comprehensively and with consummate skill and great affection. It was the 48th in our series and the first in Lincolnshire. Maybe one day soon, we'll produce the fourth edition. I hope and believe it will continue and flourish in many more.

And that is what I hope for David, that he will continue and flourish far beyond his four score years, because he deserves much longer to do all those things yet to be done, and Louth and Lincolnshire and all his family and friends deserve much more of his practical passion and informed achievement. May he, with Lamb, proclaim: 'Damn the age: I will write for Antiquity!'.

David is now the doyen of Lincolnshire and Louth academe, O-rganiser of B-est E-ffects, M-aster of Sc-enarios, a man for all reasons and one I am proud to call friend.

Write Tight – David Does!

Peter Chapman

The alliance of scholarship and popular journalism is vexed. First, it requires a determination not to write down to the audience. Second, the message must not be allowed to suffer. It is an art … and it requires a basic belief that the popular press is the vehicle for ideas and campaigns, good stories and awareness to be relayed to the unenlightened.

It was when I returned to Lincolnshire in 1968 that I first met David Robinson. Roy Faiers, the then proprietor of *Lincolnshire Life* had asked me - at the suggestion of Colin Carr the celebrated Grimsby artist and illustrator - to edit the magazine. One of its principal ingredients was a column called 'Poachings', contributed monthly by David, and which continues to this day. The column was serious but never tedious - academic but never boring. Its tone was exactly correct for straightforward people who wished to know. David's pitch was sure.

The years went by and I left Lincolnshire Life - but David's contributions didn't. Soon, I found myself reviewing his several books and they too disguised his obvious mastery of his subjects. In particular, his book on the county's seaboard - *The Lincolnshire Seaside* - by adept choice of word and phrase (which had, if I may say so, the common touch) translated the arcane into the clearly understandable in very readable prose.

I knew, of course, that David was a lecturer and tutor and a man in close contact with 'the people', but it was his lack of condescension which appealed to me. The book he wrote in 2001, concerning William Brown and the Louth Panorama, was breathtaking for its extravagance, panache and production. Never had a local subject had such munificent treatment – or been so readable.

David Robinson never patronises. He conveys his considerable knowledge to whomsoever has the pleasure of reading it, leaving them amused, absorbed and better informed. Over many years he has always been ready and willing to help me in my quests for specific answers or general information and I am most grateful to him.

His life in journalism is a lesson to us all. David would not wish me to labour the point or over-egg the pudding - he never does!

Lincolnshire Humour

John Lill

Lincolnshire: The county is 'one of the most brute and beastley of the whole realm'

Henry VIII

Humour: The mental faculty of discovering, expressing, or appreciating ludicrous or absurdly incongruous elements in ideas, situations, happenings or acts; droll imagination or its expression: distinguished from wit as less purely intellectual and having more kindly sympathy with human nature and is often blended with pathos: that quality in a happening, an action, a situation or an expression of ideas which appeals to a sense of the ludicrous or absurdly incongruous.

Webster's New International Dictionary

Having recorded the words of Henry VIII and having defined the true meaning of humour - or 'humor' as our North American cousins would have it, we can now proceed.

One can understand Henry's total dislike of the county when one thinks of all the trouble we caused him. To present him with the Pilgrimage of Grace on top of all his matrimonial problems was bound to cause a spontaneous hostile reaction. No wonder heads had to roll. But enough of history - we are here to look at humour.

And this of course is where our problems begin.

Lincolnshire is a very big place. Edward Campion claims four main dialect areas in the county while my friend Alan Stennett in his book – *Nobbut A Yellerbelly* – claims six. As yellerbelly humour is closely intertwined with our dialect and that dialect varies across the county, it is quite possible that what causes a wry smile in Barton on Humber may produce a belly laugh with tears rolling down the cheeks in Sutton Bridge.

There is possibly a PhD in this somewhere, but unfortunately I think the time to research this has virtually gone.

Where has our dialect gone and our own brand of homespun humour to go with it?

Fifty years ago we could have got on our bikes and cycled gently over to Owmby by Spital, Muckton or even Whaplode, calling at the local hostelries on the way and for the price of a couple of pints wallowed in the banter and cross talk of true experts speaking the dialect and dispensing true Lincolnshire humour. This is no longer so. Other areas of potential research have also ceased to exist: the local cattle market, the Corn Exchange full of farmers swapping news and views on stock, grain, feed and the price of 'artificial' while their wives traipsed round the town stocking up with enough food and sundries to see them through until they came into town again next week.

Who and what can we claim caused this demise? How did all this come about? What has caused the demise of our dialect and our humour? I blame the wet battery accumulator!!

In the 1930s and 1940s when many country areas still had no electricity we sat in the farm kitchen of a night in front of the old black range, the room lit with the paraffin lamp, listening to 'In Town Tonight', Radio Luxemburg, 'Dick Barton - Special Agent', not forgetting 'ITMA'. That is until the battery ran out and someone was despatched on their bike down to the local garage to swap the flat battery for one on charge.

This was the beginning of the insidious brainwashing over the next 60 years by dint of many and varied electronic communicative devices which have standardised both the way we speak and the way we think. Our speech and our sense of humour now conform to standard middle English patterns while those things which once we held so dear have all but vanished, and probably more so in a wide ranging agricultural county like Lincolnshire.

Large centres of population where people are in constant contact both at work and play find no difficulty in maintaining their own individual pattern and rhythm of speech. Not so in the smaller, more isolated villages in a county like ours which by nature, prompts the old adage 'there's a lot of it out of doors' - a county which is the fourth least populated in the United Kingdom.

With no large towns or cities, we have, for instance, no Music Halls to produce and promote Lincolnshire comedians. In this changing world Cockneys, Scouses, Yorkies, Taffs, Jocks and West Country 'O Aahs' proliferate each with their own brand of humour and regional turns of speech. Not so Lincolnshire, but at least we can say nobody ever laughs at us! At least not very often!

But this does not mean that we have no sense of humour, far from it! We can laugh as long and as loud as the rest of them, but we do it in our own way. If you analyse our pre-media humour it has one very special quality: it has an underlying gentleness and finds fun in the everyday happenings of what at that time was a predominantly rural, agricultural existence.

Webster identifies this in his definition of humour, or humor as the case may be.

> *'Droll imagination or its expression: distinguished from wit as less purely, intellectual and having more kindly sympathy with human nature and is often blended with pathos'.*

Not for us the bitter, snide, hurtful humour, the demeaning and disparaging humour with the need to get our laughs at someone else's expense whatever the cost. True 'yellerbelly humour' is of a much softer and gentler nature, laughing at ourselves and our own faults and idiosyncrasies. Going back to my childhood days of the 1930s and 1940s, humour also expressed itself not only in words but also in a practical way. Here again not the hard, disruptive, wanton damage of today. We probably annoyed a few people, particularly if they had annoyed us, but it was all done with a sense of fun and seldom, if ever, to 'score one back' or to do wilful damage or harm.

The original true Lincolnshire Humour is basically centred around the village and went on in that environment of farming, the village pub, W I, church and chapel (the vicar was often fair game) and the situations and happenings in the local area. This is not to say that the humour was simple or even childlike. It could be and was extremely funny, and on occasion had an underlying thread of logic or wisdom. This is beautifully illustrated in Tennyson's poem 'The Northern Farmer (New Style)' where the father is explaining love and marriage to his 20 year old son who is in love with the impoverished parson's beautiful daughter.

V

Do'ant be stunt: taäke time: I knaws what maäkes tha
    sa mad.
Warn't I craäzed fur the lasses mysén when I wur a
    lad?
But I knaw'd a Quaäker feller as often 'as towd ma
    this:

'Doänt thou marry for munny, but goä wheer munny
    is!'

VI

An' I went wheer munny war: an' thy muther coom
    to 'and,
Wi' lots o' munny laaïd by, an' a nicetish bit o' land.
Maäybe she warn't a beauty :- I niver giv it a thowt -
But warn't she as good to cuddle an' kiss as a lass as
    'ant nowt?

Another time, another place – where would you go today to find logic for the lovelorn so concisely dispensed, and this I think is the problem. All traces of our dialect are finally being eroded away under a scathing mass of media speak. The younger generation have no place for it, it is not 'cool' or 'wicked'. They have their own 'clan' speak.

They have no knowledge or use for:

Dumplin' Dust	flour
Battle Twigs	earwigs
Gawming	staring about
Kelter	rubbish
Pot-noddles	tadpoles (not a snack)
Artificial	manufactured fertiliser

There are now few true exponents of the Lincolnshire dialect and when they have gone, they will not be replaced. Some of us try to imitate them, but it does not have that genuine authenticity of the style and humour of the real thing. The only record of its existence will be in the written word and unfortunately there is very little of that although what there is, is very good.

If our dialect is very nearly gone, what future is there for our humour? Here I think the news is considerably better. Geographically we are still somewhat isolated from the rest of the country. What a blessing the M11 Motorway was never built from Cambridge to the Humber Bridge. This partial isolation has allowed us to retain a number of those qualities passed on to us by our predecessors, a sense of humour being one of them. We are not raving extroverts or avidly outgoing. When 'foreigners' meet us for the first time, they may find us slightly reserved but this reservation soon gives way in normal circumstances and a long conversation can and very often will ensue.

I suppose you could argue that the transition from local to national humour is now just about complete. We laugh at the same things as the rest of the country – 'Dad's Army', 'The Two Ronnies' and 'The Vicar of Dibley', but we can still laugh at ourselves and each other in that gentle way inherited from our ancestors.

We are Lincolnshire people but we don't shout it from the housetops, we don't make a great song and dance about it and we don't want to attract a lot of attention to ourselves, but when you get to know us you will find that we do enjoy life and have a good time and I promise you, you'll find plenty to laugh about.

LATE ARRIVALS AT THE LINCOLNSHIRE STUFF BALL

Mr & Mrs Thorpe and their daughter Mabel

Mr & Mrs Fleet and their son Wayne

Mr & Mrs Nook and their daughter Donna

Mr & Mrs Kington and their son Rus

Mr & Mrs Con and their daughter Lyn

Mr & Mrs Ingham and their son Will

Mr & Mrs Terton and their daughter Wyn

Mr & Mrs Vendale and their son Ray

Mr Toft and his Brother

Mr & Mrs Ingsby and their daughter Con

Mr & Mrs Enderby and their daughter Mavis

Mr & Mrs Berland and their son Tim

Mr & Mrs Norton with the Bishop

Mr & Mrs Worth and young Benny

Mr & Mrs Willingham and their daughter Cherry

Mr & Mrs Hill and their daughters Amber and Penny

Mr & Mrs Ford and their son Al and their landlord Rigsby

Mr & Mrs Holbeach with their saintly sons John, Mark and Matthew

Likewise the Suttons with Edmund and James

Brian Ansell and the Ceres Carving at Louth Museum

Frank Marston

I have known David Robinson for about fifty years, first as a colleague in the teaching profession and then as a very dear friend.

There is no doubt in my mind that David is a 'Renaissance Man' when both the depth and breadth of his interests and knowledge are considered. He is also a man of letters as well as a man of science with many years of involvement in the production of the 'Lincolnshire Life' county magazine behind him and numerous books on many aspects of Lincolnshire life and history.

One project very dear to his heart, I am sure, was the refurbishment and development of the Louth Museum

Fig. 1: Brian Ansell at work in his workshop at Riby

which still continues. His enthusiastic pursuit in acquiring some of the works of Peter DeWint for the museum illustrates his keen interest in the visual arts. On the exterior of the museum is a superb carving of the goddess Ceres, the goddess of the harvest, which is a replica of the statue originally adorning the old Louth Corn Exchange which has now disappeared. The goddess Ceres was an obvious choice for a Corn Exchange particularly in a county renowned for its arable farming.

The craftsman chosen to carry out the carving of the goddess was Brian Ansell who I have known both as a friend and mentor for about ten years.

Brian Ansell is a Suffolk man and now lives in his home town of Bury St Edmunds. Leaving school in 1966 he first became a trainee joiner but in 1969 entered into an apprenticeship in General Masonry with A H Hanchet. From 1973 he entered the workshop of I S M Masonry where he developed his skills in ornamental masonry. Between 1977 and 1983 Brian worked for H L Perfitt on monumental masonry. For the next four years he was with J C Welham and Son, now specialising in architectural and monumental masonry. During this time Brian was gaining experience in the art of carving and was involved in numerous projects in the Suffolk area.

In 1987 he returned to the workshop of H L Perfitt for a year before finally arriving in Lincolnshire to work for the Dean and Chapter of Lincoln Cathedral. Brian's years of hard work and training were now to pay off as he began working in the Masons' Yard close by the Cathedral in Eastgate. He was, however, a man of so diverse talents that he initially spent some time working in the quarry where stone is extracted for restoration of the Cathedral. This is the self-same quarry from which the medieval masons took stone to build the original cathedral. Taken from here is a beautiful limestone which exists in several layers showing somewhat different colours and exhibiting different characteristics for carving. The Cathedral Authorities had acquired a new stone cutting machine and Brian was for a time the only one who was familiar with its use.

During the four years he was at Lincoln Cathedral Brian produced some outstanding pieces of carving in various parts of the building. His work can now be seen, apart from here and there on the building, on the West Front

Fig. 2: Piece carved by Brian Ansell for York Minster west front restoration

and on the pinnacle at the south east of the Chapter House. Those still there who remember him are full of praise for the quality of Brian Ansell's work.

After a short period of less than a year in Ivett & Reed's workshop in general masonry, Brian entered the Masons' Yard of York Minster on 28 September 1992. Here he was very much involved in restoration work for the Minster. His colleagues told me how much he was admired as a craftsman and that he did some superb work while in York. It was in December 1994 that Brian had to leave the Minster as he was finding travelling to and from Stallingborough where he was now living too much. He decided to go freelance and set up a workshop on a farm near Riby. It was when he was working there that I met him for the first time and where he began to teach me stone carving. I was able to observe this talented man at work on a good number of projects. It was obvious he was an expert at lettering on stone and well able to work on any type of stone. He was able to help out local monumental masons who were pushed to carry out commissions for grave stones. Also, he carried out a commission for a war memorial for airmen who flew out of Hemswell. This was done in black slate,

Fig. 3: Brian Ansell's carving of the 'taxman' now on a pinnacle on the west front of York Minster

the carving being beautifully sharp and crisp, and is well worth seeing. When I first met Brian he was carving a replacement for the War Memorial at Dalderby, near Scrivelsby Court, home of the King's Champion. A passing motorist had carelessly collided with a telegraph pole which fell, demolishing the memorial. It was observing this replica develop under Brian's hands that taught me how a carving grows from very simple forms and basic shapes to the final state of detail and complexity. This was pointed out to me many times by my mentor. He would give as an example the repetition of a basic motif over and over again by medieval carvers to produce the effect of an extremely complex pattern from simple beginnings.

During the period when Brian was working at Riby he carried out some extensive work on the church, of which the most important was the complete replacement of the north east pinnacle of the 500 year old tower. The pinnacles were fifteenth century (*c.* A.D. 1420) and Brian took the

Fig. 4: Brian Ansell's carving of 'Ceres' on Louth Museum

dimensions for his new pinnacle from the old one he had dismantled and brought to his workshop. One morning I arrived to find him very excited by some marks he had discovered carved onto the upper surface of one of the lower stones making up the old pinnacle. These markings were identical to the ones he had already made on the new piece he was about to start carving. After over 500 years the method of measuring out from a centre point on the stone employed by the medieval masons was still the method taught and used today. That day Brian felt closely in touch with his fellow craftsmen of centuries ago.

On another occasion I came to the workshop to find my friend in an uncharacteristically furious temper. It was the time when the taxman (or perhaps more correctly the Government) had decided that businesses should not only pay their taxes for the past year based on what they had earned but should also predict what tax would be due from them during the coming year and pay that as well. A double tax bill that year! It so happened that Brian had been asked by the authorities of the Minster in York to carve a pinnacle with a couple of heads featured on two corners of the stone. The Minster was undergoing an extensive restoration of the West Front, particularly the west door surround, but had not

Fig. 5: My carving 'Grieving Woman' done under Brian's tuition

enough carvers in the masons' yard to complete the work in time for the Duke of York to dedicate the restoration work. Before the bombshell from the taxman, Brian had already completed one head - a medieval lady. When he started in on the male head he gave full vent to his anger by carving him with the ugliest and most disagreeable expression imaginable. It was the 'taxman' and his portrait is placed on the west front of York Minster for almost evermore! When I told the carvers in the masons' yards of Lincoln Cathedral and York Minster they laughed and said it was precisely what the medieval carvers had done when they wanted to get back at a Canon, Bishop or other member of the Clergy or even, one of them said, their own wives! Another piece of beautiful work Brian did for the Minster restoration at this time was a triple finial, this time with no heads with sour expressions.

The superb carving of Ceres was carried out in Brian's workshop at Riby. It was carved from a massive piece of limestone which all but filled his workshop. As with the

Dalderby carving, I was able to observe the progress of the work from the blank block of stone to the finished piece. The way in which Brian moved large pieces of stone was remarkable to me. Using a system of levers and wooden rollers he was able to manipulate the heaviest piece with, it seemed, miraculous ease.

When I marvelled at his skill in this he simply shrugged and reminded me of what he had told me many times - the ancient builders had quite simple means to lift and move great blocks of masonry and that most often these techniques were passed down the generations of craftsmen from the dim and distant past. To appreciate what they achieved without our modern industrial machinery, just look at the Egyptian pyramids.

The Ceres carving was started by carving the figure in simple blocked out shapes and, as with the Dalderby carving, slowly the detail would appear. A comment many make about the carving process is 'what happens if you have almost finished your masterpiece and you accidentally knock off the end of the nose?'! The answer Brian always gave was that you begin with the end of the nose and work backwards into the stone and if the nose end is damaged the carver is able to work back into the stone again as he always leaves plenty of room for this. Fortunately, as expected, there were no accidental knockings off Ceres whilst Brian was carving back into his stone!

Another interesting comment Brian made was to do with the fact that many, if not most, pieces of sculpture were destined to be exposed to the elements. This means that the design must provide for rainwater to completely run off the piece and not accumulate in little pockets where in frosty weather it would expand on freezing and split the stone. I carried out a piece for the grave of an old tutor of mine and Brian stressed this point before I started on the work, a 'Grieving Woman' in a beautiful block of Portland stone.

Brian was fond of relating his sometimes amusing trials and misadventures. He spoke of the tremendous winds that blow up there on the tallest pinnacles of a cathedral and of how he had to tie himself on to prevent being blown away at times. On one occasion he was working high up in the interior of Lincoln Cathedral when he pushed his hand deep into a crevice in the masonry to steady himself and felt a sharp and painful bite by some unknown creature lurking there. For a few days afterwards his hand and lower arm felt numb from the bite and he was convinced some very ancient and medieval spider had made known its objection to the intrusion!

On 9 December 2005 an Architectural Festival was held at the Minster in York. Brian felt honoured to be invited to be there. There were readings by the actors Ian Carmichael and Jane Lapotaire. Brian and Jane had known each other for a good while and she had great sympathy for him knowing of the disability from which he now suffers and which prevents him from making use of his talents. She read a poem by John Ormond, 'The Cathedral Builders', in his honour.

More recently Brian has been able to visit North Africa and has had the opportunity to consort with some of the Moslem stone carvers there. He greatly admired the wonderful craftsmanship these men exhibited. He told me of one inscription carved on a piece of Islamic masonry which moved him very much and which seemed to epitomise every stone carver's philosophy. It read ES SABRE GAM EEL which translated means – 'Patience is Beautiful'.

No more able to practise his craft due to a crippling illness Brian Ansell has now worked in an advisory capacity in his home town of Bury St Edmunds and has actively encouraged young carvers and helped in finding them positions. I have heard that one of the apprentices he taught whilst working at the Masons' Yard at Lincoln is now making a valuable contribution as a carver at Salisbury Cathedral. Brian Ansell's skill and influence live on through this young carver and the evidence of it through the superb carving of Ceres on the Louth Museum in Lincolnshire.

Acknowledgements

My thanks to Paul Atkin in the Masons' Yard, Lincoln Cathedral; Alan Drury at the Quarry, Lincoln; Steve Mills and Geoff Butler at the Stone Masons' Yard York Minster, for their help in researching Brian Ansell's history.

Fig. 6: The head of the repaired War Memorial at Dalderby carved by Brian Ansell

The Legend of Havelock

Bill Meek

In the late 1950s, so dusty documents and even dustier memories would have us believe, the Geography Department at Havelock School, Grimsby, was almost null and void. The earth science ramparts were manned, but by a force of only one: Head of Department D N 'Robbie' Robinson. Teachers were in short supply and only short supply teachers were available.

Desperate trawling of dole queues, low taverns, National Service dodgers and the Pontoon Stand at Blundell Park produced for the school four tattered UB40 holders who were willing to take the CEO's shilling and join Robbie in his avowed intent to bring drumlins, coastal erosion, and the exports of Madagascar to the unsuspecting victims of Havelock. John Parsons, Paddy Powell, Keith Parkinson and Bill Meek were all young, gifted and mad. Robbie was a brilliant organiser who was able to channel their enthusiasms and ideas, tolerate their anarchic jokes, and enjoy their Milliganesque humour. He was nicknamed 'The Chief' and he and his Indians launched their pupils on a tsunami of fieldwork the like of which has probably never been equalled in the area. For more than five years every school holiday and half-term saw the British landscape infested with Havelockians.

They took over Camp Schools in the Southern Uplands where they did Geography, Geology, Art, Sport, and Hill Walking; panned for gold; had their own radio station; and created the unforgettable 'Havelockness' Monster. They explored North Wales, the Yorkshire Dales and Moors, the North East of England, and their native Lincolnshire. They

forged links with Grimsby Nautical School and learned sailing, seamanship and navigation. Today when pupils of that era meet it is never long before the conversation turns to the adventure and camaraderie of those trips with The Chief and his dedicated generals. Other teaching staff were drawn into taking part and adding their expertise, and the excursions became an integral and integrating part of the life of the school.

Robinson, Parsons, Powell, Parkinson and Meek were also a team socially, and frequent get-togethers were hosted by Robbie and his wife Joyce. These were usually occasions of great hilarity but between the jokes and anecdotes plans were laid for bigger and brighter field trips to more and more sites of interest. It was a great time at Havelock, and Robbie led a revolution in fieldwork from which hundreds of pupils benefitted.

The times changed as times do: Robbie's right hand men were young and seeking promotions, and The Chief himself ambitious to move into adult education. By 1965 the team had been broken up and within a very short time all had moved on. But a school generation had walked the countryside of Britain, learned to live and work and laugh together, and to appreciate all the kaleidoscopic pieces which make up the evolving landscape. The whole country had become their classroom. In this they had been led and encouraged by a group of inspirational lunatics. And they in their turn had been led, encouraged and directed by The Chief … D N Robinson Esquire, Geographer Extraordinaire.

Couple reminiscing in an old people's home:-
'I'm so owd hive fergotten 'ow ode I ham.'
'Tak' off yer clothes and bend ower'
(he does) … 'You're seventy foower.'
'Ow do yer know?' … 'Yer told me yisterday'
(John Lill)

Some Havelock History

P K Parkinson

The summer of 1959 was very similar to the summer (July) experienced in 2006; hot sunny days, little or no rain, rock-hard ground, with the British making heavy weather of the conditions, as they do when the climate becomes even a little extreme. In spite of the adverse conditions, a very special growth was fostered – Robbie's Geography Department at Havelock School in Grimsby.

The members of the department were a varied bunch. The eldest was John Parsons, a very sound man, of great common sense, who became a headmaster in Nottingham later in his career, and three raw recruits from the ranks of the National Service Re-Direction squad. Towards the end of the 1950s, National Service was coming to an end, and the 'bulge', the post-war rise in the birth rate, was hitting the secondary schools causing major shortages of teachers. Consequently, qualified teachers and good honours graduates were moved to 'approved schools' to shore up the gaps in the teaching staff, instead of doing square-bashing etc. So, Bill Meek, Keith Parkinson, and Paddy Powell found themselves under the direction of David Robinson (Head of Department). We did have a lady teacher as well, but she objected to men who displayed their braces to a lady (which we did frequently as it was hot, and we were allowed to work without our jackets on) so she left in disgust! Paddy Powell died two years ago, so Bill Meek and Keith Parkinson are left to tell the tale from the local area, and we have dealt with 'Robbie' ever since in a variety of ways, and he certainly proved to be a major influence on our lives and careers.

The rules of engagement of 'conscripted' teachers were, that you were expected to teach anything that you were told to, and that you must stay in teaching until you were 26 years old, otherwise it was back to the Navy, mob, or whatever! Paddy and Keith were geographers with geology and maths, and Bill was an honours geologist with biology and natural history. Bill was also a good soccer player and, being of a slight build (if you stood him sideways you could mark him absent!), he was a capable cross country runner, carrying no weight. Keith was a swimmer, high board diver and hockey player and of totally the opposite build. John Parsons was a very good cricketer, and David Robinson also played hockey in a kamikaze fashion, similar to his

driving! It was marginally advantageous to be on the same team as Robbie – but only marginally!

In our first meeting of the autumn term of 1959, we realised what we were up against: not enough teachers, up to date textbooks, chairs, desks or even rooms. If a class or two were not doing games, or in the hall, we could not sit everyone down in a room. We had no proper changing rooms or showers and no sports ground except a public field fifteen minutes walk away. I can still see a lad with size fourteen feet, who eventually played in goal for Manchester City, trying to wash the mud off himself in a small wash basin, which was the limit of the facilities (20 basins maximum). The average size of class was around 40, and we even made our own maths books of duplicated questions bound in covers of old Cornflakes' packets. I supervised the squad who sewed these together with figure of eight stitch – a task which occupied pupils for whom the devil would otherwise have found evil work! The general hardship that everybody suffered, pupils and staff alike, did however develop a sort of 'Dunkirk Spirit'; we were all in it together, and we either sank or swam.

Robbie, as head of department, had to forge this disparate (or was it desperate?) group into a working unit under these adverse conditions. We were told they were desperate for teachers, but Robbie must have wondered what he had let himself in for. Luckily his organisation was excellent. He made a very rigid syllabus, right down to the last page number in the text books, film strip/films from the town film library, and whatever handouts we could beg, borrow or steal from local industries and the like. This production-line approach allowed us to make maximum use of our meagre resources and deal with the serious over-crowding which we were up against. We rapidly had to learn from Robbie that without preparation and organisation, there was no such thing as a quiet life.

Robbie had one other major policy which basically hinged round the idea that an hour in the field, was worth several hours in the classroom. Apart from being a sound idea in aiding understanding, it made very good sense, as it alleviated the 'standing room only' situation we had in the school. So we went round local industries, mapped anything in sight - you name it, we did it. We fostered relationships with local industries for the school-leavers – the boys in particular joining the fishing fleet, which Grimsby still had then, so I spent some considerable time 'down dock' as they say in Grimsby.

The idea of not always being in the classroom was not universally popular with staff and departments but it had a major effect on us as new teachers, something that we all continued with for the rest of our careers. When you take children out of school, problems are always going to arise – accidents occur, people get lost, are late back, lose things etc. It is very easy to criticise anyone who takes on any out of class activity, forgetting the organisation and preparation that is involved, and the pitfalls that are there waiting for you. Robbie had to take a fair amount of flak himself, and for us, which we were possibly unaware of at the time, in order to keep us enthusiastic. The 'going out' did not stop at the end of term. Robbie organised all sorts of field weekends, camp schools, etc, so most wives/girlfriends were convinced we were 'crackers', and especially the organ grinder! Robbie had his critics both within and without.

As part of our extra-departmental duties we had to teach our own form R E, not having a resident 'sin bosun'. So we followed the Robbie pattern – the two chapters of the Bible per term cycle – rather like the Norfolk four course rotation: namely - first week, read the chapter and talk about it; second week, discuss the chapter and answer any questions arising therefrom; third week, write about it and fourth week, draw a map of it using a mapograph outline, as this took a long time to accomplish with a big class. Fifth week, have a test on it. Sixth week, pray that it was half-term or there was a concert/house match/lecture/fire practice, etc. The next half term followed the same lines.

Bill and I also did our share of P E and games, being young and fit, unlike the P E staff who were either war veterans or non-swimmers. Bill had a soccer team and helped with the cross-country. I took the swimmers (boys and girls) with the economics teacher and when the only games-mistress left, the maths master and myself took on the girls' hockey team. They became a formidable group, much feared in the district, on a par with Havelock the Dane and the Viking raiders that the school was named after. Robbie helped us out when he could, and what the team lacked in skill, they gained in élan and determination!

As time went on, the various strengths and qualities of Robbie's department became apparent. We were probably the youngest and most active of the departments, taking our fair share of staff matches, Friday night badminton with the senior pupils and treasure hunts (a very serious and highly contested business and an opportunity for Robbie to excel himself at cross country driving, long before the era of 4x4s). Robbie had to balance all this youthful energy and exuberance within his department with sound academic progress and also explaining/covering up, or just stoically putting up with some of the 'clangers' we dropped as a result of our relative youth and inexperience. Some staff were very critical of our energy, possibly even jealous of it, while others were keen to recruit us to help in their departments. Robbie had to plough a fairly difficult furrow through all of this, and I think we only realise now how well he did it - something that later in our careers, we in our turn, had to do for others.

The winter of 1963 acted as a catalyst of change in the department. From mid January until the end of the spring term, the temperature rarely got above freezing point – the whole school was positively Arctic. The Geography Room, Robbie's HQ, was the coldest room in the place. This added burden caused cracks to appear in the department. Robbie was keen to widen his horizons into adult education. Bill Meek and myself were coming up to 26, so could leave and join any educational establishment. Advancement within the school seemed impossible, so we eventually left and joined the local grammar school. Paddy and John Parsons remained after Robbie left, and so the whole department moved on, as it does in all establishments. We all left a lot wiser, with ideas and systems established in our minds which were to shape our futures. Robbie remained in contact and whenever the phone rang, you knew he was after information, help, gossip, or on the 'cadge'. Even now, after 40 years, we still use each other to draw on our various skills and knowledge. Many of the pupils who are now 'getting on a bit' mention the features they liked and the way the school operated under difficult conditions. I think they thought all schools operated under duress, but realised later how Robbie and his team made the best of it.

Botanists at 160 Eastgate……

If you arrive at 160 Eastgate by car it's possible to find yourself approaching the property from the back.   Your entrance is via a tall snecked green painted door of vertical planks through which you will enter an unexpectedly large beautiful garden, the empire and retreat of Joyce.   Failure to look to your left will mean you will not notice carved stones, features that David has saved here – a pinnacle from a restoration of Louth St James, a quatrefoil from William Allison's 1876 excavation of Louth Park Abbey.   The boundary opposite your entry is a length of high brick wall built (well built, according to David, because of Joyce's tea and cakes!) in 1980 when a supermarket was grafted onto the Robinson abode.   Turning towards the house the path will take you round or across an area of lawn, David's only responsibility here, past a summerhouse, along the washing line to a large camellia, wrapped up in cold periods, to the back door of the house.

Finding herself the owner of this ground in 1965, Joyce has here developed her scientific expertise, planting hundreds of herbs, shrubs and herbaceous plants.   The Lincolnshire Wildlife Trust and other local charities have benefited through its being occasionally open for visits.   Her care of and interest in her garden has meant that it is to her that David refers when he sometimes says, 'I have my own botanist!', fielded as a defence and excuse for there being one thing Lincolnshire that he hasn't studied in depth!

Some Thoughts on Plants

Joyce E Robinson

What image comes to mind with the word 'botanist'? Is it an earnest and bespectacled chap, or a stout tweedy woman, rejoicing over a seemingly insignificant weed, to a chant of incomprehensible Latin? Or is it an intrepid plant hunter risking his life in some far-away place to bring back exciting new plants for his patrons? Or maybe the plant ecologist, striving to develop stronger, or tastier, or more disease-resistant food crops for an ever hungry world? Add to these the plant historians, the students of particular periods and styles of gardens, and the gardeners - highly skilled and immensely knowledgeable men and women - plus many more, studying specialised aspects of plants, from white-coated scientists to garden centre staff serving the ever increasing appetite of garden lovers for the unusual and rare, - or the top twenty popular flowering plants. We are fortunate to have so many branches of plant studies, catering for all interests.

In the distant past, when people were trying to understand their world, they learned from observation and trial and error. They knew that food, warmth and shelter were only to be had in return for effort. At that time, we believe men were hunters and women developed the knowledge needed to gather plants, nuts and fruits for food. With time and perhaps unfortunate experiences they discovered that some plants were good to eat while others were poisonous; that

some had healing and curative qualities but others were narcotic or debilitating; and while a few had special uses for making fibres or containers, many had no practical uses.

With the development of farming, human societies began to live more settled lives and it became possible for some individuals to develop specialised knowledge. All communities had wise men (or wise women), some perhaps thought of as shamans or witches. These were the people who knew the rituals to ensure good crops. They knew the healing properties of plants, and how to extract and use them. Some even knew how to brew unpleasant potions, guaranteed to make a curse work. They passed their special knowledge on from generation to generation and were important, and sometimes feared, individuals. Plants and places were believed to have their indwelling spirits and the medicine men and medicine women knew of them and knew when they were kindly disposed to people. It is difficult for us in our modern 'scientific' times to comprehend the influence and power that these men and women held in their communities.

By the fourteenth century in Britain, many plants had a mass of beliefs attached to them. These included some real knowledge, but mostly superstitions drawn from Greek, Roman, Celtic, and Christian beliefs. Every invader of these shores brought new beliefs with them, which were gradually absorbed into local traditions and their sources forgotten. In a similar way, a great diversity of religions, gods and goddesses had touched our national traditions. Each brought new connections for places, mountains, springs, trees and plants to different deities, some of which survive to this day. For instance, certain plants are connected to or dedicated to particular gods or goddesses:

> Venus has myrtle, violet, rose and daffodils among others;
> Apollo, the sun-god, musician, poet and athlete, has bay, peony and golden sun-like flowers;
> Jupiter, the ruler of the gods, has the oak-tree, although Druids earlier claimed the oak especially when it bore mistletoe;
> Pluto had cypresses, dark evergreens, and mint;
> Ceres has wheat and poppies.

The reasons why these connections are made may be fanciful, but some are probably attempts to explain puzzling questions about natural phenomena:-

Ceres, the goddess of harvest, was heart-broken when her lovely daughter Proserpina was abducted by Pluto to be his queen in the underworld, Hades. Ceres searched everywhere but eventually, weary and exhausted, fell deeply asleep in a cornfield full of flowering poppies. In gratitude for her much needed sleep, she decreed that poppies should always flourish in cornfields, - as indeed they do! Proserpina was permitted to pass six months of each year above ground, when the earth rejoiced in her presence, flowering and fruiting. It became cold and frozen with few plants surviving, when she returned to Hades, thus giving an early explanation of the mystery of the seasons.

Venus, the goddess of love, listened to the desperate pleas of Myrsine, an ill-used Athenian girl, and changed her into a myrtle bush, a fragrant evergreen and therefore a symbol of fertility, which in summer is covered in white flowers, a symbol of purity. These aspects have come down to us, in that a bride's bouquet should include a sprig of myrtle, which would be planted by the door as a symbol of constancy. In Wales there should be a myrtle bush on either side of the door.

Venus, like the other deities, could be as vindictive as she could be caring. Her son, Cupid, very much liked the white violets which Zeus had conjured up to provide fodder

Fig. 1: In gratitude for her much needed sleep, Ceres decreed that poppies should always flourish in cornfields - as indeed they do!

for the heifer, Lo, formerly a maiden he had pursued, but whom he had transformed to protect her from the wrath of his wife, Hera. Venus, in a fit of pique, changed the violets from white to blue, knowing that Cupid liked them. Because violets hang their heads, they were considered an emblem of modesty.

The Christian church, spreading in strength and influence, took over and modified ancient beliefs, including the plants which had been dedicated to pagan deities. Venus' flowers became rededicated to the Virgin Mary. Simple, easy to memorise, rhyming couplets, fixed the new concepts in untutored minds:

> In the Myrtle's fadeless green
> Mary's constancy is seen

Another couplet which was surely consoling to people whose lives were haunted by fear of the supernatural, and the necessity to divert witches or sorcery:

> Rowan tree and red thread
> Put the witches to their speed

Rowans have red berries, and witches cannot abide red. The rowan was considered a highly magical protection against evil, and twigs of it were carried for protection.

Hawthorn bushes, with their thorny, twisted branches were obviously not good, especially if they were single ones growing on a mound as these were doorways to the fairy kingdom. Hazel twigs were pliable and were useful for holding in tension for divining. Apart from their more mundane use for locating water, they were used in medieval courts for discovering guilty thieves and murderers.

To anyone interested in legend and folktales, almost every native British plant has some story connected with it. Some have elements of truth behind the tales, others are apparently innocent and beautiful. When ill-health was thought to be caused by cursings, spells, or ill-wishing, then health could be restored by counter-spells, and blessings. Now, in these more enlightened times, many cards are written or conversations ended with 'All the best', 'All good wishes', 'Good luck', 'Kind regards', or 'With love'. What are these but warm thoughts sent to surround the recipient and protect them from illness, malice or jealousy? The remedy for ill-wishes!

A great many people (who do not consider themselves to be botanists) derive enormous pleasure from finding and recording wild plants in their habitats. At day schools or weekend courses, anyone can discover the wide variety of plants that are to be found in their own neighbourhood or in the rich variety of habitats that exist. To those brought up on acid soils, a visit to the limestone Burren in Ireland, or the chalk Wolds, can be breath-taking, for the new varieties of plants to be found. Similarly, a visit to Australia, is simply bewildering because every indigenous plant, from herbaceous to shrub to tree, is so different from anything growing 'at home'. It makes you realise how amazed and excited the early botanists, such as Sir Joseph Banks, must have felt when faced with such wonders. Studying the exploits of the early plant hunters as they faced extraordinary situations and unfriendly natives, can give great vicarious enjoyment.

These days, immense enjoyment may be gained from the number and variety of books on plants, and flowers: beautifully illustrated floras, detailing all the wild flowers of the British Isles; floras with keys to track down specimens; simpler books showing the more frequently-seen varieties; and books on every area from mountains in Scotland to the nature reserves of England

We are a great nation of gardeners and the range of plants and information available has grown enormously of late with the rapid expansion of industries supporting this interest. Outings to garden centres have become a major leisure pursuit. Amongst the gardeners you might find at the garden centre, some will be seriously knowledgeable, knowing the Latin names, hybrids and cultivars of their plants, while others are happy to know their plants by the relatives and friends who gave them their specimens. Thus, Fuchsia magellanica alba to one, is Aunt Janet's fuchsia to another. Some people are collectors of many plant species, the rarer and more difficult to grow, the better. Others develop a passion for a single genus, and hold national collections of all available species; a useful source of reference and knowledge for interested gardeners.

Garden design has altered greatly through the centuries. There have been formal Paradise gardens, as still seen in Persian carpets, which show walled gardens with water features, trees and flowers. There are Moorish gardens, as still preserved in the Alhambra in Spain. In England we have a background of carefully laid-out formal parterres, followed by landscape gardening on a vast scale, later developing into Georgian and Victorian public gardens of carpet bedding, or ferneries and grottoes, some even with live-in 'hermits'.

Modern garden design, as seen in gardens at Chelsea Flower Show, seems to emphasise hard landscaping to the exclusion of many flowers. The freedom of prairie-style grasses, or the strict formula of a Japanese garden, are other choices, but the British herbaceous border, plus the shrubs and trees now permitted, is still dear to gardeners, from suburbia to the great gardens. There will always be highly specialised fun gardens: Mary gardens, with all the plants and flowers associated with the Virgin Mary; physic gardens of medicinal plants; herb gardens perhaps inter-grown with vegetables (so difficult to keep under control); magic and sinister gardens with plants of ill-repute; Bible plant gardens, and of course always there will be much-loved gardens with plants growing where they thrive and look happy, with probably more plants crammed in than should be, but all giving great pleasure and satisfaction to their gardeners. Lincolnshire, a predominantly agricultural county, is rich in fine gardens, large and small. The more one studies the plant kingdom, the more one must admit that it is full of wonders, mysterious, almost incredible, yet one on which the whole of the animal kingdom ultimately depends for its existence.

David Robinson and 'Lincolnshire Life'

Judy Theobald

Back in the 1950s, when David was working as a schoolteacher, he founded a magazine called 'The Lincolnshire Poacher'. Unfortunately, the company which printed the Poacher went out of business and its publication was brought to an end. However, in 1961, when a freelance Grimsby journalist named Roy Faiers founded 'Lincolnshire Life' magazine, he asked David to become involved with this new publication and on the early editions of the magazine, the masthead read: 'Lincolnshire Life, incorporating The Lincolnshire Poacher'.

David's involvement was far more than providing part of the title; he was asked to produce a regular feature, 'Poachings', a hotchpotch of county news, history, traditions, dialect, anniversaries, memories, snippets and gleanings about life in Lincolnshire.

'People said I'd never find enough to fill it,' he said. However, more than 500 editions later, 'Poachings' is still a monthly feature in 'Lincolnshire Life' magazine. Among its many roles, the page has provided a vehicle for David's collection of 10,000 Lincolnshire postcards, enabling them to be enjoyed by a wider public, as well as providing a forum for discussion and enlightenment on many county topics. Photographic mysteries, alleged apparitions and queries about past events have all been solved through the 'Poachings' page.

David also appeared in the magazine in 1969 as 'A County Personality' and his involvement with 'Lincolnshire Life' increased further in 1970 when he became its editor, a post he held for thirteen years, making him the longest-serving editor in its history.

His contribution continues today – as well as writing the 'Poachings' page he is a much valued editorial consultant providing insight and information on any topic with a Lincolnshire connection, including dialect, history, archaeology, wildlife, geography, geology, personalities, the church, and many more. Articles sent to him for perusal and correction are always returned, marked, in his red schoolmaster's pen but always guaranteed to be accurate after his knowledgeable eye has passed over them.

It was journalism, as well as his services to the community in Lincolnshire, which earned him the award of Officer of the Order of the British Empire (OBE) in 1997. Like all of us working on the magazine, he is looking forward to making a contribution to the fiftieth anniversary edition, in April 2011.

Fig 1: The first edition of Lincolnshire Life magazine in Spring 1961.
David Robinson has written the 'Poachings' page since it began and was editor of the magazine from 1970 – 1983

Waiting Patiently for God

David is a master of time management: to arrive early is to waste your own time; to arrive late is to waste everyone else's. Furthermore, there is an optimum travel time to and from all points in Lincolnshire.

The following cartoon and accompanying text appeared in The Methodist Recorder some years ago, but we are unable to ascertain the date or the identity of any of those involved....(Eds)

'I was heading for John Wesley's own county (Lincs) where I was preaching at two services later that day as part of what is charmingly known as 'The Louth Aggregate'.

'My mind was still full of the morning conversations as the train sped towards Newark. But it was soon emptied of all such thoughts on the road to Louth. My driver went like the wind. If I'd shut my eyes, I could have imagined myself at Brands Hatch or Silverstone. Every turn in the road became a chicane and my driver treated every vehicle ahead of us as if it were a Grand Prix straggler needing to be overtaken with disdain. When it started raining I half expected a pit stop for a quick change of tyres.

As a result of this Formula One race against the clock, I was delivered to Louth Methodist chapel on the stroke of 4.30 p.m. I stepped out of the car and into the pulpit, all without passing GO. And I preached my heart out to a gorgeous and enthusiastic congregation on the subject of "waiting patiently for God".'

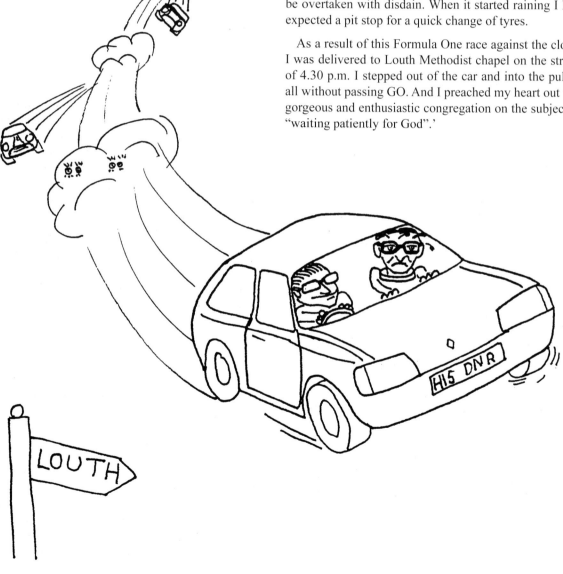

School Magazines

Pearl Wheatley

Queen Elizabeth's Grammar School, Horncastle, like most such establishments, has a small archive store. Among the treasures therein are various series of school magazines dating back to 1893. There is not a continuous run up to 1897 but from those remaining it seems they were published and professionally printed each month, including August. They were entitled 'Banovallum', the so called Roman name for Horncastle.

By 1914 the name had changed to 'The Horncastrian' and as such appeared in 1914 and 1915. In the 1930s it changed again to 'The Elizabethan' a name which was to stick. Some of the early numbers in this series are home produced and had serial numbers, volume and number. Very few remain in the school archive no doubt due to the problems of printing within the establishment. The war years also affected issues there being a shortage of paper and possibly teachers to help and advise. Readers might be interested in two that survive: Vol 4 No 2 and Vol 4 No 3, both of 1944. They have home made covers of maroon thick paper - maroon being the school uniform colour. Each have 8 quarto pages - now very yellow - of typed news and articles. The editor had a problem in obtaining articles. In one editorial he writes:

'Again I am confronted with the brain-tiring task of writing this article, a constant worry, even to brains like mine.(?) I do not wish to pass any remarks on No 1, but I will leave that to you. I must say that the response to the call for contributions was not very heartening. I hope, on behalf of the Magazine Staff, you will respond better in future, or it will be an impossibility for us to carry on the Magazine on our own. Well, bear in mind what I have said, but, in the meantime - read on!'

One would not be surprised to learn this editor became a teacher and suffered many such problems over many years as editor of this and that.

It seems the teaching staff and headmaster gave support by awarding prizes for competitions. Adams of Form 5 gained 2 shillings for solving the code problem. He had correctly de-coded a paragraph about the Baltic States and relations between Germany and Russia in 1939. The headmaster gave 3 prizes each of 5 shillings for competitions for a story, a verse and a cover design. The headline is

GRAND COMPETITION
GENEROUS OFFER BY HEADMASTER!
OPEN TO ALL FORMS!

The editor gave ample space for jokes and limericks:

French girl sees the Falls of Ledore
(She never had seen them before.)
"But where is the gold?"
She asks, "I was told
I should see Les Cascades de l'Eau d'Or!"

And another:

Maths Master, 'Now boys, this is a very difficult problem. Watch the board carefully while I go through it.'

There are reports on games successes, critical comments on drama productions, examples of pupils' poetry prowess, lists of pupil howlers and news of past students and those serving in the armed forces. The editor soon followed these last and then set out on a career of teaching, writing and editing on a much grander scale. But would these be any harder for DNR than a school magazine produced under difficulties of poor quality paper, pupils who failed to support and teachers who sat on the side-line!

David Knows

Judy Theobald

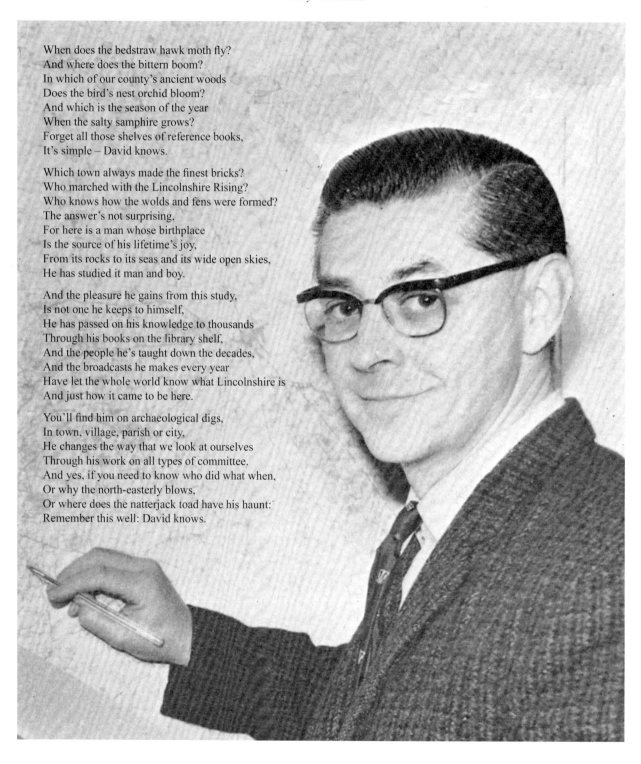

When does the bedstraw hawk moth fly?
And where does the bittern boom?
In which of our county's ancient woods
Does the bird's nest orchid bloom?
And which is the season of the year
When the salty samphire grows?
Forget all those shelves of reference books,
It's simple – David knows.

Which town always made the finest bricks?
Who marched with the Lincolnshire Rising?
Who knows how the wolds and fens were formed?
The answer's not surprising,
For here is a man whose birthplace
Is the source of his lifetime's joy,
From its rocks to its seas and its wide open skies,
He has studied it man and boy.

And the pleasure he gains from this study,
Is not one he keeps to himself,
He has passed on his knowledge to thousands
Through his books on the library shelf,
And the people he's taught down the decades,
And the broadcasts he makes every year
Have let the whole world know what Lincolnshire is
And just how it came to be here.

You'll find him on archaeological digs,
In town, village, parish or city,
He changes the way that we look at ourselves
Through his work on all types of committee.
And yes, if you need to know who did what when,
Or why the north-easterly blows,
Or where does the natterjack toad have his haunt:
Remember this well: David knows.

STUDIES

Continuing Erratic Progress

John Aram

'Man is not satisfied, like the brute, in seeing things which are; he seeks to know how things have been, and what they are to be.'[1]

Introduction

Many centuries ago the inhabitants of Lincolnshire recognised that there were large blocks of rock that appeared different from those with which they were more familiar. The larger stones were often given names, or fired the imagination to create stories to explain their presence or give them significance[2]. Many such stories linked them with buried treasure, gods, battles, dragons, witches, druids and evil spirits, whilst smaller ones were often simply called 'blue stones'. Historically, stones that got in the way of agriculture but were too large to be moved were often buried, whilst smaller ones might be dragged to the edge of fields to act as markers or boundary stones. Several of the larger stones found in towns and villages were used as foundation stones for buildings or as bases for market crosses, whilst others simply served to identify meeting places. Even smaller stones, depending upon their shape, frequently found their way into local buildings, boundary walls and rockeries. A few of the smaller stones with distinctive properties or appearances have been used since prehistoric times as hammer-stones, hone-stones, 'pot-boilers' and probably as charms or ornaments.

More recently, two stones each weighing several tons, have been moved from the route of a pipeline trench to mark the entrance to a farm near Bardney. In 2000 a large stone in Sudbrooke was set up to mark the Millennium, with a plaque explaining its glacial origin. (Fig. 1)

Glacial theory

The claim that glacial ice had once been widespread in Britain was made by the Swiss geologist Agassiz to a sceptical audience at the British Association for the Advancement of Science (BAAS) meeting in Glasgow in 1840[3]. Further evidence for the past existence of glacial ice in Northern Britain was presented by Agassiz, Buckland and Lyell at a meeting of the Geological Society of London (Geol. Soc.) later in 1840, at which they were all strongly criticised by Murchison and other eminent geologists of the day. Even as late as 1873 the president of the Geol. Soc. was still challenging the idea that glacial ice was able

to erode rocks and supporting the 'diluvial theory' that all British gravels and loams had been deposited during the great Biblical Flood. When the Geological Survey of Great Britain was founded in 1835 the 'diluvial theory' was still widely accepted, consequently all such materials were classified and mapped as 'drift', a term that is only now being removed from British Geological Survey (BGS) maps.

In Lincolnshire the first geological maps were not surveyed and published until the final quarter of the nineteenth century, by which time the glacial theory had gained much wider acceptance. Maps at a scale of one inch to the mile scale were printed and hand-coloured, each sheet being accompanied by a memoir containing detailed

Fig. 1: A large glacial erratic erected at Sudbrooke near Lincoln in 2000 to commemorate the Millennium. Originally derived from rocks in the north of Lincolnshire or the North Yorkshire Moors

descriptions of all the beds that had been encountered in that area. These memoirs include the first published records of 'glacial erratics' in Lincolnshire in their descriptions of Boulder Clays.

Geological Survey records of glacial erratics in Lincolnshire

In the Witham valley south of Grantham, surveyors recorded huge blocks of rocks that had been glacially transported[4]. The largest block, of Lincolnshire Limestone, was exposed along the side of the railway cutting at the south end of Stoke Tunnel, measuring 430 feet long and 30 feet thick, with more than seven feet of boulder clay exposed below it. Further large erratics recorded in the area included a block of Marlstone more than 100 yards long and twelve feet thick near Castle Bytham; an erratic near Ingoldsby of Cornbrash, eight feet thick, that was being quarried for roadstone, and another block of Cornbrash more than 200 yards in diameter capping a hill near Swayfield (Fig 6). In the same area the surveyors recorded 'far travelled boulders' that did not reach such large sizes, consisting chiefly of Coal Measures Sandstones, Millstone Grit and Carboniferous Limestone. The surveyors' task was simply to map and record their findings; interpretation of the deposits was not part of their official role.

Whilst the memoirs distinguished between Older and Newer Boulder Clays, the differences between them were not recognised at a sufficiently early stage in the mapping to allow them to be separately distinguished on the published maps. Jukes Browne, a senior geological surveyor involved in the mapping of large parts of Lincolnshire, was convinced of their separate existence and identified a location near Welton le Wold where their age relationship might be proven[5]. Unfortunately large parts of Lincolnshire have not been mapped since the nineteenth century so the full distribution, characteristics and relationships of the different boulder clays, now called tills, is still not known in detail.

Lincolnshire Naturalists' Union Boulder Committee

When it became accepted in the late nineteenth century that large parts of the British Isles had been glaciated, attention focussed on identifying source areas for the ice and determining how far glaciers had extended. J Cordeaux, President of the Lincolnshire Naturalists' Union (LNU) in 1895, suggested that they should establish a Boulder Committee for Lincolnshire ' to take observations

relative to the erratic or ice-borne blocks of Lincolnshire, their character, position, size, origin and height above the sea'[6]. The committee membership included; F M Burton, J H Cooke, Percy F Kendall, H Preston, A W Rowe, and A E Woodruffe-Peacock, with the Revd Tuckwell, acting as secretary.

By November of 1896 the secretary had received over 200 'boulder' reports, although the definition of 'boulders' must have been taken quite loosely since the reports include a number of cobbles and pebbles only a few inches in dimensions. Their origins as glacial erratics must have come either from their inclusion in boulder clay deposits, or the distinctive smoothing, polishing and striation frequently seen on the surfaces of softer materials that have been subject to glacial transport. (Fig 2)

Fig. 2: A polished and striated pebble from the Devensian Till at Welton le Wold, near Louth. Originally derived from rocks in the Scottish Borders

Fig. 3: The Drake Stones, outside the churchyard at Anwick, near Sleaford. The small diamond shaped face on the nearest end of the larger stone is where Henry Preston described glacial polishing and striations

A published list of 102 specimens includes a pebble of Shap Granite collected from the Humber bank near South Ferriby Hall[7]. This was believed to be the first record of an erratic transported by Lake District ice being found south of the Humber, although they were known in the cliffs along the Holderness coast[8]. (Fig 4) Two larger Shap granite specimens were reported: the largest from near Barton, measured two feet six inches by one foot by one foot; the smaller specimen was found built into the garden wall of the rectory at Irby. Sheppard also records three boulders of Shap Granite from near Goxhill, but noted that a boulder recorded near Yarburgh, previously believed to be of Shap Granite, had been mis-identified[9]. Several other 'red granite' boulders and pebbles were listed, whilst a 'bluish granite' was recorded at South Elkington. Many 'blue-stones', had rusty coloured exteriors and dark crystalline interiors, being recognised as varieties of basalt, dolerite and diorite. The suggested source areas for these dark coloured, basic igneous rocks were the Whin Sill, the

Northumberland coast, or the Central Valley of Scotland. (Fig 4). Sedimentary rock records included Millstone Grit, sandstones, ganister and 'glaciated' and 'ice scratched' Carboniferous Limestones, all again suggesting a north-east of England source area, whilst coarse greywackes and a few slaty rocks were probably derived from the Southern Uplands of Scotland. Metamorphic rocks, including gneiss and mica-schist, were more likely to have been derived from the Scottish Highlands, but could possibly have originated from Scandinavian source areas.

The first clear evidence for Norwegian Ice eroded materials to be found in Lincolnshire came from a glacially scratched boulder of augite syenite, on the Lincoln road from Louth. Measuring approximately two feet in diameter it was identified by P F Kendall, member of the LNU Boulder Committee and Secretary of the British Association Erratic Blocks Committee, as being a characteristic Norwegian rock. A similar rock

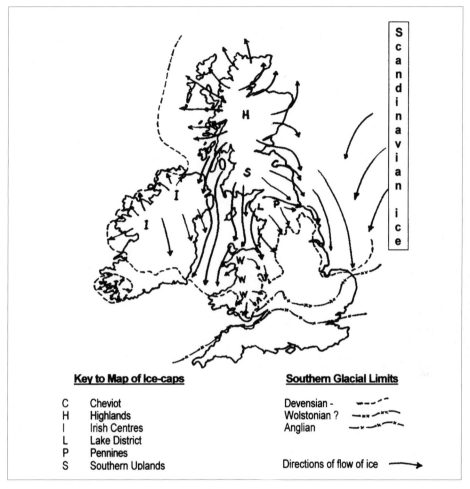

Fig. 4: A map illustrating the main source areas for glaciers reaching Lincolnshire, with lines of flow indicating routes taken

more than three feet in diameter was also recorded near the carpenter's shop in Benniworth, whilst five smaller distinctive rhomb porphyry specimens of a southern Norwegian type occurred as 'small boulders' at South Ferriby, Louth and Kirmington. Taken together these rocks clearly indicate that at some stage the eroded products of a Scandinavian ice-cap had reached Lincolnshire. Several different types of porphyritic rocks are also listed that could be of Scandinavian origins, but might have been derived from The Cheviot or the Scottish Highlands.

The LNU reports of glacial erratics and their possible source areas were all framed within the belief that there had been a single glacial event in Britain, with several different, approximately contemporary ice-caps and outlet glaciers.

The Drake Stone

The Drake Stone at Anwick illustrates the changing beliefs, attitudes, explanations and methods of investigation of these stones over the last few centuries. Local folklore suggests that the name was derived from a time when farmers unsuccessfully tried to move a very large stone near Anwick. During their attempts what was seen as the stone's guardian spirit, in the form of a drake, was seen to fly away, thus giving the stone its name. Unable to move the stone, it was buried by excavating around and underneath it, where it remained until excavated by Dr Oliver in 1832. He recorded two stones, the larger supported by a smaller one, before back-filling the excavation. His view was that the name came from the Celtic word 'Draig', a deity represented by a dragon, and he suggested that the hollow on the upper surface had been used by the Druids to collect uncontaminated rainwater for ritual purposes[10]. This possible Druid connection may help to explain why even now both the Drake stones are located just outside the churchyard in Anwick. (Fig. 3) The two stones were re-excavated in 1872 by Trollope, an engraving was made and a fuller description made before they were again re-buried. The larger stone, formed of a mass of dark reddish grey sandstone full of sea shells, was measured as nearly five feet long, three feet wide and of a similar depth, whilst the smaller piece had 'evidently been broken from it'. Trollope distanced himself from the earlier explanations, quoting its partly smoothed appearance as evidence that it had been transported to its present location by the action of water.

In 1912 Preston reported that two large erratics called 'The Drake Stones' had recently been excavated and placed on Anwick Green[11]. He recorded that they had been recovered from beneath the surface of a field a mile north of the church, where they had sunk following an earlier attempt to pull them out using a yoke of oxen. The larger stone, he measured as more than six feet long, six feet wide and four feet thick, with an estimated weight of five tons. His geological examination of both stones revealed that they were made of a fine-grained calcareous grit or sandstone and contained numerous casts and moulds of fossil shells. The smooth upper surface of the larger stone and a small triangular area with striations and grooves convinced him that they had been transported to the area by glacial ice. Plate glass photographic slides of these distinctive features were taken both to illustrate his talks and lectures as well as being published in his report. By comparing the boulders with specimens of rocks from the Willingham and Horncastle districts of the Lincolnshire Wolds he concluded that the Drake Stones were probably derived from an un-weathered part of the Spilsby Sandstone and transported across the county during the 'Great Ice Age'.

Lincolnshire Naturalists' Union reports

The Lincolnshire Boulder Committee's records and findings continued to be published, with a Mr Jordan of Doncaster recording a 'large block of Shap Granite' from Spital Hill, Gainsborough, also a block of 'greenstone' that he believed to be a dolerite[12]. Following the First World War new findings of glacial erratics and reports concerning glacial deposits were published in the Geological Section of the Annual Transactions of the LNU. The report for 1920 includes an account of a large block of Marlstone ironstone

from south-east of Colsterworth, with a suggestion that it had been excavated from north of Grantham and moved to its present location by ice flowing to the south[13]. The same report includes the record of a well sinking two miles south-east of Great Ponton, that passed through 54 feet of Chalky Boulder Clay, the greatest known thickness of that material in the Grantham area. The largest rocks encountered during the excavation were reported to be about six inches in diameter and included deeply scratched and striated pebbles of chalk. During the Second World War new records of 'islands' or 'rafts' of Northampton Ironstone and different varieties of Lincolnshire Limestone were made by Kent in an old pit east of Hougham station[14]. Lying nearly horizontally within Boulder Clay they were interpreted as having been transported as more or less rigid entities frozen into the sole of a moving glacier, with the ice movement following the general north to south direction along the strike of the beds in Central Lincolnshire[15]. In the same report Kent suggested that Cretaceous materials, including flint and chalk derived from East Lincolnshire, now frequently found in drift deposits in Leicestershire, indicated a flow from the north-east during a later stage of the main glaciation.

Harmer's analysis

All the LNU Boulder Committee reports were eventually drawn together by Harmer and integrated into his own extensive field studies of erratics and glacial deposits in East Anglia and Lincolnshire. His unfinished work was published posthumously, having been edited by Kendall, and accompanied by a map showing glacial erratic and Boulder Clay distributions in England and Wales[16]. Harmer divided the glacial deposits of Lincolnshire on the basis of erratic contents and clay matrix into a North Sea Drift and two types of Chalky Boulder Clay, one with a chalk matrix and another with a Jurassic matrix. The chalk matrix variety occurred over the solid Chalk areas of the Lincolnshire Wolds and extended south-eastwards beneath the Fens, whilst the Jurassic matrix variety formed a roughly parallel strip to the western side of the Wolds over Upper Jurassic clays. Partly based upon his work in Norfolk Harmer interpreted these two varieties of Chalky Boulder Clay as the deposits of two contemporary ice streams moving southwards over land areas. By contrast he considered that The North Sea Drift had originated in Scotland, the Lake District, Tweed, Cheviot and Teesdale areas. These English glaciers had initially flowed eastwards until deflected south, down the present-day

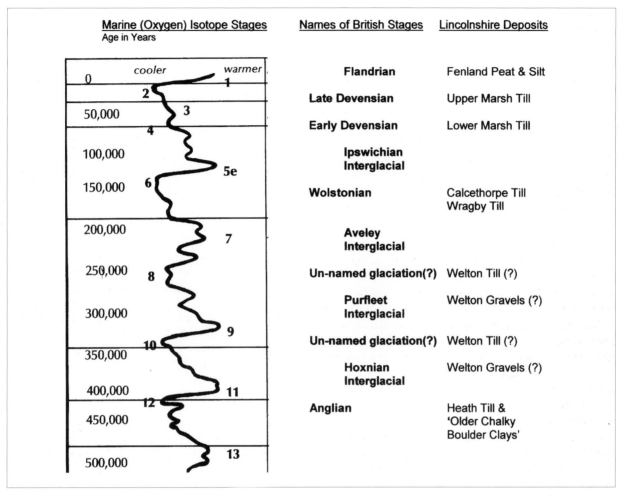

Marine (Oxygen) Isotope Stages Age in Years	Names of British Stages	Lincolnshire Deposits
	Flandrian	Fenland Peat & Silt
	Late Devensian	Upper Marsh Till
	Early Devensian	Lower Marsh Till
	Ipswichian Interglacial	
	Wolstonian	Calcethorpe Till Wragby Till
	Aveley Interglacial	
	Un-named glaciation(?)	Welton Till (?)
	Purfleet Interglacial	Welton Gravels (?)
	Un-named glaciation(?)	Welton Till (?)
	Hoxnian Interglacial	Welton Gravels (?)
	Anglian	Heath Till & 'Older Chalky Boulder Clays'

Fig. 5: Chronology of Lincolnshire glacial deposits related to the Marine (Oxygen) Isotope Stages derived from ocean cores

North Sea area, by a larger Scottish ice-sheet. At a later stage he postulated a much larger Scandinavian ice-sheet had pushed the combined Scottish and English ice-sheets westwards, across the lower ground in Holderness and East Lincolnshire. Harmer's studies in Lincolnshire were later closely followed by Professor H Swinnerton in his Presidential Address to the LNU[17]. Harmer's work also bears a distinct similarity to both recent computer modelling of patterns of glaciation[18] and earlier models of the last ice sheet, about 15,000 years ago, during the late Devensian[19].

The Second World War period, and after

Geological investigations of iron ore deposits in the county during and after the Second World War led to a renewed interest in the overlying glacial deposits. Work in South Lincolnshire led to the recognition of valley-floor bulging and valley-side cambering as being related to processes of glacial loading, erosion and unloading.[20] A borehole programme to delimit the iron-ore beds south and east of Grantham identified several west to east valleys filled with tens of metres of Boulder Clay. The routes of these valleys were all previously unknown since they lacked any present day topographic expression.[21] The origins of sand and gravel deposits found beneath the till in the South Witham to Thurlby valley must have pre-dated the major glacial event in the area.[22] From South Witham sands and gravels deposited by the newly named 'Bytham River' have subsequently been traced across East Anglia to the Thames valley.[23]

Correlation and dating

When the LNU published the first major geological account of Lincolnshire[24] Chapter XIV, The Pleistocene, was written using the terminology of Chalky Boulder Clay and North Sea Drift related to two glacial events. This did not relate easily to the four or five glacial advance stages of the Alpine model then gaining acceptance in Britain. Straw, who had originally divided the Lincolnshire tills into only two different types based upon their erratic content and matrix materials[25] revised this view[26] based upon his own research in the Lincolnshire Wolds[27] and the work of Harrod in the south of the county[28]. Straw had mapped the Calcethorpe, Belmont and Wragby Tills as having quite different distributions, and like Harmer he appreciated that each matrix closely related to the bedrock over which the ice had been passing. With the geological grain of the Wolds aligned approximately north-north-west to south-south-east, and the ice flowing approximately in the same direction, where Chalk lay beneath the ice's passage the matrix of the overlying tills consists mainly of finely ground chalk, as in the Calcethorpe Till, and had a Jurassic clay matrix where they were the bedrock, as beneath the Wragby Till. Many problems of the glacial chronology of Lincolnshire were resolved when Straw assisted Kent in the revision of Chapter 14, The Pleistocene Deposits, in the Second Edition of Geology of Lincolnshire[29].

Welton le Wold

Part of Straw's revision can be related to the period 1969 to 1973, when a sand and gravel quarry to the west of Louth yielded a small number of stratified animal bones, teeth, tusks and flint hand-axes[30]. Immediately above the gravels a greyish till that was not otherwise known to occur in the Wolds was named the Welton Till, whilst a very chalky, yellow till widely distributed over the central and southern Wolds, that lay above the Welton Till was named the Calcethorpe Till. The eastern part of the quarry had a third, reddish till capping, recognised by Straw as Marsh Till. Relying upon the archaeological dating from the hand-axes both the Welton and Calcethorpe Tills were designated as Wolstonian in age, whilst the Marsh till was attributed to the Devensian glaciation. (Fig 4 Table 1) Unfortunately, shortly after the finds were made and before further investigations could take place, the quarry changed ownership, was closed and largely back-filled[31].

Geological Society of London Quaternary Correlations

The Wolstonian and Devensian stage names used by Straw came from a Geological Society publication intended to formalise the rapidly expanding post-war terminology and British names for Alpine stages[32]. In Lincolnshire the deposits in different parts were described and correlated by specialists from the adjacent areas and published under the adjacent area sections of the Report. Not surprisingly several confusing and internal conflicting correlations resulted, with the Calcethorpe, Belmont, and Wragby tills in north Lincolnshire being grouped with the Heath tills of south Lincolnshire and allocated to the Wolstonian stage. In south-east Lincolnshire the Chalky Boulder Clay that underlies the Fens and appears to be a continuation of the Calcethorpe Till of the Wolds, was given an Anglian age.

Marine (Oxygen) Isotope Stage Dating (MIS)

Arising from these problems[33] and combined with new techniques and data, a Revised Correlation of Quaternary Deposits of the British Isles was published in 1999[34]. The problems of relating discontinuous lithostratigraphic units to any geochronology were well known, but the potential of using an independent absolute chronology derived from the differing ratios of the principal isotopes of oxygen from a continuous ocean sediment core was recognised. Whilst it was still considered premature to offer firm correlations to marine oxygen isotope stratigraphy they did give the Welton Gravels and the Welton Till of Straw 1974 'Formation' status, and a tentative Marine Oxygen Isotope Stage 6 (MIS 6) age; i.e. Wolstonian. Unfortunately they also suggested that the overlying Calcethorpe and Wragby Tills were members of the Lowestoft Formation, and therefore the much older MIS 12, i.e. Anglian age. Not surprisingly this anomaly of older tills apparently lying on younger tills without any evidence of tectonic thrusting was noted[35].

Lincolnshire RIGS Group

Much of the glacial history of Lincolnshire might have remained a subject of speculation and theory had the Lincolnshire Trust for Nature Conservation (LTNC) not taken a lead in the identification and designation of Regionally Important Geological and Geomorphological Sites (RIGS) in the county during the last decade of the twentieth century. Under their guidance a group of volunteers were given the task of identifying appropriate

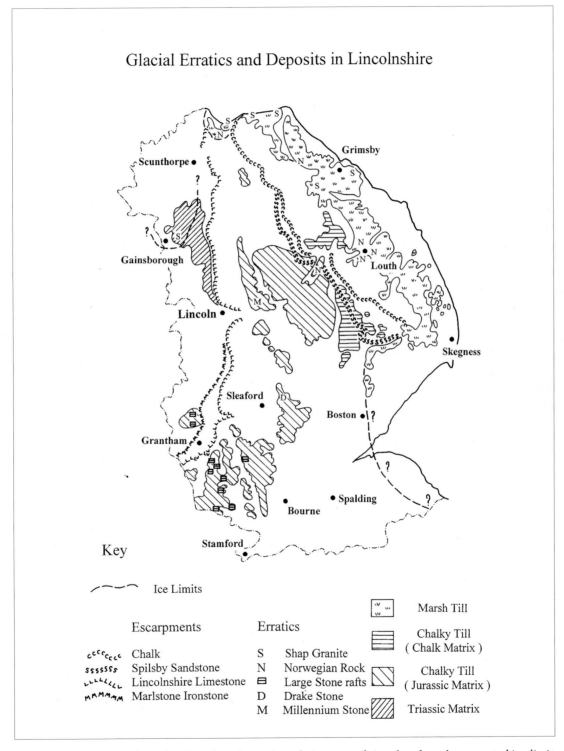

Glacial Erratics and Deposits in Lincolnshire

Key

Fig. 6: Map of Lincolnshire showing glacial erratics relative to traditional and newly suggested ice limits
(drawn by David Hopkins, Heritage Lincolnshire)

sites for notification to the local planning authorities. Since the Lincolnshire Wildlife Trust (LWT) evolved from the LTNC they have continued to recognise and support the RIGS group work. A RIGS display of glacial erratics was mounted in the LWT marquee at the Lincolnshire Show where leaflets were distributed to the public requesting information concerning any large stones or boulders. The Show event was also linked to an article concerning the work of the RIGS group and publicising the erratics project in the LWT magazine[36]. Together this resulted in more than 30 previously unrecorded glacial erratics being notified, nearly all of which have subsequently been measured, described, photographed and their locations recorded.

Reflecting a renewed interest in the glacial history of the county the LWT RIGS group obtained funds from English Nature (EN) Facelift Fund for clearing a small section of the glacial deposits in the Welton le Wold Geological SSSI [37]. In conjunction with Heritage Lincolnshire they also obtained funding from both English Nature and English Heritage to create a permanent exposure of the glacial deposits in the eastern part of the SSSI[38]. Located on land purchased by LWT this now forms the basis for a Geological Reserve regularly visited by geological societies and groups of geology and geography students from local schools and universities. Undergraduate students have already completed supervised projects at the site, whilst post-graduate and research students are currently involved in projects concerning climate change, British glacial and early human history.

The problem and its solution

Deposits scattered in a patchwork of isolated locations have always been the bane of any traditional stratigrapher's life. Since Quaternary deposits can rarely be seen in a simple vertical sequence, determining their relative ages by the use of superposition can seldom be applied, hence the significance of the Welton le Wold site. Similarly correlation by tracing the lateral continuity and relationships of beds to resolve such issues has also only a very local value due to rapid facies changes in glacial deposits [39]. Because the severe climate during glacial periods restricted the variety of life and due to the short time periods involved, very few new distinctive species have evolved, so even the use of fossils is limited. Whilst pollen and beetles have both been used, they suffer from the relationship between climate, vegetation and life being almost repeated during each successive glacial-interglacial-glacial sequence. A further major complication is that due to the topographic controls on temperature and precipitation successive ice sheets tend to develop in the same geographical areas during subsequent cold glacial periods. Ice-lobes consequently follow similar topographically restricted routes, resulting in each later glacial advance eroding, re-working and incorporating some of the deposits of its predecessors[40]. In Britain it is really only tentatively possible to differentiate deposits of the last half million years, when it is believed that successive ice advances reached progressively less far from their source areas. Even this is complicated by stationary ice-front positions and localised re-advances occurring during a retreat phase of an interglacial[41].

It is with an awareness of these problems and difficulties that Fig 6 has been compiled, incorporating the evidence from glacial erratics to illustrate possible interpretations of ice-limits and till types in the county[42]. In this interpretation the evidence is weighted towards the larger and more unusual rock types on the basis that they are somewhat easier to identify and less likely to have been reworked from previous glaciations compared with the much more difficult work on heavy mineral grains[43] or palynomorphs[44]. Alternative dates for the Welton Till and Welton Gravel Formations shown in Table 1 arise from the recognition by the author of a shear surface between the Welton and Calcethorpe Tills at Welton le Wold and the continuing or inconclusive alternative dating of both the archaeological and vertebrate remains from the underlying gravels. Hopefully results from recent optically stimulated luminescence (OSL) dating of sands at Welton combined with new research at the site into MIS 6 will help to resolve these issues.

After more than a century of study, these exotic stones are now contributing to a very different kind of treasure from that envisaged in the folklore stories.

Notes:

1. J Hutton, *Theory of the Earth,* Transactions of the Royal Society of Edinburgh (1788) pp.209-305.

2. E H Rudkin, *Lincolnshire Folklore,* (1936) pp.56-70.

3. R J Price, *Glacial and Fluvioglacial Landforms*, Geomorphology Text 5 (1973)

4. A J Jukes-Browne, *The geology of the south-west part of Lincolnshire*, Memoir of the Geological Survey of England and Wales, Sheet 70 (Old Series) (1885b)

5. A J Jukes-Browne, 'The boulder-clays of Lincolnshire', *Quarterly Journal of the Geological Society* Vol.41 (1885a) pp.114-132

6. W Tuckwell, The Lincolnshire Naturalists' Union Boulder Committee. (1896) pp.349-353.

7. T Sheppard, 'Lincolnshire boulders', *The Naturalist* 257 (1896b) p 373.

8. T Sheppard, 'Notes on the occurrence of boulders of Shap granite, etc. in Lincolnshire', *The Naturalist* 257 (1896a) pp.333-339.

9. T Sheppard, 'Notes on the Geology of South Ferriby,' *Transactions of the Lincolnshire Naturalists' Union,* 1905 pp.61-68

10. E Trollope, Sleaford and the Wapentakes of Flaxewell and Aswardhurn, in the County of Lincoln, (1872) pp.187-188

11. H Preston, 'Geological Report', *Transactions of the Lincolnshire Naturalists' Union,* 1912 pp.23-26.

12. E Hull, 'Erratic blocks of the British Isles – report of the Committee', *Report of the British Association for the Advancement of Science for 1900.* pp. 343-346

13. H H Preston, 'Geological Report for 1920', *Lincolnshire Naturalists' Union Transactions* 1920 pp.130-132

14. P E Kent, 'Glacially transported Inferior Oolite at Hougham', *Transactions of the Lincolnshire Naturalists' Union,* 1943 pp. 40-41.

15. J Aram, '1993a Solid Geology', in *An Historical Atlas of Lincolnshire*, edited by S Bennett and N Bennett pp.4-5

16. F W Harmer, 'The Distribution of Erratics and Drift – a paper and contoured map', *Proceedings of the Yorkshire Geological Society* (1928) 79-150

17. H H Swinnerton, 'The Physical History of East Lincolnshire; 1936 Presidential Address to the Lincolnshire Naturalists' Union', *Transactions of the Lincolnshire Naturalists' Union,* 1937 pp.1-10

18. G S Boulton, A S Jones, K M Clayton, & M J Kenning, 'A British ice-sheet model and patterns of glacial erosion and deposition in Britain', in *British Quaternary Studies, Recent Advances,* edited by F W Shotton (1977) pp.231-246

19. K M Clayton, 'The differentiation of the glacial drifts of the East Midlands', *East Midland Geographer* 1 Pt 7 (1957) pp.31-40.

20. S E Hollingworth and J H Taylor, 'The Northampton Stone Ironstone, stratigraphy, structure and reserves', *Memoir of the Geological Survey.* (1951)

21. R J Wyatt, A Horton, & R J Kenna, 'Drift-filled channels on the Leicestershire-Lincolnshire border', *Bulletin of the Geological Survey of Great Britain* 37 (1971) pp.57-79

22. R M Bateman, & J Rose, 'Fine sand mineralogy of the early and middle Pleistocene Bytham Sands and Gravels of Middle England and East Anglia', *Proceedings of the Geologists' Association,* 105 (1994) pp.33-39

23. J Rose, J A Lee, I Candy, & S G Lewis, 'Early and Middle Pleistocene river systems in eastern England: evidence from Leet Hill, southern Norfolk, England', *Journal of Quaternary Science* 14 (4) (1999) pp.347-360

24. H H Swinnerton, and P E Kent, The Geology of Lincolnshire, Lincolnshire Natural History Brochure No.1 (LNU 1949) pp.94-105

25. A Straw, 'The glacial sequence in Lincolnshire', *East Midlands Geographer*, 2 (1958) pp.29-40.

26. A Straw, 'Pleistocene events in Lincolnshire: a survey and revised nomenclature', *Transactions of the Lincolnshire Naturalists' Union,* 17 (1969) pp.85-98

27. A Straw, An examination of surface and drainage in the Lincolnshire Wolds, with a brief consideration of adjacent areas. Unpublished PhD thesis, University of Sheffield (1964)

28. T R Harrod, Investigation of major events in the geomorphological evolution of south and central Kesteven. Unpublished PhD thesis, University of Sheffield (1972)

29. H H Swinnerton, and P E Kent, The Geology of Lincolnshire, Lincolnshire Natural History Brochure No.7 (2nd edition LNU 1976) pp.84-93

30. C Alabaster and A Straw, 'The Pleistocene context of faunal remains and artefacts discovered at Welton le Wold, Lincolnshire', *Proceedings of the Yorkshire Geological Society*, 41 Pt 1 (1976) pp.75-94

31. A Straw, Glacial and Pre-Glacial Deposits at Welton-le Wold, Lincolnshire, (2005)

32. G F Mitchell, L F Penny, F N Shotton, & R G West, A correlation of Quaternary deposits in the British Isles. Geological Society of London, Special Report No.4 (1973)

33. R M S Perrin, J Rose, and H Davies, 'The distribution, variation and origins of pre-Devensian tills in eastern England', *Proceedings and Philosophical Transactions of the Royal Society*, Vol. 287, Series B, Vol. 1024 (1979) pp.535-570.

34. D Q Bowen, A revised correlation of Quaternary deposits in the British Isles. Geological Society Special Report No.23 (1999)

35. A Straw, "Some observations on 'Eastern England'", in *A Revised Correlation of Quaternary Deposits in The British Isles* edited by D Q Bowen, Quaternary Newsletter, 91 (1999) pp.2-6

36. D N Robinson, 'At The Rock Face', *Lapwings* (LWT Magazine) May 2000 p8

37. J Aram, 'Geological Facelift', *Lapwings* (LWT Magazine) January 2002, p18

38. A Straw, 'Research at Welton le Wold', *Lapwings* (LWT Magazine) Spring/Summer 2004 p9

39. J Catt, 'Till facies associated with the Devensian glacial maximum in Eastern England', *Quaternary Newsletter,* 30 (1980) pp.4-10

40. J R Lee, Testing the case for a Middle Pleistocene Scandinavian glaciation in eastern England: evidence for a Scottish ice source for tills within the Corton Formation of East Anglia, UK. *Boreas* 31 Pt 4 (2002) pp.345-355

41. E A Francis, 'The Devensian limit in England: general considerations', *Quaternary Newsletter* 31 (1980) pp.25-28.

42. J Aram, '1993b Drift Geology', in *An Historical Atlas of Lincolnshire*, edited by S Bennett and N Bennett, pp.6-7

43. P A Madgett and J A Catt, 'Petrography, stratigraphy and weathering of Late Pleistocene tills in east Yorkshire, Lincolnshire and north Norfolk,' *Proceedings of the Yorkshire Geological Society,* 42 Pt1 (1978) pp.55-108

44. J B Riding, A palynological investigation of the Quaternary glaciogenic sediments of Welton le Wold quarry, Lincolnshire, British Geological Survey Internal Report IR/05/052 (2005) 11pp

The Life, Legacy and Letters of Sir Joseph Banks

Julia Bruce

Introduction

There can be no doubt that during his lifetime, Sir Joseph Banks (1743–1820) was a giant figure in Georgian England. There can have been few of his contemporaries who had never heard of the gentleman explorer and naturalist, turned panjandrum of science, who had fingers in pies as diverse as Cook's voyages of exploration, the colonisation of Australia, the draining of the Lincolnshire fens and the supervision of the King's botanic gardens at Kew. As one Banks scholar described him he was a 'naturalist philosopher, agriculturalist, medallist,

Fig. 1: Joseph Banks shortly after his return from the Endeavour voyage. Banks is surrounded by curiosities from his voyage, and wearing a Maori cloak.
(Lincolnshire County Council: Art and Archaeology in Lincolnshire)

geographer, associate of the great and heaven knows what else'. His influence was felt worldwide – as his admirer and contemporary, Robert Hobart asserted: 'as wide as the world is, traces of you are found in every corner of it.'

Yet, despite this contemporary fame, today Banks's name does not rank equally alongside those of other notable Georgians, such as Humphry Davy (1778–1829), Samuel Johnson (1709–1784) and James Cook (1728–1799). Even within a relatively short time, perhaps only 50 years after his death in 1820, his name had slipped into relative obscurity. This is almost certainly due, at least in part, to the nature of Banks's written legacy.

While Banks wrote much, he published little. The reasons for this are many. One could cite, for instance, Banks's dilettantism, his lack of scholarship and his lack of desire to be immortalised in print. His one major publishing project, the great *Florilegium*, a massive work of life-sized engravings and detailed botanical descriptions of all the plant species collected on the *Endeavour* voyage, whose publication would have guaranteed his immortalisation, fell foul of economic strictures and was never published in his lifetime. This article will look at Banks's life and at his private, rather than his public, written legacy – his huge corpus of correspondence.

Biography

But who was Sir Joseph Banks? He was born plain Joseph Banks in London in 1743, the son of William – a comfortably off landowner with estates in Lincolnshire and Derbyshire, and Sarah – daughter of one William Bate of Foston, Derbyshire. He spent much of his early life at the family home Revesby Abbey near Horncastle. By all accounts his was a happy childhood, with much time spent running wild in the fen country around his home. Nothing, it seemed, pleased him more than searching for natterjack toads, or fishing for trout.

This all came to an abrupt halt when he was packed off first to Harrow, at the age of nine, and then to Eton. Formal schooling didn't suit the young Banks, who was once described by an exasperated master as an inattentive boy with an 'immediate love of play'. But even if his Latin and Greek were not up to scratch, Banks did take one

Fig. 2: Revesby Abbey near Horncastle in Lincolnshire. (Engraving by Howlett)

thing from his school days, and that was a determination to study the natural world around him. His early years of freedom in the Lincolnshire countryside had given him an abiding love of natural history. By chance he had discovered his mother's copy of Gerard's *Herball* one holiday and set about learning the names of plants from it. He later recounted a story of walking back from a river swim when he was at Eton and noticing all the plants in the hedgerows around him. He decided that these were as worthy of study as Latin and Greek, setting the course of his education from that point on. He went up to Christ Church, Oxford as a gentleman-commoner in 1760 and, finding that the University's august professor of botany, Humphrey Sibthorp, did not lecture to undergraduates,

set about engaging the services of Israel Lyons, a botany tutor from Cambridge, paying him from his own pocket. By this time, Banks was a very wealthy young man. His father, William, who had been an invalid for many years, died when Banks was just eighteen, leaving his estates and substantial fortune to his young heir. Banks took his responsibilities as an estate owner seriously, learning as much as he could from his uncle, who managed his affairs until Banks took over on reaching his 21st birthday.

Banks left Oxford in 1765 without taking a degree and moved to London. He used his money wisely, if unusually, to forward his self-education in natural history. He became a regular visitor both to Chelsea Physic Garden and to the fledgling British Museum, and forged a lifelong friendship with Daniel Solander, the Museum's keeper of natural productions. Solander, a Swede, was an expert botanist and protégé of the great taxonomist, Carl Linnaeus.

Banks famously rejected the notion of going on the Grand Tour around Europe – then popularly undertaken by many wealthy young men of his time. He remarked that every blockhead did that, and ambitiously stated that instead he intended the whole globe to be his Grand Tour. True to his word, in 1766 Banks managed to get a passage on the survey ship HMS *Niger* bound for Newfoundland and Labrador, with the purpose of studying the botany of those areas and bringing back specimens for his own herbarium. He returned to London in 1767 as an experienced field botanist and with a substantial botanical collection. This experience would prove invaluable to him very soon.

Two weeks after his return, Banks was admitted as a Fellow of the Royal Society. Soon afterwards the Society proposed an expedition to observe the rare astronomical phenomenon, the Transit of Venus, from the recently discovered South Pacific island of Tahiti. Banks put himself forward to accompany the voyage as a botanist and collector, financing his own team of scientists and assistants. Among these were the artist, Sydney Parkinson, and his friend Daniel Solander. The personal cost to Banks of this undertaking has been estimated at ten thousand pounds – equivalent to at least a year's income from his estates.

The expedition left England in August 1768 on HMS *Endeavour* under the command of Lieutenant James Cook. They sailed west, stopping at Madeira, Brazil and Tierra del Fuego, successfully rounding Cape Horn on the fourth attempt. They arrived in Tahiti in good time for the Transit, and all enjoyed the island's many and varied pleasures. After successfully observing the Transit, Cook opened secret orders, given to him by the admiralty on his departure. His instructions were not to return home but to turn south and look for *Terra Australis Incognita*, the great southern continent that it was widely believed existed in the southern hemisphere. His voyage of exploration took him to New Zealand, which he charted with great care and accuracy, and on up the previously unknown eastern coast of Australia. Banks accumulated enormous collections of plants, animals and birds on this voyage, and his artists recorded it all in fantastic detail. After many adventures, the *Endeavour* returned safely to England in 1771. Banks and Cook were heroes. Banks became the toast of London society with his exciting accounts of kangaroos, native

Fig. 3: Daniel Solander, botanist "disciple" of Carl Linnaeus and lifelong friend of Joseph Banks.
(Courtesy of the Linnean Society of London)

princesses and near shipwreck on what we now know as Australia's Great Barrier Reef. Banks's unrivalled natural history and ethnographic collections from this trip formed the basis of the herbarium and museum that he housed at his new London home – 32 Soho Square, an address that was to become one of the foremost scientific and social centres in Georgian London.

Banks did not join Cook on his subsequent voyages and, after a short voyage to Iceland in 1773, settled down from the age of 29 to assume new responsibilities at home at the heart of scientific life. His fame following the *Endeavour* voyage had brought him into contact with no less than the King himself, George III. The two men were of an age and got on well, sharing enthusiasms for farming and economic botany. Banks became unofficial director of the King's Royal Gardens at Kew, and under his care they became the foremost botanical gardens in the world. Banks was fascinated by the prospect of translocating plant species, both for economic purposes and to enhance British horticulture. He ensured that any voyage of discovery setting out from Britain would bring back exotic plant specimens for the King's garden.

Banks was involved in most British voyages of discovery of his day. He helped organise both the ill-fated *Bounty* voyage under William Bligh, 1787 to 1790, and Bligh's more successful *Providence* voyage, 1791 to 1793 to translocate breadfruit plants from Tahiti, to grow as a food staple for slaves working in the West Indian plantations. It was also Banks who recommended establishing penal colonies on the east coast of Australia, believing that with sufficient supplies and skills people would prosper there. Banks supervised much of the detail surrounding the sending of the First Fleet in 1788. He also supervised the circumnavigation of Australia in HMS *Investigator* by Matthew Flinders, incidentally another son of Lincolnshire, between 1800 and 1805. The famous Swedish botanist, Carl Linnaeus was keen that this newly demarcated southern continent should be named Banksia, but Banks politely refused such a suggestion. This is an example, perhaps, of the reticence that would result in his name slipping out of the public consciousness after his death.

In 1779 Banks was elected President of the Royal Society, a position he held for the remainder of his life – a total of some 41 years – during which time he rarely failed to chair a Society meeting. In London, his house at Soho Square with its unique collection of plants or his enormous library, was open to all interested parties, and it was here also that Banks entertained people of eminence from all walks of life. From his comfortable study he maintained a huge and lively correspondence with friends and associates across the world on a breathtaking range of subjects. In 1781 Banks was made a baronet, and in 1795 received the order of Knight Commander of the Bath; two years later he was made a Privy Councillor.

There is not room here to enumerate all the projects that Banks concerned himself with during his long and fruitful life but to give a flavour, those interests included the establishment of the Ordnance Survey; the affairs of the Royal Mint; the founding of numerous learned societies including the Linnean Society of London, the Royal Institution and the Royal Horticultural Society; the drainage of the Lincolnshire fens and diplomatic missions to China. Banks's role was as a systematiser and facilitator. He was very much a man of the Enlightenment and a major supporter of the internationalist nature of science, being actively involved in both keeping open the lines of communication with continental scientists during the Napoleonic Wars and in introducing the British people to the wonders of the wider world. All these interests are reflected in his wide-ranging correspondence.

Throughout his adulthood, with the exception only of a couple of years towards the end of his life when he was crippled with gout, he made an annual pilgrimage to Revesby to oversee his estates there. He was High Sheriff of Lincolnshire from 1793 to 1794 and was always proud of his Lincolnshire roots. Banks would also make annual visits to his Derbyshire estate at Overton and kept a close eye on all matters affecting both these interests.

Sadly, Banks and his wife, Dorothea Hugesson, whom he married in 1779 never had children. By all accounts theirs was a happy union, and they shared their life with Banks's unmarried sister, Sarah Sophia, herself an avid collector – of coins and curiosities. Dorothea outlived Banks, who died in his country residence at Spring Grove in Isleworth in 1820. In the years following Banks's death, the world swiftly moved on, and Banks rapidly became a figure of the past – the symbol of another age. This was compounded by his own self-effacing desire not to be commemorated by a grand funeral or ostentatious memorials – he once said, 'I earnestly request that my family will not erect any monument to my memory' – and the fact that he left very little in the way of a tangible published legacy. Consequently his memory faded with the deaths of those who knew him.

When Banks died in 1820 the beginning of the Victorian era, that period of unprecedented change, was only seventeen years away. Science and empire that Banks had done so much to encourage in lifetime would flourish; railways and industry would transform both the landscape and the social structure of the country. The population would begin a steady migration from the countryside to burgeoning towns and cities, and fiscal and political patterns we still recognise today were set. And a small boy, only ten years old when Banks died, would change the world forever less than 40 years later with his publication of *On the Origin of Species*. That small boy was, of course, Charles Darwin. It is worth noting that Darwin came by his insights on natural selection during his time as a naturalist on the navigational vessel *Beagle*, a precedent set by Banks when he organised and financed the first true scientific party on a voyage of exploration when he sailed with Cook on the *Endeavour*. One could argue that without Banks, there might never have been a Darwin.

Banks's publications

Some have queried why Banks published so little. Some cite this as evidence that he was a dilettante, with no real scientific acumen – a butterfly who flitted from project to project without gaining any depth of knowledge.

In some sense this may be true. Banks was a poor scholar, never took his degree and never made any great scientific discovery. There is no doubt that Banks was not an academic – and he never pretended to be one. His was a broad knowledge that spanned all the known natural sciences and more besides. A close friend of his, Charles Hatchett, commented after his death that while he 'never pretended to be deeply versed in any branch of science, he possessed, nonetheless, no small share of scientific knowledge and was a living index of facts, especially pertaining to the skills and knowledge of others.'

He was indeed a member of the Society of the Dilettante, a group composed predominantly of landed gentry and peers of the realm whose wealth and independence allowed them to indulge their interests as scholars, savants and collectors. But to be thought a dilettante in the eighteenth century meant something very different from the rather derogatory meaning of the word today. The eighteenth century dilettantes were gentlemen of some learning, connoisseurs with a love of the fine arts.

There are many different motivations that urge people into print. One of these must be a certain pride and a desire to be remembered. Banks was singularly lacking in this desire. Personal fame seemed to matter very little to him. His motivation was always one of practicality. His published works were limited to modest writings, penned mainly to be of utility to others. He wrote some 51 papers for journals, such as *The Annals of Agriculture* and the *Transactions of the Horticultural Society*, on subjects including the spread of plant pests and the cultivation of cranberries as an important contributor to the economy of the family (and this in 1808, over 30 years before cranberries began, in America, to be commercially produced).

The *Florilegium*

Banks did have one major publishing project, the great *Florilegium*. This was a massive work of life-sized engravings and detailed botanical descriptions of all the plant species collected on the *Endeavour* voyage. Banks returned from the expedition with thousands of plant specimens and hundreds of drawings. His collections

Fig. 4: The Fly-catching Macaroni –
Banks was robustly lampooned during his lifetime.
(Courtesy of the Linnean Society of London)

included 110 new plant genera and 1,300 new species, all of which needed describing and publishing. Banks was determined to make this publication the best it could possibly be, and the botanical world waited on tenterhooks for its appearance. Banks spent a fortune on this project. He employed the services of the best plant illustrators of the day to finish the artworks that his artist Sydney Parkinson, who died on the *Endeavour* voyage, had been unable to complete. Then a total of nineteen master engravers were set to work to make state of the art engravings of the finished artworks. Banks's plan was to publish them in black and white with detailed plant descriptions that he, and more particularly Daniel Solander, would prepare. Sadly, both the engraving and the text took much longer to prepare than perhaps Banks had originally bargained for. The pressure to publish from the rest of the botanical world that had originally been so anxious to see the new species

Fig. 5: Banksia serrata – just one of the stunning images from the Editions Alecto printing of Banks's Florilegium.
(Editions Alecto/Natural History Museum 2006)

in print, lessened as time went on. As more people went out to Australia, New Zealand and the Pacific, others began to publish details of the new species Banks had collected. A downturn in Banks's financial fortunes in the lead up to the Napoleonic Wars made it difficult for him to complete the expensive project, which it is estimated cost him in the region of £7000. The death knell of the *Florilegium* finally came in 1782 when Solander died suddenly and unexpectedly of a stroke. Banks shelved the enterprise, and it was never completed. The original copper plates finally found their way to the Natural History Museum in London where they languished for almost 200 years. Then, in 1982, a joint project between the Museum and specialist publisher Editions Alecto led to their final publication in a

collectors' edition of just 100 copies. Indeed, Alecto went one better than Banks and, in a development of which he would surely have approved, printed the images in colour, using a technique called *à la poupée*, whereby the coloured ink is applied directly to the plate. The results are stunning.

If Banks had managed to publish his *Florilegium* within a short time of his return from the *Endeavour* voyage, his fame would have been assured from that alone. Instead, others forged ahead and published his discoveries, either from new collections or, ironically, from specimens in Banks's own herbarium. Banks was generous in giving access to his collections and in sending out duplicates of his specimens to genuine researchers.

Man of letters and entrepreneur of the sciences

Another factor in the delay and eventual non-publication of the *Florilegium* was that Banks could not devote anything like enough time to it. He was simply too busy with a myriad other things. Banks was ever the man of action, be it as an explorer of the unknown in his early years or as a facilitator of science in his later ones. He was more interested in getting things done and forwarding the interests of science, country and empire through his own actions or those of others, than publishing his works or thoughts for personal gain or aggrandisement. The French scientist Cuvier said of him that although he published 'only a few sheets' whose 'importance was not greatly superior to their extent' his name would 'shine with lustre in the history of the sciences'. For Cuvier recognised that science depended not just on its practitioners, but also its facilitators and organisers. Banks was the entrepreneur of the sciences, making things happen, financing projects, sponsoring individual collectors, putting the right people in touch with each other, and keeping the scientific lines of communication open with continental Europe in the throes of war. As Banks himself commented, 'It has, indeed, been always my wish to promote the scientific intercourse among nations, notwithstanding any political divisions which might subsist between them.'

It is this great spread of scientific interest, plus innumerable exchanges on topics as diverse as uprisings against conscription in Lincolnshire and concern over the health of the king, that we see reflected in Banks's real legacy – his correspondence. Gavin de Beer, former Director of the British Museum (Natural History) and scholar of Banks's correspondence once noted: 'there can

Fig. 6: Banks at the height of his powers.
(Courtesy of the Linnean Society of London)

be no aspect of British public life in the reign of George III which is not represented at first hand by the correspondence of Sir Joseph Banks.' He further commented: 'It is curious that Banks should not yet have been recognised as one of the greatest letter-writers in the English language, but such he clearly was.' Banks's correspondence spanned the known and emerging world. Wherever there was European settlement or exploration between the years 1779 and 1820, you can be certain someone was writing to Banks. As another of Banks's biographers, John Gascoigne, has said: 'Banks was so much the centre of the scientific, institutional and imperial concerns of his day that his voluminous correspondence provides a way of understanding the broader currents of his age.'

The letters and their writers

Through his correspondence, Banks received the latest information on new discoveries in science and exploration, on politics, on industry and agriculture, on current affairs both at home and abroad, on economics, navigation and natural history, and in languages equally as diverse as their subject matter. French and Latin were the most common after English but less expectedly were letters received in Swedish, Russian and even Icelandic.

His correspondents were as varied as their topics, ranging from the lowliest sailor or estate worker to the most eminent scientists of the day, politicians, artists, writers, engineers, mercantilists, nobility and even royalty. It is this wide range of subject matter and correspondents, which makes this particular series of papers so very important as a primary research tool. It should also be remembered that Banks was writing through the French Revolution, the Napoleonic Wars, the American War of Independence and the beginnings of the Industrial Revolution. Study of this material can reveal unique insights into contemporary opinion of these events as well as providing a mine of information about those events in which Banks was more actively involved, such as the colonisation of Australia and the breadfruit voyages of William Bligh.

Estimates of just how many letters Banks sent and received in his lifetime vary but a rough figure of 50,000 is often quoted, although this is probably a conservative one. About 20,000 of these are believed to be extant, of which some 14,000 are written to Banks by around 3,000 correspondents, and 6,000 are from him. These figures give the impression that Banks received more letters than he sent out at a ratio of about 3:1 but although it is likely that he did receive more letters than he replied to, his outgoing letters are more difficult to trace, being necessarily diffuse, and it is certain that a large proportion of them have simply been lost.

Banks's correspondence was unusually focused, such that each letter tended to be pertinent to just one particular subject although of course some did span several topics. It is, however, possible to break down his letters into specific themes. The most recent figures for the extant correspondence can be summarised thematically as follows:

Indo-Pacific	1,973
County matters	1,701
British science	1,479
Foreign science	1,474
Sheep and Wool	1,460
Estates	1,458
Current Affairs	1,251
Social and Domestic	1,114
Agriculture and Horticulture	762
Royal Society	387
Societies and Institutions	347
Arts	296
Royal Botanic Gardens, Kew	283

Middle East and Africa	278
Iceland	275
Library and Herbarium	249
India and England	209
Political and Diplomatic	136
Privy Council	123
North America and Arctic	106
Board of Longitude	94

This list gives some idea of how wide-ranging Banks's correspondence was. Some of the more interesting subjects include the health of George III, the smuggling from Spain of fine-woolled Merino sheep for the royal flock, and what defensive measures to take in the event of a French invasion. Banks's abiding interest in agriculture, particularly as it pertained to his Lincolnshire and Derbyshire estates, is evidenced in a corpus of more than 750 letters. These letters, which include among their correspondents poachers, tenants, stewards, farmers and other landowners, record in detail agricultural practice over more than 60 years. These were years that saw unprecedented change brought about by fen drainage, land enclosure and the beginnings of mechanisation

But Banks wasn't just a man of science, agriculture and all things practical. He had a literary flair too. He wrote several poems, including a eulogy of the Lincolnshire countryside as it was before the fens were drained. His correspondence also hints at his interest in art and literature and his letters to his friends, his wife and his sister, and their replies to him, give us a window into Banks's domestic life. Many of these letters show an enduring affection for those close to him.

Banks's literary style

Despite this huge corpus of correspondence that he wrote and received during his lifetime, Banks never really regarded himself as a man of letters in the literary sense, seeing them more as a tool than a vehicle for literary pretension. He once commented, although no doubt with his tongue firmly in his cheek, 'I know myself too well to suppose myself a proper member of a Society of Belles Lettres. I am scarce able to write my own language with correctness, and never presumed to attempt elegant composition either in verse or in prose, in that or in any other tongue. It is fitting, therefore, that I continue to confine myself, as I have hitherto done, to the dry pursuits of Natural History.'

Certainly, compared with the ramblings of some of his contemporaries. Banks's letters are mercifully short; 85% of his known letters are under 500 words and half are under 200 words. He occasionally succumbed to a flowery phrase or metaphor, particularly in letters to friends, but more usually got straight to the point! He was an assured writer, with a firm and succinct style, and one gets the impression that he often wrote at speed. His prose is generally unencumbered by punctuation, although he liked the comma, which he used somewhat randomly. Full stops are rare, but capital letters abound – whether they are needed or not. His spelling is often phonetic and his words frequently abbreviated. He often rather endearingly doubled letters in certain words such as *cabbin* and frequently missed out the 'e' in words such as *furnishd* and *askd*. But he was writing at a time when Dr Johnson's dictionary was still a novelty, and English spelling was still relatively fluid. Banks also often misspelt the names of his friends and acquaintances, for instance Bolton for Matthew Boulton, Clarke for Charles Clerke and Blythe for William Bligh.

Corrections and crossings out pepper his writings, and one gets the impression he did not want to waste time producing a work of perfection but just get down the substance of what he needed to communicate as quickly as possible. One might hazard a guess that he often wrote as he would have spoken. What a pity we cannot tell from the written word whether that speech was delivered with a Lincolnshire accent. Although at least one Banks scholar, John Gascoigne, has commented: 'Banks could be a little too direct for some Fellows [of the Royal Society]. He spoke the robust language of the Lincolnshire Fens just as well as the polite conversation of London Society.'

Few of the physical idiosyncrasies of his writing, however, make his letters difficult to read and none detract from their content, which offer the reader a cornucopia of information about any number of aspects of eighteenth and early nineteenth century life. It is this breadth of subject matter that makes the correspondence so fascinating, not only for the historian of the period but also for the general reader.

The organisation of the correspondence

Banks probably first started systematically to organise his correspondence after 1776 when he moved to 32 Soho Square, with its ample accommodation.

Fig. 7: 32 Soho Square – Banks's main London residence. (© *The Natural History Museum, London*)

This move marked a distinct change in his way of life. His travelling days were over and he began to establish a pattern of life which would remain essentially unchanged until his death in 1820.

Within three years of moving he had both married and been elected president of the Royal Society, and the Society's timetable would set the pattern of his year. While the Royal Society was in session, through the winter and spring, he and his household (wife Dorothea, sister Sarah Sophia, and a succession of librarians and assistants) would be domiciled at Soho Square. In the summer the family would move to their country residence at Spring Grove in Isleworth. In the autumn, they would travel up to Revesby, often via Banks's Derbyshire estate at Overton Hall near Ashover. This pattern remained unchanged until gout and ill-health prevented Banks from making his Lincolnshire pilgrimage in 1813, 1816 and 1818. He last visited Overton in 1812.

With his new stability and increasing eminence, his correspondence increased and he was at pains to put it into some sort of order. Banks would often write the date of receipt on his incoming letters and the name of the correspondent. Sometimes he would draft a reply or simply annotate a succinct comment on the originals themselves. These notes have proved of immense interest to historians where the actual reply has since been lost. Banks kept together letters he received within a given year, arranged alphabetically by correspondent's name. He bound the letters into two main series, 'General' and 'Foreign', by year. He foliated them in the top right-hand corner and provided each volume with an index of names. It has been estimated that there would have been a total of 120 of these volumes containing about 200 letters each, but only seven of them, part of the foreign correspondence series, are known to have survived intact in the bequest under the second codicil of his will to the British Museum. He also appears to have bound letters by year under the general heading of 'Science' and certainly separated out

Fig. 8: Banks's herbarium at 32 Soho Square.(© *The Natural History Museum, London*)

others into dossiers organised by theme; for instance Cook's second voyage and the voyages of William Bligh. These collections placed in folders made of thick, grey, herbarium paper also included files on the cultivation of hemp, sheep and wool, his family history, coinage, and the Royal Society.

Banks also carefully organised his papers at Revesby. Here documents relating to his estate and to the county of Lincoln were kept in numbered drawers in the so-called Evidence Room behind a fireproof door. When Banks's Revesby Abbey was demolished in the mid nineteenth century, this room was the last part of the old building to be torn down, and was left standing presumably until the transference of the documents to new accommodation could be arranged. The papers would have covered a wide range of subjects including fen drainage, enclosures, Acts

of Parliament, the supplementary militia, his tenure as High Sheriff (1793 to 1794), county history and archaeology, agriculture, animal breeding, details about his tenants and probably a large collection of maps and plans.

Banks visited his other country estate at Overton in Derbyshire for two to six weeks almost every year between inheriting it from his uncle in 1792 and his last visit in 1812. The estate included a share in the Gregory lead mine. As he was there, on average, for only two weeks a year it is unlikely Banks would have kept a large documentary archive at Overton – perhaps just papers pertaining to estate matters and information on mining. The house, left to Lady Banks, passed out of the family immediately after her death in 1828.

Banks also organised his correspondents into an efficient cataloguing system. Arthur Young the agriculturalist described his experience of the Banksian database thus:

'There is a catalogue of names and subjects in every drawer so that the enquiry was … scarce named before a mass of information was before me. Such an apartment and such apparatus must be of incomparable use.'

The Dispersal of the Correspondence

At Banks's death there were many thousands of items filed at Soho Square and in the Evidence Room at Revesby. Unfortunately, despite Banks's careful cataloguing, these papers and correspondence were broken up and gradually dispersed. Banks's marriage was childless and when he died at his Spring Grove home in 1820 his will and its subsequent codicils left the task of sorting out the Soho Square papers mainly to his fourth executor, his nephew Edward Knatchbull, (son of Dorothea's sister Mary). Banks requested that Knatchbull go through these papers and distribute them at his discretion as follows: papers of relevance to Lincolnshire and his estate should go to Revesby; Royal Society papers should be deposited with the Society; papers on coinage should go the Royal Mint; foreign correspondence both bound and unbound, should be given to the British Museum and finally any other papers in his handwriting should be burnt.

It is not known if Knatchbull did destroy anything but there is no doubt that he effectively did nothing with any papers that remained. He delivered some of the foreign correspondence to the British Museum in 1828 but nothing to the Mint or to the Royal Society. Over the next 60 years papers were shunted between various prospective biographers, the most notable of whom was Dawson Turner, the antiquary and acquaintance of Banks. He held the papers for some thirteen years, during which time he had copies of around 2,000 of the letters made by his industrious daughters, Hannah and Mary. Regrettably, the task of writing a biography proved too much for Dawson Turner and he eventually returned both the originals and the copies to the Knatchbull family. Thankfully, his daughters' copies, bound into 23 volumes, found their way to the Botany Department of the British Museum (Natural History) where they remain to this day in the Botany Library. The Dawson Turner copies are sometimes the only record that a letter existed, the original having been lost in the intervening years.

It was not until 1880 that any real action was taken with the papers. By this time Knatchbull had died and ownership had passed first to his widow and then on to his second son, Lord Brabourne. Against the wishes and advice of several interested parties, Brabourne finally decided to sell the majority of the material. He auctioned some in 1880, and in 1884 sold another batch privately to the New South Wales state government offering the remainder to the British Museum for £250. The British Museum refused and Brabourne proceeded to auction them in two sales at Sotheby's in 1886, where they realised less than £200. The result of these and subsequent sales has been that what was once a unique, ordered corpus of material was split up and scattered all over the world. There are now large collections in Australia, USA (particularly Yale University and the Sutro Library, San Francisco), New Zealand and Canada. In addition there are substantial collections in many UK repositories.

Quite apart from Banks's own letter archive there are also all the letters he sent out during his lifetime. These can also be found all over the world in museums, libraries and private collections and are a far less coherent corpus than Banks's own archive. It is thus very hard to say how many of Banks's papers are still extant. Regrettably many papers would have been lost through destruction by autograph dealers and we will never know how much if anything Edward Knatchbull destroyed. The intervening 100 years since the first sales must also have seen the loss or destruction of some of the original corpus.

The Documents after Dispersal

This dispersal of the documents both at the original sales and from subsequent resales, diluted not only the raw material but also the memory of the man who created it. Early biographers had failed to publish and now, without a coherent corpus of documents to work from, the writing of a definitive biography became virtually impossible. By the end of the nineteenth century there was no one who remembered Banks from life, and his reputation and achievements slipped slowly into obscurity. Although several biographies were written in the first half of the twentieth century (for instance by the Australian historian, J H Maiden in 1909) all were working from only a portion of the material, and none of them explored Banks's life and character in any depth. Several more specific studies were made of aspects of his life from single documents or collections. Examples include works by A M Lysaght and H B Carter on Banks and Newfoundland and Banks's sheep and wool correspondence. But to get a true overview of Banks the man the papers have to be viewed as a

Fig. 9: Banks the President of the Royal Society, the position of which he was the most proud.
(© The Natural History Museum, London)

whole, and for that to happen they have to be found and brought together. This was not an easy task considering how far flung they have become over the years. In 1958 Warren Dawson made an impressive stab at the problem in his calendar of all the Banks letters known in British repositories, but further work on a more holistic view of

Banks was still hampered by the physical separation of the original documents.

The correspondence today

Thankfully, in more recent years, there have been strenuous efforts to find and organise Banks's correspondence. Since the 1990s the Banks Archive Project at the Natural History Museum in London has pursued the ambitious aim to reconstruct the Soho Square and Revesby archives by bringing together, in copy form, (mainly photocopies and microfilms) the dispersed correspondence. In addition it also endeavours to add the outgoing letters where they can be found, the ultimate goal being to catalogue and publish the letters and produce a detailed computer database. The Project, which is jointly administered by the Museum and the Royal Society, has published three volumes of correspondence, and its founder, Harold Carter, published the most comprehensive biography of Banks to date in 1988. The computer database is virtually complete and indexes the name of the correspondent, date, address, repository, whether it is an autograph letter or a copy, language, and keyword names, places and subjects. Alongside the letters database is a biographical database with details of Banks's 3,000 correspondents. The net result of this activity is a central resource for all interested scholars and researchers, at last making Banks's greatest legacy available to all.

It is not just in the UK that Banks's correspondence is being given the prominence it deserves. Large collections in the United States of America include those at the Sutro Library, California, Yale University and the University of Wisconsin. Appropriately, the National Library of Australia in Canberra and the State Library of New South Wales in Australia both hold major collections of Banks papers. A project at the State Library NSW has electronically imaged some 10,000 manuscript pages. The library is arranging its holdings in much the same way as Banks would have done with the intention of reflecting the way the papers were used and accumulated by Banks in his lifetime. The project's aim is to improve intellectual access to the papers by digitising them and making them available on the Internet, so that the user can gain quick access to a single document or to a related series of documents. Access to the documents is through a combination of free-text searching and subject indexing based on the content of documents. This aim surely mirrors that of Warren Dawson in his calendar compiled 50 years earlier, 'to revive and emphasise the recognition of the great services to science and progress rendered by Sir Joseph Banks'.

Detailed information about Banks and his papers are available on the websites of all these institutions. Banks would surely have loved email and the Internet, gaining an enormous amount of pleasure from something that made communication so easy and information so widely available. Work continues on Banks's papers at these and other institutions – both in terms of making the raw material more widely available through cataloguing, indexing and publishing and by researchers now being able to study these resources and use them to draw new insights about Banks and his world. Although Banks stated many times that he had no desire to be remembered, if he had known how valuable his papers would be to future generations, one can only hope that this is an outcome of which he would have approved. Banks worked tirelessly for the good of his country and for science during his lifetime, and even almost 200 years after his death, his papers are still of utility to others. In his own words, 'a man is never so well Employd as when he is labouring for the advantage of the Public: without the Expectation, the hope or even a wish to derive advantage of any kind from the result of his exertions.'

Selected Reading

Joseph Banks: a global perspective (edited by R E R Banks *et al*) The Royal Botanic Gardens (Kew 1994).

G De Beer, *The sciences were never at war*, Thomas Nelson and Sons (1960).

H B Carter, *Sir Joseph Banks,* British Museum (Natural History) (1988).

The Letters of Sir Joseph Banks: A Selection 1768–1820 (edited by N Chambers) Imperial College Press (2000).

The Banks Letters: A calendar of the manuscript correspondence (edited by W R Dawson) British Museum (Natural History) (1958).

J Gasgoigne, *Joseph Banks and the English Enlightenment*, Cambridge University Press (1994).

A M Lysaght, *Joseph Banks in Newfoundland and Labrador, 1766*, Faber and Faber (1971).

J H Maiden, *Sir Joseph Banks: "The Father of Australia"*, NSW Government Printer (1909).

P O'Brian, *Joseph Banks: a life*, The Harvill Press (1987).

Henry Winn: A Wander through Life

Jean Burton

Henry Winn was a Victorian man renowned throughout Lincolnshire for his knowledge of local history and his poetry which regularly appeared in print. In 1914 the *Stamford Mercury* described him as the 'Grand Old Man of Lincolnshire', a well deserved sobriquet for someone who spent much of his time recording fascinating information about life in his native county.

High up in the Lincolnshire Wolds Henry was born on 23 January 1816, the first child of Richard and Sarah Winn. His father was a cobbler and shoemaker in Fulletby where Henry enjoyed a comfortable childhood. His parents were literate and ensured that all their six children received a basic education. Henry was enrolled at a dame-school in the neighbouring village of Belchford where he attended until he was ten years old.

Life was pleasant although Richard's ill health did cause the family serious concern. Henry remembered his father as someone who spent much of his time in bed, taking many different potions in an effort to relieve his symptoms. In December 1824 Richard travelled to Lancashire for specialist treatment and in one of Henry's manuscript books he recorded a letter received by Sarah in January 1825. The following is an extract describing the type of treatment he received:-

> ....they have done nothing at me yet but blistering and I have four or five sorts of stuff to take in a day. They put a blister one side of my neck and when that is took off and scrubbed, about two days, they then put one the other side. When that is dried up a little they put another under my chin and so they keep going on so that I have always two going together.
> My doctor is upon the drinking line, he has not attended a dressing since Monday morning. I went three times this morning before he was up to ask him what he thought to me and whether he could give any idea when I could return home. He said he could not tell. It was an ulcerated throat and it will take longer bringing forward than a wound on the outside. I said can it be cured and he said it will get better but it will take a long time. He does not like being asked too many questions so I left him. My anxiety to be at home is very great. I want to see you and my children. You are ever in my thoughts a week seems to be as long as a month.

Richard returned home a few weeks after sending this letter but his condition did not improve. He died on 9 August 1826 leaving Sarah to support six children, the youngest Matthew only six months old.

Fig. 1: Henry Winn in 1913, aged 97
(Photograph: W Winn Marshall)

The effect on the family was devastating. Unless someone could be found to run the family business Sarah would be destitute and reliant upon Parish assistance. It was Henry's grandfather who came to the rescue. He vacated his home in Belchford to live in Fulletby, where he helped his daughter in law maintain the shoemaking business. Henry reluctantly left school and worked with his grandfather helping to provide financial stability for the family.

The early termination of full time education did not prevent Henry from pursuing his love of books. He continued to find reading material and so impressed the Reverend Matthew Pierce that he invited Henry to visit his library at the Rectory. Attending the Sunday school, established by Revd Pierce in 1826, also helped to improve his scholastic skills.

A measure of Revd Pierce's confidence in Henry's ability is indicated in 1830 when he asked him to become the Parish Clerk (the elected member Mr Staves was illiterate). Four years later he offered him the position of Sunday school teacher at one shilling per week. At the young age of eighteen Henry was already becoming an important member of the community.

In his youth he, like many young men, enjoyed a drink, and in his diaries he occasionally refers to over indulgence resulting in headaches and nausea. When he reached his 22nd year his attitude towards alcohol changed radically, and on the 30 March 1838 he took 'The Pledge' at the Wesleyan Chapel in Fulletby. He became a fierce advocate of abstinence as can be deduced from a diary entry on 27 December 1840:

> Participated in the sacrament of the Lord's Supper. I thought seriously that the institution was dishonoured by intoxicating wine being used as a symbol of the blood of our Saviour. Should rejoice greatly to receive the sacrament in the pure juice of the grape.

Following Richard's death his mother married Joseph Blackbond of Belchford, eventually moving there. In 1840 the 24 year old Henry married Maria Maltby of Belchford, and on 21 May she came to live in Fulletby. The following year they suffered the effects of a virulent fever. Maria, Henry and his youngest brother Matthew, who lived with them, became victims of the epidemic. They were so ill Sarah had to return to her former home to nurse them. About 100 people were afflicted in the village, and nine died as a result of this highly contagious disease that physicians were unable to identify.

During the family's illness the shoe-making business ceased to trade and consequently, by the time Henry recovered, they were nearing financial ruin. The couple considered their situation and gauged this to be an opportune moment to embark upon a new venture. They partitioned off part of their living room, borrowed £10, acquired credit for £20 and commenced a grocery and drapery trade. To help augment their income Henry also farmed on a small scale, was occasionally employed as an auctioneer's clerk, became an expert at paper hanging

Fig. 2: Henry Winn's home at Fulletby. He lived here for over 90 years
(Photograph: W Winn Marshall)

and taught himself land surveying. In a letter to a friend in 1879 he states

'I refused no employment that would earn me an honest sovereign'.

The shop enabled Henry to put his poetical skills to work. He wrote a series of poems which he had printed onto labels, and then attached to packets of tea. He not only provided his customers with refreshment but a little pleasure too.

The Lincolnshire Wolds

I love the hills, the Lindsey hills,
   Where healthy breezes blow;
And bubbling fountains feed the rills,
   That through the vallies flow.

Not lofty mountains, rugged, steep,
   And cloth'd with endless snow;
But gentle rises white with sheep,
   Or broken by the plough.

Such hills as form my native Wolds,
   Where plenty spreads her charms;
And every vale a village holds,
   Encircled round with farms.

Tis pleasant in the Marsh to roam,
   And in the well drained fens;
But more I love my le-Wold home,
   My native hills and glens.

Among the hills my home I make,
   And when this life shall close,
Under a hillock green I'll take
   My last, my long repose.

Having recovered from the fever and successfully established his shop, fatherhood entered his life. In February 1843, Maria gave birth to Sarah Ann, followed by Selina in June 1844. Unfortunately these happy events did not continue. During her 28 years of marriage Maria gave birth to 21 children, but only four survived to adulthood. Emily, born in 1849, tragically died of consumption twenty years later, Margaret, the last of the Winn children to survive, was born in 1868. The sadness felt, by Henry and Maria is expressed in his diaries as this entry indicates:

Last night our dear little boy expired in my arms at 11.45 p.m. aged only nine days. He was in convulsions from about 9 a.m. I should like to have kept him but the Lord's will he done.

Maria was seventeen years old when she married, but she did not seem to fully recover from the fever of 1841.

She died at the young age of 46 on the 11 December 1869, just a few months before her daughter Emily.

Henry's diaries mainly record his thoughts and activities but this one gives a rare glimpse inside his home. It is dated 5 February 1846:

At about 11p.m. we were alarmed by a fire breaking out. The girl had drawn the clothes horse, full of clothes, near to the grate which had a small quantity of fire left. She hung her own frock on the child's chair which was so near to the grate that it caught fire and spread to the clothes horse. We had not been in bed long when we heard some books fall off the shelf. The shelf hung in the recess suspended by a cord. I ran downstairs to find the room filled with smoke. I realised what had happened so picked up a bucket and ran to the well in the yard for some water. Maria called our neighbour Ranson to assist us and we managed to put the fire out between us.
The room was badly damaged, all the clothes and chair were burnt, many books were destroyed as were most of the pictures and curtains. I estimate the loss at about £5. It was lucky we had not been in bed long as the damage would have been worse. We shall have to work hard and be very economical to make up the loss.

Henry enjoyed travelling round the county jotting down interesting facts and unusual events. In the summer of 1849 he took his oldest daughter, six year old Sarah, on one of these tours. From Fulletby the two of them walked to Hatton where they stayed overnight. The next day they made their way on foot to Langworth and after a night's rest they caught a train to Lincoln. While there they visited the cathedral, castle and Newport Arch, after which they caught the steamer to Boston and stayed with friends. They began their homeward journey on the steamer to Kirkstead, and then walked to Horncastle where they were offered a lift in a cart on its way to Fulletby.

Henry was addicted to the pen and he recorded information in every possible guise; essay books, letter books, diaries, poems and scrap-books. Nothing seemed to escape his attention: family situations, changes in social attitudes, farming methods, inventions, education, religion, history and even anecdotes found their way into his manuscripts.

Conversations were recorded for posterity as exemplified by the following:

He recounts the occasion when a village shopkeeper was convinced that monies collected at her missionary meetings seldom found its way to the mission field. In order to test her theory she marked several coins and placed them in the collecting box. The next morning the Vicar called at the shop and paid for his purchases with money that included the coins she had marked. This she believed proved her suspicion. Henry, however, did point out that the money could have been transferred through the bank or post office.

Another relates to a wealthy merchant who was also a very religious man. He regularly made very long prayers at the family altar for his sick and distressed neighbours, whose suffering was rarely relieved. One day his young son expressed a desire to possess his father's wealth, and when asked what he intended to do with the money the little boy replied 'I will answer all your prayers father'.

In one of his letter books there is an amusing entry recording the correspondence he sent with his Income Tax Exemption Claim on 22 February 1843.

> I am a shoemaker by trade, as all my neighbours know,
> And where I carry business on the top of this will show.
> I've searched my books until I'm tir'd and yet it does appear
> That from this source I have at most but sixty pounds a year.
> Also a cottage, garden, shop, myself doth occupy,
> In annual value about six pounds, situate in Fulletby.
> The holy Sabbath to improve, has always been my rule,
> And two pounds ten, I yearly draw, for teaching Sunday School.
> Look o'er these items, one by one, and cash them up, and then
> You'll find my yearly income is but sixty-eight pounds ten.
> Thus, as required I have set forth a full and correct statement
> Of what my annual income is without the least abatement
> For bad book debts, expense of tools, land tax, repair of premises, –
> Poor rates, and boons, fire, food and clothes and numerous etceteras.

Henry kept large scrap-books in which he pasted pictures from newspapers and books together with published articles and poems. In 1857 he cut out a letter which had been published in a local newspaper giving an account of life in Fulletby.

> Dear Editor,
> With your permission I will give you a brief sketch of our little village which it situate about four miles east of Horncastle and contains 300 inhabitants.
> There is a nice little church dedicated to St. Andrew, it has five stained windows, a stone pulpit, carved reading desk, a beautiful mosaic floor and good harmonium well played, resident clergyman who preaches twice on Sunday. A clerk well up to the mark for he is a grocer and draper, land surveyor, tax gatherer, paper hanger, a noted poet and staunch teetotaller. One Wesleyan Chapel, one Primitive Methodist Chapel, two Primitive preachers of the right sort - not female - one public house the Axe and Handsaw and one beer house the Black Horse. One carrier who has no tilt to his cart, three hagglers, one rat catcher very cunning one miller an honestish chap, no doctor but two doctoresses one of whom sells her powders by the pound, three midwives very handy. I am going to say three sons of St. Crispin but one is a daughter, no barber but one hair cutter and bunion shaver. No resident butcher, one pig killer, there were recently two but one has given up the trade. No dressmaker but a good fit would do well to come amongst us. No policeman though one is sometimes wanted, two charwomen, one nurse who understands her business. A few female smokers and several Laudanum takers, plenty of newsmongers and backbiters; two wheelwrights one very clever at mending old pumps and the other at mending windows. One beehive maker fond of his bacca, one amateur barrow maker a very swaggering chap, one well sinker and land surveyor who can talk for a week and be none the worse. Six farmers some of them good to the poor, two cottagers four old maids, three bachelors. Two gamekeepers quietish fellows, one blacksmith who is also a carver in wood and stone and headstone letterer second to none, no tinker.
> One church school, one school mistress who was a good singer before tunes came up, one Roman catholic. One mangle house with a patent mangle, one hawker of cows foot jelly, two bake houses very punctual in time, one gardener who knows a thing or two, one letter box emptied at four, three coal sellers, twenty-four thatched and mud houses, one brickyard, four widowers and six widows.

Home and family were at the heart of Henry's existence. In his letters he acknowledges the support and comforts his two spinster daughters brought to his life after Maria died. Later in his life he provided a secure future for Selina and Margaret by placing the shop and house in their names.

I'm a King in my own Chimney Corner

I'm a King, I'm a King, though I wear not a crown;
  And a queen is my wife gentle Alice;
I've the neatest, and happiest home in the town,
  And that home, though a cot, is my palace.
My subjects are Charlie, and Willie, and Ben,
  Little Mary, and Maggie and Annie;
Besides a ring-dove, and a handsome pet hen,
  And a faithful old dog we call Fanny.

> You may say this is folly and sneer at my song,
> But 'tis thus I repel every scorner :-
> Unsought by a fawning and flattering throng,
> I'm a king in my own chimney corner.

Every morn, at my levee, are constantly found
  Health and joy, and contentment, and beauty;
Where my dear loyal subjects are gather'd around,
  To present me their love, and their duty.
I consult with my senate on matters of state,
  And defer to each honest opinion;
And I toil at my calling both early and late,
  For the good of my little dominion.

> You may say this is folly and sneer at my song,
> But 'tis thus I repel every scorner :-
> Unsought by a fawning and flattering throng,
> I'm a king in my own chimney corner

Every subject of mine is well taught, and well fed,
  The result of my patriot labour.
Through strife or ambition I never am led
  To encroach on the rights of my neighbours,
As I'm friendly dispos'd other monarchs agree

Fig. 3: Fulletby: the church, the school and an old farmhouse, the latter now gone
(photograph W Winn Marshall)

To respect both my person, and borders;
And my people are happy, contented, and free,
    Without pensions, or titles, or orders.

    You may say this is folly and sneer at my song,
    But 'tis thus I repel every scorner :-
    Unsought by a fawning and flattering throng,
    I'm a king in my own chimney corner.

Henry's knowledge of Lincolnshire was extensive and he became a celebrity in the county. In 1904 an article appeared in a local newspaper which illustrates the respect he was accorded during his lifetime:

Mr. Henry Winn of Fulletby near Horncastle Lincolnshire who has been Parish Clerk at Fulletby for seventy years visited Lincoln on Tuesday last. Mr. Winn is 89 years of age and he was appointed clerk of his parish at an early age. He is at present on a visit to his daughter Mrs. Marshall of Branston and a few days since he travelled by train from Branston to Burnley in Lancashire in order that he might see his sister who has attained a great age and is considered the oldest inhabitant in Burnley. Mr. Winn still enjoys the full vigour of his mental facilities and his keen interest in antiquarian matters is unabated. Mr. Winn has wielded a prolific pen and the majority of his many publications being in verse. His poetry is richly melodious and it is perhaps in his vivid historical pictures and in his portraiture of rural splendours that he appears at his best. His knowledge of history and lore of the county is very extensive and he is the possessor of a library of books relating to Lincolnshire of considerable value. In books and literature generally Mr. Winn from an early age has taken great interest and nothing gives him more pleasure at the present time than to recall many a quaint and curious volume of forgotten lore.....

In one of his essay books there is this extract which highlights the many changes that he had witnessed in his long life:

I am now in the 88th year of my age and have resided in Fulletby all my life. I have lived in five reigns, one of them the longest in the annals of England, and of course have seen many and great changes. On looking back it seems like a new world since I first knew it. I remember the time when we had no railways in England, when the powers of steam and electricity were scarcely known beyond the laboratory of the scientific chemist, when we had not gas to light our towns, and of course no electrical trams or bicycles. There was no Union workhouse, no rural police, no penny postage. These things are such necessities now that we should not know how to do without them and are as familiar in our mouths as household words.

Ten years later on 23 January 1914 Henry celebrated his 98th birthday and he wrote a poem which he sent to his many friends thanking them for their thoughts and gifts.

Birthday Thoughts and Thanks
January 23rd, 1914

I heartily thank all my friends and my God,
　For many bright gleams on the road I have trod;
And I feel truly thankful to find I am here,
　As I enter this morning my 99th year.

Old age is a blessing by many desired,
　Yet where much is given, there much is required,
This calls for reflection and heart searching too,
　Have I done the work well I was given to do?

If the good things above are apportioned to all
　For the good work done here, then my portion is small;
But so little I know of the doings above,
　My future I trust to God's mercy and love.

Many thanks for the blessings I've had in this life,
　A kind careful mother, a true hearted wife,
Good children, kind neighbours, and fairly good health,
　And for one mercy more, the absence of wealth.

With my heart free from envy, my tongue turned to praise
　I cheerfully wait for the close of my days;
Many thanks to my friends for their tokens of love,
　May we all meet at last in the mansions above.

From Henry Winn
To...

This was to be Henry Winn's last birthday. The Grand Old Man of Lincolnshire died on 17 October 1914. His death was mourned throughout the county and obituaries appeared in newspapers across Lincolnshire, but perhaps this simple tribute is the statement he would have appreciated most

.................The funeral took place on Wednesday afternoon in the churchyard opposite the house, the grave being within a few yards of the road. There was a large attendance, practically the whole of the villagers being present to pay their last tribute to one whom they had respected for so long, while many friends from the surrounding villages were in attendance. The Rector Revd. Robert Barker. Rural Dean officiated.

Fig. 4: The two Winn brothers c.1906:
Richard (standing) and Henry
(Photograph W Winn Marshall)

Considering Henry's dedication to the power of the pen I feel the last words should be written by him, and this seems a fitting epitaph to a man who surrounded his life with books and manuscripts.

Words

The highest art that man on earth can reach
Is rightly to employ the part of speech.
The greatest power the world has ever known,
By which the monarch mind upholds his throne;
Secures his conquests o'er the realms of thought,
And makes of use the crude ideas caught,
Is words; - so easy formed, so glibly spoken,
So wild and way-ward when their checks are broken.

Like to an eastern despot on his throne,
The mind can freedom boast, and it alone.
And as his abject slaves, and vassals stand,

To do his sovereign will, and dread command,
So words of every sort, and grade, we find,
Are but the promptings of the ruling mind:
Harping of gentle peace, and firm alliance;
Or trumpet notes of war, and stern defiance.

Words spoken are but breath, and hence we find
They bear resemblance to the changing wind.
Soft soothing words are zephyrs, light and gay,
Fanning the wanderer on his sultry way.
The stirring words of love we may compare
To summer whirlwinds driving through the air.
Kind words like gentle breezes after showers,
Come thickly laden with perfume of flowers.

Rude words are winds surcharg'd with sleet and hail;
While angry words drive on, a fearful gale.
Sarcastic words bite keen as northern blast,
When winters icy frowns o'er earth are cast.
Loud boist'rous words are fitful as the gales
Which in the stormy month of March prevails.
Hot ireful words produce an irritation;
And warlike words blow up a conflagration.

'Tis with the pen the mighty mind records
Its flights and fancies in the form of words.
This sage advice I give to old and young,
Guard well the flow of words from pen and tongue.

Dyke near Boston
(Drawn by Hilary Healey)

John Speed's Map of Lincoln

R A Carroll

The first printed map of the City of Lincoln was published by John Speed in 1611. The original drawing made by Speed in 1607 has recently been found in an Oxford College. This paper discusses the significance and historical setting of this find.[1]

From the onset of the project by John Speed (1552-1629) to produce a work to rival William Camden's *Britannia* he envisaged a set of county maps to accompany his text. Speed's earliest interests were in theology and it is significant that when he helped Hugh Broughton to publish *Concent of scripture* in 1588 to 1589, it contained maps, one engraved by William Rogers and one attributed to Jodocus Hondius. In 1595 he published a wall map of Canaan and around 1598 he presented maps to Queen Elizabeth and obtained from her a post in the Customs, possibly on the recommendation of Sir Fulke Greville. Three further maps were presented by him to the Merchant Taylor's Company, of which his father was a member and of which Speed himself had been made free in 1580.[2]

By 1600 Speed was becoming more involved with genealogical, historical and topographical research and he mixed with the circle surrounding the early days of the Society of Antiquaries. Members at that time included William Camden, Sir Robert Cotton and William Smith. Speed certainly made use of the books and manuscripts in the libraries of Cotton and Camden. Smith was involved with the preparation of a series of county maps in 1602 to 1603 but only twelve maps are known and most are based on the earlier maps of Christopher Saxton and John Norden.[3] Camden's great work *Britannia* was first published in 1586 in Latin and without maps, although there are indications that a series of accompanying maps was contemplated for the 1589 edition. In 1607 a new edition appeared with maps of all the English and Welsh counties; they included little that was new, 41 of them being ascribed to Saxton, six to Norden and the remaining ten being largely unsigned.[4] In that edition the text remained in Latin; only with the 1610 edition was Camden's work translated into English, the year before Speed's English language work.

Nearly ten years before the eventual publication of *The Theatre of the Empire of Great Britaine: presenting an exact geography of the Kingdomes of England, Scotland,* Ireland and the Iles adioyning... a start had been made on the design of the first of Speed's county maps. William Rogers (a native of Cheshire, like Speed himself) who had engraved one of the maps for the Broughton work referred to above, now engraved a map of their own county. Since it has the arms of Queen Elizabeth as part of its surrounding design it must have been created before 1603. Rogers died in either 1604 or 1605 and would probably have been engaged to provide more of the planned series of county maps. A new set was begun including a new plate for Cheshire; thirty-three of the maps are signed by Jodocus Hondius and he or others under his supervision engraved all the plates in his workshop in Amsterdam. The work took until 1611 to 1612, the dates on the title-pages of the final published work.[5]

By the beginning of the seventeenth century a growing interest in town plans had begun to develop in England, perhaps spurred by the pioneering work on the continent by Georg Braun and Frans Hogenberg whose *Civitates orbis terrarum* had begun appearing in 1572. It had town plans of important places in Europe, being itself based on a series of maps of Dutch towns prepared from 1558 by Jacob van Deventer for Philip II of Spain. While, in their first volumes, they had no plans of English towns several surveyors had started to make plans of English towns; these included Norwich (1559), London on twelve or fifteen copper plates (date not known precisely, since the complete map has not survived though three of the plates have come to light, but between 1553 and 1559), Bristol (drawn 1568), Cambridge (1574) and Oxford (1578).[6]

When Speed came to compile the atlas part of his work he used county maps already in existence to provide the basis for the newly engraved plates. The bulk of them derive from the surveys of Christopher Saxton, first published as a collection in 1579 but he also used two manuscript maps of William Smith, Symondson's map of Kent (1596) and five maps previously prepared by John Norden; four other maps are derived from local contributions including the map of Rutland prepared by John Harington.

What is original is the inclusion on the county plates of some 73 inset town plans. The address to his readers by Speed, concerning these plans, includes the phrase: 'some have bene performed by others, without Scale annexed, the

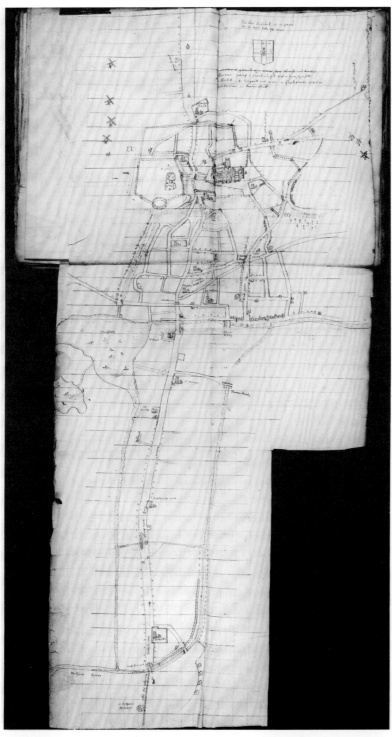

Fig. 1: The first printed map of the City of Lincoln was published by John Speed in 1611.
This original drawing made by Speed in 1607 has recently been found in an Oxford College.
The drawing measures 102.2 cm x 45.5 cm at its widest

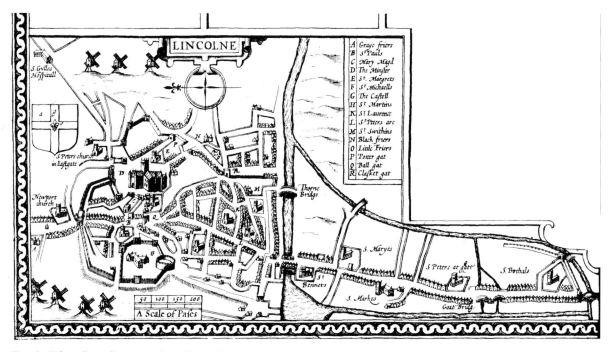

Fig. 2: When Speed's town plan of Lincoln was engraved next to his county map it was turned through ninety degrees to fit in the lower left-hand corner of the plate and also lost some detail at its extremities

rest by mine owne trauels, and unto them for distinction sake, the Scale of paces'. While there has been much discussion of whether Speed did actually survey so many towns these words do not leave much room for doubt that Speed claimed the credit for such survey work. Evidence now makes it more clear that he did work his way around England and Wales, but not Scotland, and the 50 town plans that have 'A Scale of Paces' or a similar phrase can now be assigned to original work done by Speed.[7] The recent discovery of 33 manuscript maps in Merton College, Oxford removed any doubts about the authenticity of the greater part of Speed's claims, since five bear the initials I.S. or (Newport, Isle of Wight), John Sp. Their similarities to the plans that have no signatures make it clear that Speed with his son (also John) drew the others.

From the dates on the surviving drawings it is possible to trace a great deal of Speed's itinerary. The earliest date shows that he was in Winchester on 14 to 16 August 1606, moved on to Dorchester (Dorset) and was in Hereford on 1 September before surveying Brecon, Cardiff and Carmarthen. In 1607 it is probable that Speed was in Warwick on 17 June (the date he was given official permission to conduct a survey – the drawing has not yet been found); he was in Ely on 5 July before journeying to

Huntingdon, Peterborough, possibly Stamford and Oakham, before arriving in Lincoln on 19 July 1607. Subsequently, his travels took him to North Wales, northwest England before returning to the Midlands (Stafford and Lichfield). Further work in 1608 is known now to have produced maps of Bedford, possibly Hertford and Newport (Isle of Wight).[8] This year, therefore, marks the 400th anniversary of the drawing of the first known plan of the city of Lincoln..

One incidental result of this find is thrown up by the plan of Stamford, which Speed did not incorporate on the Lincolnshire plate but had engraved on the plate of Rutland. From the above itinerary it is clear that Speed was in Peterborough on 8 July [1607] and had reached OUKHAM (as it is spelt on the Rutland plate) on the 13 July 1607. The scale on the plan of Stamford is in paces – a clear suggestion of Speed's own surveying. It would seem reasonable, therefore, to assume that Speed passed through Stamford on his route and drew his plan between those two dates although the manuscripts that have now been found do not include Stamford (or STAMFORT as it appears on the proof copies).[9]

The drawing of Lincoln is on sheets of paper stuck together to allow Speed to include the whole of the then city area from *Gray friers* in the north to *St Kathrens Nunorye* in the south (figure 1 – all names on the drawing are given as spelt and in italic). Speed is believed to have used a plane table to make his drawings. Such a table would have measured 30.5 x 38 cm and have allowed the surveyor to use a full sheet of foolscap paper, measuring 34 x 43 cm. That Speed felt the need to add pieces of paper to his basic sheet is, of course, because of the peculiarly elongated nature of Lincoln's shape This means that the final drawing measures 102.2cm from the top to the bottom and 45.5cm at its widest. So many of his other drawings easily accommodate the fairly regular rectangular shapes of our more ancient county towns, such as Dorchester (Dorset), Canterbury and Northampton without additional pieces of paper being necessary.

We can only deduce from the finished products how well trained Speed was in surveying practice. He made life easier for himself by preparing a grid of red lines at one inch (2.5cm) intervals on his working paper – a system that many children learn to adopt when copying a drawing or plan on to another sheet. Speed tried to indicate the steepness of the hill below the cathedral by drawing a wavy line (rather like barbed wire) from just south of the castle to the eastern outskirts of the city.

One slightly unfortunate result of Lincoln's 'irregular' shape is that, when it came to engraving and placing the plan within the framework of the county's delineation Hondius, the engraver, would not allow the inclusion of the plan to disturb the design he had organised for the left-hand side of the plate (a series of ten heraldic shields of the county's great and good). He turned the plan round ninety degrees to fit it into the lower left-hand corner of the plate, with the result that north on the plan in its final engraved state is to the left (figure 2).

Space considerations obviously forced the engraver to make some alterations from Speed's original (figure 3); two immediately noticeable changes are that Newport/Church is now the most northerly point and the bridge over the unnamed Sincil Drain is the southern limit. This also means that Speed's original words at the top of the drawing have been 'lost'; above the city's heraldic shield they read:

Lincolne described at 50 paces/ to the inche Iuly 19. 1607 and below it: *This citie governed by a maior, tow* [sic] *sherefs and twelve/ Aldermen, having a sword and hat before themselves/in scarlet, 4 Sergants with mace a Sword bearer, recorder/Chamberlain and towne Clerke/.*

On the west side of the city the fuller extent of *Bradforth* (i.e. Brayford Pool) on Speed's original is curtailed and

its link to a large mass of water to its west disappears. To the north-west Speed showed four windmills in a roughly north-south line and to the north-east three more in a short diagonal array; Hondius included them in his engraving but the constricted space in which he was working has forced him to foreshorten their positions so that they appear much nearer the city's environs than Speed intended. Foreshortening especially affects the elongated form of the area south of *Thorne Bridg* as far as *SouthBargat* and beyond; while the distance from *Newport Church* to *Thorne Bridg* is roughly one third of that from *Newport Church* to *South bar gat* on the drawing, the distance, as it was finally engraved, is only just under a half. The engraved depiction of Steep Hill, The Strait and the road as far as High Bridge is more or less a straight line. Speed's drawing is a much more subtle delineation of that thoroughfare's slight changes of direction and curves.[10]

Many features of the present city are clearly drawn, especially the churches but also some of the street names. One notable variation is that the present Steep Hill is here labelled at its upper portion *Bore hill* – perhaps a reference to a well since the present-day Well Street is close by. Another unusual feature of the drawing is the inclusion of two sets of figures seine fishing – one group with both men in boats on the Brayford and the other pair on the water adjacent to the Brayford, a figure on the shore holding a line out to another in a boat. The delineation of swans and other sea birds on the Brayford is an enjoyable extra. Features that are delineated but have disappeared include a representation of a pillory to the east of *St Benet*, stocks just north of *Goats Bridge* and *St Laurenc(e)* church (to the east of The Strait). Reference has been made to one notable feature that Speed drew on his plan but has not appeared in the engraved result – *St Kathrens Nunorye*. At the time of Speed's visit the site of St Katherine's Priory must still have shown signs of its former existence – it was only seventy years since Henry's dissolution of the monasteries after all.[11] Curiously, the Malandry or Hospital of the Holy Friars, which stood on the east side of the road leaving the city's southern gate (and opposite the Priory) is not drawn by Speed; two oddly shaped marks may indicate the site but they are unnamed. Much else on the drawing has its own historical interest. Attention has been drawn to the bridge at the end of the lane by St Mary's which might have been a simple wooden affair.[12] Along the modern High Street the only buildings noted are *St Peters ye gat*, *Goats bridge* and *st Botthalls*. For goat read gowt while the latter equates to St Botolph's. Interestingly, what is often referred

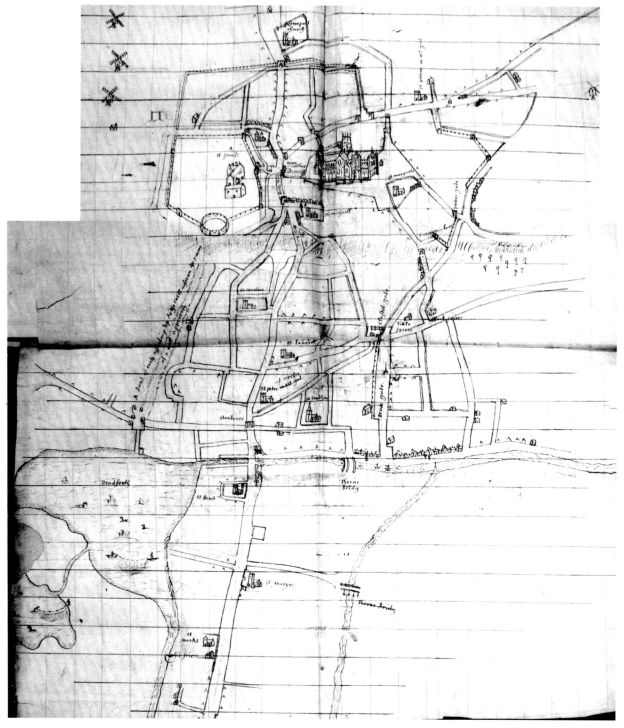

Fig. 3: Detail from Speed's survey drawing of Lincoln in 1607

to as John o' Gaunts Palace is not drawn or identified here. Among other features on the drawing that are altered on the final engraved result are *St Benet* (becomes St Bennets); *Brode gate* (is not listed; the whole road has been named as Clasketgate when Speed only drew Clasket gate as a gate at the northern end of *Brode gate*); *whit friers* and *Stan bowe* have both been omitted. Conversely, Speed did not include a compass but Hondius has engraved one prominently below the city name. The most significant change between the drawing and the engraving relates to the depiction of houses. Only under close scrutiny can small inverted letters v be discerned as Speed's marks for domestic habitation, the v meant to indicate a house's upper gable. Hondius in his engraving shows a large number of houses in a bird's eye view and may have, thereby, exaggerated the city's housing stock particularly along the modern High Street. Speed's marks only extend from the southern gate as far north as *St Marks* with one more 'arrow head' just south of *St Maryes* and three more on the north-west corner opposite that church.

How the Speed drawings arrived at Merton College, Oxford is a matter for speculation. Dr Bendall[13] puts forward the theory that Sir Henry Savile, the Warden of Merton at the end of the sixteenth century, and whose brother was a founder member of the Society of Antiquaries and was himself a great friend of William Camden, moved in circles that overlapped Speed's. Probably through that congruity of interest Savile acquired the volume containing the drawings. Until 1998 the volume was housed in the College's Sacristy and never appeared in any earlier catalogues of the college books or manuscripts.

Although Speed's drawing and the subsequent engraving are together the earliest indication we now have of the city's late medieval appearance a suggestion has been put forward [14] that the symbolic representation of Constantinople in the Luttrell Psalter (1345) is based on Lincoln. That, if true, would give the modern historian some idea of what the city looked like some 250 years or so earlier than when John Speed made his historical trip to Lincoln in 1607.

I am grateful to the Warden and Fellows of Merton College, Oxford for permission to reproduce their manuscript of Speed's drawing, to Dr Julia Walworth, Fellow librarian, Merton, who provided facilities to examine the drawing; and also to John Gibbons, who took the photographs of the original drawing.

Notes:

1. D R Mills and R C Wheeler, *Historic town plans of Lincoln,* 1610-1920. (Lincoln, 2004), pp. 3-4 includes discussion of Speed's map, the text of which (by R A Carroll and Dr J A Johnston) had been prepared before the paper reporting the discovery of the original drawing (see note 8 below) came to the attention of the authors.
2. Dictionary of National Biography: www. Oxforddnb.com/articles/26/26093 –article.html?back=
3. R A Skelton, *County atlases of the British Isles, 1579-1703: a bibliography* (1970) pp. 19-22.
4. *op. cit.*, pp. 25-30 (and later editions, pp. 67-68).
5. *op. cit.*, pp. 30-44 (later editions up to 1695 are discussed throughout the work; for seventeenth century editions see D Hodson, *County atlases of the British Isles published after 1703*: volume 1; atlases published 1704 to 1742 and their subsequent editions, Tewin, (1984), pp. 40-49 and 60-70; R A Carroll, *Printed maps of Lincolnshire, 1576-1900* (Lincoln 1996), pp. 18-26.
6. C Delano-Smith and R J P Kain, *English maps: a history,* (1999), pp. 190 and 280; J Howgego, *Printed maps of London, circa 1553-1850*; second edition (1978), pp. 8-9, 32 and 43 – at the time of publication only two of the three surviving plates were known.
7. R A Skelton, 'Tudor town plans in John Speed's *Theatre*'. The *Archaeological Journal*, vol. CVIII, (1952), pp. 109-120.
8. Sarah Bendall, 'Draft town maps for John Speed's *Theatre of the Empire of Great Britaine*'. *Imago Mundi*, volume 54, (2002), pp. 30-45. The shelf mark of the collection of drawings found in Merton College, Oxford is D.3.30.
9. Proof copies are held in British Library (Maps C.7.c.5) – dated to c.1608 - and (prepared slightly later but before 1610) in Cambridge University Library (Atlas 2.61.1 and Royal Geographical Society (265 G 25)). The only difference between the proof copies and the final engraved plan is the inclusion of letters on the city's heraldic shield, intended to aid any colourist, i.e. o = or = gold; a = argent = silver, g = gules = red. These indicators are present on Speed's original drawing, except that Speed puts *ar* for argent.
10. Mills and Wheeler, *op. cit.*, pp. 1-4 for discussion of the city's growth and decline and estimates of its changing population.
11. Sir F Hill, *Medieval Lincoln*; re-issued [enlarged] edition. (Stamford, 1990), pp. 343-352; *Victoria History of the County of Lincolnshire*, volume 2, (1906), pp. 188-190; M Jones, D Stocker, and A Vince, *City by the Pool*, Oxford (2003), *passim*.
12. Jones, Stocker, and Vince. *op. cit.*, p. 246. Although St Mary's Lane is not actually named on the original or the subsequent engraved plan K Cameron notes that this is the earliest reference to the name – see *Place-names of Lincolnshire*, volume 1, (Nottingham, 1985), p. 95.
13. Bendall, *op. cit.*, pp. 41-42.
14. J Harvey, 'Symbolic plans of a city, early 15th century' in R A Skelton and P D A Harvey, editors, *Local maps and plans from Medieval England* (Oxford, 1986), pp. 342-343.

Standing on the Shoulders of Giants: William Fowler and Thornholme Priory, an Early Venture in Lincolnshire Archaeology and its Sequel

Glyn Coppack

In the days when it owned the greater part of the Roman town of Ancaster and the Cistercian monastery of Kirkstead, there was a time when Nottingham University thought of Lincolnshire as its own, a place of great opportunities and remarkable potential where it could encourage its graduates to get involved. I was sent there in 1970 by Maurice Barley to become a proper archaeologist, entrusted to the care of Tom Baker, and advised to listen carefully to Ethel Rudkin and David Robinson. Little did I know that, apart from a brief excursion into my native county of Yorkshire, I would still be here 36 years later. My career, and my love of the county, spring directly from Professor Barley's advice and the support and advice I was so freely given. To paraphrase an early Lincolnshire polymath, Sir Isaac Newton, it is easier to see when you are standing on the shoulders of giants.

My involvement with Lincolnshire was cemented, and my career established by a lucky accident. In 1974 I was asked to undertake a rescue excavation at Thornholme Priory at Appleby where the site was being damaged by unauthorised cultivation. Thornholme was one of those wonderful sites that Lincolnshire hides away; remarkable archaeology, fascinating buildings, and a wide open field of research[1]. Thornholme was a house of Augustinian canons, founded by King Stephen in 'his wood of Appleby' in the Ancholme valley to the east of Scunthorpe. Never important in its own right, unlike the Yorkshire monasteries it led me to, it was typical of the majority of smaller monasteries in England, and perhaps more significant, typical of monastic houses in Lincolnshire. The excavation was to continue until 1981, and unwittingly, I found myself being guided by another early Lincolnshire giant, the architect and antiquary William Fowler of Winterton. I say unwittingly because I had no idea he had been there before me though I knew someone had, because we kept finding old excavation trenches. Research for the Humberside Archaeological Survey of 1979 produced a possible date of 1873 for this intervention[2], which would have been completely unremarkable. Then, sixteen years after the completion of the excavation, Kevin Leahy sent me copies of some papers he had found in the Fowler archive and everything was suddenly clear. There was not

very much – two documents totalling 680 words, some sketches, and a plan. There was also a date, March 1818. It is probably the earliest monastic excavation for which we have a contemporary written record and drawings by someone who was present during the work. To put it in context, the excavation of Jervaulx Abbey by John Claridge between 1805 and 1807 was not recorded until 1845[3], Martin Stapylton's excavation at Byland Abbey undertaken between 1818 and 1820 was recorded by a third party in 1823[4], and Charles Pelham's excavation at Thornton Abbey, which was recorded by the excavator at the time, was not completed until 1835.

The church at Thornholme Priory

Looking at the surviving documents it is not immediately obvious where the early nineteenth century excavations at Thornholme were made, and only in the first instance why they were commissioned. Re-excavation provides the benefit of hindsight – the two areas examined were the priory church and the great gatehouse. For the church there is no plan but there is a good description. Interest in the site was occasioned by a chance discovery, recorded in William Fowler's hand:

> This was being discovered on the intake of C. Winn Esq. at Thornham near the river Ancholme, a Stone coffin a very little below the surface of the ground. A labourer was cleaning a ditch and found some opposition to his pursuit which led to the exposure of this piece of antiquity. There was formerly a Priory here which is quite demolished with the exception of the foundations and some parts of the walls that are now overgrown with the sward – the ground form of the building may yet be traced and Mr Winn has opened a part where he discovered a doorway and some fragments of window tracery etc.
> This coffin lay in the usual direction having the feet towards the east and was placed in a S. E. direction at a distance of a few yards from the chancel end. The top was composed of small rough unhewn slabs cemented with lime mortar, and the receptacle contained a perfect skeleton imbedded in earth which appeared to have lain [illegible, ?without] disturbance. The coffin is of one stone and cut as if it had been designed for fitting the corpse. A round part 10in diameter is sunk for the head; the part for the neck is 7½in wide, immediately below the width increases to 1 - 5 [17ins] for the shoulders and gradually tapers to the feet where it is only 11in wide within. There is something peculiar in the formation of the bottom of the coffin. It has a curvature similar to the outline of a man's back, and is 8in deep at the head, 11in deep from shoulders to the lower part of the back, 8in deep at the knees, and 10in deep at the feet, and at the two hollow places near the lower part of the back and the feet are two

holes cut through the bottom of the coffin, each about 1in in diameter. The outer dimensions are 6 - 8 [80ins] in length, 2 - 1 [25ins] at the top and 1 - 5 [17ins] at the bottom in width and 1 - 2 [14ins] in depth without the cover.

Appended is a sketch of the coffin in plan and perspective (Fig. 1), with the following notes:

Arris off round the head
Head 9in deep
Shoulder 11in deep
Knees 8in
Feet 10in deep
Sides cut down perpendicular
Rough hewn

No standing masonry was noted apart from that unspecified part of the site opened by Mr Winn, but Fowler observed that 'the ground form of the building may yet be traced' from the clear earthworks that largely survive today, and his reference to the 'chancel end' left no doubt that he thought the coffin lay within the priory church. It must have been the discovery of the coffin and its contents that led to Charles Winn opening the site further. A record of Winn's excavation, made at the time and transcribed by Fowler's son Joseph in 1868 and associated with drawings in William's hand follows:

Thornholm Priory (Excavations)
3rd Augt 1868

Observed several foundations cleared and plinths of jambs etc., with two patches of encaustic tiles, and one of flag pavers. All the former being glazed and laid alternated of yellow and dark brown, but some of a greenish cast. The one patch being in squares 7x7, and the other 9x9, whilst the limestone (oolite) pavement is in squares 15x15. Many disjointed parts of a zigzag arch, with fragments of jambstones, mullions, tracery, dripstones, round shafts, and numerous mouldings in good preservation and relief. A very fine early English capital, also with other indications of the transition from Norman to early English as well as evidences of construction of a later date. Several human bones were found and decently reburied, and some larger bones, probably of an ox, were lying beside one of the diggings – round and bleached. From two or three pieces of flat red tile, each having a perforation, it is inferred that the building was covered with this material so common in mediaeval times. Some lumps of a metallic composition resembling fused and corroded bronze and iron were also collected, together with several ~~pieces~~ bits of sheet lead whitened by their long subjection to corrosion.

The glazing of the encaustic paviors is quite clear as if unused, though it appears that later work has been set on one part of ~~the~~ a floor, and that all the tile and stone pavements were laid with joints parallel to the walls, as none of any sort are seen lying diagonalwise, *in situ*. The undersides are flat – not sunk for holding more firmly in cement. Semicircular stone, probably the head of a narrow Norman window, - chamfered on the outside at the aperture.

Wm Winn, Watson, Lee, my Father, old Tommy, etc.

24 March, 1818. At Thornholm.

The excavation of the north transept, the northern third of the presbytery, the crossing, and eastern bay of the nave in 1975 and 1976 as an exercise in community archaeology

Fig. 1: The coffin from Thornholme Priory recorded by William Fowler in or before 1818.

encountered clear evidence of an earlier excavation (Fig. 2), narrow trenches following the inner and outer faces of the walls and running through the north transept into the crossing. At the time it was thought they dated from the late nineteenth century, though at the time no precise record could be found of an earlier excavation. These trenches had penetrated floors, and in their backfilling were a number of architectural fragments which included elements of the late twelfth century arch referred to in the record. Evidence of shallower excavation within the choir area was probably removed by machine stripping and not observed in excavation, but the floor of the choir and the north transept chapels with their limestone paving remained largely *in situ*, as did the floor tiles on the north side of the nave, their dimensions being identical to those recorded by Fowler. In the nave, the tiles were laid square to the building, and were laid above an earlier mortar floor, suggesting that these were indeed the tiles observed by Fowler. They were also completely unworn. The modern

Fig. 2: The church at Thornholme Priory, looking east, at the conclusion of excavation in 1976.
The depressions in the unexcavated demolition rubble to the right of the excavated area are
unemptied trenches from the 1818 excavation

excavation revealed a monolithic stone coffin with a female burial on the north side of the presbytery, undisturbed though it had lost its cover, lying below later medieval choir stalls, some six metres from the east wall. To its east was a child burial below a cut-down waster thirteenth century grave marker with an incised floriate cross. Neither of these burials was the one recorded by Fowler, for the woman was in a coffin with a flat base which retained a part of its lid and the child was buried in a stone-lined grave. Fowler's burial was found in clearing a ditch, and it is not without significance that the road that runs across the site down to the River Ancholme lies at a slight angle over and just outside the south wall of the church. The south transept gable survives as a substantial earthwork immediately to the south. Fowler recorded the burial 'a few yards from the chancel end' suggesting it lay on the north side of the road in the ditch that is still apparent on the surface. This would place his burial on the south side of the presbytery, opposite or to the east of the burials found in 1976. The

fact that the coffin was capped with rough limestone slabs would suggest it was originally covered with a raised tomb and not a simple ledger like the grave to the north, though this would have been removed when the late medieval choir stalls were inserted into the western half of the presbytery. The northern burials had been covered by the northern bank of stalls in the later Middle Ages.

As Fowler says, the excavation was conducted by Charles Winn within his intake or enclosed land. This was prior to the cutting of the West Drain on the west side of the Ancholme valley in or before 1836[5], the cultivation of the valley floor and the subsequent shrinkage of the peat that surrounded the cornbrash limestone outcrop on which the priory stood. It also predated the construction of the small courtyard farm built by the Appleby Estate in the 1860s or 1870s to the north and west which has substantially obscured the earthworks of the church. Its barn, now ruinous, was built of reclaimed materials,

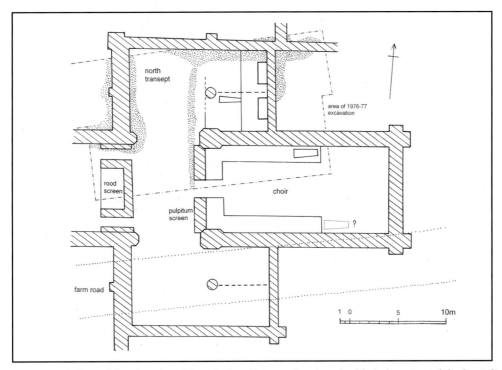

Fig. 3: Reconstructed plan of the church at Thornholme Priory, showing the likely location of the burial recorded by William Fowler as dotted line coffin. Stipple indicates the location of the 1818 trenches

including elements of a window with reticulated tracery recorded by Fowler and presumably recovered from Winn's excavation and left on site. Almost certainly, other material from Thornhome was included within the folly and 'medieval cottage' that Fowler built in his garden at 53 West Street, Winterton in 1827 to 1828[6].

If this had been the total of Fowler's interest in Thornholme Priory it would have been important enough. No plan has been traced in the Fowler archive, but the excavation of the 1970s provides a perfectly good framework in which to understand William Fowler's careful observations. Indeed, it is possible to reconstruct the plan of the eastern part of the church with a fair degree of accuracy from the walls excavated in 1976 to 1977 and its surviving earthworks and to place Fowler's observations in a meaningful context (Fig. 3). The modern excavation revealed the whole of the north transept, a little over half of the first bay of an unaisled nave with the base of a late medieval rood screen, almost exactly half of the crossing and pulpitum screen, and the northern bank of stalls at the west end of the presbytery. Apart from the rood screen nothing stood more than two courses above floor level. What is represented is a fairly typical canons' church,

Fig. 4: Reticulated tracery from an early fourteenth century window at Thornholme recorded by William Fowler. Some elements of this window survive in the west gable of the ruined barn of Thornholme Priory Farm.

unaisled, and with shallow two-bay transepts each with two eastern chapels. What Fowler did not realise, though it was immediately apparent from the construction of the walls, is that although the west wall of the north transept was contemporary with the north wall of the nave (they actually bonded) and the north wall of the presbytery, the north and east wall of the transept were a modification. Originally, the transepts did not have eastern chapels, and a robber trench for a north-south wall seen in the west end of the grave in the southern chapel of the north transept was almost certainly the original east wall of the earlier transept. The first phase of the church was dated to about 1170 by a lancet window that had fallen virtually complete from the upper part of the west wall of the north transept and by a mass of Transitional architectural detail; pottery from construction levels suggested that the transepts had been rebuilt in the first quarter of the thirteenth century. Fowler's 'disjointed parts of a zigzag arch' and 'evidences of construction of a later date' (Fig. 4) also recovered when the church was re-excavated indicate that he was

recording architectural detail that belonged to the building. He was right, too, about the church being roofed with tile, though perhaps he was stretching the evidence of 'two or three pieces' a little. Thornholme was a relatively modest monastery, built for a community of 12 to 15 canons, but typically had high quality decorative carving that belies its simple plan. Its development follows that of Kirkham in Yorkshire, where a simple cruciform church of the 1140s was extended and updated in the 1180s[7], the only difference being that the Thornholme church lags 30 years behind the development of Kirkham, showing that the Augustinians were as conservative in their planning as the Cistercians were after them.

The great gatehouse

The excavation of the great gate of the priory between 1976 and 1979 revealed a building which had been substantially robbed in the 1830s when the West Drain was cut through the site and a bridge built across it to carry the road that still runs through the fourteenth century gate passage. Presumably the robbing was to provide infill for the spandrels of the brick bridge, and it rather implies that the building was visible at the time the bridge was being built. Robbing had not quite destroyed the evidence of earlier excavation, and the discovery of a measured plan with dimensions (Fig. 5) in the Fowler archive proves beyond doubt that he returned to the site and examined the gatehouse. The plan is in the hand of Joseph Fowler,

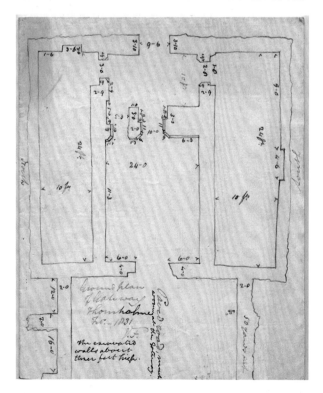

Fig. 5: Fair drawing by Joseph Fowler of the dimensioned plan of the great gatehouse of Thornholme Priory taken from an original made in 1831.

Fig. 6: The southern part of the mid fourteenth century great gatehouse at Thornholme Priory as excavated in 1976, seen from the west, showing its relationship with the farm road and bridge of 1835 to 1836 over the west drain. Note the almost total removal of masonry which was present when Fowler planned the building

Fig. 7: The northern part of the mid fourteenth century great gatehouse, seen from the north, with its detached latrine tower and the northern precinct wall. Mid fourteenth century and later floor levels and the damp-proof membrane of blue clay have been removed to reveal the surviving footings of the gate and the north wall of its predecessor.

and it appears to be a fair copy of an original site drawing, possibly made around the time of the 1868 transcription above. The notes on the plan, which is dated February 1831, indicate that some three feet of masonry remained above the foundations, and Fowler was able to record the location of doors and wall fireplaces that no longer existed when the site was re-excavated. As with the church, it was the walls that interested him, not the floors within or deposits outside the gate.

Thornholme's great gatehouse was rebuilt in the mid fourteenth century to the standard plan of a central porch and gate hall flanked by guard chambers, virtually identical in plan and dimensions to the contemporary great gate at Bardney Abbey and only slightly smaller than the surviving great gate of Bridlington Priory. Because the access road still runs through the porch and gate hall the building had to be excavated in two parts, and the southern side was excavated first (Fig. 6). Thus, we were unable to see the whole of the building at one time or to investigate the porch and gate hall. Virtually all masonry had been removed from the southern half of the gatehouse and had been robbed down to a damp-proof course of blue clay on its north side, and the roadside ditch, present only on the north side of the roadway, cut into the robbing of the north wall of the gate hall (Fig. 7). Only walls that ran below the road were not robbed of good building stone, presumably to retain a firm bed for the road as it approached the bridge, and they could not be re-examined. Fortunately Fowler had not been so constrained in his work.

Excavation revealed that the gate was a complex structure (Fig. 8); indeed it was the third gatehouse to be built and incorporated the remains of the second gatehouse, built early in the fourteenth century. It also had contemporary buildings against its west wall flanking the late medieval road into the precinct. These buildings, however, had been demolished to ground level or below at the suppression and

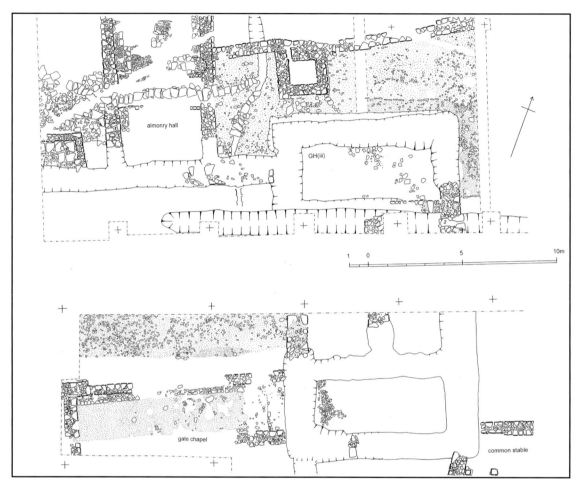

Fig. 8: Plan of the great gatehouse at Thornholme Priory as excavated between 1978 and 1980, with the almonry hall to the north west, the gate chapel to the south west, the detached latrine tower and precinct wall to the north, and the common stable to the south.

cannot have been visible when the gatehouse itself was planned or robbed in the nineteenth century. Fowler was only drawing standing masonry, and was unaware of adjoining structures to the west and south. At the time of his work, the road did not run through the gatehouse. Excavation was to show that it had been diverted around the north side of the building, and the removal of the ruin was to permit it to run in a tolerably straight line. Thus the robbing of the building, the construction of the road and its northern ditch across it, and the construction of the bridge across the West Drain were all part of the same operation.

Thornholme's great gatehouse, the entrance to the inner court and the church and cloister beyond it, was a monumental structure 17.5m wide and 10m deep,

designed to impress visitors, and was approached along a walled lane, not the free-standing building that Fowler supposed. It stood in the north-west corner of a walled precinct at the end of a short causeway that brought the entrance road onto the island. The almonry stood on damp ground on the north side and the gate chapel stood on the south side of the road immediately to the west of the gate on a slightly raised bank of wind-blown sand. The guest stable stood immediately to its south east. Within the gate was a substantial paved yard, bounded to the north by the precinct wall that followed the edge of the island. To the north of the gate was a detached latrine tower that was clearly related to it, the two separated by a narrow passage into the enclosed almonry yard. Thus we can see the gate in context, the point at which access was restricted to the inner

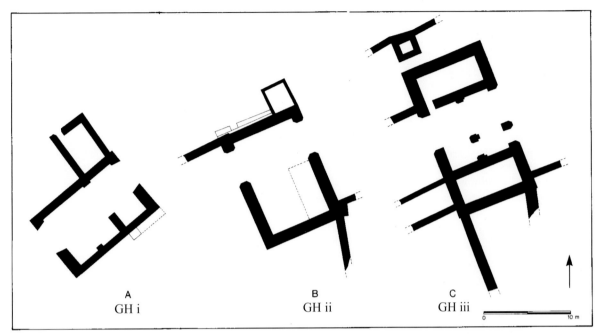

A
GH i

B
GH ii

C
GH iii

0   10 m

Fig. 9: The sequence of great gatehouses excavated at Thornholme Priory. Note that the latest phase (C) was drawn without the knowledge of Fowler's dimensioned plan and places the pedestrian access on the south side of the gate passage and a door into the northern guard room from the gate porch.

court, the poor, most women, and the destitute excluded, and alms distributed.

From Fowler's plan it is clear that he saw it as a distinct building, apparently of a single building phase, and it was not immediately clear on re-excavation that he was wrong. On the south side of the access road virtually no masonry had survived, but the construction trenches of the external walls were all clearly contemporary. It was only the untangling of the archaeology of the northern side of the gatehouse that showed it was two buildings and not one. The earlier building Fowler had barely seen at all because the evidence for it apart from a butt joint in the east wall was all buried below the undisturbed floors of the northern guardroom. It remains the case, however, that we would not have understood how the building was extended and reconstructed without the early nineteenth century plan.

What was not understood until the 1970s was how gatehouses related to the monastic enclosure, and this was partly a result of their common survival to serve post suppression houses while their attendant buildings rarely survived the 1530s. They tended to be elaborate buildings, often decorated with the arms of the founder and other patrons, and almost exclusively late medieval buildings or re-buildings. How the plan had developed was not known, and until the re-excavation of the Thornholme gate and the excavation of the Kirkham gatehouse[8] in 1978 and 1982, untested by excavation. Thornholme[9] provided the perfect typological development of the monastic great gate (Fig. 9) – a tower-like gate with an off-centre passage way of the end of the twelfth century (GH i); a passage way and single guard chamber of the early fourteenth century like that of Kirkham Priory (GH ii), and a mid fourteenth century gatehouse with paired flanking guard rooms like Bardney or Bridlington (GH iii). The first gate was a free-standing building at the entrance to a ditched precinct enclosure; the later gates were an integral part of a walled precinct, something which does not appear to have been common before the early thirteenth century in Britain.

The two fourteenth century gates at Thornholme really need to be seen as one structure that was substantially enlarged within a generation of its building. The earlier building, known since its excavation as gatehouse GHii, was a rectangular structure of two storeys, its upper floor of unknown use accessed by a stair outside the south wall. The entrance road ran through its northern half, and the porter occupied a timber-partitioned cubicle in the south-east corner. Its southern two thirds was built directly onto a thick build up of pitched limestone roads and had no need of foundations, but its northern third was built into the butt end of a pre-existing precinct ditch and required substantial foundations and northward projecting buttresses. Within its footings was an opening with a segmental arch of undressed limestone voussoirs that drained the ditch where it lay below the gate. The whole building was constructed of coursed limestone rubble set in dense blue clay and grey sand, but all that survived of it above contemporary ground level was its north-eastern corner and buttress. Against the north wall and within the precinct ditch was a small timber-framed building set on narrow stone cill walls that provided accommodation for the porter.

When GHii was reconstructed in the mid fourteenth century as gatehouse GHiii, a rectangular guard chamber was partitioned in its southern third, and a second guard chamber was added against the north wall of the earlier building. That wall was then taken down to its foundations and a narrower wall built in its place. The west wall of GHii was similarly taken down to footing level and rebuilt of rubble limestone set in gritty orange clay. It was built around a surviving stub of wall that extended westwards from the north-west corner buttress of the old gatehouse and was of one build with the narrower north and east walls of the new guard-room which were similarly bonded, and which butted up against the surviving north-east corner buttress of gatehouse GHii. The northern guard chamber was then levelled up and a surface of hard, off-white mortar, the finished floor, was laid. The new wall that separated the porch and gate hall from the northern guard chamber appeared to stop one metre short of the west wall of the gate, suggesting a door at that point, though no door was recorded there by Fowler, and it may never have existed. A second door in the north wall was marked by an area of external paving. No original floor or evidence of doors

survived in the southern guard chamber, and there was no evidence inside the building of a stair to the upper floor. The early fourteenth century stair against the south wall must have been retained. Of the upper storey, the only evidence was a detached latrine tower built in the old precinct ditch and which must have been reached by a timber bridge. It implies a domestic use for the upper floor, and the contents of the latrine included the bones of a sparrow hawk, goose, duck, pigeon, and domestic fowl as well as exotic pottery and a bone whistle signifying high status. In contrast, the debris on the floors of the ground floor guard rooms suggested that the porter enjoyed more basic fare.

Once the enlarged gate was completed, there were no apparent changes to its structure before the monastery was suppressed in 1536. It was however modified inside. In the late fourteenth century a new floor of pitched limestone was laid in the south guard chamber, removing all earlier deposits down to the underlying road surfaces, and in the mid fifteenth century a new floor of orange-brown clayey sand incorporated the remains of a cill wall for a partition cutting off the east end of the northern guard chamber. Within the partitioned space was a hearth of flat stones and a spread of ash.

William Fowler had a good eye for detail, equalled by few antiquaries before 1850. It has to be admitted that his work at Thornholme Priory was hardly of national significance, in spite of its early date. However, that view is only possible with hindsight. But for a lucky accident, the site may never have been revisited. Then it is the only evidence we would have had for the priory's buildings apart from its earthworks. What it does show is that his observations were acute and to the point, and rather ahead of their time. Re-excavation has shown that he can be 'trusted', perhaps the greatest compliment one archaeologist can pay to another.

Notes

1   G Coppack, 'Thornholme Priory, the development of a monastic Outer Court' in *The archaeology of rural monasteries*, edited by R Gilchrist, and H Mytum, (BAR British Series 203, 1989) pp. 185-222.

2   N Loughlin and K Miller, *The Humberside Archaeological Survey*, Humberside Libraries (Hull, 1979) p 182

3   J Stopford, *Medieval Floor Tiles of Northern England*, Oxbow (Oxford, 2005) p 304

4   E Baines, *History, Directory, and Gazetteer of the County of York*, *Vol. 2* (Leeds, 1823) p 422

5   W Andrews, *History of Winterton and the adjoining villages* A D.English (Hull, 1836) pp. 47-48

6   N Pevsner, J Harris and N Antram, *The Buildings of England: Lincolnshire* Yale University Press (London and New Haven, 2002) p 805

7   G Coppack, S Harrison and C Hayfield, 'Kirkham Priory, the architecture and archaeology of an Augustinian house' in *J British Archaeol Assoc* 148, (1995) pp. 63-70 and figs 2-4

8. *op. cit.* pp. 105-118 and figs 15-19

9. G Coppack, *Abbeys and Priories* Tempus (Stroud, 2006) pp. 132-134 and fig. 81

The Withern Cottage Project – goes on

Rodney Cousins

During October 1980, beside the busy Mablethorpe Road in Withern, an old brick and tiled cottage had started to be demolished. Adjoining the cottage was a recently built bungalow, and the intention was that the bungalow would replace the cottage on the site. However, the cottage was far from ordinary: as the brick wall was removed a mud and stud building was revealed, and under the roof tiles was the original thatch. There it was, encased, hidden and yet protected by its relatively modern outer shell. Staff at the Museum of Lincolnshire Life were alerted to the situation, to enable at least some recording to be done before the cottage was destroyed. On a grey, drizzly day elementary recording began and the cottage revealed its complete timber framework from within. The learning curve also began; just how many mud and stud buildings were still in existence? Was there a possibility of reversing the demolition order? Were there any other alternatives? Clearly more advice was required, and Nottinghamshire Buildings Preservation Trust expertise, with Prof. Maurice Barley and architect and timber frame specialist John Severn, came to the rescue. Their advice was to create a project team to carefully dismantle and record the cottage. If all went well, John Severn suggested, it could be saved by re-erection elsewhere. The rest, as they say, 'is now history', and within eighteen months, the cottage had been dismantled with the support of Community Action Project Skegness (CAPS), and re-erected at Church Farm Museum, complimenting the existing farm buildings, and providing a new attraction.

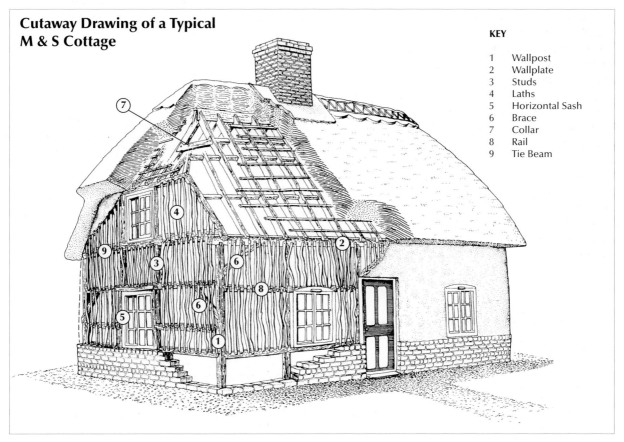

Cutaway Drawing of a Typical M & S Cottage

KEY

1	Wallpost
2	Wallplate
3	Studs
4	Laths
5	Horizontal Sash
6	Brace
7	Collar
8	Rail
9	Tie Beam

Fig. 1: Cutaway drawing of a typical mud and stud cottage (drawn by David Hopkins, Heritage Lincolnshire)

In addition to saving and reconstructing the building, the Withern Cottage Project highlighted a number of other related issues. How many mud and stud (M&S) structures survived? How many had been destroyed within living memory? Were there others, like Withern Cottage, under threat of demolition? What level of protection did they have? Clearly, the Withern Cottage Project had only finished the first stage; a platform to raise awareness of this unique form of Lincolnshire building was urgently required. Visitors, publicity and John Scoley (Lincolnshire's master thatcher who put the golden crown of thatch on the Cottage) added to the floating information. A working list of M&S properties that required recording was prepared, followed by a successful bid by the Museum, to appoint a photographer/recorder, Ken Walker. At the end of the year, Ken Walker and the museum staff mounted an exhibition entitled 'Timber framed Views of Lincolnshire'; and invited all the M&S owners and other interested parties to the opening. The exhibition was opened by John Severn and the enthusiasm from owners gave 'mud and stud' a new

buzz-word status; 'wattle and daub' was a term locally on the decline. Owners wanted more information, contacts, support, and above all a support group. Other M&S phases were about to begin. First, an M&S register was begun by the writer, listing all known M&S properties, existing and demolished. The register total grew rapidly at first, passing 400, then 500 and, after several years, up to nearly 900.

Meanwhile the owners' needs helped to bring about the creation of the East Midlands Earth Structures Society[1] (EMESS). The interest in earth as a building material was gradually gathering pace within the UK and abroad both as a historical technique and a modern 'eco-alternative'. EMESS was the third regional 'earth buildings' based group to be established in the UK. The Devon Earth Building Association (DEBA) was established in 1991, with a direct interest in the thousands of cob buildings, with the greatest concentration being in Devon. In 1994, the carefully chosen acronym, EARTHA was coined for the East Anglian Region Telluric Houses Association covering

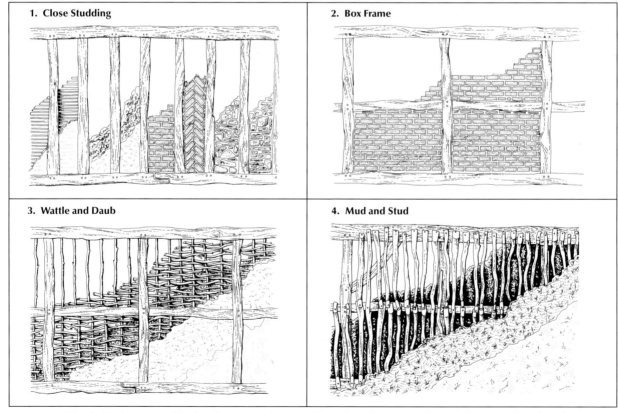

Fig. 2: Techniques of timber framing - close studding, box frame, wattle and daub, mud and stud
(drawn by David Hopkins, Heritage Lincolnshire).

Fig. 3: Withern Cottage 1980, demolition started and halted. Cottage now at Church Farm Museum

the area that includes the clay lump tradition. The UK has a surprisingly wide range of earth building techniques which include 'clom' in Wales, 'wychert' centred in Buckinghamshire, more cob in the East Midlands, 'clay dabbins' in Cumbria and even 'stake and rice' in Scotland. Some of these techniques are in serious decline, with little protection. EMESS quickly established itself as a very practical 'hands on' group, made up of owners, conservators, architects and historians, together a powerful resource of support for M&S. EMESS currently has a membership of around forty, holding four or five meetings per year at different locations. They also arrange talks, village walkabouts and their popular demonstrations at the Lincolnshire, Heckington, and Spilsby Shows.

English Heritage maintain the national register of 'listed' buildings which designates those buildings considered to be of 'special architectural or historic interest'. In the early 1980s only about thirty M&S buildings were listed, and they were mostly recorded only because they were 'timber framed'. One outcome of the Withern Project and the new M&S register was the ability to lobby for M&S to be recognised as a local Lincolnshire technique, and for the best examples of that technique to be listed. Following a visit to Lincolnshire by the Royal Commission on the Historic Buildings of England, mud and stud finally received recognition and was considered by the Royal Commission to be 'of national significance'. During the mid 1980s Lincolnshire was 're-listed' with the number of M&S listings rising to 166. There are 113 in East Lindsey, thirteen in West Lindsey, seventeen in South Kesteven, seven in NE Lincolnshire, six in Boston, four in North Kesteven, three in South Holland and three in North Lincolnshire. The re-listing has effectively halted the trend for demolition, although sadly, several

Fig. 4: The Old Vicarage, Billinghay, now restored by North Kesteven District Council

*Fig. 5: Greetham, Beech Farm 1985, before restoration
and dendrochronology proved its real age.*

George Pasks, Lowthorpe, adjoining the Perseverance, now replaced
by Willow Lodge

*Fig. 6: Southrey, the Old Perseverance Public House,
one of many M&S revealed in recent parish histories.*
(from Southrey, not the back of beyond Marjorie W Woodcock 1998)

disappeared between the recording phase and the official
notice of listing.

Photographic resources

The Hallgarth collection[2], then at the Welholme
Gallery, Grimsby, contained a wonderful collection of
Lincolnshire photographs amassed by the local historian
Bill Hallgarth. The collection is now housed at Grimsby
Library, Local Studies, and may be viewed by appointment.
Over 170 mud and stud buildings, most of them now
demolished, are recorded in this fine collection. The
National Monuments Record, based in Swindon[3], also
has an extensive photographic collection. Here, as in

most collections, photographs are stored by parish,
and in three days you can just about get through all the
Lincolnshire box files. Anyone undertaking a parish or
building study, is strongly recommended to view this
magnificent collection. Lincolnshire County Council's
recently developed Illustrations Index[4] has a wide ranging
collection which, significantly, recognises M&S as a
specific subject classification.

The M&S register is still maintained as an ongoing
project by the writer. To date it has around 900 M&S
entries. These include approximately 385 existing
buildings, and over 500 buildings demolished within
living memory. By district, East Lindsey has over 70%
of those known and almost 80% of those still surviving.
Other district tallies are:- South Kesteven: 60, of which 26
are existing; West Lindsey: 50+ with twenty existing; NE
Lincolnshire: 54 with thirteen existing; North Kesteven:
53 with thirteen existing; Boston: 29, with six existing;
South Holland: nineteen with seven existing, and North
Lincolnshire: eight with four still existing. Individual
parish leaders are:- (with a special fanfare!) Mareham le
Fen with 57 on the M&S register and with 42 still existing.
This amazing total means Mareham has over 10% of our
county's M&S heritage, and I feel whilst, perhaps not of
World Heritage status, it does deserve special recognition
and support. Picturesque Thimbleby has twelve registered
and ten existing, Hagworthingham has eighteen with
nine existing, Belchford has eleven with eight existing,
Bolingbroke has ten with six existing and Coningsby has
seventeen, with five still existing. Other parish notables
are, in West Lindsey, Bardney (& Southrey) with seventeen
(five existing), Middle Rasen with 26 (three existing),
Thurlby(SKDC) with twenty and six existing. North east
Lincolnshire leaders are - Humberston with eleven and two
survivors, and Grimsby recorded with ten, but sadly with
none existing. Finally in Heckington (NKDC), fourteen
with four still existing.

Following early retirement in 1998, the writer had
the perfect opportunity to put all this accumulated data,
including the M&S register, many photographs and the
story of the Withern Cottage Project, into a publication.
The resultant book 'Lincolnshire Buildings in the Mud and
Stud Tradition' was published in May 2000 by the Heritage
Trust of Lincolnshire and was another by-product of the
Withern Cottage project. The book launch date coincided
with an International Conference, 'Terra 2000', held in
Torquay, with EMESS participation. Thus M&S went
international and much experience was gained and shared,

Fig. 7: Fulstow, Poultry Farm Cottage 1999, one of many cottages restored with EMESS expertise

with earth structures as the common bond. The M&S book is now out of print, but it has done its job. It has spread the story of Lincolnshire mud and stud techniques and has ensured that our unique vernacular architecture receives the recognition it deserves.

During 1995 to 1996, an M&S restoration project at Beech Farm, Greetham, incorporated a dendrochronological survey. Prior to this project, the property was described as 'a mid seventeenth century listed building … probably timber framed … internal evidence suggests a number of posts survive'. The survey proved the structure was mainly fifteenth century, and incorporated some timbers from the fourteenth century. So the original estimate was up to 250 years off the mark. The restoration scheme located an almost complete timber frame. As this is the only M&S property to have had a dendrochronological survey, one wonders how many others can be proven to be much earlier than at present assumed? A representative selection of other M&S properties, would add a great deal to proving M&S is a technique locally well known in medieval times. I feel another M&S Project is overdue!

Restoration of over 30 M&S buildings over the past twenty years, mainly by EMESS members, has widened the experience of conservators, architects and specialists who have questioned the best, or the traditional, methods of mixing mud, the ratio of components, method of application, mud and lime finishes, the use of tallow in limewash to improve waterproofing etc. Experience and time will prove the best methods. Thatching too has been examined in some detail nationally - reed or straw, preferences, availability and design. Re-thatching often poses a problem of whether to restore 'like for like', or 'following the local style'. There are a number of regional differences, particularly with the ridge, and certainly Lincolnshire labourer's cottages with their fairly plain ridge had no sign of a straw pheasant running along the thatch!

The millennium brought a welcome upsurge in village publications, recording parish life for posterity at this important milestone. Most are well researched and illustrated, with a number including a glimpse of their present or former vernacular architecture. Villages with a

Fig. 8: Mareham le Fen, Hawthorne Cottage, a shining M&S jewel in this special village

good representation of M&S within their content include, Bilsby, Coningsby, Heckington, Maltby le Marsh, Old Leake, South Kyme, Southrey, Tetford, Willoughby and Wrawby.

Notes:

1. East Midlands Earth Structures Society (EMESS), c/o David Glew, 20 West Parade, Lincoln LN1 1JT
2. The Hallgarth Collection – Local Studies, Grimsby Library, Town Hall Square, Grimsby, DN31 1HG
3. NMR, National Monuments Record Centre, Great Western Village, Kemble Drive, Swindon, SN2 2GZ
4. Illustrations Index – c/o Lincolnshire Archives, St Rumbold St, Lincoln LN2 5AB

PARISH	DETAILS OF M&S STRUCTURE	DIST
Bardney	Barn, adj Silver Birch Fm	WL
Belchford	Barn, 'Flint Hall'	EL
Bicker	Cottage, School Lane adj Sch	B
Deeping St James	46 Bridge St	SK
Dogdyke	Cottage, W Riverbank, Chapel Hill	EL
East Kirkby	Cottage, The Wagon, Fenside	EL
Goxhill	Barn, Littlewick Fm, South End	NEL
Great Carlton	Old Hall, interior wall	EL
Halton Holgate	Cottage, Wold View	EL
Harrington	Cottage, behind Woodman's Cott.	EL
Heckington	April Cottage, Fen, Kyme Rd	NK
Hemingby	The Cottage, Mill Lane/New End	EL
Holland Fen	Sunnybank (not seen)	B
Horncastle	72-74 West Street	EL
Hundleby	Brown's Cott, North Beck Lane	EL
Ingoldsby	Old Shop	SK
Langton by Wragby	Barn, Hoop Lane Farm	EL
Mareham le Fen	Woodview Cott., Birkwood Lane	EL
Mareham le Fen	Cottage adj Fish shop, Main St	EL
Mareham le Fen	Former Woodman's Rest, Main St	EL
Mareham le Fen	Horseshoe Cottage, Main St	EL
Mareham le Fen	Primrose Cott/Toft Hurn Moorside	EL
Mareham le Fen	Sandy Nook, Main St	EL
Mareham le Fen	Bldg behind Old White Horse, Main St	EL
Mareham le Fen	Spring Villa, Fieldside	EL
Mareham le Fen	Unnamed Cottage, Fieldside	EL
Mareham le Fen	Cott. next to Clark Butcher, Main St	EL
Mareham le Fen	Cottage behind Levine Cottage	EL
Middle Rasen	Old Vicarage, Low Church Rd	EL
Minting	Mill Cottage	EL
Mumby	Mill House	EL
North Somercotes	Outbuilding, Church Farmhouse	EL
North Thoresby	Cottage, Dickinsons Lane	EL
Orby	Barn, opp lane to Church	EL
Revesby	Gamekeeper's Cottage	EL
Sibsey	Jay's Cottage (not seen)	EL
South Willingham	The Forge Cottage (Listed)	EL
Stickford	Ashton's Cottage	EL
Stickford	Warren's Cottage	EL
Surfleet	Bldg nr Golf Course, Park Lane	SH
Tetford	Brookside Cottage	EL
Tetford	Old Post Office, opp White Hart PH	EL
Tetford	Cottage, Mill Lane	EL
Thimbleby	Post Office, Main St	EL
Thornton	Ox Pasture Farm	EL
Thornton	Thornton House	EL
Thurlby	Barn	SK
Waltham	Cottage now Café near Windmill	NEL
Waltham	Bramble Cottage	NEL
Waltham	Cottage, next to PO, High St	NEL
Welton le Marsh	Rea Farmhouse	EL
Willoughby	Willoughby Arms PH	EL
Wyberton	Cott. West End Lane nr Chain Bridge	B

Table showing mud and stud structures located since the publication of Lincolnshire Buildings in the Mud and Stud Tradition in May 2000, and thus not included in the gazetteer within the book.

Points of Reference (& Reverence) in the Lincolnshire Landscape

Rex Critchlow

A local historian told me that Lincolnshire spires were all deliberately sited to be navigation aids for travellers. My own feeling is that they were for the most part not deliberately planned or sited, but were placed in the centres of established communities and became points of reference in the landscape over time and were useful navigation aids in pre sat-nav days.

In some cases roads and redevelopments have occurred that make churches form a central focal point in a village. However, I consider towers and steeples were really built for reasons of symbolism and status, thus demonstrating the dominant influence of the church.

In Lincolnshire (and I mean the old County) there remain over 700 churches and chapels serving a county whose population at one time was the second highest in the land. When most of the population left the county (along with much of the money) during the industrial revolution, the residual population were blessed with a rich heritage of buildings including the best collection of spires in the world.

One characteristic that is constant is that each of the county's spires is distinct. This is a helpful aid for travellers as they cannot be confused by 'look-alikes'. (Exceptional in this regard is Haugham which seeks to copy Louth).

Some of our spires have features and materials in common, and these often reflect a local fashion or a shared master mason who up until the Georgian period often acted as unnamed architect. Some spires compete for quality and embellishment with the use of clip on details – see the crockets at Louth, Brant Broughton, Stamford All Saints and many others as they endeavour to 'out crocket' each other. Some regard size and in particular height as lending status to a parish or indeed a whole town. Louth and Grantham vie with each other in the height stakes, whilst Stamford has a fine pair of spires and many pinnacles. Perhaps this stems from its early ambitions to be a university town of dreaming spires – the third Oxbridge.

Clearly at one time the most prominent spires in the county were the three on Lincoln Cathedral, removed, like other less well known examples, for safety reasons. Indeed spire building techniques in the Middle Ages were largely experimental and predate the calculation of wind loads. By way of example, Chartres Cathedral was said to have fallen down six times before the final structural solution was found.

Lightweight copper, shingle or lead covered spires built on permanent timber frames are more susceptible to wind damage, but were a favourite form when a spire was to be added to an existing masonry tower in order to achieve the much desired 'steeple status'.

Apart from a local desire and need for each spire to be its own icon in the landscape, I assume that all church builders and benefactors would prefer to have a complete steeple, rather than having to stop short and only have a tower. Then, as now, the need to cut costs at the design stage or during construction was a real factor. Nothing has changed over the centuries except that in modern terminology 'cost cutting' is termed 'value engineering'!

The selection of spires I have chosen illustrates the extraordinary diversity of shapes, sizes and details to be seen in Lincolnshire. One day somebody may compose a 'Good Spire Guide'. Such a guide would tell by star rating which spires, first seen in the distance, were worth homing in on so the visitor could search for the key and enjoy the body of the church and its star rated contents.

Top of my list and always worth a detour is Caythorpe, located on what I call 'the spire run' from Navenby to Grantham. Let its sugar-loaf form draw you to its fascinating interior so that you can puzzle over how a church ends up with arcade columns located in the centre of the nave. It also puzzles me why Temple Moore should deliberately copy this apparent accident of evolution at his 1913 church in Walesby – now there's a church that needs a spire!

These notes can only give the reader a taste of what could become an absorbing fascination; with increased mobility and few people in the way we can all enjoy this unique collection of 'pointers in the Lincolnshire landscape'.

INDEX TO THE SELECTION

For glossary of terms see any volume of *The Buildings of England* by Nikolaus Pevsner.

A SELECTION OF LINCOLNSHIRE SPIRES

Lincolnshire Landscapes

Stuart E Crooks

Lincolnshire is not particularly well known for its landscapes. Though the Fens and the Wolds are referred to in a variety of literature where wildness and remoteness are often the dominant themes, the true variety and richness that the county has to offer remains, to many people, obscure. Often it is the great expanse of the fen with its cloudscapes that is most readily conjured up as an image of the county, but in reality the fen represents only one of many Lincolnshire landscapes, and at that one that is rather misunderstood.

To the outsider Lincolnshire seems scarcely to exist at all. Somehow England's geography is distorted in the popular mind so that the land between the Wash and the Humber, if there is indeed anything perceived between Norfolk and Yorkshire, is *terra incognita*. Vaguely, there may be some recognition that there is a zone of flat land somewhere in the vicinity of the Wash.

Though fenland occupies no more than one quarter of Lincolnshire, it has come to symbolise the county, perhaps more strongly than in some neighbouring counties such as Cambridgeshire which have little else. Why this should be so is a slight mystery, for the county is in truth highly varied and the major communication routes that pass through Lincolnshire – the Great North Road (the A1), Ermine Street and Barton Street – all tend to follow the higher ground of the limestone and chalk.

The underlying geology on which the county's diverse countryside is founded is quite simple, with rocks of the Jurassic and Cretaceous gently dipping eastwards, the Oolitic Limestone and the chalk standing out as highlands with west-facing scarp slopes, features which run roughly north to south. But underlying clays, and superficial glacial sands and boulder clay – all manipulated by the great forces of the Ice Ages – serve to add complexity and local detail which in turn lend the county great variety and character.

Despite the county's fame for potatoes and bulbs, the prevalent landscape is a rather typically English scene with gently undulating countryside, hedged fields and scattered hamlets. Stamford and the villages of the Lincoln Edge are built of limestone, giving a resemblance to the Cotswolds rather than eastern England. In the eastern half of the county there is a dearth of good building stone, so that the Wolds market towns and villages are mostly of brick.

Lincolnshire is one of England's least wooded counties, yet it has – a little known fact – some fine woodlands of national significance. Ancient woodlands with a more or less continuous wooded history since the last Ice Age are widely scattered, but there are three prominent groups worthy of note. On the eastern flank of the Wolds, woods of ash and oak, many with a coppice layer of hazel, are scattered between Louth and Alford. In the Kesteven clay vale there is another group of similar woods with added variety of lime and service. And in central Lincolnshire around Bardney there are the famed Lincolnshire Limewoods where the small-leaved lime, a scarce tree in England, is the dominant species.

Attempts at formalising a division of the county into distinct landscape types or natural areas have had to cope with intricate complexities of local geology and their attendant wildlife habitats. Neither lend themselves to simple categorisation. Of course, bold features such as the chalk wolds and the fens are obvious enough, but it is not so easy to do justice to the scattered sand deposits, or smaller but significant features such as the Spilsby sandstone. The second edition of *The Geology of Lincolnshire* by H H Swinnerton and P E Kent, published by the Lincolnshire Naturalists' Union in 1976, contains a map compiled by D N Robinson which provides an excellent overview of the county. It illustrates, more than anything, that little about Lincolnshire's structure and scenery, save the solid geology, is simple.

Nevertheless, there are clear boundaries between the chief features, so that a useful simplification can be made as an aid to interpretation. In 1999 English Nature published its analysis of *Natural Areas* for each of the government regions in England. At about the same time the Countryside Commission produced its own maps based chiefly on landscape character. Later these two approaches to the problem were combined, resulting in *Joint Character Areas*. These are now widely accepted, and have been adopted by the consortium of statutory agencies, local authorities and non-governmental organisations which has published the *Lincolnshire Biodiversity Action Plan* (Second Edition launched October 2006). Lincolnshire is covered by ten *Joint Character Areas*. Some recognise the marine environment as an eleventh area.

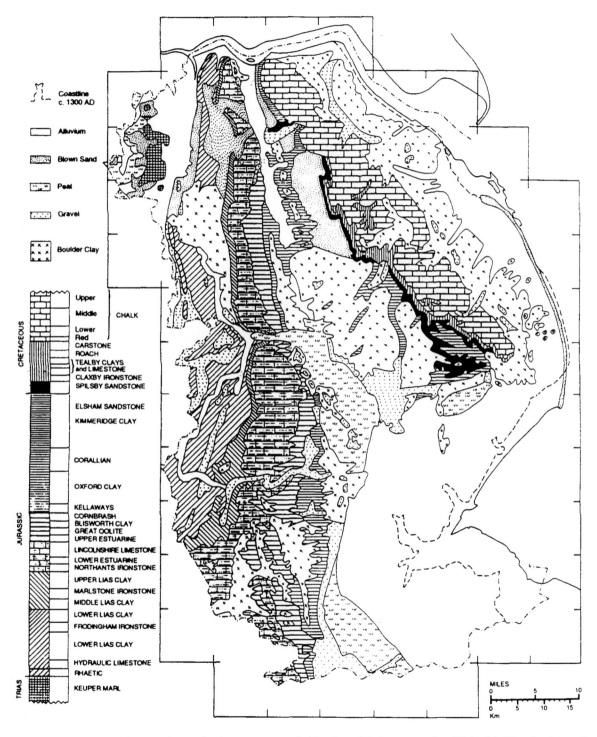

Fig. 1: This geological map of Lincolnshire was compiled by David Robinson and published in The Geology of Lincolnshire (second edition) by H H Swinnerton and P E Kent, in 1976

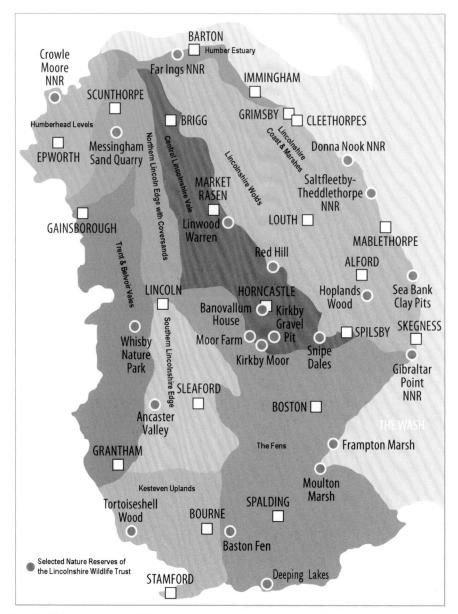

Fig. 2: The Lincolnshire Character Areas map with selected LWT nature reserves added

Useful though the Joint Character Areas are, they overlook many important landscape and wildlife features as illustrated by the maps at Figs. 2 and 3 which should therefore be viewed in tandem. Whilst the first shows the broad brush of the *Joint Character Areas*, the second paints in a little of the detail, showing the fragmentary nature of the Coversands, the continuity of the Lincoln Edge or Heath, the fen edge, and the division of the marsh into the

boulder clay of the Middle Marsh and the marine deposits of the Outmarsh.

The western border of the county is bounded by the north-flowing River Trent with its attendant clay vales and siltlands - the *Joint Character Area* known as the **Trent and Belvoir Vales** - a level landscape looking eastwards to the steep scarp of the Lincolnshire Limestone. The **North Lincolnshire Edge with Coversands** to the

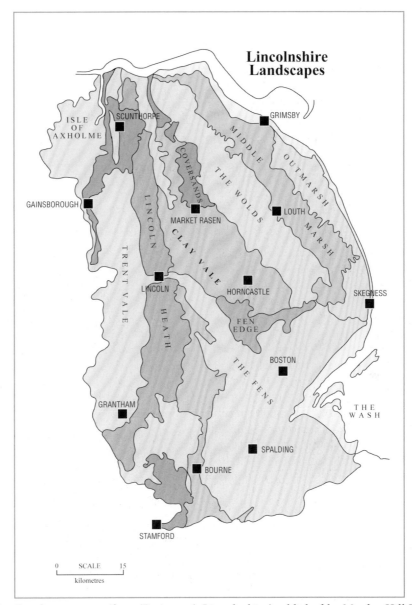

Fig. 3: Lincolnshire Landscapes map (from 'Betjeman's Lincolnshire' published by Morden Hill Press for the Lincolnshire branch of the Betjeman Society in 2006)

north of Lincoln, and the **Southern Lincolnshire Edge** and **Kesteven Uplands** to the south form an almost continuous ridge from north to south of this large county, broken only by the gaps at Lincoln (through which flows the modern River Witham) and at Ancaster (formed by an earlier glacial version of the Witham). Anyone who claims that Lincolnshire is flat should be walked up Lincoln's Steep Hill. It is no accident that the top of this hill was chosen for the site of the Cathedral. From the top there are commanding views of the Trent Vale and, because of the gentle dip slope to the east, there are fine views of the Cathedral to be had from many parts of mid-Lincolnshire and the Wolds. To the north of Lincoln the limestone ridge (or 'Lincoln Cliff') is narrow, but to the south it broadens to form the Lincoln Heath. Further south the limestone is dissected by other valleys where it presents the more broken landscape of the old county division of Kesteven.

Abutting the limestone to the east is an extensive clay vale, which runs down to the southern fen.

From the limestone the view to the east reveals the long low outline of the **Lincolnshire Wolds**. In reality, once one is among these hills, they seem not so low. Indeed, they take in the highest ground in eastern England south of the Humber, rising to some 550 feet at the highest point near Acre House, Normanby le Wold, and include some outstanding landscape features, with a broad rolling upland in the north, and a more dissected area in the south where there are some deep combes. Little of the chalk appears at the surface: most is blanketed by glacial deposits, but here and there fragments of downland survive.

A prominent chalk ridge in the southern Wolds carries the Bluestone Heath Road, an ancient trackway which runs a good way north. But in the south it follows a more or less east to west internal scarp, south of which the chalk has been stripped by glacial action to reveal the underlying Spilsby Sandstone. This southern part of the Wolds, stretching to Spilsby, and almost as far as Horncastle – known sometimes as the 'Spilsby Crescent' – has its own distinctive character. The porous sandstone sits upon a layer of impervious Kimmeridge Clay, giving rise to numerous spring-lines with fretted valleys, always difficult to drain and to farm. It is in this part of the Wolds, close under the chalk ridge, that Tennyson was born and grew up, lending the name 'Tennyson Country' to this attractive intimate landscape set around Somersby, Bag Enderby and Tetford. Tennyson's poems are full of references to his childhood haunts and the 'Calm and deep peace on this high wold…'. Here, too, is Tennyson's Brook – several in fact – that join up to drive the millwheel at Stockwith Mill.

> *I come from haunts of coot and hurn,*
> *I make a sudden sally*
> *And sparkle out among the fern,*
> *To bicker down a valley.*

To the east of the Wolds lies the **Lincolnshire Coast & Marshes**. The marsh is divided into the Middle Marsh and the Outmarsh. Oddly, there is no 'inner' marsh. The marsh is based on a platform cut into the chalk by wave action at a time of much higher relative sea levels. The wave action also created a line of chalk cliffs – rather like today's white cliffs of Dover – which has since been eroded, giving the false impression of an eastward-facing scarp. This is the hill which ascends steeply westwards from the market towns of Alford and Louth. Like the other market towns of the Wolds, they are set at the foot of the hill, on the

perimeter of the Wolds. The Middle Marsh, running up to the foot of the degraded cliff-line, has a capping layer of boulder clay of glacial origin, giving it a somewhat 'lumpy' character, quite different from the flatter marine deposits of the Outmarsh and the absolutely flat fen.

Between the Wolds and the limestone ridge there is the **Central Lincolnshire Vale**, an area mainly of boulder clay and blown sand. In several of the larger valleys, deposits of sand and gravel give rise to other landscapes, where sandy soils lend a 'heathy' character. One of the most extensive of these is the Fen-edge around Woodhall Spa and Kirkby on Bain. These sands and gravels were spewed out by the putative River Bain – the main tributary of the Witham – flowing from the heart of the Wolds, through Horncastle into the edge of the glacial fenland lake. This heathy district includes special places such as Kirkby Moor and Ostler's Plantation, and the two championship golf-courses of the English Golf Union.

Around Market Rasen and Scunthorpe, and extending into the Isle of Axholme (that isolated division of Lincolnshire lying on the wrong side of the Trent), are areas of blown sand known as the Coversands, which also give rise to heathy landscapes and some fine, but fragmented, grass and heather heaths such as Scotton Common and Linwood and Risby Warrens.

The Isle of Axholme is also characterised by the **Humberhead Levels**, a vast expanse of raised bog extending into south Yorkshire. Here, Crowle Moor, an area extensively exploited in the past for peat, is a part of a National Nature Reserve which is home to a range of scarce wildlife. Together these levels are said to be the largest tract of land in England without a road.

Turning now to the last of the chief terrestrial landscapes of Lincolnshire, let us not forget that the south-eastern quarter of the county – the old Holland division – does indeed consist of level fenland. Surrounding the great estuary of the Wash, **The Fens** once formed a vast wetland, drained to provide some of the country's richest farmland. The last large area to be drained, the East Fen, lying between Wainfleet and Stickney, was drained only 200 years ago. Fen is, properly, a watery environment, but the drainage of south Lincolnshire was so thorough that not a vestige remains of the great wetlands that once supplied Londoners with plentiful wildfowl from the ten or more fen decoys. Only the name, and the great cloudscapes, remain, and now the name fen is taken to describe the vast acres of level farmed landscape hedged with ditches and given over to intensive arable production and bulb growing around the principal fenland towns of Boston and Spalding. But not all drained fenland is the same. Look more closely, and one may make the distinction between the silt fen and the peat fen. Also, running around the southern Wash is a slight ridge of raised ground characterised by medieval villages such as Moulton, Whaplode, Holbeach and Sutton, and distinguished by an organic road network. To landward the fen drainage is marked by straight roads and ditches. To seawards, the land has been reclaimed from saltmarsh by building new, and ever larger and higher, sea walls.

Thus we arrive at the last of Lincolnshire's great landscapes – the sea coast. From Trent Falls at Alkborough (where the River Ouse meets the River Trent to form the prodigious estuary of the Humber), to the Norfolk border, close to the outfall of the River Nene in the Wash, is a distance of some 105 miles. Now that Lincolnshire is part of the East Midlands Region, it is worth observing that Lincolnshire possesses the entire regional coast (and a good part of that of the Yorkshire and Humber Region as well).

The two estuaries, the Humber and the Wash, with their attendant sand and mudflats, and fringing saltmarsh, are landscapes in their own right. Here the rivers carry their load of silt to the sea, giving succour to one of our richest environments – biologically more productive than the best farmland. These great wild places are home to teeming wildfowl and wading birds, fuelling stops on the long migration routes. The **Humber Estuary** also has an important fringe of wetland formed by the excavation of clay for cement and brick making and, especially, the tileyards of Barton and Barrow. Many of the claypits are now nature reserves, including the National Nature Reserve at Far Ings. Managed realignment of sea defences at Alkborough and Chowder Ness have added new inter-tidal habitats to the Humber fringe.

Between the two estuaries – from Killingholme to Gibraltar Point – there lies a sandy stretch of coastline,

known to thousands from holiday trips to Cleethorpes, Mablethorpe and Skegness. The developed holiday coast may have its attractions, but in between the towns there is a lesser-known landscape of sand-dunes, saltmarsh and seashore. The broad dunes and marsh of Donna Nook and Saltfleetby (both National Nature Reserves) form the largest unbroken section where the gently sloping beaches mean that the sea is generally a long way off. But as one travels southwards the shore narrows and bulges gently into the North Sea, so that between Mablethorpe and Skegness there is no saltmarsh, only a steep beach mostly flanked by concrete sea walls built to protect this vulnerable part of the coast.

South of Skegness the accreting shore broadens once more. Here lies Gibraltar Point National Nature Reserve, a complex of seashore, saltmarsh, freshwater marsh and dunes on the north-west corner of the Wash. At the apex, where the shore turns sharply south-westwards into the Wash, there is the unusually placed feature of a river outfall – the small un-navigable Steeping River or Wainfleet Haven. This is the outfall of what is known upstream as the River Lymn which carries the tributaries of 'Tennyson's Brook' from the Wolds. The accretion of successive sand and shingle ridges has pushed the shoreline eastwards, so that the old coastguard station now has only distant views of the sea. On a clear day there is a view across the mouth of the Wash to the Norfolk coast of Hunstanton and Sandringham, which has the mysterious appearance of a North Sea island, the low land disappearing into the flatlands of the southern Wash.

All of the distinctive landscapes of Lincolnshire can better be understood and appreciated by considering the extra layers of soils, vegetation and human history. Each has its characteristic human settlements and wildlife habitats, moulded by a combination of geology, ecology, climate and land-use history, which blend to produce a subtle but enduring identity. This big county – the second largest in England and perhaps the least known – has riches and diversity which repay exploration.

A Primitive Way of Life

Linda Crust

2007 is the 80th anniversary of David Robinson's birth and the 200th anniversary of the birth of Primitive Methodism at Mow Cop in Staffordshire, the first English Camp Meeting. In 1808 the 'Primitives' were expelled by the Wesleyan Methodists 'for setting up other than ordinary worship'. By 1812 they had formed a new connexion of Primitive Methodism. The two great leaders of the Primitive Methodist movement were Hugh Bourne, a millwright, and William Clowes, a potter.

It has been said that there must be more to religion than religion: there must be an element offered to adherents other than the spiritual. What is it? Would religion survive if it offered post-mortem salvation alone? Belief is hard to explain; its acquisition is a mystery - so what else does religion offer? Hope is desirable and helpful to humans: 'Blessings all thine and bright hopes for tomorrow.'[1] Tomorrow might be in this world or the next. Ritual is another item on a human want list. Early Methodists decried the Catholic ritualistic Latin mass - yet they

Fig. 1: This commemorative plate celebrating 100 years of Primitive Methodism shows Mow Cop, the scene of the first camp meeting, along with the camp organisers Hugh Bourn and William Clowes

composed their own ritual in a different cultural context - yearly national conferences and Love Feasts in rural villages. Charisma works well and attracts in any culture; Catholics have the pope; evangelicals have American telly-preachers; early Methodists had a hypnotic little man from Lincolnshire called Wesley and a subsequent army of passionate open-air preachers. It is the cultural elements of religion in the context of class and time that I will explore in relation to Primitive Methodism.

I do not seek to explain the attraction of Methodist theology, nor that of the broad scope of Christian ethics, but the human manifestations (emotional and physical) of Primitive Methodism as its adherents used it to mould their lives in nineteenth century England. The Primitive Methodist Connexion was not created in a cultural void; like all religions it absorbed and exploited the contemporary social needs of its followers.

The name 'Primitive Methodism' indicated a desire to return to the spirit and methods of early Methodism under John Wesley. John Wesley's words at Chester, in 1790 were

> ....if it be two or three under a hedge or a tree, preach the gospel; go out quickly into the streets and lanes of the city and bring in the poor and the maimed and the halt and the blind - and yet there is room.. ..and this is the way the primitive methodists did.'[2]

Fervour and religious passion were evident but there was a certain wildness about the early meetings of the newly formed Primitive Methodists, a lack of literacy and a return to the superstitions of old England in the first decades of Methodist ministry. According to E P Thompson, Jabez Bunting, a spiritual successor of Wesley, was intent on ushering Methodism 'to a seat on the right hand of the Establishment'.[3] Bourne and Clowes were of the working people and were intent on redeeming the souls of the labouring masses. Bourne wrote: 'Our chapels were the coal-pit banks, or any other place; and in our conversation way, we preached the Gospel to all, good or bad, rough or smooth'.[4] In other words the Primitives spoke the language of the working man and wished to include him and give him the means of eternal salvation.

At the beginning of the nineteenth century Methodism was already prone to some local divisions. Wesleyan Methodism was hugely successful nationally and already giving much scope for laymen to give voice in the government of the denomination. Primitive Methodists wanted a more revivalist, emotional, style of preaching, prayer and public confession in the form of testimonies. An American preacher, Lorenzo Dow, was visiting England between 1805 and 1807 and it was he who inspired Bourne and Clowes to organise the pivotal Mow Cop meeting on the lines of American Camp Meetings which he had held in his own country and reported upon in *The Wesleyan Methodist Magazine.*[5]

Primitive Methodism soon became an alternative to Wesleyanism. New members were gathered in by the camp meetings and some Wesleyan members preferred the new, exciting approach of the Ranters as 'Primitive' Methodists were nicknamed. One such was Samuel Sharp a thatcher from Messingham. He joined the Primitive Connexion in 1819 with other Wesleyans.[6] One couple, in 1848, explained why they had transferred their membership from a Congregational Church to the Primitive Methodists because they were: '...so plain and willing to stoop so low, as to go out into highways and hedges and compel the Poor and needy and outcasts of society to come into the field of Christ.'[7]

Prayer was often loud and, perhaps, exhibitionist. A Lincolnshire minister, Revd Parkinson Milson wrote, 'Many people, flashing, thrilling, and transforming glory.'[8] On another occasion he recorded, 'two persons fell to the floor during the sermon; in fact, the whole congregation was broken down.' Billy Paddison of Saltfleetby, writing in his diary, told of a Mrs Drury who, '...became wonderful woman to pray. She would shout and her whole person seemed to be lifted up in the air.'[9]

Thomas Cooper, who later became a well-known Christian preacher himself, wrote of the advent of the Ranters into Gainsborough in 1819 when he was fourteen years old.

> One morning, I ran out, with a crowd of the neighbours, to hear two men who were singing aloud as they walked along the street,... 'Turn to the Lord and seek salvation!' They were called 'Ranters' by the crowd; but I soon learned that they termed themselves 'Primitive Methodists'. These men remained in the town for some weeks, and preached in the open air, and held meetings in houses; and the crowd, young and old, were greatly affected. Soon a society was formed, and they began regularly to preach in the very small chapel which John Wesley himself caused to be built.[10]

Cooper himself became a Primitive Methodist for a time but he had a rich intellect and read widely and enjoyed many types of music. The attitude of other members of the Primitive Methodist society eventually caused him to rebel and he returned to 'the argumentative preaching' and 'warm, discourses' of the Wesleyan chapel in Gainsborough. This is an indicator that, at that time, the Primitives were rather ignorant, although sincere, men. Cooper wrote that, '... some of the members of the Society - poor men who knew little of books, but who found happiness in prayer, and in hearing others read and preach about the goodness of God demurred to my reading any book but the Bible unless it was a truly religious book.'[11]

The ignorance of early adherents of Primitive Methodism was inevitable given their lack of education at the time and it was also just as inevitable that they carried old traditions with them. Cooper wrote of an old man who was an inveterate cock-fighter being converted by the Ranters and thenceforth living a Christian life. 'Nor was his case a solitary one. On the other hand there were some fearful backslidings.'[12] Just as the medieval stone carvers in Lincoln cathedral expressed their old beliefs in folklore, in monsters and green men translated into figures in a Christian cathedral - so did the early, embryo Primitive Methodists retain their belief in supernatural visions. This is not surprising - did not the French peasants of the fourteenth century adhere to the holiness of Joan of Arc as a result of her visions?

At the start of the nineteenth century a group of men in Delamere Forest, including Hugh Bourne and William Clowes, belonged to a sect of people known as Magic Methodists. The group which was almost entirely local, was led by James Crawfoot and it centred around him until his death in 1839. Crawfoot was somewhat in the nature of an English rustic mystic figure. He was born about 1758 and lived for 81 years. Writing of his childhood:

> 'One day, being alone, a thought crossed my mind that I should look up to the skies, and as I looked I wondered what they were, and what they were made of, and who made them; it struck my mind that God made them; then, I thought, he must be great. After this my understanding was opened respecting God and the Devil, life and death, heaven and hell, rewards and punishments after this mortal life is ended.'

From the age of twelve he was said to have had visions, usually involving thrones and angels and Satan. His preaching must have been extraordinarily exciting and charismatic. One of his dreams, or visions, concerned his wish to attend a cock-fight - but he saw that the Devil would seize him if he went so he desisted.[13] The Magic Methodists preceded Mow Cop and survived long after the Primitive Methodists became established. Hugh Bourne visited and, at one time, admired James Crawfoot but later became somewhat embarrassed by his association with the Magic Methodists as he wanted order, respectability and gravitas to be connected with the Primitive movement. To the simple people (many of them illiterate) of Delamere Forest however the visions they experienced gave them great succour. Many of the entranced visionaries were

women and, among the most popular visions, were images of favoured preachers arranged on a ladder equipped with trumpets (a sign of the preaching office) and holding cups (a sign of spiritual gifts). The preachers were arranged in order of preference, usually with James Crawfoot at the top, Lorenzo Dow below him and Hugh Bourne lower down in the hierarchy. Women preachers, who appeared to be strong in Magic Methodism, generally appeared on a separate, slightly lower ladder than the men. On one occasion Crawfoot had a vision of a yew tree which enfolded and comforted him. It would be true to say that more established denominations regarded the Magic Methodists with mildly amused derision - yet the Bible is full of visionaries. Did not Abraham's grandson, Jacob, have a vision of angels ascending and descending a ladder? No Christian sect queries the event on the road to Damascus. The Magic Methodists must have enjoyed their visions and their fellowship and the sect certainly brought colour to the lives of its followers who were usually reported to have lived good, moral lives. Crawfoot did some preaching for the Primitive Methodists but in 1813 he was expelled. Bourne said that he, 'fell into sin,' though we have no details. His followers stayed with him, however, and he continued preaching until his death in 1839.

The Ranters had an effective publicity machine which consisted of shouting and singing in the streets to the glory of God on public occasions, such as the day of Queen Charlotte's funeral. They were also reported as singing hymns at public executions where there was a large gathering of people. But it was at the camp meetings that they caused greatest fear and offence in the hearts of the respectable population. It should be remembered that in the early decades of the nineteenth century many of the middle class, particularly landowners, were feeling the cold worry of a revolution such as the French had suffered within living memory. The population was increasing, industrialisation was incipient, many labouring men feared for their livelihoods as machines took on their work in factories and on the land. Luddites and Captain Swing were real threats to farmers and industrialists who were therefore suspicious of large gatherings of working class people in an emotional state. Hence, in the early days, the camp meetings were regarded with horror by some. Camp meetings were an innovation from America (and therefore rowdy and vulgar?); they were not field preaching meetings in the style of John Wesley the founder of Methodism but more democratic gatherings at which many people might preach and pray and give testimonies.

There are several accounts in local newspapers of camp meetings in Lincolnshire. In the early years all reports are derogatory, a manifestation of the fear felt by Tory editors for the possible outcome of a disorderly rabble. In 1819 *The Lincoln, Rutland and Stamford Mercury* reported on a meeting in the county:

> The praying was conducted by individuals who took the lead alternately; and at other times, the whole of the more active members of the fraternity were engaged together, working upon each other's enthusiasm, and presenting to the astonished ears of the passengers whom chance or curiosity brought to the spot, a very Babel of broken exclamation with 'cries and groans and shrieks that rent the air'.[14]

The Anglican clergy were alarmed and one gentleman living in the Spalding area in 1820 wrote:

> ...the Church is openly assailed by an organized banditti of strolling Methodists, vociferating Ranters, and all that impious train of et coeteras [sic] who without either the substance or form of Christianity, nestle under the wings of, toleration and hurl defiance at all constituted authorities..... [15]

This prejudice did abate as the nineteenth century progressed and all Methodist adherents, Primitive, Wesleyan and others, became better educated and more respectable. Indeed Methodism itself was a great factor in the education and discipline of the working classes and the offering of education (through Sunday Schools and day schools) and a structure of an orderly way of life.

Other causes, such as teetotalism and temperance, were embraced with vigour, particularly by Primitive Methodists. The Temperance Societies, Bands of Hope and Rechabites started in the late 1830s. This was a positive movement away from the old drinking culture and a route to respectability and decency. A poster advertising the seventh

Fig. 2: The Primitive Methodist Chapel at Tetney Lock, founded in 1864. It is now a house

anniversary of the Laceby Temperance Festival held in the Primitive Methodist Chapel in 1845 offered declamations on Teetotalism and Rechabitism following the public tea. Signing the pledge of abstinence was a serious step taken by many thousands (and still taken seriously by many who signed this pledge a century later). The Barton Temperance Society's pledge promised abstinence from 'rum, brandy, gin, whiskey, ale, porter, wine, cider and spirit cordials, except for medicinal and sacramental purposes.'[16] By the 1840s virtually all Primitive Methodist congregations promoted the virtues of temperance at the least but, preferably, abstinence from alcohol. The Primitives were moving away from a perceived, unlettered, rowdy mob towards public approbation; by this date, their piety and temperance were, on the whole, applauded. Even camp meetings were seen as decent, orderly, Christian gatherings. Temperance festivals and parades gave a ritual and drama in an acceptable form. A description of a parade in Alford described:

> 'Medals, ribbands and sashes, the badges of temperance, were attached to scores of reformed drunkards who were eager to assist in the reclaiming of those with whom they had associated when intemperance used to drown their senses and empty their pockets....'[17]

In Horncastle the Temperance Festival started with a service in the Primitive Methodist chapel and continued with a procession from The Wong led by a band and marchers with banners. [18]

The Primitive Methodist Magazine gives hundreds of examples of poor, ill-educated people becoming 'saved' by their religion. I would suggest that the salvation encompassed a broader (perhaps incidental) meaning than the saving of the soul by Christ's sacrifice. They were saved from a miserable life of toil and lack of dignity to be given trust and respect. One typical example is that of Thomas Butterfield:

> Thomas Butterfield was born at the Mountain, about the year 1823. He was brought up in ignorance, and at an early age was sent to labour in a coalpit, where much wickedness was practised. But about the year 1844 he was induced to go to hear brother G Lee, and was thereby brought to the knowledge of the truth. Pitying the state of his fellow-men, he soon after began to tell them words by which they might be saved. He was put upon our local preachers' plan of the Pembroke mission, and when able, was diligent in attending his appointments. He was neither learned nor gifted, but he did what he could, and was of some service in the cause of God. [19]

Such accounts give credence to E P Thompson's assertion that Methodism saved Britain from a revolution such as the French suffered.

Methodists were socially active among their members in other aspects of self-help. Many were members of Oddfellows and Free Gardeners and in Gainsborough there was a Sick and Dividing Club run by Primitive Methodists. The Agricultural Trade Union had a large Methodist membership in the 1870s and 1880s. By the end of the nineteenth century photographs give proof of well dressed chapel members enjoying anniversaries and teas and Sunday School outings.

Love Feasts were a ceremonial meal of water and bread or seed cake, even biscuits, that unified gatherings by simple ritual. Prayers, readings and public confessions (testimonies) were given on the same occasion. This may have been a substitute for the sacrament which in country areas was usually celebrated only yearly. Whatever the purpose it was a satisfying piece of togetherness and drama, an occasion when all could participate. This was in contrast to the secret confession of Roman Catholicism and a priest-led ritual. The following is a description of a Love Feast at Tetney in 1837.

> The Spirit of God went through the congregation like fire. The speaking was with a great liberty; and behold, a shaking, and a cry for mercy; and after a long and hard struggle, the Lord converted five souls. And at a late hour we returned home, weary in body, but rejoicing in spirit.' [20]

From the start, music was always an important part of Methodism with Charles Wesley, a great musician and hymn writer, supplying the thirst for communal singing that goes with harmony of souls. In the 1880s sacred songs of a different nature flooded through camp meetings and chapels thanks to the visit from America of evangelists Moody and Sankey. As Lorenzo Dow had inspired the Primitive movement in 1807 so did these other Americans fire up the souls of Primitive Methodists some eighty years later. Many of the hymns emphasised the Protestant means of salvation through Christ's blood and others stressed the humility and hard lives of lowly Christians who yet had cause to hope for something wonderful in the afterlife.

'Work, for the night is coming; Work, through the morning hours... .etc.'; [21] 'When by sorrow pressed down, I long for my crown In that beautiful land on high... .My Jesus is there, He's gone to prepare A place in that land for me...' [22]; 'There is a home, a glorious home, a heavenly mansion fair; And those we loved so fondly here Will bid us welcome there.'; 'Call them in the poor, the wretched, Sin-stained wand'rers from the fold; Peace and pardon freely offer...' [23] One of the best-known 'blood' songs has the instruction to sing 'Joyfully' - 'Just on the borders of the silent grave, Shouting Jesus's power to save, Washed in the blood of the Lamb.' [24] Overall the hymns empowered a poor but decent crowd of people to feel togetherness and hope coupled with a spiritual faith.

Primitive Methodism served people's needs for over a century. In the early days of the nineteenth century its members and adherents were predominantly working class - in this county they were mainly farm labourers. The years before 1850 were described as 'the heroic age' by Obelkevitch. [25] This was the period when evangelism was at its peak and the saving of souls by conversion was the most important thing. Magic Methodists, the forerunners of Primitive Methodists, had their own versions of religious phenomena. The old culture of cock-fighting and wife sales was giving way to new forms of leisure such as the camp meeting and the love feast. Anglican church festivals were largely ignored. Primitive Methodism became a way of life for many. Around the mid-nineteenth century prayer meetings generally became less boisterous as a more educated congregation sought decorum and respectability. But the spontaneity and heart-felt emotion of religion still continued with extemporaneous prayer and the emphasis on a 'good death'. Much energy was, by then, channelled into fund-raising for buildings and a calendar prompted by anniversaries and Sunday School treats. The spiritual element became more muted outwardly and the epithet *Ranters* was no longer heard, but prayers, hymn singing and conversions continued. In 1907 a commemorative plate claimed 4,905 Primitive Methodist preaching places and 4,209 Sunday Schools. It was no fly-by-night minor cult but a major force in British life.

Primitive Methodism officially ended in August 1932 with Methodist Union. The last Primitive Methodist Class card neatly accepted the transition with a Bible quotation which recorded the inevitability of progress. 'He taketh away the first that He may establish the second'.[26] Methodist Union served the purpose of, in some cases, consolidating people and buildings but the Primitive Methodist ethos is gone forever. Have we lost a valuable part of spiritual and cultural life or should we now regard Primitive Methodism as a phenomenon of its day and age?

A new sect is not born into a void - nor does it stay the same but changes as the lives of its followers change. Sometimes it merges with another group but the basic rules of a way of life are retained. It is the culture that changes around the rules to make the practice of religion suitable for the times and the people who live in the times.

Fig. 3: Goxhill Primitive Methodist Chapel, founded in 1891
(Drawing by R Russell)

Notes:

1. *Hymns and Psalms*, The Methodist Church Hymn Book, 66.

2.. John T Wilkinson, *Hugh Bourne 1772 – 1852*, Epworth Press (1952) p92.

3. E P Thompson, *The Making of the English Working Class*, Pelican (reprint 1970, first published 1963) p436.

4. Wilkinson, op. cit. p32.

5. R W Ambler, *Ranters, Revivalists and Reformers: Primitive Methodism and Rural Society South Lincolnshire 1817-1875*, Hull Univ Press (1989) p29.

6. *op. cit.* p38.

7. Leonore Davidoff and Catherine Hall, *Family Fortunes, men and women of the English middle class 1780-1850*, cited by D Bebbington, *Victorian Nonconformity,* Headstart History (Bangor, 1992) p22.

8. J Obelkevitch, *Religion and Rural Society: South Lindsey, 1825-1875*, Clarendon Press (Oxford, 1976) p225.

9. LAO miscellaneous deposits 738.

10. Thomas Cooper, *The Life of Thomas Cooper,* Leicester Univ (1971) p37.

11. *op. cit.* p37-8.

12. *op. cit.* p38.

13. Henry D Rack, *James Crawfoot and the Magic Methodists*, Englesea Brook Chapel and Museum of Primitive Methodism (2003) p1.

14. Ambler *op. cit.* p39.

15. Ambler *op. cit.* p46.

16. Rex Russell, *The Water Drinkers in Lindsey 1837-1860,* Barton-upon-Humber WEA (1987) p38.

17. Russell *op. cit.* p6.

18. *Lincoln, Rutland and Stamford Mercury*, 11 June 1841, cited by Russell, *op. cit.* p38.

19. *Lincoln, Rutland and Stamford Mercury*, 18 June 1841, cited by Russell, *op. cit.* p38.

20. *The Primitive Methodist Magazine* (Thomas King, 1854) vol. XXV, p59.

21. Ira D Sankey (compiler), *Sacred Songs and Solos* (Marshall Pickering, 1990) no. 66.

22. *op. cit.* no. 67.

23. *op. cit.* no. 197.

24. *op. cit.* no. 58.

25. Obelkevitch, *op. cit.* p230.

26. *The Bible*, Hebrews ch.X v.9.

Two Songs and a Singing Game

from the collection of Brian Dawson

'The Owls and the Mice' was remembered by Mrs Ethel Rudkin of Toynton all Saints *c.* 1980 when she was in her late eighties.   Mrs Rudkin said it was the only song she remembered learning as a little girl in the early 1900s.

A missing line, verse 2, line 2, has been taken from a Virginian version with a quite different tune published in 'Folk Songs of the Blue Ridge Mountains' by Herbert Shillans, Oak 1968.

The Owls and the Mice

1. There were three little owls sat a-singing in a barn
       Dinga dinga doo dum day
   And they huddled up together just to keep
           their bodies warm
   Dinga dinga doo dum day
   And the song that they sang I will now tell you
   It's a song that begins and ends too-woo
   And a very, very pretty little song it is too.
       Dinga dinga doo dum day.

2. There were three little owls sat a-singing in a barn
       Dinga dinga doo dum day
   And the owls eat mice and the mice eat corn
       Dinga dinga doo dum day
   The moon it shone in the sky so bright
   That it made the whole world look quite light
   And owls as you know only sing at night.
       Dinga dinga doo dum day.

3. There were three little mice sat a-listening to that
           song
       Dinga dinga doo dum day.
   Though they knew what they were doing was very,
           very wrong
       Dinga dinga doo dum day.
   For the old mouse said "Little mice beware
   When the owls are a-singing 'too-woo' take care
   For their song is nothing more or less than a snare"
       Dinga dinga doo dum day.

4. Now those three little mice they thought they'd
           have a lark
       Dinga dinga doo dum day.
   So they crept out softly as soon as it was dark
       Dinga dinga doo dum day.
   And they found that song 'too-woo' so nice
   That closer and closer crept the three little mice
   Till the owls came and gobbled them all up in a trice
       Dinga dinga doo dum day.

5. Then those three little owls flew back into the barn
  Dinga dinga doo dum day.
And they said "Those little mice have made us feel so
    nice and warm"
  Dinga dinga doo dum day.
Then again they began a-singing 'too-woo'
Now I don't think much of this song. Do you?
The only thing is that it's all perfectly true.
  Dinga dinga doo dum day.

'Hooray for the Beer' was sung and written down for me in dialect by Mr George Chester in 1989. Mr Chester was brought up at Mareham le Fen and picked up songs sung by local residents in the late 1930s. He learnt this song from the singing of Harry Roberts who sang it at the Foresters Club Supper in 1939.

Versions were found extensively throughout England and there are other Lincolnshire examples. In spite of the title the song is a warning against spending too much money on beer and tobacco.

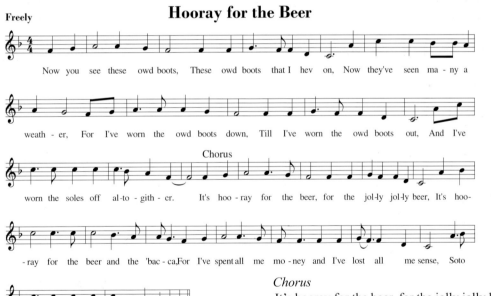

Hooray for the Beer

Freely

Now you see these owd boots, These owd boots that I hev on, Now they've seen ma - ny a

weath - er, For I've worn the owd boots down, Till I've worn the owd boots out, And I've

Chorus

worn the soles off al-to-gith-er. It's hoo-ray for the beer, for the jol-ly jol-ly beer, It's hoo-

-ray for the beer and the 'bac-ca, For I've spent all me mo-ney and I've lost all me sense, So to

cross the bri-ny ho-cean I must goa.

1. Now you see these owd boots,
  These owd boots that I hev on,
  Now they've seen many a weather,
  For I've worn the owd boots down,
  Till I've worn the owd boots out,
  And I've worn the soles off altogither.

Chorus
It's hooray for the beer, for the jolly jolly beer,
It's hooray for the beer and the 'bacca,
For I've spent all me money and I've lost all me
    sense,
So to cross the briny hocean I must goa.

2. Now you see this owd cap,
  This owd cap that I hev on,
  Now it's seen many a weather,
  For I've worn the owd cap down,
  Till I've worn the owd cap out,
  And I've worn the beak out altogither.

3. Now you see this owd coat,
   This owd coat that I hev on,
   Now it's seen many a weather,
   For I've worn the owd coat down,
   Till I've worn the owd coat out,
   And I've worn the ames out altogither.

4. Now you see this owd shirt,
   This owd shirt that I hev on,
   Now it's seen many a weather,
   For I've worn the owd shirt down,
   Till I've worn the owd shirt out,
   And I've worn the lap off altogither.

5. Now you see these owd trousers,
   These owd trousers I hev on,
   Now they've seen many a weather,
   For I've worn the trousers down,
   Till I've worn the trousers out,
   And I've worn the seat out altogither.

'Isabella' was given to me by Mr William H Houlden of Bunkers Hill, Thornton le Fen. It was sung by the young people in the vicinity of Sandy Bank Methodist Chapel for the game of 'Kiss in the Ring' played late in the evening of the Monday following the school Feast Weekend.

The Kissing Ring used to be a common feature of school feasts and for many was the highlight of the event as it gave the participants a great opportunity to 'play the field'. Many romances started with the first kiss in the ring and for some this would eventually lead to marriage.

Sandy Bank Methodist School Feast, held in a tent near the chapel, was the last in the area and the local tradition was that if you hadn't got a sweetheart by the time Sandy Bank's ring closed you had missed your chance for that year.

Mr and Mrs Houlden took part in the 1953 ring and the romance which blossomed led to their wedding in 1956 and a lifetime together.

Locally the tradition died out in the 1950s and now sadly Sandy Bank Methodist Chapel has closed too.

Isabella

When the trees are all cov-ered, all cov-ered, all cov-ered, When the trees are all cov-ered, all

cov-ered in green. Last night when we part-ed she was nigh brok-en heart-ed, 'Tis a bell-ow, 'tis a

bell-ow, 'tis a bell-ow for me. Then give me your hand love, your hand love, your hand love, Then

give me your hand love and a sweet kiss for me.

When the trees are all covered, all covered, all covered
When the trees are all covered, all covered in green.

Last night when we parted she was nigh broken-hearted,
'Tis a bellow, 'tis a bellow, 'tis a bellow for me.

Then give me your hand love, your hand love, your hand love,
Then give me your hand love and a sweet kiss for me.

Acknowledgement

   The editors wish to acknowlege the assistance of Steve Adamson with
the musical typesetting.

'Crow and dead tree' (Drawn by Hilary Healey)

Grasby in 1873

Roger Evans

Anglican subscribers to *The Day of Rest*, an illustrated journal of Sunday reading, would no doubt have found some pleasure in the front cover (shown here, fig.1) of the issue dated 8 February 1873. The whole page is given up to a fanciful picture of a fine, solid Church of England cleric in dignified garb with a passing resemblance to W E Gladstone. His gaze carries us beyond the gate to a humble village, a collection of cottages that Wordsworth would have described as 'green to the very door'. Smoke rises from chimney pots and the rising sun shines valiantly from a hilly horizon. Its glow significantly emanates from a spot immediately above the little steeple of the village church. It is a scene of concord and tranquillity.

" 'The Faithful Pastor'- See Page 62" reads the rubric beneath the picture. On page 62 we find that the illustration accompanies a sonnet by 'the Revd Chas [Tennyson] Turner'. It was receiving its first publication and here it is:

The Faithful Pastor
At dawn he marks the smoke among the trees,
From hearths to which his daily footsteps go;
And hopes, and fears, and ponders on his knees,
If his poor sheep will hear his voice or no:
What wholesome turn will Ailsie's sorrow take?
Her latest sin will careless Annie rue?
Will Robin now, at last, his wiles forsake –
Meet his old dupes, yet hold his balance true?
He prays at noon, with all the warmth of heaven
About his heart, that each may be forgiven;
He prays at eve; and through the midnight air
Sends holy ventures to the Throne above;
His very dreams are faithful to his prayer,
And follow, with closed eyes, the path of love.

The journal's rendition of the author's name is clumsy. He was, in fact, simply the Reverend Charles Turner but the circumstances of his life had clouded the issue and created error.[1] He was born 'Charles Tennyson', elder brother of Alfred, the future Laureate, at Somersby in 1808 but, in deference to the will of his great-uncle, the Reverend Samuel Turner of Caistor, he changed his name by royal licence from Tennyson to Turner in 1835. All his later volumes of verse - *Sonnets* (1864), *Small Tableaux* (1868) and *Sonnets, Lyrics and Translations* (1873) – were published over the name 'Charles Turner'. His quite frequent appearances in journals from 1860 onwards, however, are marked by editorial whim with regard to his name, the form 'Charles Tennyson Turner' being the most common. We can perhaps sympathise with the editors who had the brother of the Poet Laureate, a supremely successful and famous Laureate to boot, gracing their columns and they rarely failed to blow this little trumpet.

Turner himself was in fact quite unworldly and he had no truck with publishers' wiles. Since 1835 he had been Vicar of Grasby, a village on the north-western slope of the Lincolnshire Wolds, half-way between Caistor and Brigg. The nearest railway station today is that at Barnetby. His days and the days of his wife Louisa were occupied with his ministry and, although he retired from the offices of the church in 1866 as a result of illness, handing over his church duties to the curates, he continued for the rest of his life to minister to the bereft, the sick and the dying and joined his flock in their devotions on their knees in the church he so lovingly restored at his own expense in 1868 to 1869. It would be a mistake, nevertheless, to imagine that 'The Faithful Pastor' is a self-portrait: Turner was too modest to suppose himself such a model of benevolence. The poem does, however, present an ideal which he cherished. But what are these 'hopes and fears' he speaks of? What of these 'poor sheep'? Had he particular cause for concern? Were things not quite right in his own village of Grasby? Does the illustration accompanying his poem lack something? Are we getting the whole picture?

Grasby was, and is, an attractive village untroubled by the more extreme advances of nineteenth century industrialisation or urbanisation. It had had its struggles: the rural economy held many villagers in the grip of poverty and nonconformist dissent had indeed created divisions in their number, but by 1873 church and chapel were managing to live cheek by jowl with only subdued murmuring. Village life had its charms and the annual pursuits were managed and enjoyed with enthusiasm. 'The great events in the summer were the Village School Treats', records one observer. 'The one at Grasby was the most popular because Mr Turner always took such an active interest in all the activities of the young people'.[2] Turner himself captured the spirit of these genial events in his sonnet 'After the School Feast'[3], published in 1873.

After the School Feast

The Feast is o'er - the music and the stir -
The sound of bat and ball, the mimic gun;
The lawn grows darker, and the setting sun
Has stolen the flash from off the gossamer,
And drawn the midges westward; youth's glad cry -
The smaller children's fun-exacting claims,
Their merry raids across the graver games,
Their ever-crossing paths of restless joy,
Have ceased - And, ere a new Feast-day shall shine,
Perchance my soul to other worlds may pass;
Another head in childhood's cause may plot,
Another Pastor muse in this same spot,
And the fresh dews, that gather on the grass
Next morn, may gleam in every track but mine!

The first half of 1873 passed peacefully enough for
Turner. He published his last volume, *Sonnets, Lyrics
and Translations*, at the end of April and received fine
commendation from the Bishop of Lincoln: 'Your sweet
songs breathed from your quiet vale have been a great
refreshment to me', he wrote.[4] Public notice was growing
and he was to see a sympathetic survey of his old and new
work in *The Contemporary Review*.[5] In July Turner and
his wife had a holiday at Sea Mill, near Ardrossan and
afterwards, refreshed, they continued their pastoral duties,
indefatigably ministering to the sick and needy in Grasby.
They are captured in their daily round in an oil painting,
done by their neighbour the Revd T J M Townsend, the
Vicar of Searby. It shows them in a lane by the church,
talking to a villager (fig.2). This does indeed look like
an idyll but ominous rumblings were to be heard. The air
was to become agitated and then turbulent. By the end
of the year the village was in a storm! From concord and
tranquillity we move into a veritable uproar!

A source of the trouble was the Reverend T J M
Townsend himself. He was not only the Turners' neighbour:
he was a good friend. Turner and Townsend met frequently
at convivial 'club meetings' where Turner would call
himself 'Torneutes' and Townsend would call himself
'Poleostelos'. The Vicar of North Kelsey, the Revd W
F Chambers was known as 'Thalamon', all these being
absurd renderings of their names in Greek. Townsend
was a High Church man and indeed declared his hand in
early 1873 by having a pamphlet about doctrinal practices
printed over his name and describing himself as 'an English
Catholic priest'.[6] He lectured on the subject in his own
village and also in Grasby. He was one of many much
occupied at that time with matters of form, display, ritual

*Fig.1: The front cover of The Day of Rest,
Vol. 1 no. 6, Saturday, February 8, 1873.
(Reproduced courtesy of The British Library.)*

and symbol. Their concerns embraced such subjects as the
practice of both clergy and laity turning to the east when
reciting the Creeds, the significance of various forms of
church vestments, the adornment of the altar – indeed the
position of the altar in the church, and the use of music. The
arguments revolved around the proposition that the church
should re-embrace pre-Reformation practice. All this was
explosive in a Protestant land and in rural Lincolnshire,
a district of deeply-founded dissent and old fashioned
Georgian habit, it could scarcely be countenanced.

Turner himself expressed little opinion on the subject,
but it must be noted that he chose an architect of High
Church persuasion, Charles Buckeridge of Oxford, when
he rebuilt the church in the 1860s. Also Turner's curates
were indulgent in their ritualist ways: indeed many
members of the congregation had felt uncomfortable
about the introduction of plainsong for responses by the

previous curate, John Wilberforce Doran, who was once found - to Turner's horror - exorcising the church flowers and who also went on to publish the 'Te Deum Laudamus' to Ambrosian Chant in 1879 .

The matter came to a head between Wednesday 12 November and Saturday 15 November when a 'Retreat for Ladies' was held in Grasby. The programme[7] ran like this:

Wednesday

6.30 pm	Tea
7.15 pm	Introductory Address
9.00 pm	Supper
9.30 pm	Compline

Thursday & Friday

8.00 am	Prime
8.15 am	Holy Communion
9.00 am	Breakfast
10.00 am	Matins
10.45 am	Terce followed by meditation
12.30 pm	Sext followed by instruction
1.30 pm	Dinner
2.00 pm	Recreation
3.30 pm	None followed by meditation
5.30 pm	Evensong
6.30 pm	Tea
7.15 pm	Meditation
9.00 pm	Supper
9.30 pm	Compline

Silence was observed throughout the retreat and no letters were to be opened unless in a case of extreme emergency. Accommodation, which came under the supervision of Mrs Turner, was provided as near the church as possible, even in The Cross Keys, the Grasby public house – an establishment, it should be noted, which was owned by Turner and managed by a churchwarden. The event was conducted by the Revd Dr Robert Linklater of St Peter's, London Docks. He was later to become a locum curate at Grasby and was to officiate at Turner's funeral in Cheltenham in 1879. He was also to become an immensely vigorous and respected worker among the poor in Landport, Portsmouth.[8] The moving spirits behind the retreat, however, were the Grasby curate, the Revd H W Holden, and Townsend, the Vicar of Searby.

The reaction to all this was predictable. Among many there was bewilderment. 'Breakfast, dinner, tea, and supper… one can understand', wrote one local inhabitant to the editor of *The Mercury,* 'but what means "terce", and

"sext", and "recreation", and "none"?' The programme, he said, 'might as well have been in Chinese characters'. Reports in the press, however, reveal that the event raised more scorn than bewilderment:

> At a neighbouring village, where the practice of auricular confession gains ground, the wives of the clergy and their female relatives to the number of 16, not wishing to lag behind the nobler sex in a manifestation of pious zeal, have just been having a 'retreat' among themselves, under the auspices of the Rector [sic] of the parish, or rather of his wife and Curate, the latter of whom is well known as a ritualistic diamond of the first water. On the arrival of those 16 un-wise virgins last Wednesday week they were all conducted to lodgings, two of them having to be domiciled at the village inn, to insure isolation from husbands, children, and every duty of domestic life, whilst they endeavoured to realize the charms of conventual existence, arising from an imposed silence of six hours each day, etc. Their progress from lodgings, with lamps well trimmed in their hands, to church in the evening, where they were joined by a 'father confessor' from London, immediately on his arrival, naturally excited the curiosity of the villagers to know what it was all about. Some of them attempting to enter and see were repulsed almost by force; but looking through the windows a sight could be obtained of the reverend gentleman bedizened in curious vestments and seated in the chancel, with the postulants kneeling before him. A spirit of persecution thus became excited in the minds of the ruder sort, who afterwards, and every night until 'the retreat' came to an end, hooted and yelled obscenities of language after the devoted 'nuns', stretched cords for them to fall over in the streets, threw cabbages, sods, and other missiles, set loose a cat and a terrier dog to raise a disturbance, and a flock of sparrows to knock out the lighted candles in the church[9]

What gave particular offence was the fact that villagers were barred from entering the church and had had to resort to peering in through the windows (presumably those which are quite low in the north aisle). In defence, Townsend explained that 'As … the services for the retreat were private, there was no necessity to admit others, and every reason for excluding a scoffing rabble'.[10] This response merely stoked the fires, prompting tart replies: '…if there be a number of people properly called "rabble" in a small village like Grasby, it speaks unfavourably for those clergy who have had the well-paid spiritual oversight of the parish from time immemorial'.[11] Insults flew back and forth. '…the village boys showed better sense than the "silly women" who gathered together for the glorification of an apostate Romanizing priest', wrote one correspondent in the newspaper columns[12] and another '..if, instead of treating such disturbers of peace and order to a few rotten cabbages, they had treated them like ill-mannered curs, tied a tin-kettle to each of their tails and hooted them out of the place, they would only be serving them as they richly deserved'.[13] The more serious charge, however, was that summed up in another newspaper column: 'The whole affair is part and parcel of the bold attempt now being made

Fig.2: Grasby Church, showing the Revd Charles Turner and his wife, an oil painting,
dated 1868, by the Revd T J M Townsend, Vicar of Searby. Detail.
(The Tennyson Research Centre, Lincoln. Reproduced courtesy of Lincolnshire County Council.)

throughout the land to un-Protestantise the Established Church'.[14] This was, of course, the nub of the matter.

And where, we may ask, did Turner, the Vicar of Grasby, stand in all this? In the columns of the press, no whit of blame was apportioned to him. He was seen as 'aged and past active duty'. It was Townsend who bore the brunt of the attacks and he was seen as one interfering in the affairs of another parish. 'As the mistletoe attracts attention only by fastening itself to the giant oak', wrote 'a Caistor Protestant', 'so do those insignificant human parasites attract attention only by associating themselves with some noble character, such as the humble-minded, the amiable and accomplished incumbent of Grasby. They know full well from his modesty, his goodness, and his patient endurance that they are pretty safe in his parish…'[15]

The incident at Grasby reflected the concerns of the Church of England at large in 1873. The Bishop of Lincoln felt constrained to make his views quite clear in the following year when he declared that 'it ought not to be left to individual Clergymen to choose by an eclectic process what rites and ceremonies they please, from ancient, mediaeval, or modern Churches, and to import them into their own Churches, and to impose them onto their own congregations …'[16] but, in 1875, in fear that there may arise a schism among the clergy, he granted that certain practices adopted in, for example, the celebrating of Holy Communion 'might be lawfully regarded as an open question'.[17] What the Bishop was unable to remove was the deep seam of suspicion that rankled and seethed among the Church's flock. 'These are days of suspicions, and of separations consequent on suspicions', wrote one pastor in December 1873.[18] Were these the thoughts of

Turner when he wrote of the Faithful Pastor's 'hopes and fears', pondering whether 'his poor sheep will hear his voice or no'?

Notes:

1. Roger Evans, 'Charles Turner'. *The Oxford Dictionary of National Biography*, OUP (Oxford, 2004).
2. Sir Charles Tennyson and Hope Dyson, *The Tennysons: Background to Genius*, Macmillan (1974), p.128.
3. Charles Turner, *Sonnets, Lyrics and Translations*. Henry S King & Co, (1873) p.54.
4. John Henry Overton and Elizabeth Wordsworth, *Christopher Wordsworth, Bishop of Lincoln* Rivingtons (1888) p.315.
5. Henry G Hewlett, 'English Sonneteers: Mr Charles Turner'. *The Contemporary Review*, 22, September 1873, pp.633-642.
6. Revd T J M Townsend, *A Lecture on Popery*, Geo. Parker (Caistor) and G J Palmer (1873).
7. *The Lincoln, Rutland and Stamford Mercury*, 5-12 December 1873, *passim*.
8. Robert R Dolling, *Ten Years in a Portsmouth Slum*, S C Brown, Langham & Co (1903).
9. *The Market Rasen Weekly Mail and Lincolnshire Advertiser*, 28 November - 12 December 1873, passim.
10. *The Lincoln, Rutland and Stamford Mercury, op. cit.*
11. *The Market Rasen Weekly Mail, op. cit.*
12. *The Lincoln, Rutland and Stamford Mercury, op. cit.*
13. *The Market Rasen Weekly Mail, op. cit.*
14. *The Lincoln, Rutland and Stamford Mercury, op. cit.*
15. *The Market Rasen Weekly Mail, op. cit.*
16. Christopher Wordsworth, Bishop of Lincoln, *A plea for toleration by law, in certain ritual matters,* Lincoln: James Williamson and London: Rivingtons (1874) p.4.
17. Christopher Wordsworth, Bishop of Lincoln, *Results of an inquiry on ritual with remarks*. Lincoln: James Williamson and London: Rivingtons (1875) p.7.
18. Revd John H Snowden, *An Address to the Congregation of Christ Church, Woburn Square, Bloomsbury,* (Privately printed, 1873) p.12.

(Drawn by Hilary Healey)

Lincolnshire's Two American Annes

John Haden

It could be argued that the most significant change in the democracies of the developed world in the last century is the achievement by women of the right to vote on equal terms with men. Before 1928, women in the United Kingdom were denied full equality in their right to be heard politically. But much earlier than that, in the early years of England's expansion into the New World, two strong minded and interesting Lincolnshire women, Anne Bradstreet and Anne Hutchinson, made their voices heard in the world of their day. Both names are well known in the USA, particularly in New England and amongst those interested in the study of the role of women in society. In Lincolnshire, the county in which they both grew up, their stories are less well known. This paper offers an opportunity to remember these two women, both of whom made a significant contribution to the story of early English speaking North America. It is also the 400th anniversary of the founding of the USA with the first English speaking colony at Jamestown, and of the first attempt by the Pilgrim Fathers to escape from England, which gives all the more reason to tell their story.

In the north aisle of Boston's parish church of St Botolph, there is a memorial window which has in one panel the image of a young woman. She wears the demure dress of an early seventeenth century Puritan and holds in her arms what appears to be a basket of fledgling birds. The window is a tribute to Anne Bradstreet, poet and one of the few women who left a record of their experiences in the early days of the Massachusetts Bay Colony. Although born in Northamptonshire, Anne spent her formative years in Lincolnshire when her father, Thomas Dudley, became Steward to the Earl of Lincoln. Dudley had fought in the Protestant cause of Henry of Navarre in France, returned to England and married Dorothy Yorke. He entered the service of a nobleman with strong Puritan views, Lord Saye and Sele, and impressed his employer by his integrity and efficiency. His daughter, Anne, was born in 1612 into a family committed to the Puritan way of godly living and hard work.

In the early seventeenth century, many of Lincolnshire's leading families were deeply sympathetic to the Puritan point of view. The Clintons at Tattershall, the Berties at Grimsthorpe Castle and the Hickmans at Gainsborough,

Fig. 1: Anne Bradstreet depicted in a window in the north aisle of St Botolph's Church, Boston. She is in Puritan dress and holds a basket of fledgling birds

all supported their local Puritan clergy in their struggles with the Bishop and employed Puritan supporters in their households. At Tattershall, when Thomas Clinton, third Earl of Lincoln died in 1619, his nineteen year old son, Theophilus, became the fourth Earl. The estate was in debt and the young Earl had four unmarried sisters each of whom would need a dowry. His widowed mother, Elizabeth, Countess of Lincoln, sought advice from her late husband's cousin Lord Saye and Sele who recommended Thomas Dudley as a suitable person to administer the Lincoln's estates. The link between the two families was further strengthened when the young Earl married Bridget, Lord Saye and Sele's daughter, and set up his household at Tattershall, while his mother and sisters moved to the family's house at Sempringham. Dudley was already 43 when they moved to Tattershall in 1619. Anne was seven, about the same age as the youngest daughter of the Dowager Countess.

Throughout her early life, Anne's health was poor. Soon after moving to the damp air of the fens at Tattershall, she was bedridden with rheumatic fever. How do we know this? Because Anne had a passion for writing, and she wrote an account of '*God's dealing with me from my childhood to this day*', for the benefit of her children, a typical Puritan work of pious introspection.

> 'In my young years, about 6 or 7 as I take it, I began to make conscience of my ways, and what I knew was sinful, as lying, disobedience to parents, etc., I avoided it. If at any time I was overtaken with the like evils, it was as a great trouble, and I could not be at rest 'til by prayer I had confessed it unto God…In a long fit of sickness which I had on my bed I often communed with my heart and made my supplication to the most High who set me free from that affliction.'

To join the household of one of the great families of England was to share their way of life. Anne would have spent much of her time with the Countess's daughters and their tutors, gaining an education very different from that of her female contemporaries in the village of Tattershall. Grammar Schools were for boys, but Anne's privileged situation would have ensured that she learnt to read and write and to become relatively fluent in Latin and a little French. With access to the family library, she learnt of the history of Ancient Greece and Rome, read the poetry of Sir Philip Sidney and the French Huguenot, du Bartas, and Raleigh's *History of the World*. Above all she would have had access to the Geneva Bible, and the other book which so influenced the Puritan movement, John Foxe's '*Acts and Monuments*' or the Book of Martyrs as it became known.

Anne Hutchinson was born in Alford in July 1591, the third child of the Revd Francis Marbury and Bridget Dryden, a relative of the poet. Marbury was Cambridge educated and ordained into the ministry of the Church of England. He was soon in trouble. Described as an 'overthwart, proud puritan knave' largely for his relentless attack on the Bishops as 'ministers unfit for their calling', he moved to Alford to take up his post as 'Lecturer' at the parish church of St Wilfrid. This was combined with the role of master of Queen Elizabeth's Grammar School. Marbury's outspoken views provoked the Bishop of Lincoln into depriving him of his living and his school-mastering. With time on his hands and constrained to remain at home, he found a willing pupil in his daughter, Anne. This gave her an education far beyond that of other girls of her time, and she became a biblical scholar, well versed in both the Geneva Bible and the extreme Puritan theology which it promoted.

By these accidents of personal history, two young women in very different circumstances gained the means to make their voices heard in a world in which women were expected to be quiet. From her mother, Anne Marbury as she then was, gained another skill, that of a midwife. Bridget Marbury had sixteen children, all of whom survived infancy. From helping at her mother's many confinements, Anne learnt the skills of midwifery, which gave her entry to the homes of her Alford neighbours and to the most intimate aspects of their lives. After his battles with the Bishop of Lincoln, Francis Marbury decided that conformity with an imperfect church was preferable to constant arrest and imprisonment and moved with his large family to the living of St Martin's Vintry in London in 1605. He held several successful appointments in London and when he died in 1611, he was sufficiently well off to leave £200 to each of his twelve living children. Anne's mother died about 1645, also in London.

As her father had decreed that his daughters were to stay with their mother until they were 21, it was not until 1612 that Anne married a mercer from Alford, William Hutchinson, in London. William is described as a 'man of mild temper and weak parts', but he was a successful merchant. Together, the couple returned to Alford where William developed his business interests and Anne had the first of their children, Edward, in 1613. Fourteen more followed Edward, Susan in 1614, Richard in 1615, Faith in 1617, Bridget in 1619, Francis in 1620, Elizabeth in 1622, William in 1623, Samuel in 1624, Anne in 1626, Mary in

1628, Katherine in 1630, William in 1631, Susan in 1633 and Zuriel in 1636.

In contrast with the robust health of the Hutchinson household at Alford, Anne Dudley remained a sickly child in the much more privileged setting of Tattershall Castle. It was there that she first met the son of another minister who was as uncompromising as her own father had been. Revd Simon Bradstreet, another Puritan product of Emmanuel College, Cambridge, had been Vicar of Horbling since 1596. His son, also Simon Bradstreet, was born there in 1603, the year that Queen Elizabeth died. As the new king, James I, made his leisurely journey south from Scotland to claim his throne, the Puritan clergy in the Church of England gathered signatures for their great Millenary Petition asking for reform of the practices which they believed smacked of 'popish rituals'. Bradstreet would have been as disappointed as any of his colleagues when James decided to insist on absolute conformity to the requirements of the Prayer Book and gave them just six months to accept the use of ceremonies and vestments against which they had objected so strongly. If they did not conform, they would be driven out of their livings. Bradstreet would not conform. He refused to wear the surplice, he refused to make the sign of the cross over a child at baptism, and he refused to insist that the good people of Horbling knelt to receive communion. When the Bishop of Lincoln's visitation came to Horbling in 1611 to report on the practices of the vicar, Revd Simon Bradstreet was described as 'of good behaviour saving he is unconformable'. He was allowed to continue in his Puritan ways for another ten years, until his death in 1621.

Meanwhile, Thomas Dudley was demonstrating his genius for administration in his service to the Earl of Lincoln at Tattershall. Sturdy, autocratic and irascible, he was at the hub of the Earl's affairs, running his huge estates from the Steward's room on the ground floor of Tattershall Castle. His vigorous management soon turned the estates to profit and his family to prosperity. Dudley's eldest son, Samuel, went up to Emmanuel College, Cambridge, at roughly the same time as Simon Bradstreet followed his father to the same college. There was another link through Dr John Preston, who had been tutor to Theophilus, the young Earl, when he was also at Cambridge, and also guardian to Simon Bradstreet when his father died. It is not surprising that Simon Bradstreet was himself invited to join the Earl's service as Assistant Steward, working under Thomas Dudley.

From about the age of nine, Anne Dudley would have known the able young Cambridge graduate. By her early teens, as she became more interested in the young men of the household, Simon Bradstreet must have made a deep impression on her. In her own words,

> 'But as I grew up to be about 14 or 15, I found my heart more carnal, and sitting loose from God, vanity and the follies of youth taking hold of me.'

But her health remained poor and she again became very ill just before her sixteenth birthday, this time with the often fatal and usually very disfiguring disease of smallpox. In her fever, it seems that she promised God that if He spared her life and gave her a sure conviction of forgiveness, she would marry Simon, and become his devoted wife.

> 'At 16, the Lord laid his hand sore upon me and smote me with the smallpox. When I was in my affliction, I besought the Lord and confessed my pride and vanity, and He was entreated of me and again restored me. But I rendered not to Him according to the benefit received. After a short time I changed my condition and was married.'

They were married in 1628, probably by John Cotton in Thomas Dudley's own house in Boston, as there is no record of the marriage in the parish church records. Her father had by then retired from the Earl's service and was living in the town, and worshipping at St Botolph's Church. As Anne and Simon set up home in Boston, the Earl of Lincoln and his close associates faced growing pressure from both King and Church.

Three years before, England had lost James I, or the 'wisest fool in Christendom' as the French King had described him. He died leaving his favourite, Buckingham, his hatred of the Puritans, and his crown to his handsome, fastidious and self-willed son, Charles. In the following year, 1626, Charles tried to raise a forced loan from his subjects to finance his military adventures without first getting the agreement of parliament. In the eastern counties, and especially in Lincolnshire, very few of the gentry agreed to subscribe to the loan. The young Earl of Lincoln refused and was imprisoned in the Tower for his impertinence. Thomas Dudley was also reported for refusing the loan, but escaped imprisonment. Eventually the Earl was released, but the threat both to the security of the nobility and the authority of parliament was clear.

Leading Puritans faced another threat. Charles had married the Catholic Princess Henrietta Maria, sister to the French King Louis XIII and she was allowed to practise her faith in private without censure. As a condition of the royal marriage, the anti-Catholic recusancy laws were suspended. Worse still, the King and Buckingham favoured the increasingly influential theologian, William Laud. He had preached that obedience to God meant obedience to the King, as no power but God could judge the King. Laud was the leader of a growing movement within the Church of England that followed the theology of Jacobus Arminius. This Dutch theologian had taught that the Calvinist insistence that only the 'elect' would be saved by grace, was wrong. God could be persuaded by the good works of the sinner. To the Puritan's thoroughgoing Calvinism, this seemed little better than the Catholic doctrine of salvation by good works and a denial of the Reformation itself. To King Charles, the anti-Calvinist Arminian position offered a helpful broadening of the Church and a way of binding up old wounds.

With King and Parliament locked in opposition over the King's need to raise money and the Puritan and Arminian parties in the Church battling for control of the leadership, the future of Puritan clergy and laity alike looked increasingly threatened. It was a time of turmoil, when, in the words of George Herbert,

'Religion stood on tiptoe in our land
Ready to pass to the American strand.'
(The Church Militant)

The Mayflower Pilgrims had first tried to escape from the oppression of King James I in 1607. They succeeded in reaching Holland in 1608 and then left the Old World for New England in 1620. By that time, the group of leading Lincolnshire Puritans based at Boston and Tattershall had been joined by like-minded gentry from Suffolk, and were planning another new 'planting' on the coast of New England. A start was made in 1623 with the small settlement at Salem, and the Massachusetts Bay Company was set up with backers from Dorchester and from Lincolnshire to develop a colony. The Company was granted a patent from the King for 'a planting between the Matachusets Bay and Charles River on the south and the River of Merimack on the North' and the leading shareholders of the company backed a much more ambitious 'planting'. They met at Cambridge and signed a 'compact' which committed them to 'passe the seas under God's protection to inhabite and continue in New England'. At the heart of the Massachusetts Bay Company, was a group of families bent on the foundation of a community where a Puritan church, governed on Congregational principles, would be free from all interference from the Bishops and the King. Instead of remaining in the control of a Company based in England as was the case with the Jamestown Colony, the

leaders of the Massachusetts Bay Colony planned to take their charter with them and to be entirely self-governing from the beginning.

In October 1629, John Winthrop was invited by the General Court of the Company to serve as Governor, Thomas Dudley was chosen to be his Deputy, and a number of Assistants or Magistrates were elected. Ships were bought or chartered and the fleet crossed the Atlantic to Massachusetts Bay in 1630, carrying over seven hundred passengers. On the *Arbella,* named for the Countess of Lincoln's daughter, the Dudleys and the Bradstreets sailed with a large Lincolnshire contingent.

The journey of 'close quarter, raw nerves, sickness, hysteria and salt meats' that took them from the English Channel to Massachusetts Bay must have been appalling, particularly for the families. The *Arbella* had no proper passenger accommodation, just small timber partitions for the women and children on one of the decks, with no sanitation and little privacy. Sixty two days after leaving their last English port of Yarmouth on the Isle of Wight, the fleet arrived off Salem on the North American coast.

It was a miserable place, not more than forty houses, few really habitable, mostly cabins and wigwams, or even burrows in the hillside. It was full of the sick and dispirited survivors of a hard winter that had taken eighty of the earlier settlers. Rejecting Salem, Winthrop ordered the fleet to sail south along the coast to Charlestown. But the drinking water there was poor and the main group of colonists moved south again and met up with William Blackstone who led them to his Trimountain area, which had a good source of water. The newcomers named it Boston in honour of the Lincolnshire town from which so many of them had come. The Dudleys and the Bradstreets settled at Newtown, just northwest of Boston, which was later renamed Cambridge, Massachusetts, in honour of the fact that so many graduates of that university were amongst the early settlers. There they built simple timber houses and began to adjust to a very different life from that which they had left in Tattershall and Boston. Although at first dismayed by her new surroundings, Anne Bradstreet soon reconciled herself to the conditions.

'I found a new world and new manners, at which my heart rose up in protest. But after I was convinced it was the way of God, I submitted to it and joined to the church at Boston.'

Within two years of arriving at Newtown, Anne Bradstreet began to write poetry, at first little better than doggerel. One of her earliest conscious attempts to turn her thoughts into verse, records the time when she was again ill and thinking she was near death.

> 'Twice ten years old, not fully told,
> Since nature gave me breath.
> My race is run, my thread is spun,
> Lo here is fatal death.'
> (Upon a fit of sickness. 1632)

For a woman of the early seventeenth century, to even attempt to create poetry was an extraordinary thing to do. Her role, in the eyes of her contemporaries, should be limited to the family and the home, the dutiful wife and fertile mother. But Anne had no child and the first three years of her married life must have been a painful time. She wrote:

> 'It pleased God to keep me a long time without a child, which was a great grief to me and cost me many prayers and tears before I obtained one, and after him gave me many more, of whom I now take the care' (from 'To my dear Children')

Her first son, Samuel, was born in 1633, to her in a very real sense an answer to her prayers. In 1635, Simon and Anne Bradstreet moved to an area about fifteen miles north of Salem, a place the Indians called Aggawam. There they helped to establish a settlement which they called Ipswich. This was a frontier outpost, where settlers carried arms at all times and agreed to build their houses within half a mile of the meeting house. It was a tough place for a mother with a two year old son and a new baby daughter, to establish a home. Encouraged by her father, husband and the pastor of the Ipswich settlement, the Revd Samuel Ward, Anne took up her pen again, although she clearly struggled to commit her thoughts to verse recording her self-deprecating comments and frustration.

> 'I'll leave thy praise to those shall do thee right,
> Good will, not skill, did cause me bring my Mite.'

Yet, she persevered, and produced a series of long poems following the fashion for 'Quartets', on the themes of the Four Elements, the Four Humours, the Four Ages, and the Four Seasons. These ambitious poems run on for hundreds of lines, and the last ends with a sigh of despair as Anne struggled to find the words to express her thoughts.

> 'My subject's bare, my brain is bad,
> Or better lines you should have had:
> The first fell in so naturally,
> I knew not how to pass it by;
> The last, though bad I could not mend,
> Accept therefore of what is penned,
> And all the faults that you shall spy
> Shall at your feet for pardon cry.'
> (The Four Seasons of the Year)

As her family grew over the next six years, Anne went on writing poetry. Sarah was born in 1638, the year that Simon moved Anne and the family further west into the wilderness along the banks of the Merrimack River where they built the new settlement of Andover. By 1642, when the Civil War broke out in England, the tide of the Great Migration which had brought twenty thousand settlers to New England slowed to a trickle. Anne was clearly very much aware of these iconoclastic changes when she wrote 'A dialogue between Old England and New concerning their present troubles'. She heard of the savage punishments meted out to those who first opposed the King, and of Parliament's retribution as Lord Strafford was executed and Archbishop Laud imprisoned.

> 'These Prophets mouths (alas the while) was stopped,
> Unworthily, some backs whipped, and ears cropp'd;
> Their reverent cheeks did bear the glorious marks
> Of stinking, stigmatising, Romish Clerks'
>
> They took high Strafford lower by the head,
> And to their Laud be't spoke, they held i' th' Tower
> All England's Metropolitan that hour.'

While Anne Bradstreet was busy with the life of a wife and mother, her father Thomas Dudley had found that he needed to be nearer the seat of government and subsequently moved back from Ipswich to Roxbury on the edge of Boston. He built a house on the west side of Smelt Brook, at the foot of the hill where the road that runs up to the First Church joins the Town Street. His strict Puritan insistence on integrity and conformity in matters of religion informed all his activity and especially that as a magistrate. The 'proud, insolent Thomas Morton' of whom many complained 'for injuries done by him both to the English and Indians', could expect short shrift and little mercy. 'We caused his hands to be bound behind him and set his feet in the bilboes, and burned his house to the ground – all in the sight of the Indians – and kept him prisoner till we sent him to England'. One of the ironies of early Massachusetts is this wish to rid themselves of criminal behaviour and dissenting voices, by banishment, much as the Elizabethans had planned to ship their 'idle poor' as far overseas as possible. Thieves and a bigamist were sent back from Massachusetts, on the next ship to 'Old England'.

Dudley and John Winthrop, the Governor, continued to have a stormy relationship, quarrelling on many occasions and being called before the General Council to account for their differences. The records show that when this happened, both sides claimed that there was no conflict,

Fig. 2: Both Annes attended St Botolph's church in Boston where they were inspired by the 'honey-tongued' preacher, Revd John Cotton

from Boston in the early years of the Massachusetts Bay colony was Anne Hutchinson.

Before leaving England, the two Annes may well have known each other as both had attended Revd John Cotton's church in Boston, Lincolnshire. The Hutchinsons had become enthusiastic members of Cotton's congregation at St Botolph's, travelling on a Sunday from Alford twenty four miles south to Boston to listen to the 'honey-tongued' preacher as he led his four hour Sunday afternoon service. Inspired by his sermons, Anne Hutchinson took Cotton's message of God's absolute grace back to Alford, to share with the women who met in her house. These meetings touched many who sought Anne's help as they prepared for the birth of their children and her combined skills of teacher and midwife made her an effective evangelist.

In 1629, Will Hutchinson's sister, Mary, married the Vicar of nearby Bilsby, the Revd John Wheelwright, another Puritan preacher whose sermons Anne Hutchinson enjoyed. A year later, the town of Alford suffered a virulent outbreak of the plague and cut itself off from the outside world until the epidemic had passed, leaving more than a quarter of the population dead. The Hutchinsons lost two daughters, Susan and Elizabeth, and were lucky not to lose more as Anne was actively involved in nursing the sick and helping the women of the town. They suffered a further blow when John Wheelwright was thrown out of his living at Bilsby, to join the ranks of underground preachers, including John Cotton, hiding from the church authorities. For a time, it seemed that Anne Hutchinson had no minister in England whose preaching she completely respected. She turned to the Scriptures for guidance.

The answer came sooner than she may have anticipated, from Isaiah Chapter 30. If she had consulted the Geneva Bible, the version favoured by the Puritans, she would have read:

> 19. Surely a people shall dwell in Zion, and in Jerusalem: thou shalt weep no more: he will certainly have mercy upon thee at the voice of thy cry: when he heareth thee, he will answer thee.
> 20. And when the Lord hath given you the bread of adversity, and the water of affliction, thy rain shall be no more kept back, but thine eyes shall see thy rain.
> 21. And thine ears shall hear a word behind thee, saying, This is the way, walk ye in it'

That may seem strong enough as a message from God, but if she had consulted the 'new' version authorised by King James I for use in all English parish churches, she would have read an even clearer message in verse 20:

> 'And though the Lord give you the bread of adversity, and the water

but the fact that Dudley and Winthrop chose to live well apart, suggests otherwise. Dudley was the more inflexible of the two, able to win approval for his ideas by strength of argument and force of personality, but seldom to win affection. As magistrates, they both took a firm line with any who dared to dissent from the community's orthodox belief and practice, any who challenged the religious authority of the clergy of the Colony. These were punished mercilessly, before being cast out into the wilderness, to survive as best they could. The growing number of Quakers, or 'Friends', were dealt with with particular severity. One 'Friend' who left Massachusetts for the more tolerant colony of Rhode Island described the fate of those who tried to stay and speak out for their form of faith. 'Three were martyred, and three had their right ears cut off. One hath been burnt with the letter H. Thirty one persons have received 650 stripes … one lieth in fetters condemned to die.' Amongst the many who were banished of affliction, yet shall not thy teachers be removed into a corner any more, but thine eyes shall see thy teachers:'

As soon as Anne had recovered from the birth of Susan, her fourteenth child in 1634, the Hutchinsons left England with ten of their children, and were welcomed to Boston, Massachusetts, by John Cotton. Will Hutchinson had become a man of means and soon established himself as a merchant and leading citizen of Boston, while Anne began both a midwifery role and a meeting in their house for the women of Boston, much as she had done in Alford. Revd John Wheelwright joined them two years later and was invited to preach to the Boston church, where John Cotton already served, alongside their pastor, Revd John Wilson, who did not share Cotton and Wheelwright's views. Wilson felt that his authority was undermined by this divisive invitation and contrived to block it by claiming that the appointment of Wheelwright had to be by unanimous vote. Winthrop as Governor sided with Wilson and Wheelwright was appointed to a church outside Boston where Wilson and Winthrop believed he would cause less trouble.

But the conflict deepened with the arrival in the Colony of a young man with impeccable royal connections, Henry Vane, son of the chief adviser to Charles II. Vane lodged with Cotton and was soon attending Anne Hutchinson's meetings. These had become so popular that she started a second meeting open to men, held in her house just across the street from Governor Winthrop's own home. Both meetings provided an opportunity for those attending to discuss the sermons that had been preached over the previous week. They also gave Anne a platform from which to comment on the theology of the preachers. Matters came to a head when the young and inexperienced Vane, heavily influenced by Anne Hutchinson and John Cotton, was elected Governor in Winthrop's place and Wilson's congregation began to voice their disapproval of his sermons. They claimed that he had lapsed into preaching a 'covenant of works' rather than a 'covenant of grace'. This, to the committed Puritan, seemed little better than the system of earning salvation through what you did that had for so long been at the heart of Catholic doctrine. Wilson, his accusers claimed, was no better than the 'legal preachers, Baal's Priests, Popish factors, Scribes, Pharisees and Opposers of Christ Himself.' Those who made such accusations were labelled 'Hutchinsonians', or Antinomians, accused of undermining the stability of the 'new Jerusalem'. The 'city set on a hill' founded as a community of the saints was irreparably divided, and those who quite genuinely cared for its future were convinced

that only by purging itself of the canker of error would it survive.

In the hot summer of 1636, Thomas Shepherd, the minister at Cambridge, opened hostilities with a letter to Cotton couched in terms of 'brotherly affection', but warning Cotton of being influenced by Familist and other erroneous teaching. Without naming Anne Hutchinson, he warned against those who claimed a direct link with God through prophecy, and who like Jezebel had proved to be the enemies of the true servants of God. Cotton's equally brotherly reply rejected this warning but the ministers were not satisfied. In October 1636, they called a gathering in Boston to meet Cotton, Wheelwright and Anne Hutchinson 'in private'. Cotton was required to provide a 'short and plaine answer' to sixteen questions, the opening round of an exchange of theological broadsides which continued well into the winter, without solving the conflict.

Faced with this continuing dissent in their 'earthly paradise', the General Court of the Colony called a fast day in January 1637. Rather than calming things down, Cotton invited Wheelwright to preach in the Boston Church. Adding fuel to the flames, Wheelwright chose texts and themes which focused on 'spiritual combat' and 'being ready to fight'. This aggressive stance led to his being hauled before the General Court in March on charges of sedition and contempt, crimes for which he was sentenced to banishment from the Colony. But his supporters did not give up quietly, raising a petition in his support just at the time when elections for the governorship were about to be held.

By holding the elections in Newtown (Cambridge), rather than in Boston where support for Cotton, Wheelwright and Hutchinson was strongest, Winthrop engineered a return to power. Wheelwright was banished and travelled north to found New Hampshire. Those who had signed the petition in his support were accused of sedition and warned that they would meet the same fate if they did not conform. If they wished to remain in the Colony and to exercise their right to vote, they must accept the authority of the Governor and the Court. The defeated Henry Vane returned to England and became a leading member of the Commonwealth government under Cromwell. When the monarchy was restored, Vane was convicted of high treason and beheaded in spite of the fact that he had not supported the execution of Charles II.

With Wheelwright gone, the Court attempted to silence Anne Hutchinson. Women could meet to pray, but not to be

Fig. 3: In November 1637 Anne Hutchinson was brought before a court at Newtown and found guilty of heresy and sedition. She was banished from the Massachusetts Bay Colony

addressed by one of their number in a 'prophetical way'. She ignored the ban. In November 1637, Anne Hutchinson, the 'troubler of Zion' and the 'American Jezebel' was brought before the Court at Newtown. There are two surviving accounts of her 'examination' or trial before the all-male General Court. One is the version written by the Governor, John Winthrop, as part of his 'Short story of the Rise, reign and ruine of the Antinomians, Familists and Libertines'. This account by the man who was determined to rid the Colony of a woman whom he regarded as 'the breeder and nourisher of all these distempers' can hardly be regarded as unbiased. Winthrop described Anne as 'a woman of haughty and fierce carriage, or a nimble wit and active spirit, and a very voluble tongue, more bold than a man, though in understanding and judgement, inferior to many women'. The second and fuller account is from the *'History of the Colony and Province of Massachusetts Bay'* (Boston, 1767), written by Anne's great great grandson, Thomas Hutchinson, who was also a Governor of the Colony. Clearly sympathetic to Anne's point of view, it records her spirited defence and parrying the accusations of her accusers with a wit and verve that at first reduced them to confusion.

She could not be charged with sedition as she had not signed the petition supporting Wheelwright. No woman could sign a legal document as her signature had no legal status. She could be accused of 'harbouring and countenancing' those who had signed, but, she claimed, that was a matter of conscience and thus no crime. Winthrop next tried to show that she had broken the fifth commandment by opposing the ministers and leadership of the colony who were the 'fathers and mothers' of the Commonwealth. Getting nowhere with this, Winthrop turned to the holding of meetings in her house. Anne admitted holding weekly meetings for discussion and prayer, but claimed that these were for women, citing scripture in her defence as 'elder women should instruct the younger'. When both Simon Bradstreet and Thomas Dudley as members of the Court joined in the questioning, they pursued the question of whether any man had attended her meetings. She admitted that there had been two meetings, one for women only at which she had spoken, and a second for both men and women, but denied ever having spoken at the meeting which included men.

Having failed to get Anne to admit to the charge of teaching men, and having noted that in questioning her they had fallen into the trap of actually inviting her to teach them in court, her accusers then turned to the more important matter of what she had said about the ministers of the churches. Six of them testified that she had accused them of preaching a covenant of works and had criticised their sermons. This she flatly denied and challenged them to give this evidence under oath, with details of when and where she had said these things. This affront to their integrity threatened to reduce the hearing to disorder. John Cotton was finally called to give evidence of what she had said to him, but he claimed not to remember, refusing to support or to condemn the woman who had been his most faithful follower since the early years in Lincolnshire. Anne was clearly winning the verbal exchanges when Winthrop decided to adjourn the matter overnight.

What happened to her as she read through the transcript of the day's proceedings we shall never know, but in the Court again the following morning, she began to do what she had been accused of doing, she began to teach. She gave what would today be called her testimony, her account of how in her journey of faith, she struggled with the choice of staying within the Church or becoming a Separatist, as the Scrooby Congregation had done before they became the Pilgrim Fathers. Without being questioned, Anne was preaching, to a court-room of men, using her considerable knowledge of the Bible to illustrate her theme. Winthrop let her continue as she described how 'having none to open the scriptures to her but the Lord', she had become convinced that only through Cotton and Wheelwright could she hear 'the voices of my beloved Jesus Christ'. She went further, claiming as Abraham had done, and Jacob and Daniel, that 'the Lord did reveal himself to me'. She knew that she was now in God's hands because this was much more than the Court needed to condemn her. Direct revelation was heresy in a world in which ministers saw themselves as essential interpreters of God's word. That she had condemned herself was clear, but what were they to do with her? With none of the ministers, not even John Cotton coming to her defence, the Court found Anne guilty of heresy and sedition and 'unfit for our society'. She was to be held in custody over the winter until the sentence of banishment could be carried out in the milder conditions of the Spring, that much was conceded to her feminine weakness.

While Anne was held at Roxbury, south of Boston, her husband William and others who had supported her were planning for the future. Roger Williams, who had been banished from Boston earlier, encouraged them to set up a new 'plantation' on Aquidneck Island, south-west of Boston. Will and about another twelve men signed an agreement to become jointly responsible for the new settlement on Aquidneck, which was also called Rhode Island, a community which from the start guaranteed religious freedom. They purchased land on the Island from the chief of the Narragansett, whose people agreed to leave it vacant by the next winter. Clearing land and finding good water on the north end of the Island, they established a settlement which they named Portsmouth and William waited there for Anne's banishment from Boston to be implemented.

But before that physical eviction could take place, Anne had to face a second trial. She was brought before the congregation of the church in Boston, for them to decide whether she had shown any signs of repentance following her conviction. The leaders of the church confronted her with long lists of her 'errors' and demanded that she answer. The issues centred on what was believed about the soul and the spirit. Much of this had not been raised at her earlier trial and although Anne did her best to satisfy them with her answers, she failed. Eventually, her accusers returned to the charge that she was a Familist and a believer in free love. This she had consistently denied. Her long and secure marriage to William gave the lie to this charge, but they would not be satisfied. For them it was but a short step from the freedom of the spirit to liberty from the law and the licentious behaviour which challenged all their social norms. Even John Cotton accepted that she held many 'unsound and dangerous principles' and urged her rid herself of any 'evil or poison' by making speed to 'vomit it up again and to repent of it'. Alone and exhausted from the ordeals of her trials and her advancing sixteenth pregnancy, Anne was found to be in error and unrepentant, and the Revd Wilson proceeded to the act of excommunication.

> 'Forasmuch as you, Mistress Hutchinson, having transgressed and offended,.....and troubled the church with your errors....in the name of Jesus Christ and in the name of the Church, ... I do cast you out and ... deliver you to Satan, that you may learn no more to blaspheme, to seduce and to lie.. Therefore, I command you in the name of Christ Jesus and of this church as a leper to withdraw yourself out of the congregation...'

Anne got up and walked out, and as she left, Mary Dyer took her hand and walked out with her, the same Mary Dyer whom she had helped with an earlier miscarriage and who would become a Quaker and eventually return to Boston to be hanged for her 'errors'. Anne made her way with her son Edward, the rest of the family and her supporters including the Dyers through the March snow to a new life on Rhode Island. She went into premature labour in May 1638 and delivered a mass of tissue which would now be called a hydatidiform mole, but which at that

time was further evidence for Winthrop and her enemies of her errors and her alleged promiscuity. Dissent also followed her to Rhode Island. The new community split, with the Hutchinsons staying at the northern settlement of Portsmouth and a new breakaway settlement of Newport being established in the south of the Island. Massachusetts supported this breakaway group and threatened to take over the whole of the Rhode Island colony. When Will Hutchinson died in 1642, Anne decided to move again, as far as she could from the influence of Massachusetts Bay, to the Dutch settlement of New Amsterdam.

With seven of her children, she settled on Pelham Bay, Manhattan Island, where she and her children cleared land and planted their crops. She was warned about an imminent Indian attack but stayed in her house, believing that she and her family had always got on well with the Indians and could trust in God's protection. While her Dutch neighbours fled, she and her children were caught and scalped, their bodies burned in their houses. But one child, Anne's nine-year-old daughter, Susan, survived, adopted by the same Indians who had killed her mother. She later returned to Boston to join the three older Hutchinson sons and two older daughters who had remained in New England.

In the years after Anne Hutchinson's banishment and death, relative peace returned to Boston and as the colony grew, Simon Bradstreet's career developed. He had to travel widely between the new settlements of Massachusetts as he helped to establish the 'United Colonies of New England'. Frequently left on her own, Anne Bradstreet found time between her domestic duties and entertaining visitors to write. She began to find her own poetic voice as she reflected on family life, and her love for Simon and her children.

> 'To My Dear and Loving Husband'
>
> 'If ever two were one, then surely we.
> If ever man were lov'd by wife, then thee;
> If ever wife was happy in a man,
> Compare with me, ye women if you can.'

This simple touching poem, one of the best known of all Anne's writings, would probably have been lost with all her other work had not her brother-in-law, John Woodbridge, found them and secretly copied them. Travelling back to England, Woodbridge took the manuscript of Anne's poems with him and found a publisher. In 1650, her work was printed in London, without her knowledge or approval as 'The Tenth Muse Lately sprung up in America, or Several Poems, compiled with great variety of wit and learning,

Fig. 4: A statue to Anne Hutchinson stands outside the State House in Boston, Massachusetts. The inscription reads: In memory of Anne Marbury Hutchinson Baptised at Alford, Lincolnshire, England 20 July 1595. Killed by the Indians at East Chester, New York, 1643. Courageous exponent of civil liberty and religious toleration

full of delight, by a gentlewoman of those parts'. It was by all accounts a success. Anne is therefore the first published American poet.

As an introduction to her poems, Woodbridge invited a number of men to write verses as a preface. Given that most seventeenth century men simply assumed that women would not be capable of such intellectual activity as writing poetry, as they lacked the opportunity for education, it is not surprising that some of these verses are less than supportive. In his preface to Anne's book, the preacher Nathaniel Ward wrote, 'It half revives my chill frost-bitten blood, to see a woman once do ought that's good'. This was the same Nathaniel Ward who had once likened women's brains to those of squirrels!

When Anne discovered that her work had been published, and was given a copy of the 'Tenth Muse', her reaction was furious. She wrote a poem 'The Author to her Book':

'Thou ill-form'd offspring of my feeble brain,
Who after birth dids't by my side remain,
Till snacht from thence by friends, less wise than true
Who thee abroad, expos'd to public view,'

But she was sufficiently astute to prepare a draft of a second edition of the book, which included this preface, together with many of her later and more successful poems, including a defence of her right to set down her thoughts in poetry, pleading that women too should be heard.

'Let Greeks be Greeks, and Women what they are,
Men have precendency, and still excel,
It is but vaine, unjustly to wage war,
Men can doe best, and women know it well,
Preheminence in each and all is yours,
Yet grant some small acknowledgement of ours.'
(Prologue of the Tenth Muse)

Simon and Anne Bradstreet continued to live at Andover and Anne continued to write poetry. Although her early poems seem naïve and wooden, as if she was striving too hard to emulate the poetry she admired, in her later work, she could stand back and comment on her own efforts with wit and a telling turn of phrase which shows much greater sophistication.

'I am abnoxious to each carping tongue
Who says, my hand a needle better fits,
A poet's pen, all scorn, I should thus wrong.
For such despite they cast on female wits;
If what I do prove well, it won't advance'
They'll say it's stolen, or else it was by chance.'
(The Prologue)

Anne's later poems are also rooted in her experience of life in seventeenth century New England, as a mother, and wife to a busy administrator. They are full of warmth and frank humanity, preoccupied with the reality of death and the need to live within God's will. These lines, written to her husband just before the birth of one of her children, are typical of this introspection, which may seem morbid to us but which expressed the reality of the hazards of childbirth in the early seventeenth century.

'How soon, my Dear, death may my steps attend,
How soon't may be thy lot to lose thy friend,
We both are ignorant, yet love bids me
These farewell lines to recommend to thee,
That when that knot's untied that made us one
I may seem thine, who in effect am none.......
And when thy loss shall be repaid with gains
Look to my little babes, my dear remains.
And if thou love thyself, or loveds't me,
These O protect from step-dames injury......

Fig. 5: The site of the Bradstreet's house in Ipswich, Massachusetts

And kiss this paper for thy love's dear sake
Who with salt tears this last farewell did take.'
  A.B.

In her old age, Anne wrote a sequence of 'Meditations Divine and Moral', short aphorisms full of good advice on how to live a Christian life and how to bring up children in the fear of God.

> 'The finest bread hath the least bran, the purest honey the least wax, and the sincerest Christian the least self-love'.
> 'Some children (like sour land) are of so tough and morose a disposition that the plough of correction must make long furrows on their back and the harrow of discipline go often over them before they be fit soil to sow the seed of morality much less of grace in them. But when by prudent nurture they are brought into a fit capacity, let the seed of good instruction and exhortation be sown in the spring of their youth, and a plentiful crop may be expected in the harvest of their years.
> *Meditations Moral and Divine 1665*

Her views on children may seem extreme today but her devotion to her family is expressed most tenderly in the lines which are illustrated in that window in the Parish Church of Boston, Lincolnshire:

> 'I had eight birds hatched in one nest,
> Four cocks there were, and hens the rest.
> I nursed them up with pain and care,
> Nor cost nor labour did I spare.
> Till at the last, they felt their wings,

Mounted the trees and began to sing.'

Since the rise of feminism and the interest in courses in Women's Studies, Anne Bradstreet's quietly subversive insistence on the right of women to be heard in a world of male power has won her a following. Her great heroine was Queen Elizabeth I, whose life had ended before her own began, but whose qualities and courage she so admired.

> 'Now say, have women worth, or have they none?
> Or have they some, but with our queen is't gone?
> Nay, masculines, you have taxed us long;
> But she, though dead, will vindicate our wrong.
> Let such as say our sex is void of reason,
> Know this a slander now, but once was treason.'
> *(In Honour of Queen Elizabeth)*

Anne's health, never good, got worse in her late 50s and shortly after she herself contracted tuberculosis, she lost her daughter, Dorothy. Consoling herself that Dorothy was now in a better place, Anne prepared to die, accepting that this would not be long in coming. Her long battle with illness came to an end on 16 September 1672, in Andover, just after her 60th birthday. There is no record of where she was buried. After Anne died, Simon married a young widow, thirty years his junior, Ann Downing. He too eventually served two terms as Governor, and was also chosen by the

Fig 6: The inscription at Bradstreet's house in Ipswich, Mas, reads 'On this spot was the house of Simon Bradstreet, Governor of Massachusetts Bay 1679 to 1686 and 1689 to 1692. His wife Ann, daughter of Governor Dudley was the first American poetess and lived in Ipswich 1635 – 1644'

Colony as their envoy to congratulate Charles II on his accession to the throne, travelling back to England and then returning to Massachusetts. He served the Colony for over 62 years before his death in 1697, at the brave age of 94, and a portrait survives, as well as his tomb in the North Point Burying Ground. Of his first wife, Anne, Thomas Dudley's daughter, there is no portrait, no grave, no house, just an extraordinary collection of prose and poetry, steeped in the theology and religious practice of the Puritans.

East Fen Experience

Hilary Healey

North and north-west of Boston lie the former East, West and Wildmore Fens. The East Fen alone before enclosure and drainage, contained upwards of 12,400 acres (opinions vary in the detail according to different writers). This included extensive deep water areas or meres, originally created by medieval peat digging, although at the time of its reclamation some 2,000 acres were left still under water. Despite drainage proposals that began to take shape in the reign of Charles I, the main thrust of enclosure and reclamation took place between 1802 and 1808. It was one of the last large areas of the Lincolnshire fen to be drained.

In view of its size it is not surprising that all the surrounding parishes formerly intercommoned in the fen. There were 21 of these altogether. Upon enclosure land was allocated on a proportional basis, allocating a considerable amount to the 'undertakers', who had invested their money in the project. Drains and roads and bridges were constructed, new farms, cottages and manufactories were built. One important element was the inns, built to encourage the navvies, or 'bankers' as they were known, from going off to town in their spare time!

Exactly two hundred years ago, with the undertakings nearly complete, the newly enclosed and drained landscape would have looked very different from today. Land was still being cleared and planted. New brick was everywhere and by 1812 seven new parochial townships had been officially created. Their churches followed modest Georgian structures, starting with Carrington (1816). The last one to be built, Eastville (1840), was influenced externally by the medieval revival, and sports a traditional medieval style tower, but the interior still feels Georgian. When

Fig. 1: Marfleets Bridge, Friskney.
Derelict cottage (now demolished). This was a typical brick, one-up, one-down cottage. In some parts of the fens these are called 'half-houses'. Access to the upper room was by a ladder and the garden was a typical fen garden full of sheds.

Fig. 2: Friskney Decoy.
One of the massive ancient sycamores in this wood.
The use of the duck decoy came from Holland in the
seventeenth century and before drainage there were
several in the Friskney and Wainfleet area. Drainage
and peat erosion have left the decoy drier and more
isolated now. The trees today include many planted
specimens, and the site is a nature reserve belonging to
the Lincolnshire Wildlife Trust.

Fig. 3: Stickford .
The remains of the tower mill,
seen against early blackthorn blossom.
This mill was built in 1820 and worked until 1925.

the Hobhole Drain had been completed a longitudinal section of the soils was drawn in 1810. This section serves to remind us that at this time a depth of up to six feet of peat was still present in much of the East Fen, amongst the meres.

Over the last two centuries the peat has eroded through shrinkage and windblow, and many trees and shrubs have been removed. As the peat shrinks, structures settle and

many of the original buildings have collapsed or been taken down. In the last twenty years the pace of change has been greater than ever, and the landscape is losing many features that connect with its history, but there is still a distinctive atmosphere. The etchings here form part of a project to capture some of that atmosphere in and around the East Fen area.

A New War Memorial for Fulstow

Jean Howard and David Start

It may be felt that the First World War was so long ago that its relevance to today's population is fading – but memories run deep in Lincolnshire. Some three years ago a new resident in Fulstow was observant enough to note the absence of a village War Memorial. Her questions about why this was so, met with initial reluctance until a story of village unity and a long-felt sadness emerged.

Fulstow's sons had indeed answered the call and ten had not returned. In the aftermath of the war there had been plans to erect a memorial. However, the plan stalled when it was made clear that one sacrifice could not be recorded. The issue had been so sensitive that the parish church had never held an Armistice Sunday service.

The matter surrounded the death of Private Charles Kirman of the Lincolnshire Regiment's 7th Battalion. Kirman had already done military service prior to the outbreak of war, when he was recalled. He went to France as part of the British Expeditionary Force and fought in some of the bloodiest battles of the conflict, including Mons, Bois Grenier and the Somme. Wounded for a second time, he was sent home to recuperate.

Returned to France, he first went AWOL in November 1916. After a court martial he was returned to his unit but, unable to face being sent again to the front line, he

absconded twice more, each time turning himself in after a few days. At his final court martial his testimony included, 'My nerves are completely broken down. I suffer with pains in the head when I am in the line. Sometimes I don't know what I'm doing.' Convicted of desertion and going absent without leave he was shot on 23 September 1917.

His contemporaries in Fulstow understood his suffering. After the war there was a united stand by the families of all who had died: their sons grew up together, knew each other and all their names should be on a memorial, or a memorial was not wanted.

In 2005, while the government was still considering lifting the taboo attached to such punishment of those suffering shell shock, Fulstow again acted in concert, to finally honour all those who made the ultimate sacrifice. The village hall had been built in memory of the three men and two women from Fulstow killed in the Second World War. Close to the entrance door a plaque was erected listing all names from both wars.

Having received publicity in The Daily Telegraph the campaign to fund the plaque was augmented by donations from America, Canada, France, Italy, Australia and Hong Kong, so additional plaques were also put up in the parish church of St Lawrence and the Methodist Chapel. On

Fig. 1: The village hall at Fulstow was built in memory of the five men and women of Fulstow who died in WWII but no memorial had ever been erected to the ten men lost in WWI.
In 2005 a plaque commemorating those who fell in both wars was finally installed.

Sunday 13 November 2005 a joint service of Anglicans and Methodists began in Fulstow chapel. After hymns and prayers conducted by David Robinson in the chapel, the worshippers joined the assembly outside at the Memorial, where proceedings continued under the Anglican priest Revd Keith Tomlin. Members of the Western Front Association, dressed in full uniform, provided a guard of honour. Thirteen young men and two young women, all village residents, spoke, each representing a fallen serviceman of their own age. The words of Binyon were shared between the last remaining resident who saw service in the Second World War, and a serving Lieutenant Colonel, home from Basra. The Last Post was sounded by another local; he had last played the cornet at school, and had practised for weeks for this important moment with a borrowed bugle.

November 2006 was a low key occasion, partly in reaction to all the media coverage of the previous year. But Fulstow will mark Armistice Day henceforth.

A Song for Fulstow

For well over ten years, Radio Lincolnshire has run an annual song-writing competition called 'Write a Lincolnshire Folk Song'. The competition is designed to encourage the composition of new folk songs relevant to our county. The songs can be on any subject at all, as long as they are about some aspect of Lincolnshire. They are submitted as performances on cassette tapes and a team of judges chooses the ten best songs. These finalists are invited to perform their songs at a concert held at Spilsby Theatre and recorded by Radio Lincolnshire. The judges choose the winners on the night and they receive a certificate and a cash prize. A one-hour radio programme of all the final entries is compiled and broadcast, usually, at Christmas.

In 2006 the competition was won by the song 'The Fallen of Fulstow'. The words were written by Mark Addison and the music by John Blanks, who also performed the song with guitar accompaniment. The story of Private Kirman and the Fulstow War Memorial caught the public imagination in 2005 and the story reached the national press bringing notoriety to this normally tranquil Lincolnshire village. In November 2005, the war memorial including Private Kirman's name was finally unveiled. The story struck a chord with writer and musician Mark Addison and this winning entry was born. It is published with the permission of the author and composer and with thanks to Kim Biggs for the transcription and to Steve Adamson for the musical typesetting.

The Fallen of Fulstow

Lyrics: Mark Addison   Music: John Blanks

The Fallen of Fulstow

This is not so much a story about the injustices of those soldiers executed for desertion in the first world war, as a tribute to the people of Fulstow, who even in those 'less enlightened' times refused a memorial to their dead until <u>all</u> their lost sons could be included on the roll of honour.

In the village of Fulstow the village hall stands
To the memory of those who've gone before,
The sons and the daughters, the Fallen of Fulstow
Who died in the Second World War.

Ten young men played in the fields of Fulstow,
Ten young men played in the fields of green,
And though nine of them died on the field of battle
There's no memorial to be seen.

But where's Pennell and Taylor, Wattam and Sherriff,
Harrison, West, Green, Marshall and Hyde?
Gave their all in the Great War, the war to end all wars,
You won't find their names inscribed.

Chorus

Charles Kirman, a soldier before nineteen fourteen,
Recalled to the field, to Mons and the Somme,
Twice wounded in battle, and with honours awarded,
He knew that he could not go on.

Chorus

So Charlie went AWOL, but he turned himself in
And he told them of the pains in his head,
'My nerves are shot to ribbons, I don't know what I'm
         doing',
Still the General sentenced him to death.

Chorus

Then come nineteen eighteen the village was told
'You may honour your dead, God rest their souls,
With a stone to your nine sons, The Fallen of Fulstow,
But Kirman's not to be on the roll.'

They said, 'Ten young men played in our fields of
         Fulstow,
Ten young men played in our fields of green,
Only nine of them died on the field of battle
But all ten have the right to be seen.'

It's eighty-odd years now, and the General's gone
There's a statue of him somewhere I dare say.
The eleventh of November, two thousand and five
Saw Fulstow's first Armistice Day.

'Ten young men played in our fields of Fulstow,
Ten young men played in our fields of green,
All ten of them died as brothers in arms
And ten names are there to be seen.'

© Mark Addison and John Blanks 2006

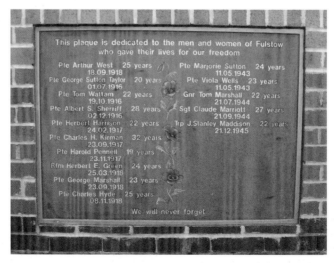

Fig. 2: The Fulstow war memorial was dedicated on 13 November 2005.
It includes the name of Charles Kirman.

'Until the Seas Boil Dry': Landscape and salt in Bronze Age Lincolnshire

Tom Lane

Preamble

David Robinson's interests are wide indeed but underpinning them all is his extensive knowledge and grasp of geology, climate and landscape. Now, as in the past, these affect us all directly by influencing what the lands around us are capable of producing and where we can or cannot live or work. Effects of climate and landscape changes large and small can be seen in and around Lincolnshire, particularly in riverine and coastal locations from the Fenland to the swathe of coastal marsh fringing the North Sea, to the Humber and the rivers of the Trent and the Ancholme. These are dynamic marshy transitional landscapes, sometimes terrestrial, sometimes aquatic, but more often in some in-between state, perhaps simply wetland.

It is to these liminal landscapes that human individuals and communities have been attracted in the past. Not for them the leisurely day at the seaside but the opportunities to gather resources specific to these harsh uncompromising coastal environments for food, shelter and items of trade. One of these resources, sea salt, is the subject of this contribution. 'Until the seas boil dry' is a line from a folk song of the 'love you 'til I die' genre. However, the 'boiling dry' of seawater to create salt has happened repeatedly over many millennia around the coast of Lincolnshire from at least the Middle Bronze Age and almost certainly earlier.

This paper will assess the emerging evidence for Bronze Age saltern sites. Moreover, there will be consideration of how *special* these creek-pierced, inter-tidal areas and salt impregnated, muddy landscapes were to the early saltmakers and how the saltmakers themselves, the people who possessed the wisdom and power to transform the sea into a valuable and venerated mineral, were regarded by others.

The Use and Power of Salt

Salt is many things. It has always been a multi-purpose mineral, used in activities as diverse as medicine and animal training, mummification and cheesemaking. In its time salt has served as currency, salary and revenue and, of course, as a major item of trade. In fact it is sometimes said to have been the only extensively traded product that was a necessity rather than a luxury[1]. Underpinning the need to win salt is the physiological requirement of the mineral by humans, although sufficient is present in most diets to survive without additional intake. Indeed, natural presence of salts in meat and fish has ensured the survival of carnivores through time. However, the introduction of arable agriculture in the Neolithic period gradually changed the balance of human dietary regimes and increased the need for a salt intake beyond that contained within meats.

In the later Prehistoric and Roman periods salt came into its own as a food preservative. Once discovered, this special conserving quality extended the crucial 'eat-by' date of meat and fish by many months. Such a revolutionary, life-changing discovery may well have created for the product the awe and esteem that tipped over into veneration. What other household product has been, and still is, central to so many ceremonies and rituals across the world? From its numerous references in the bible[2] to being part of the exchange of gifts between the Russians and Americans on the Soyuz space station[3], salt has played a key part in ceremony and ritual through time. Associations of salt with symbolism and mysticism still abound. For example, a remarkable altercation occurred in the town of Glastonbury in November 2006 when pagans had 'blessed salt' thrown at them by a visiting coach load of members of the Roman Catholic faith in an effort to 'cleanse the town of pagans'. If salt is still such a strong symbolic force in the twenty first century we can only imagine its power and potency in prehistory.

Whether this special status given to salt was transferred to its makers, or indeed the areas it was made in, has been questioned[4]. In the same way that ancient and indeed some modern societies[5] regard metalworkers as a special class - the 'magicians' who make metal out of the earth, were saltmakers, with their power to create this essential and venerated product from the ocean, regarded with the same awe, reverence and, perhaps, suspicion?

Elsewhere, the ritual and the mystical may have been associated not only with the finished product but with other aspects of salt, such as its processing and transport. In the American southwest and in Mexico salt procurement was undertaken with 'much ceremony'[6], although this was not described in detail.

*Fig. 1: Figurine in briquetage fabric from
the saltern at Addlethorpe*

Such statements, implying ceremonies being part of the manufacturing process, bring to mind the 120mm tall clay figurine (Fig. 1) made in a briquetage[7] fabric and retrieved from a buried saltern in Addlethorpe[8]. Is this merely a hastily fashioned plaything made to calm a fractious and bored child or is it more; perhaps a salt god? The latter image might easily be present on a site where a product with such a ritualistic base was being made.

In suggesting that the figurine might be a child's plaything one might cite Annie Garvey's work[9] on the transitional Iron Age-Roman briquetage from another buried saltern in Addlethorpe, this one on the line of the recent bypass. Initially fascinated by the clear fingerprints of the makers on the pedestals from the site, Garvey studied the question of the gender of the manufacturers as part of a wider study to look for any symbolic meanings embedded

in ancient technology. Although the results were not conclusive Garvey suggested, after experimentation, that these pedestals were more likely to be made by females. As pedestals needed to be made on site, as one-off pieces to stabilise the containers, it stands to reason that the makers - the females - stayed to make the salt. By association it may be that children were around too and the figurine could, indeed, be a doll.

Although Garvey's conclusions are not universally accepted there are many ethnographic parallels for women as the saltmakers. In Britain, issues of gender are tied in with 'modes of production' - the hierarchy of production systems - in ancient societies[10]. Such investigations, though necessarily theoretical, could move salt studies further down the path of understanding the full significance of this all-purpose product to the people of the Fenland and Lincolnshire coast.

Earliest Saltmaking in Lincolnshire

Our story should start when the land now known as Lincolnshire acquired its first post-glacial (Flandrian) coast. By *c.*8300BP the land between Britain and Denmark, the former Northsealand or Doggerland, had become flooded as the ice retreated and melted[11]. This resulted in a Lincolnshire 'coastline' of sorts, but one that was many kilometres east of its present location. Allied to the melting of the thick and heavy ice was a complex series of vertical movements of the land. The result of all of this was, and still continues to be, a coastline that is mobile and variable.

Fascinating as the story of the inundation of Doggerland is[12], it is the presence of that coast and not the mechanisms that created it that is important here. For here, it is the use of that coast (or, more accurately, those coasts) to make salt that is important.

Apart from it probably setting a dubious benchmark that other academics will strive to better, a recent article entitled 'The Earliest Salt Production in the World...'[13] suggests that the salt springs of Romanian Moldavia were being exploited by 6050 to 5500BC. The precise method of salt extraction there is not clear but heating or evaporation was involved with the remains at the springs comprising mounds of 'ash, charcoal and red coloured burnt soil'. The date quoted is not too far from the 8300BP for the embryonic and more easterly Lincolnshire proto-coastline, although the salt solution at the Moldavian inland springs would have been stronger than the *c.* 3% in seawater and

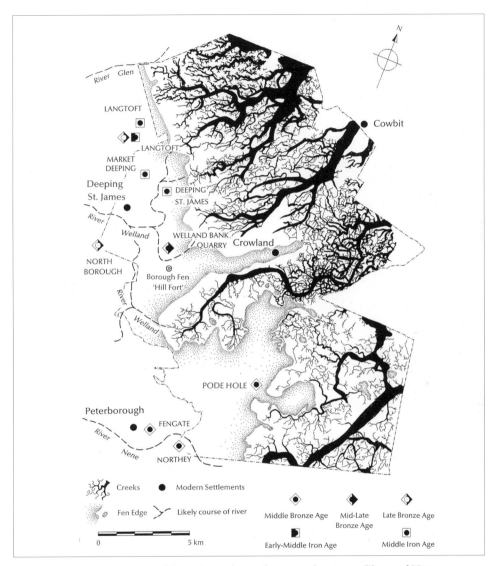

Fig. 2: Bronze Age and Iron Age salterns between the rivers Glen and Nene.

easier to process into salt. Moreover, the known techniques for extracting sea salt in the prehistoric period in Britain and around the North Sea shores involve reliance on ceramic containers which are unlikely to have been in use at this early, virtually pre-ceramic, time (although salt could have been gained by many other means at that time).

Even though salt production would have been possible, and probably desirable, by the Later Neolithic there is no known salt production of that date in Britain, the earliest being attributed to the mid second millennium BC – the Middle Bronze Age. Even this is limited to a few locations; Brean Down in the southwest[14] and on the east coast in

Essex[15]. Added to this is the Fenland and Lincolnshire coast which not only has some of the earliest evidence for salt production in the country but perhaps also the densest.

While the Late Bronze Age site at Tetney remains the best known early site in Lincolnshire it is the fen edge area between the rivers Glen, south of Bourne, and the Nene at Peterborough that has the earliest individual sites and the greatest density of Bronze Age salterns (Fig.2). This 'cradle of salt' contains four known sites containing Middle Bronze Age (MBA) briquetage, but none has features that are positively identifiable as directly related to a saltern.

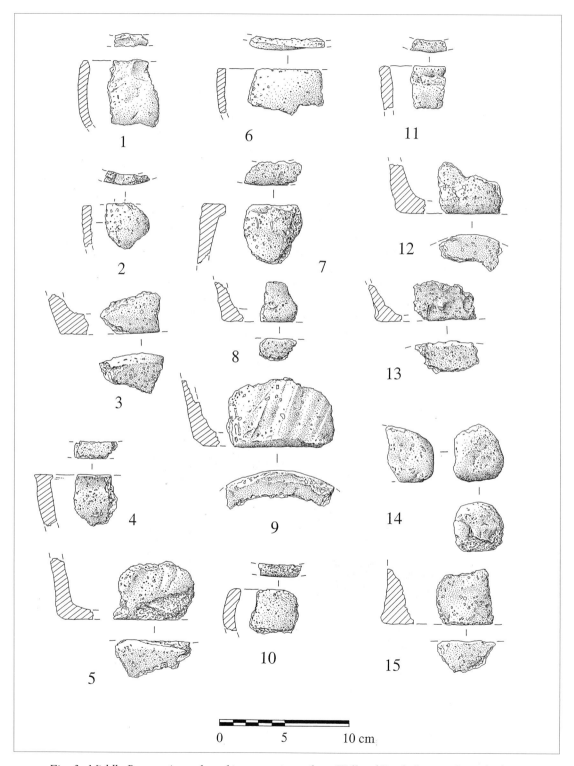

Fig. 3: Middle Bronze Age salt making containers from Welland Bank Quarry, Lincolnshire

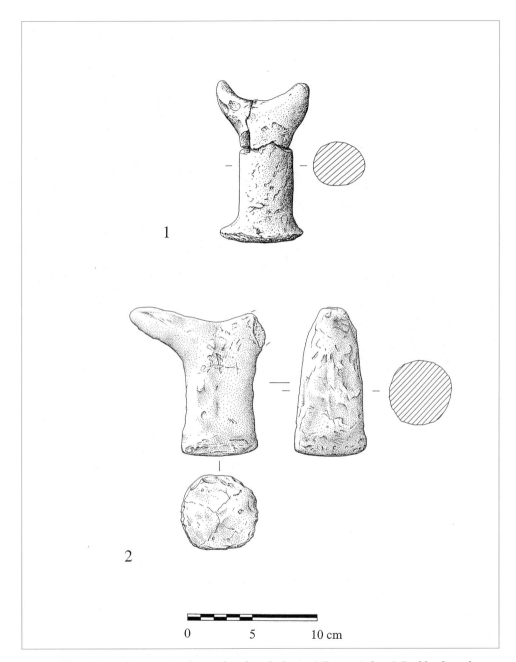

Fig. 4: Late Bronze Age horned pedestals from: 1 Tetney (after J Goddard) and
2 Welland Bank Quarry, Lincolnshire

Middle Bronze Age briquetage from the Peterborough area is known from Northey[16] and Fengate[17]. Subsequently, sites at Welland Bank Quarry on the Lincolnshire/ Cambridgeshire border (Fig. 2) and Pode Hole Quarry, Thorney[18] have yielded both Middle and Late Bronze Age briquetage. At Welland Bank the MBA briquetage was almost exclusively from a single large pit with Deverel Rimbury pottery[19]. It consisted predominantly of fragmentary container sherds from straight sided vessels. The occasional curved pieces, such as the base sherd (Fig. 3, No. 9), could be from corners. Like the MBA material the Late Bronze Age briquetage from the site was shell tempered but included various forms of support, including a horned pedestal (Fig.4, No 2) strongly resembling a published example from Tetney (Fig. 4, No 1)[20]. No definite hearth or oven structures were associated with the Welland Bank MBA briquetage, although numerous layers of ash, charcoal and burnt silt/clay, interpreted on site as redeposited structural hearth material and rake-out, came from the pit. The Pode Hole Quarry site is a new discovery and little information is available at this stage other than the presence of both MBA and LBA briquetage and that both containers and pedestals are represented.

In the same Glen-Nene fen edge areas, Late Bronze Age and/or Early – Mid Iron Age sites are known from Langtoft Outgang Road[21] Langtoft Quarry[22], Northborough[23], Market Deeping[24] and Deeping St James[25], as well as at Welland Bank and Pode Hole. All of these sites received their supplies of brine from the early multi-channelled and tidal River Welland which took several broadly contemporary routes into the Fen basin (Fig. 2). No hearths directly associated with saltmaking are known from these sites (although structural briquetage is present). The Welland Bank hearths may have been for domestic and/or industrial purposes. Striking among the briquetage were the containers described as small and 'boat-shaped' from Northborough and Langtoft Quarry. Some briquetage has parallels elsewhere, with the curious pedestals from Welland Bank (Fig. 5, Nos 1-3) resembling the Type A1 pedestals from Late Bronze Age Mucking, in Essex[26]. Both Welland Bank and Stickford, on the northern fen edge, had large quantities of burnt flint present in the immediate area and these may have played a part in the process.

Extensive peat growth in the increasingly freshwater landscape of the fen edge in the Middle to Late Iron Age saw the fen edge salterns starved of their brine supply. The response of the saltmakers was to relocate into the fen where both brine and peat fuel was available. This is best seen at Cowbit where, approximately 10km east of Welland Bank along one of the outfalls of the Welland, a series of new salterns was created. One excavated example yielded a radiocarbon date of 185-95 BC from a *second* phase of operation[27]. It is no coincidence that the Cowbit area was the location of the first of the 'in-fen', as opposed to fen edge, salterns, as it lay directly downstream from the 'cradle of salt' where operated those with the specialist knowledge and the long tradition of making salt (Fig. 2).

North of the Glen two further Late Bronze Age salterns are known (Fig.6). At Dowsby, briquetage was sealed in a ditch bottom with late Bronze Age pottery close to a contemporary stream and, 4km to the north, at Billingborough, excavations revealed the vestiges of 'two or three hearths', along with abundant briquetage from gullies and a pit with a radiocarbon date of 780-370 cal BC[28]. A broadly similar date of 815-395 cal BC came from a hearth associated with briquetage that was recorded in section on the side of a boulder clay hummock at Hogsthorpe on the Lincolnshire Marsh[29].

Some 30km to the north of Hogsthorpe, at Tetney (Fig.6), excavation of a buried saltern in advance of development yielded a radiocarbon date of 845-745 cal BC[30]. The excavator's interpretation of the methodology is more akin to the systems of collecting salt impregnated mud, washing, filtration and evaporation common in the area during the medieval period than the capture, heating and crystallising of brine that was preferred in the Late Iron Age and Roman periods. That said, most of the other Bronze Age salterns in Lincolnshire do not have sufficient features to enable a full interpretation of the methods used there at that early date.

Some indication of ritual involving briquetage on a saltern site came from the Late Bronze Age settlement and saltern site at Hagnaby Lock in Stickford (Fig. 6) on the northern Fen edge. Here, where the Hagnaby Beck ran along the east side of the Stickford/Stickney promontory, 407 sherds of Later Bronze Age pottery and 73 sherds of briquetage had been deliberately placed in a pit in a carefully arranged layered, concentric manner (Fig. 7)[31]. All the briquetage in the pit was from organic tempered containers while that from a nearby ditch was all quartz tempered and likely to be from pedestals or supports[32]. While such structured deposits involving pottery are not unknown in later prehistory the use of briquetage is rare. Again there was no real indication of the process involved in making salt on this site.

Location

The fact that pre-Late Iron Age salt production is not commonly found in Britain is sometimes regarded as an indication or confirmation of a low level of production, perhaps implying that salt at that time was used chiefly for ritual purposes and not consumption[33]. However, despite discoveries of Bronze Age salterns in Lincolnshire around the fen edge and marshland coast being rare, they hint at a much larger industry. The nature and history of the surface geology around these sites means that many doubtless

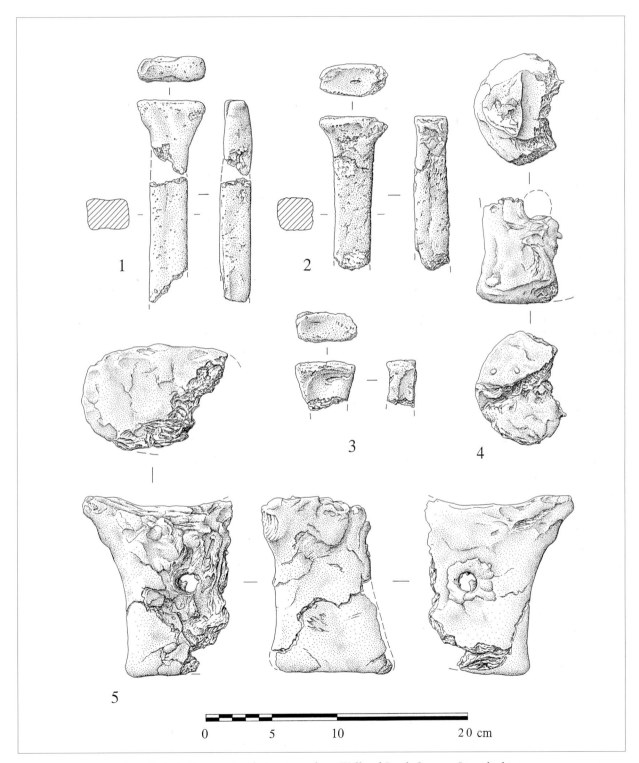

Fig. 5: Late Bronze Age briquetage from Welland Bank Quarry, Lincolnshire

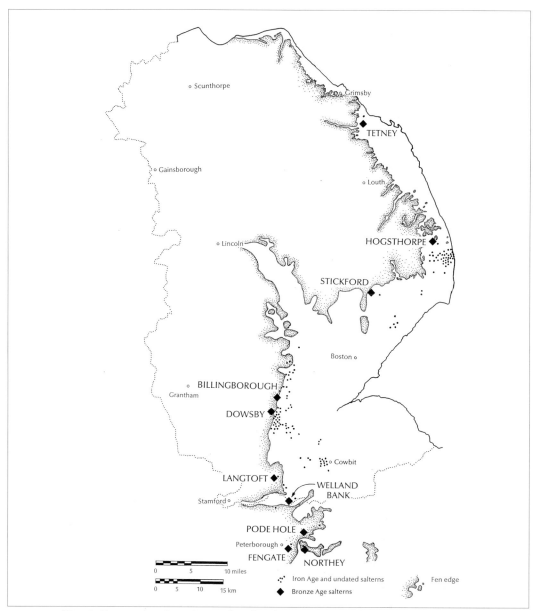

Fig. 6: Bronze Age, Iron Age and undated salterns around the Fenland and marsh

lie buried beyond the range of the usual archaeological prospecting methods. On the marsh it is the changing coastline that either buries sites with alluvium (e.g. Tetney and Hogsthorpe) or perhaps erodes other sites away. On the fen edge the extensive spreads of river alluvium around the outfalls of the Rivers Nene and Welland[34] obscure the sites. For instance, Welland Bank had in the region of 0.5m of freshwater alluvial cover. Only where there has been mineral extraction (e.g. Welland Bank and

Langtoft), development (e.g. Northborough), or research-led archaeological excavation targeting other features (e.g. Fengate, Stickford and Market Deeping) have the sites been found. Because the sites remain buried, no Bronze Age salterns have been discovered in the fen edge locations as a result of aerial photography or fieldwalking, despite the attentions of the Fenland Survey.

Once the industry had to move seaward from the fen edge then there is evidence of Iron Age salterns, in the form of

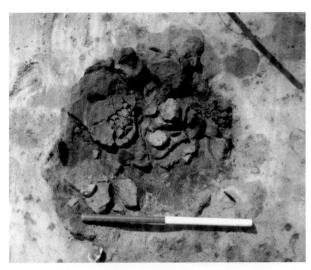

*Fig. 7: Stickford: Late Bronze Age pottery
and briquetage 'placed' in a pot*

surface scatters of briquetage, in a narrow zone seaward of the peat, before they are once more sealed by later, post-Roman, silting. This is best represented at Cowbit (Fig 2). Any number of sites could be present beneath the later coastal alluvial accretions or indeed, beneath the North Sea.

The salt industry continued to develop through the Iron Age when, with the exception of the isolated examples at Tetney and Stickford, sites were confined, by and large, to the same geographic areas as in the preceding Bronze Age (Fig. 6). While this may simply reflect the continued suitability of the conditions it may also be an indication of where the skills were based and where the saltmaking tradition was strongest. Whether these areas were 'up for grabs' by any incomer or recognised as the areas specific to established salters is not known, but these zones, where the powerful ceremonial product was 'magicked' from the muddy creeks, may have had their own ambience, resonating with the mystical and not welcoming to outsiders.

A Comment on the Romans

By the early Roman period salterns were ubiquitous across the Fenland and this is a story well told elsewhere[35] and not part of this article. The recent conclusions by Strang[36] that the '*Salinae*' noted on Ptolemy's map of Britain, compiled from data gathered prior to AD122, relates to a location in the Skegness region, broadly at the junction of the Fenland and the Lincolnshire Marsh,

is plausible. Given the known density of sites around that location it may have been the area generally and not a single specific place that Ptolemy referred to. If a single place, however, dare we suggest that it might have been Skegness itself which Leland[37] recorded as having once been a '*towne waullid having also a castelle*' but which was by the early 1500s '*clene consumed and eten up with sea...*'. Certainly there are no known documentary references of the medieval period to suggest a walled town and castle at Skegness and the description may fit better with the remains of a substantial Roman settlement.

Experimentation

Discovering how salterns operated can be aided by conducting experiments. Because of the paucity of data from the Bronze Age salterns it is difficult to recreate the process. However, for the Late Iron Age and Roman periods excavations have taken place which have yielded a typical arrangement of a hearth or oven type heating structure with flanking clay-lined pits, interpreted as 'settling tanks', all enclosed within a horseshoe-shaped ditch[38]. Repeating the much earlier experiments by David Robinson a recent experimental saltmaking day on the marsh at Wrangle, sought principally to re-create an Early Roman saltern from Wygate Park, Spalding[39]. Modern copies of the ceramic containers from Ingoldmells[40] were used with modern pedestals and clips made on-site out of local clays. At the same time a replica of a simple Late Bronze Age hearth (Fig. 8) with large pedestals based on those from Langtoft and Market Deeping, holding a single gutter-shaped trough, was fired using peat blocks as fuel and with the fire started, on the advice of David, using sea purslane, a small woody-stemmed plant growing locally on the sides of the marsh creeks. Despite the shattering of the large pedestals on the Langtoft-style hearth salt was made eventually, as it was on the wood-fired multi-container Spalding-type heating structure.

This was a one day experiment and the first of a number, but it will need time to develop strategies to monitor effectively, for example, the quantities of fuel used, the processes involved in strengthening the brine, the time spent on both resource procurement and in standing at the heating structure actually making the salt. It was apparent in the experiment that once the crystallisation process had started on the multi-container Spalding heating structure there was a need to ladle repeatedly the brine from those containers furthest from the heat source ever nearer the hottest one closest to the fire. During this period on the

Fig. 8: Experiments: The Langtoft (Late Bronze Age) reconstructed pedestals and container in a simple hearth with peat fire

experimental firing there was little time for the saltmaker to undertake any other tasks, including stoking the fire.

Obtaining the correct fuel for the experiments created problems, not least those in finding peat fuel supplies in Eastern England. All that could be obtained was in the form of compressed blocks. Useful facts did emerge from the Wrangle experiments. One is the knowledge that surprising quantities of combustible saltmarsh vegetation were washed up on the strand lines (and dried in the hot sun), although it is unlikely that the prehistoric and Roman salterns would have been sited that close to the open sea, or could operate using only such material. Nevertheless, such dry vegetable matter would have been useful in starting the fires. The second fact served to offer one explanation for the deliberate backfilling of features at the end of the saltmaking season (end of summer?) as recorded at the excavated Roman sites of Morton[41] and Middleton, Norfolk. At the latter site, Crowson[42] noted that the site had been 'conspicuously tidied in an orderly fashion' intimating a possible military involvement. In fact, at Wrangle at the end of the day, we broke up the hearth and

backfilled the settling tanks (we had not had time to dig the characteristic surrounding ditch) to avoid the possibility of the cattle which grazed on the marsh stepping in the holes and harming themselves. Perhaps this is also a reason for the 'conspicuous tidiness' in the Roman period.

Conclusions

This contribution has sought to bring to the fore just one aspect - the Bronze Age salterns - of the long and fascinating story of saltmaking in Lincolnshire. A number of Bronze Age salterns are now known and, while they are scattered widely on the Lincolnshire coast, there is evidence for a concentration on the fen edge in south Lincolnshire and north Cambridgeshire. The regions with the greatest promise of increasing knowledge of the early days of an industry that is intimately associated with the county have been identified. This will enable an awareness of that rich promise by those who advise the planning authorities on archaeological matters and, as a result, further evidence may be forthcoming in advance of any property development in those areas.

Meanwhile, the work continues towards understanding the many different aspects of a type of site that is superficially no more than an area of abandoned industrial remains, but is, in fact, a useful point of entry into the world of prehistoric work and worship.

Acknowledgements

My thanks to all those whose work contributed to this paper directly or otherwise. Dave Hopkins prepared the illustrations with usual consummate skill; Susan Unsworth produced the photographs; Betty Kirkham and Anderby Drainage Museum gave permission to include the Addlethorpe figurine; Phoenix Consulting Archaeology Ltd/Network Archaeology Ltd provided information of the site at Pode Hole in advance of publication. Brian Simmons and Steve Malone read early drafts of this report and improved it immeasurably. I find those smitten by salt tremendously enthusiastic and inspirational and in a short list that is by no means exhaustive I must include here Elaine Morris, Andrew and Annelise Fielding, who led the experimental day, Brian Simmons and, of course, David Robinson.

Notes:

1. Leacok (1971) quoted in I W Brown, *Salt and the Eastern North American Indian: An Archaeological Study*, Lower Mississippi Survey Bulletin 6 (1980) p.4.

2. see for example, J Nenquin, 'Salt: a study in economic prehistory', *Dissertationes Archaeologicae Gandenses* 6 (Bruges, 1961).

3. *A Millennium of Saltmaking: Prehistoric and Romano-British Salt Production in the Fenland* edited by T Lane and E L Morris, Lincolnshire Archaeology and Heritage Reports Series 4 (2001), p.8.

4. for instance T Lane, 'Roman and Pre-Roman Salt-Making in the

Fenland of England', in *Salt Works and Salinas: The Archaeology, Conservation and Recovery of Salt Making sites and their Processes*. edited by A M Fielding and A P Fielding, Lion Salt Works Trust Monograph Series Research Report 2, (2005) pp.19-26, and E L Morris, 'Making Magic: Later Prehistoric and Early Roman Salt Production in the Lincolnshire Fenland', in *The Later Iron Age in Britain and Beyond*, edited by C Haselgrove and T Moore, Oxford (Oxbow, forthcoming).

5. for instance D Moretti 'Ethnologic Observation: The Blacksmith', in *Wolayta: Una Regione D'Etiopia. Studi e Ricerche 1995-2004*. edited by C Cavanna, Societa' Naturalistica Speleogica Maremmana (2005)

p.131.

6. I W Brown, *Salt and the Eastern North American Indian: An Archaeological Study*, Lower Mississippi Survey Bulletin 6 (1980) p.5

7. The term 'briquetage' is specific to the equipment created for use in ancient saltmaking. It is the name for the ceramic debris from the saltmaking process and includes evaporation vessels, various supports and clips and the remains of the hearths/ovens used in extracting salt from brine. Saltmaking sites can contain large quantities of this ceramic debris and it has become an archaeological indicator for the ancient saltmaking industry.

8. Lane and Morris *op. cit.* p.409

9. A Garvey, *Who were the Saltmakers?,* Unpublished BA Dissertation, Univ of Southampton (2003).

10. E L Morris, 'Briquetage and Salt Production and Distribution Systems: A Comparative Study', in *A Millennium of Saltmaking: Prehistoric and Romano-British Salt Production in the Fenland* edited by T Lane and E L Morris, Lincolnshire Archaeology and Heritage Reports Series 4 (2001), p.394.

11. R Van de Noort and P Davies, *Wetland Heritage: An Archaeological Assessment of the Humber Wetlands* (Univ of Hull, 1993).

12. see B Coles, 'Doggerland's loss and the Neolithic', in Bog Bodies, Sacred Sites and Wetland Archaeology edited by B Coles, J Coles and M S Jorgensen, *WARP Occasional Paper* 12, 1999, 51-7 and N C Fleming, (ed), *Submarine Prehistoric Archaeology of the North Sea*, CBA Research Report 141 (2004) and in particular, for *the* concise account of the formation of the Lincolnshire coast, D N Robinson, *The Book of the Lincolnshire Seaside,* Buckingham (Barracuda, 1981).

13. O Weller and G Dumitroaia, 'The Earliest Salt production in the World: an early Neolithic exploitation in *Poiana Slatinei*- Lunca, Romania', *Antiquity* Vol 79, No 306 (2005).

14. M Bell, *'Brean Down, Excavations 1983-1987,* English Heritage Archaeol. Rep. 15, (HBMC, 1990).

15. T J Wilkinson and P Murphy, *The Archaeology of the Essex Coast, Volume 1: The Hullbridge Survey*, East Anglian Archaeology 71 (1995) p.218.

16. D Gurney, 'Evidence of Bronze Age Salt-Production at Northey, Peterborough', *Northamptonshire Archaeol.* 15, (1980) pp.1-11.

17. F Pryor, *Excavation at Fengate, Peterborough, England: The Third Report*. Northamptonshire Archaeological Society Monograph 1 and Royal Ontario Museum Archaeology Monograph 6 (1980).

18. E L Morris *pers comm.*

19. Deverel Rimbury is a name given to an archaeological culture of the British Middle Bronze Age. It is named after two sites in Dorset and dates to between 1600 and 1100 BC.

20. J Samuels, 'An unusual fired clay pedestal from a Late Bronze Age saltmaking site at Tetney, Lincolnshire', *Antiquaries Journal,* 74, (1994) pp.324-5

21. Lane and Morris *op. cit.* p.250

22. A Dickens, 'Langtoft: Life on the Edge', *Lincolnshire Unearthed*, Issue 5, (2006) pp.4-9.

23. M Knight, The Archaeological Investigation of the Anglian Water Northborough to Etton Watermain and Excavation of a Terminal Bronze Age Settlement at Nine Bridges, Unpublished CAU Report 287 (1998).

24. Lane and Morris *op. cit.* p.262.

25. Lane and Morris *op. cit.* p.279.

26. P M Barford, 'Salt Production in Essex before the Red Hills', in A J Fawn, K A Evans, I McMaster and G M R Davies, *The Red Hills of Essex: Salt-making in Antiquity*, Colchester(Colchester Archaeological Group, 1990). p.81.

27. T Lane, 'An Iron Age Saltern in Cowbit Wash, Lincolnshire', in Lane and Morris (2001) p.89.

28. P Chowne, R Cleal, A P Fitzpatrick, with P Andrews, *Excavations at Billingborough, Lincolnshire, 1975-8: A Bronze-Iron Age Settlement and Salt-Working Site.* East Anglian Archaeology 94 (2001) p.92.

29. B Kirkham, 'The Excavation of a Prehistoric Saltern at Hogsthorpe, Lincolnshire', *Lincs. Hist. and Archaeol.* Vol. 16, (1981) pp.5-10 and B Kirkham, 'Iron Age and Roman Saltmaking on the Lindsey Coast and Marshland', in Lane and Morris *op. cit.*

30. C Palmer-Brown, 'Bronze Age salt production at Tetney', *Current Archaeology.* 136, (1993) p. 136.

31. D Trimble, 'Hagnaby Lock, Stickford', in *Fenland Management Project Excavations 1991-1995*, edited by A Crowson, T Lane, and J Reeve, Lincolnshire Archaeology and Heritage Reports Series 3, (2000) p.152.

32. D Trimble, Hagnaby Lock, Stickford, in *Fenland Management Project Excavations: The Lincolnshire Prehistoric Sites* edited by T Lane and D Trimble, (forthcoming).

33. For instance, see A S Failes, *Prehistoric Fenland Salt Production: a Social Theoretical Perspective*, Unpublished Dissertation, Lampeter, (Univ of Wales 2003) p.34.

34. T Lane, 'An Iron Age Saltern in Cowbit Wash, Lincolnshire', in Lane and Morris (2001) Fig. 6.

35. For instance, see: S J Hallam, 'Settlement around the Wash', in *The Fenland in Roman Times* edited by C W Phillips, Royal Geogr. Soc. Res. Ser. 5, (1970) pp.22-113 or BB Simmons, 1980, 'Iron Age and Roman Coasts Around the Wash', in 'Archaeology and Coastal Change' edited by F H Thompson, *Soc. Antiq. Occas. Pap. n.s.* 1, (1980) pp.56-73 or D Hall and J Coles, *Fenland Survey. An Essay in Landscape and Persistence,* English Heritage Archaeological Report 1 (1994).

36. A Strang, 'Explaining Ptolemy's Roman Britain', *Britannia* Vol. 28, (1997) pp.1-30.

37. quoted in D N Robinson, *The Book of the Lincolnshire Seaside,* Buckingham (Barracuda, 1981).

38. T Lane, 'Roman and Pre-Roman Salt-Making in the Fenland of England', in *Salt Works and Salinas: The Archaeology, Conservation and Recovery of Salt Making sites and their Processes*. edited by A M Fielding and A P Fielding, Lion Salt Works Trust Monograph Series Research Report 2, (2005) Fig 4.

39. T Lane, 'The Fenland of Eastern England and the Production of Salt', in O Weller, A Dufraisse and P Pétrequin, *Sel, eau et forêt, hier et aujourd'hui*. Actes du colloque de la Saline d'Arc-et-Senans, Octobre 2006. Besançon : Presses Universitaires de Franche-Comté (collection Les Cahiers de la MSH Ledoux) (forthcoming).

40. A Crosby, 'Briquetage Containers from Ingoldmells Beach', in Lane and Morris *op. cit.*

41. A Crosby, 'Briquetage' in Lane and Morris *op. cit* pp.106-133.

42. A Crowson, 'Excavation of a Late Roman Saltern at Blackborough End, Middleton, Norfolk', in Lane and Morris *op. cit.* p.248.

Picking up the Bits: Community Archaeology in North Lincolnshire

Kevin Leahy

Archaeological field walking has a long history in Lincolnshire. People like Fred Brown and Revd Reginald Gatty were collecting in the early twentieth century, attracted by the heath land 'warren' sites which produced large quantities of prehistoric flint and pottery. In the inter-war years much work was carried out by Harold Dudley, curator of what was then the Scunthorpe Museum, and by James Walshaw and Derrick Riley, whose lunchtime involved a dash from the steelworks up to Risby Warren to see what the blown sand had revealed. Further to the south, Mrs Ethel Rudkin was carrying out her long tramps across fields in search of the past. Since the last war excellent work has been done by Rex and Eleanor Russell, who salvaged what they could from Lincolnshire's deserted medieval village sites as they gradually succumbed to 'progress' and the plough. More recently, epic work has been carried out by the Fenland Survey team in the south of Lincolnshire,

which has shown that the landscape down there might be flat, but is certainly not boring.

I suppose that one of the things that first attracted me to field walking was my curiosity about the wider landscape and the bits in between the larger archaeological sites which we already knew about. How did the larger sites relate to one another? Where did the Anglo-Saxons, whose cemeteries I had excavated, live? From the practical point of view, I had a ready team of volunteers who were seasoned survivors of long excavations and who were keen to carry on with field work. So it was decided; we would start field walking.

Our first season of field work was in 1999, based around evening classes in Kirton in Lindsey. Our study area was to be the parishes of Kirton in Lindsey and Manton. The fact that the Cleatham Anglo-Saxon cemetery (which I

Fig. 1: The North Lincolnshire team preparing for a field walking survey

had spent some years excavating) was on the boundary between these parishes was a remarkable coincidence! I did have some worries about the project; the evening class had recruited remarkably well, giving us lots of new people, but how would they take to tramping the fields? Would they learn to recognise the finds? Would the farmers be willing to let us on the land? The students also had their worries as to whether they would know what to pick up, or might miss all the important finds. In reality, of course, they turned into a super team of archaeological field walkers.

Our first problem was arranging for access to the land. I wrote to all the farmers and then followed the letter up with a phone call. Most were enthusiastic and helpful, although one was a little reticent. He didn't like 'the Council' having had a disagreement with them over something, but he eventually admitted that not everyone on the Council was bad; the blokes who took the refuse away were OK. I told him that was all we wanted to do; take the rubbish away – only ours was a bit older. He laughed and gave his permission.

Since 1999 we have field walked every year and have built up a large and knowledgeable band of volunteers. In 2003 we won a £50,000 grant from the Heritage Lottery Fund to allow us to convert a workshop at the Museum into a Community Archaeology room where finds could be processed. A second grant in 2005 allowed us to take the project into a new area. The grants also allowed us to take on a temporary member of staff to run and expand the project. Knowing how important pottery is in our work, we looked for a community archaeologist who knew something about ceramics and we were lucky to find Anne Boyle who is a specialist in medieval pottery. Anne proved very popular with the volunteers and has developed a medieval pottery type series which has done wonders for our understanding of pottery sources and dating. Anne left the project in 2005 and Ian Rowlandson, a Roman pottery specialist, joined us. It is very important to be able to give archaeological specialists just starting out on their careers, a chance to develop their expertise as we desperately need to have more people with a knowledge of pottery in Lincolnshire. In addition a number of the volunteers have developed their own special interests and are now well informed about their particular topics.

Our first study area was in the Manton/Kirton in Lindsey area on the limestone of the Lincoln Edge. We then moved onto the southern part of the Isle of Axholme to see what the archaeology was like there and, more recently, we have started field walking on the chalk lands of the Lincolnshire Wolds and on the liassic escarpment around Alkborough. The four study areas allow us to make comparisons between different historic landscapes.

Field walking methodology.

Over the years that we have been field walking we have developed our own particular methods and it is perhaps worth sharing some of our ideas with other people. First get your field. We have found that the condition of the land is very important; a freshly ploughed field is useless as it is impossible to see anything. Ideally the field should be well weathered so that the soil has been washed off the finds. These days fields are drilled soon after harvest and we don't get much time for our field walking, sometimes only days, and we have walked some fields that are still covered with stubble. This can give results, but it is much better if the field is clear.

We have found that for meaningful results field walking must be done systematically. The area to be walked is split up into ten metre wide strips (transects), and each strip is divided into four equal sections known as 'stints',

Tools needed

The basic equipment is simple and cheap consisting of:

- Garden canes, about 50 of them, each 1000mm long. These are used for setting out the basic grid. Each of these has a streamer of plastic tape tied around its top so that it can be seen across the field.

- Surveyors' ranging poles (or painted broom-sticks), used to set out the corners of the grid and the stints. You will need ten two metre and five one metre long poles.

- Setting out ropes. These are made from 8 or 10mm diameter plastic rope (cheap from builders' merchants). Before you go to the field lay out the ropes and, using a 30 or 100 metre tape, tie on alternating coloured plastic streamers at ten metre intervals. The ropes need to be kept on something like garden hose reels to stop them getting tangled.

- Plenty of plastic bags for finds. The self closing 'minigrip' type bags are the best. Each person

*Fig. 2: The whole team stay in position, pick up the rope, and walk forward –
part of the process of laying out the field walking grid*

walking a strip needs four bags, one for each
section or 'stint'.

- Labels for the bags. These are made up in advance
  and simply marked with the strip numbers (1 to 10)
  each strip having cards for A, B, C and D for the
  four stints. We have found that it is best to laminate
  these to protect them from moisture.

- Large scale maps showing the shapes of the fields
  are needed to fix the location where you have
  walked.

- Two push-along measuring wheels of the sort that
  surveyors use to record distances are very useful
  and cheap. Get ones with a large diameter wheel
  suitable for use on rough ground.

How to set out.

- Have a look at the map and the field and decide
  which is the best way to lay out the grid. A straight
  field boundary is useful to run the baseline along.
  The base line is a 100 metre long rope which is
  divided into 10 metre intervals. The intervals are
  marked by plastic tape tied round the rope.

- The length of the field from the baseline is worked
  out, either from a map or by measuring the length
  of the field with a surveyor's wheel. This distance
  is then divided by four.

- The whole team is involved in the next stage; each
  person goes to one of the coloured plastic streamers
  fixed at ten metre intervals along the baseline rope.
  Each takes a set of five canes marked with the

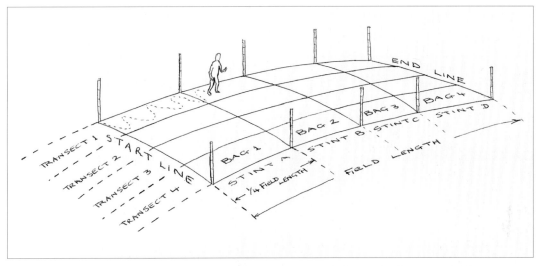

Fig. 3: Diagrammatic view of a grid of transects and stints laid out on a field

same coloured streamer as on their section of the rope. The coloured tapes alternate blue/yellow (or whatever colours you please) along the rope. The person on either end of the rope does not use canes; they each need five two-metre ranging poles and the person at the mid point on the baseline rope requires five one-metre ranging poles.

- Each person pushes their first cane or ranging pole into the ground by the baseline rope at the baseline. The whole team then stay in position, pick up the rope and walk forward. Someone at either end of the rope is measuring the distance with the surveyors' wheels. When the first quarter length is reached, the team stop. The people at either end of the rope have to make sure everyone is (more or less) in a straight line. At this point the rope is laid down and the next row of canes/ranging poles are pushed into the ground. This is repeated for three more quarter distances until the length of the field has been covered.

- This results in a grid that covers the length of the field with 10 lanes (transects) which have been divided into quarter lengths (stints). This method is quick and very effective for setting out over a large area. The transects are numbered one to ten and the stints A to D. A note must be made of this on a sketch plan.

Doing the field walking.

- Each person is allocated a transect and given four bags and a set of pre-marked labels. They start off in stint A. Beginners are usually paired up with an experienced field walker. The field walkers have to distinguish between two types of finds. 'Bulk finds' are post medieval and modern pottery, tile, items that might be archaeological or anything that might be of interest. 'Special Finds' consist of pottery that pre-dates the seventeenth century, worked flint, metalwork that is medieval or older and other special items such as glass beads or pre-modern coins. The bulk finds are collected in the bags but special finds are flagged with a cane bearing an orange coloured streamer. A small team equipped with the GPS machine then comes around to log the position of the special finds and collects them as they go.

- During walking, people use the coloured tapes on the canes to keep them on line and inside their own strip. Everyone knows that they must keep the cane with the blue tape on the right and yellow on the left which helps keep them on line. The half ranging pole in the centre also helps keep people on line - it is easier for them to see where they are when looking at five strips rather than ten.

- Everyone follows a snake walk zig-zagging from side to side up their strip picking up everything that

Fig. 4: 'Special Finds' are marked with a cane and a small team equipped with a GPS machine comes round to log their position

they see. As they move from one stint to another they change to a new bag, A, B, C, D.

• When we first started, all finds were collected and put into the stint bags but, while this gave good results, we found that things were greatly improved by using a Global Positioning System (GPS) instrument. This allows find spots to be recorded to within two metres.

Field walkers are asked to pick up everything but we do draw the line at field drain fragments or modern slag. Where large quantities of these materials occur, walkers are asked to take a sample and make a note of the size of the spread. We have had some discussions as to whether we should collect modern china and other clearly recent material. In the end we agreed that deciding that something was not old enough was a pretty poor excuse and that everything should be collected. The 'modern' pottery has turned out to be useful as it provides a guide to field conditions because we know that if we were finding willow pattern and modern glass then we would have found Roman pottery if it had been there. Modern pottery may

Fig. 5: Letting people get really familiar with the sort of stuff usually imprisoned in museum showcases

provide useful data in the future; for instance, if an aerial photograph shows a building in a area where there was a mass of Victorian pottery it rather suggests that it is not a Roman villa. It should also be recognised that we do not know as much about early modern life in Lincolnshire as we think we do. At some time in the future the study of this material may tell us about what access the people of rural Lincolnshire had to fine and exotic china.

The finds are processed by the volunteers who wash, sort and catalogue everything we have picked up. The washing is the exciting part of the process when we start to see what has been found. It also lets people get really familiar with the sort of stuff that is usually imprisoned in museum showcases. All the records are then entered onto a computer database. This is an important step as, by using a geographical information system (GIS), the computer can draw distribution maps showing finds of

different periods allowing us to see lost landscapes. More recently we have purchased equipment to allow us to do geophysical surveys. This technique allows the volunteers to take their work a step further and start to see what is under the ground. The question so often asked is 'do we want to dig any of these sites?' The answer is 'No; I just want to know where they are!'

The results

Field walking survey seems to be an all-win technique for archaeology. It involves people directly in finding out about their past and does minimal damage to the archaeological record. To begin with most people are sceptical that there

Fig. 6: The pattern of Roman finds on a field in Alkborough clearly shows the areas of activity or settlement

are archaeological finds just lying around waiting to be picked up but soon realise that this is how it is; some fields are literally covered with finds. People get the thrill of discovery in finding something that no-one has touched for hundreds or thousands of years. You never know what you might see on your next step. Field walking is a good way of getting people out into the countryside to enjoy the open air and to take some exercise.

Field walking is a non-destructive technique which does not damage the buried archaeology as we are only picking up what is lying on the surface. However, it must be realised that in one sense this is not entirely true. Even though the archaeological finds are in the plough soil, they do not move far from the buried archaeological features that are their origin. By plotting the position of the finds we can recover the shape of the buried site. To collect archaeological material, from the top-soil without properly logging its position would cause a loss of data and is something that now we would not do.

When the pattern of finds is plotted onto the map, amazing things can emerge; the site of a deserted medieval village, first ploughed during the Second World War and ploughed annually ever since, re-appears - its streets still showing up in the scatter of pottery across the field. Roman landscapes emerge - not just the big sites but what must have been little farmsteads that were only in existence for a short period of time. I have a feeling that these short-lived sites could be very important in our work on pottery. From a chronological point of view the best sites are the ones that were not in use for long so we are seeing pottery from only one period. We can get a similar effect if a settlement slowly moved over time. By looking at the pattern of use from a lot of sites we can work out, and refine, the pottery sequence and from it look in detail at the development of the landscape.

Differences are emerging between our four study areas. The sites on the Isle of Axholme are producing large numbers of fire-crack stones or 'pot-boilers'. These were heated up and dropped into wooden tanks to boil water. For some reason the people on the Isle were using a lot of hot water, were they bathing a lot or was it part of some industrial process? Fire-cracked stones are rare on the limestone at Manton/Kirton but here, we have a lot of evidence for iron smelting. What is most important from a personal point of view is that we have found a lot of evidence for Anglo-Saxon settlement around Manton and Kirton in Lindsey. The next big question is, was this typical or did it simply relate to the presence of the big cemetery? We are getting evidence of Anglo-Saxon settlements elsewhere but so far we have not found much from around Elsham where there is another large cemetery. Some of the things that we found have been embarrassing – I have stated in print that there is no evidence for early Anglo-Saxon settlement west of the Trent so it was a bit of a shock to me when we discovered lots of Saxons at Owston Ferry.

Many people have helped with this project: Mike Hemblade and Alison Williams at the North Lincolnshire Council have taken on extra work to support the field walking; Wallace Collyer has always been there with help, support and a van; and the staff at the Heritage Lottery Fund have been most helpful. I am always impressed with how obliging the farmers are. We are asking to go onto their land at the busiest time of the year when they are harvesting, ploughing and drilling, but still they welcome us. I could quite understand if they thought that we were just one complication too many but this in not the case. Finally, of course, I must mention our team of volunteers without whom none of this would be possible.

Titus Kime, Entrepreneur of Mareham le Fen, 1848-1931, and the Eldorado Potato Boom of 1903-1904

Dennis Mills

Titus Kime, a son of Thomas Kime, a Mareham grocer, became a man of many commercial interests, one of the foremost being that of seed-potato grower and merchant, and as such he was dramatically involved in the Eldorado seed-potato boom of 1903 to 1904. My interest in Kime was originally evoked by listening to 'Kime stories' told by my grandparents, Harry and Florence Major, some of them belonging to the time around 1900 when they had worked for Kime.[1]

Fig. 1: This building incorporates the house in which Kime was born and the shop kept by his parents, later used as an office. The rear of the building was converted to a warehouse, which was probably the function of the other surviving buildings.

At the 1851 census there were four Kime families in Mareham, one headed by Thomas Kime; and another by his brother Richard Kime, surveyor, timber merchant, and at different times, schoolmaster, assistant overseer and parish clerk. Titus's various interests and his involvement in parish affairs perhaps reflect the career of Richard Kime, rather more than that of his father. The other two Kime families were headed by farm labourers; that of Matthew included his daughter Maria, then a girl of eight. She married Robinson Major, one of their children being Harry Major, my grandfather. Although documentary evidence is now lacking, Kime believed that Maria was a distant cousin, and helped her when she was widowed with a large family of small children.

In 1851 Thomas Kime (aged 44) and his wife Jane (39) had in their family home six children, all below the age of eight (two more being born after the census). Jane was recorded as 'assistant in shop' and even with one co-resident servant, a girl of only sixteen, she must have been extremely hard-working. Titus was then aged two and important questions are how this very ordinary family found the means to pay for private lessons for him, and why probably only he had this privilege.[2]

Kime must have attended the National (that is, Church of England) School in Mareham, but he and three other village boys were picked out by the Revd Mark Warburton, the perpetual curate at Revesby, for special lessons in Latin and Euclid (mathematics). They were about twelve years old when this arrangement began, and this would mean that they had reached the last year or so of education offered by the village school. Warburton's stipend was only £100 a year and he had a big vicarage to maintain, with a staff of five co-resident servants in 1861, including a housekeeper and groom/gardener. Consequently he was one of many Victorian clergy who supplemented their incomes by teaching.

Kime and his companions went to the vicarage about three times a week at 8.30am to show how they were getting on with their lessons and to have more given to them. Warburton may have taught them for only nominal fees, but he would certainly have charged the parents of his upper-class boarding pupils the going rate. There were about half a dozen of them in the early 1860s, around 17 to 22 years of age (perhaps being prepared for university, perhaps making up for poor earlier progress elsewhere). Kime remembered that they were 'mostly very nice fellows, many of them bearing well-known names; some of them afterwards became famous'. Among those he named were Lord Dalmeny (later Lord Rosebery); Lord Cole (Lowry), son of the Earl of Enniskillen; Oliver Montague, son of the Earl of Sandwich; the Hon. (E) Digby; Tunnard of Frampton (a Lincolnshire landowning family); and Lord Suirdale, son of the Earl of Donoughmore.

Although the village boys did not have lessons with these aristocratic youths, there was ample opportunity for social mixing, especially on the cricket field. Kime

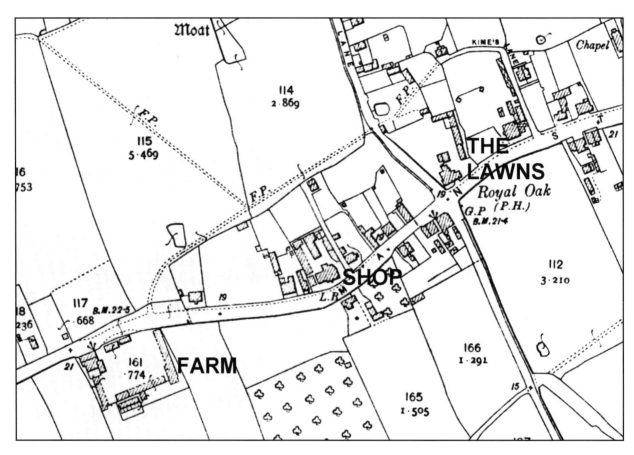

*Fig. 2: Extract from the OS 25-inch plan of Mareham le Fen (1905) showing the disposition of three of Kime's properties, in the middle the house and shop with warehouses and similar buildings at the back.
Westwards along the main road was the farmyard, and in the other direction The Lawns, Kime's residence, on the corner of Kime's Lane! Some of the buildings on the lane side were small greenhouses.
The distance from The Lawns to the farmyard is a little over 300 yards.*

describes himself as 'always a very shy nervous boy', terrified by having to field at point while the redoubtable Timms of Spilsby was batting. I find his self-portrait a little unconvincing in view of the way he 'comes over' as an adult – self-possessed and sure of himself, and brooking absolutely no nonsense as an employer, although claiming to have suffered from shyness throughout his lifetime. The older 'fellows' introduced Kime to claret, ale, champagne and smoking, and Warburton complained that they were spoiling him as fast as they could. They experienced the thrills of returning from away matches in the Spilsby direction, having had too much to drink, in wagonettes belonging to the squire and to Warburton, which were raced down Keal Hill! The squire was James Banks Stanhope, M.P., of Revesby Abbey, who on one occasion rewarded Kime with a glass of port, when he had batted dourly for

forty minutes. Kime was not overawed by keeping this company and his contacts with members of the upper class must have helped to give him the confidence to carve out the career described below. Towards the end of the century, Kime was often in Abbey shooting parties.

He had been educated beyond the needs of a boy who might join a village grocery business, was not apparently apprenticed to a craft, nor did he take the then new School Certificate examinations. So he became a clerk, then a rapidly expanding occupation, but a Horncastle solicitor's office or a Boston bank were possibly not exciting enough for him. 'In July 1865, when I was sixteen years old, I left home on a Sunday afternoon to catch the train at Tattershall station…knowing that before being fully engaged as clerk in the Railway Clearing House, London, I had to pass an examination the following Monday morning'. Kime would not have been short of good testimonials and references, but in the event he did not pass at the first attempt and had to take lessons from a coach before being successful. Following this he became one of fourteen clerks in the section dealing with passenger left luggage.[3]

It is worth recording Kime's view of the work and conditions, partly as a means of assessing his character and his attitude to life:

> I began work on a salary of 30s. a week increasing before long to 40s. and it certainly was not enough for a growing boy to live on – to pay lodgings, fuel, washing and food and clothes; but I had to make it do, and it did not do very well. I managed to keep out of debt, but often went cold and hungry to bed. Office hours were nine to four – longer if required and no pay for overtime. Clerks may have an easy time in Government, and perhaps other offices, but there is not much slacking in the Railway Clearing House, and no sinecures; we left off work at one o'clock on Saturdays. Every day I had to walk [to the corner of Euston Road and Gower Street] from Raphael Street, Knightsbridge, by Tattersalls, the Great Horse Repository. By the shortest route I could take the distance was…three miles – this was too much twice a day'.

Kime was living with cousins, a fact that might have saved him some expense, although allowance for the relatively fashionable area in which they lived has to be made. However, adult farm labourers' wages would not have been much over 10s a week back in Mareham, so it seems he had nothing to complain about, and his admission that he did not always fall into good hands – the wrong drinking pals? – suggests that he was spending too much on drink and cigars. As to the hours of work, they could hardly be described as Dickensian. Nor does three miles twice a day seem too far for a teenager to walk. Kime's association with the young bucks at Revesby, and perhaps being spoiled by his family because he was the cleverest, may have lead him to expect too much of life too soon. Of course, the contrast between rural Lincolnshire and the centre of London was objectively a difficult change for a teenager to manage. At any rate, after about two years, which included a spell at Mareham when he was 'unwell', Kime went 'home again [in 1867] with the determination to earn a living principally in the open air, and after a time managed to do so with some success'.

Kime after London

It is probable that Kime entered the family business, which is listed as shopkeeper, or grocer and draper, in various directories between 1855 and 1872. Thomas Kime, Titus's father, died in July 1872 and the next directory entry, in 1876, shows his mother as shopkeeper and Titus

as cattle-cake and seed merchant. In 1875 and at the age of 27 Kime was a member of the manorial court 'jury'[(4)], a position he would have inherited from his father, along with twelve other men whose occupations were that of farmer, or farmer with a trade, a wood dealer, and the licensee of the *Royal Oak,* where the court met. He had been accepted by both the village elders and the squire of Revesby, who was manorial lord.

On 16 May 1878 Kime and his mother entered into a formal partnership drawn up by W S Clitherow, solicitor of Horncastle. To do so was probably unusual for an ordinary village enterprise, although documents of this type are very likely to have had a poor survival rate.[(5)] The independent appearance of Kime's business in the 1876 directory is corrected, as Jane Kime was described as 'corn, cake and seed merchant and grocer and draper', whilst of Kime it was said only that he 'has assisted her for some time'. The twenty articles in the partnership agreement were essentially intended to make mother and son equal partners in all respects that they and Clitherow could think up, and to make sure that any dealings carried on outside the partnership would not impinge on its finances. Perhaps his mother did not have full confidence in her son. The terms were to be entered in the *London Gazette*, which was also used to advertise the dissolution of the partnership on 9 December 1881. The dissolution document is more interesting than the original agreement, partly because Jane's signature was much less firm than in 1878 – she was now 69, but in fact lived to be 84.

She was obviously preparing for retirement, as Kime was to carry the business forward on his own account, paying her an annuity of £26 each year. She was to stay in her own house free of rates, taxes, etc., during such time as Kime was tenant. Should he cease to be tenant he was to provide another home in Mareham at an annual rent of not more than £7 10s There were also stipulations as to how Kime should pay his mother for board and lodging – he was single at the time, but married soon afterwards. On Jane's death he was to pay her executors £100 – it is interesting that he was not an executor – and presumably this would be dispersed among his siblings. Kime entered into a bond for £200 with his mother, to be in force until he had paid her executors the £100. In other words, she let him have £200 of working capital, half of which he could retain after her death. Special arrangements were made for Sarah, Kime's eldest sister. He was to pay his mother an annuity of £3 5s per quarter for Sarah's maintenance, 'while she remains unmarried and of unsound mind'.

Perhaps it was intended that this should continue if Jane pre-deceased Sarah. On the face of it, the dissolution of the partnership marked the start of Kime's independent business life, when he was aged 33, and was followed by a rapid expansion of the business.

In 1881 the *London Gazette* entry described the Kime business as 'corn, cake, seed and general merchants'. Although Kime may have been farming some land on his own account, the entry in White's 1882 directory is again confined to the description of a merchant's business. However, about this time Kime married Georgina Sharp, the daughter of the Revd William Sharp, rector of Mareham since 1855, and this may have had a considerable bearing on Kime's career. The story goes that the rector, a Cambridge graduate and a J P, was opposed to the marriage. Sharp probably regarded Kime as too far down the social

scale for his daughter. One of Sharp's servants in 1881 was Elizabeth Kime, daughter of Thomas Kime, publican, and probably one of Titus Kime's relatives. Moreover, the rector was already widowed and dependent on Georgina for running the rectory household. However, she was about eight years Kime's senior, had already passed 40, probably had 'money of her own' and considered Kime a 'decent catch' in the circumstances.

It is necessary to jump forward to 1910, when the Estate Duty records[6] provide the only detailed picture of Kime's farm. This comprised 29 acres of his own land, 42 acres belonging to his wife and 48 acres rented from no less than five other landlords, the most significant being the Revd Lee of Benniworth (24 acres). This 119 acre holding did not possess a conventional farmstead serving an already established farm. Instead it must have been built up of

Fig. 3: The Lawns, Kime's residence, a comfortable, but modest house, sufficient in size, however, for a man who remained childless.

bits and pieces as they came to hand, which would be a reasonably easy process in Mareham, with so many small owners, especially when farming was depressed.

There were no less than six sets of buildings, including an old chapel used as a warehouse and the house in which Kime had been born, then in use as an office. The 1910 valuation recorded nine separate parcels of land, some, possibly most of them, including several fields. They were scattered about the north-western portion of the parish, some along the main road westwards from the office, but others at Moorside, further out in the same direction, and two substantial parcels running northwards up to different sections of the Wilksby boundary. The surviving physical evidence suggests that Kime did not waste a lot of money buying or renting state-of-the-art premises that would have been available on any of the large estates such as neighbouring Revesby. Mrs Kime owned *The Lawns*, possibly new at the time of their wedding, where they resided with a couple of servants, and between them Mr and Mrs Kime owned eleven cottages, at least one (Harry Major's) let to Kime employees.

By the time Kelly recorded the business in 1889 farming was included in the description: 'corn, cake, seed and manure merchant, seed-corn and seed-potato grower and agricultural implement agent'. The 1892 description in White's directory is similar, and Kime's stands in Lincoln and Horncastle corn exchanges were also recorded. In Kelly's 1896 directory 'daffodil grower' had been added to the list and in 1905, 1907 and 1909 it was followed by 'about 30 acres'. Advertisements in the *Horncastle News* in 1905 and 1906 mention the sale of horse food and Peruvian guano and that Kime was agent for Marston's ales from Burton-on-Trent across an area extending twelve miles from Tattershall station as far as Old Bolingbroke. This last activity was a means of putting his teams of horses and wagons to regular use, along with the carting of corn to Boston millers, with return loads of coal.

None of these activities could be called 'general' corn and livestock farming. He took money out of other farmers' turnover by servicing them or dealing in their produce, a much safer activity than production, or specialised in the growing of new crops where margins were much better than in old ones. He was expanding in the period of the late Victorian agricultural depression, when corn prices and even those for beast and sheep were declining. His potato acreages helped to increase the acreage of potatoes grown in Lincolnshire by 87% between 1894 and 1914.[7]

Bulb-growing

Kime started bulb-growing as an untutored hobby and commercial involvement began purely with the sale of bulbs.[8] When the sale of flowers began, he developed a range of varieties to provide a supply throughout the whole season, with tulips, daffodils and narcissi all represented. They were picked as buds and matured under glass, one greenhouse being capable of taking over 100,000 buds (later in the year the greenhouses were used for tomato production). In one week in 1907, over 30,000 bunches, weighing nearly five tons, were dispatched from Tattershall station to 'all the chief centres of the United Kingdom'. Each September, three-year-old bulbs were lifted and sold and the land returned to more conventional crops for a rest. On one occasion Kime had sent 'coals to Newcastle' by selling five tons of bulbs into the Netherlands.

This example of 'New Farming' required heavy expenditure on labour, fertilisers, bulbs, and probably some extra outlay on equipment and buildings. For example, the cost of daffodil bulbs required to plant an acre in 1914 has been put at about £75 to £100.[9] Kime himself paid three guineas for a single bulb of the *Duke of Bedford* daffodil when it was a new variety and once bid £40 for eight bulbs of another new variety, and did not get them.

Kime employed about 30 men and boys all the year round, whereas about four hands would have been sufficient for conventional farming on his acreage. In addition, about 25 extra hands, mostly women and girls, were employed in the flower season as pickers and 'tiers'. Some of the tying was done in the home and regular hands including Harry Major distributed the blooms and collected the bunches, each containing a dozen flowers, packed in boxes to take to the station by the dray-load. Pyrethrums were also grown for sale as cut flowers, and on one occasion, at least, marigolds growing as weeds in cornfields were cut and despatched to Scotland! This quirky example demonstrates how carefully Kime studied the market and how keen he was to take up the growing of new, fashionable varieties – in potatoes as well, as is told below.

Mareham parish contains a substantial area of sandy land which required plenty of animal manure to sustain both bulb and potato-growing. In his piggeries in 1907 Kime had about 150 pigs of various ages providing a continuous supply for the butcher – an intensive and 'industrialised' operation by contemporary standards. His boar, Mareham Jolly Boy, was no. 811 in the *Lincolnshire Curly-Coated Pig Breeders' Herd Book* of 1908. In 1907 pig sales

Fig. 4: Buildings that survive at Kime's main yard on the A155 just west of Mareham village.
From this evidence, it seems that Kime did not over-invest in buildings, a comment sometimes made about major
Victorian landowners by later agrarian historians.

realised £600 net, which can be compared with the annual profits of £15 to £30 an acre from bulbs.

Potato growing and the Eldorado potato boom

Kime's obituary in the *Horncastle News* during December 1931 stated that he would be remembered most of all for his great success as a potato grower. In court on 19 November 1904 Kime had mentioned that he had been growing potatoes as a speciality for 35 years, thus taking us back to c.1870, during the period when he was working for his parents. However, like bulb-growing, he probably started off in a garden and it is not until 1889 that documentary evidence of his farming of potatoes is available. On 13 August 1892 the *Horncastle News* carried an item about *Jeanie Deans,* a new second early potato, which Kime had exhibited in the *Red Lion* Hotel [at Horncastle or Revesby?]. This had been brought out by Mr A Findlay at Markinch, Fife, but Kime had thoroughly tested the new variety and now held the largest stocks in England. He took the opportunity to point out that:

> 'with wheat at 30s a quarter it is quite time that Lincolnshire farmers endeavoured to produce something that will pay better. If they grow potatoes of the first quality they will find no difficulty in disposing of them in the London Market at remunerative prices, but it is a question of quality. Those who act on our suggestion, and grow *Jeanie Deans* and *The Bruce* [a main crop variety by Findlay] will not, we are convinced, have reason to regret doing so'.

As with bulb-growing, he recommended liberal amounts of farmyard manure for potatoes, as well as the application of artificial fertilisers to include five hundredweight of kainite per acre before ridging, a considerable amount of steamed bone meal and moderate quantities of muriate of potash, sulphate of ammonia or nitrate of soda after ridging, with top dressings of the latter during the growing season.

A large proportion of Kime's crops was grown for seed, but he also bought from other farmers in his capacity as merchant, in respect of both potatoes for eating and seed potatoes. As with other activities, he left nothing to chance. For example, Harry Major remembered being sent to other farms to riddle their potatoes to make sure that the size and quality were up to Kime's specification – as grandfather riddled he would throw out the 'oughts', the misshapen and damaged specimens. Many of the farms were in the Mareham neighbourhood, but Harry once went as far as Collingham, near Newark, and spent a week on a farm there. He travelled by train, of course, but as Collingham was on the Midland Railway, and he had to take sacks and equipment, there was some difficulty at Lincoln where he changed systems. Porters at the Great Northern (surviving) station were very reluctant to let him borrow one of their trolleys to take his 'secks of secks,'[10] riddles and so forth along the High Street to the Midland Station, later St Mark's.

The greatest excitement of Kime's life was the *Eldorado* potato boom of 1903 to 1904. A reminder of those days appeared in the June 2004 issue of the *Lincolnshire*

*Fig. 5: Advertisement from Mortons' Guide
to the Royal Show, 1907.*

Gazette, which contained what was described as a 'rather uninteresting photograph' taken in 1903 of two *Eldorado* potatoes. How ironic this statement would have seemed to anyone who experienced the boom raging at the time! Fantastic prices were being given for mere handfuls of seed potatoes of this variety. For example, a few years ago Mrs Maisie Sewards supplied me with a copy of a framed report of 1904 on show in a Spilsby estate agent's window. This recorded that six tubers of *Eldorado,* weighing only five ounces, were auctioned in Spilsby for £56 3s 6d.

In his book on the subject, Kime wrote about the boom in a remarkably careful, dispassionate way, which checks out well with other sources. To start with, he called it the **Great** Potato Boom, rather than the *Eldorado* Potato Boom, as he was at pains to demonstrate the gradual build-

up to the crazy years of 1903 to 1904. He began the story in 1892 to 1893, when Mr A Findlay of Auchtermuchty[11], Fifeshire, brought out one of his first new varieties, *Up-to-Date*, a main crop variety. This helped to establish his reputation and was held in favour until about 1908, when, as was the way with potato varieties, it began to lose its early characteristics and fell out of use. At this time the average farm gate price of maincrop potatoes was about £2 to £3 a ton for eating purposes, £3 to £4 for seed, but *Up-to-Date* was soon making £10 a ton. Kime wrote: 'Really, I am anxious not to exaggerate, and I shall endeavour to put the prices at smaller rather than the larger actual figures made'.

This variety held its price to about £6 per ton, with the result that in 1894 to 1895, when Findlay brought out *Challenge,* a very good new early, he was inundated with

T. KIME,   Wholesale
                  BULB GROWER.

SEED POTATO
GROWER, &c.,

Mareham-le-Fen,

BOSTON.

ABOUT 20 ACRES OF BULBS

NOW UNDER CULTIVATION,

PRINCIPALLY

DAFFODILS

AND

TULIPS

OF THE FINEST KINDS KNOWN.

Fig. 6: Advertisement from the Horncastle Compendium and Advertiser, 1908, giving an indication of Kime's principal activities at that date.

orders. In the first year of sales he sold no more than 14 pounds to any one buyer and charged a shilling per pound, the equivalent of £112 a ton.[12] Kime explained that this stone of seed potatoes, in the hands of an experienced grower, could be made to yield enough seed to plant half an acre the next season, ten acres the year after that, and 'nearly a county' after four years. In 1896 Kime sold one ton each to only two buyers at the rate of £40 a ton – the price was going down as more seed was produced, but the acreage was going up and at ten tons to the acre the return could be £400, or four times what *Up-to-Date* had been bringing in about two or three years before.

Findlay was not the only seed grower producing new varieties, and growers had to be very careful about accepting advertisements at face value, since sometimes new varieties were insufficiently tested, or did not last many seasons owing to disease, among other factors. The

characteristics sought in a new variety included yield, flavour, cooking qualities, appearance (shape and colour), keeping qualities, freedom from disease, and for early varieties speed of growth, so there was a lot to think about. In the late 1890s two new varieties, known as *Ringleader* and *Ninetyfold,* from growers other than Findlay, were successful and helped to fuel the boom. Thus when in 1899 Findlay brought out no less than three new varieties: *Evergood, Empire Kidney* and *Royal Kidney,* growers were keen to buy. On testing these, Kime found two of them very promising, the first, a maincrop variety, and the third, a second early. He was especially pleased with his 1900 crop of *Royal Kidney,* which yielded at a rate equivalent to 18 tons to the acre, at a time when 10 tons was regarded as a good crop. For an outlay of £1 15s in 1899 he was able to sell his 1901 crop for £135. Kime advertised *Evergood* in the *Stamford Mercury* for several weeks at the beginning of 1902, stating that it was 'one of the BEST [maincrop potatoes], if not THE BEST ever raised'.

> 'And time rolled on, but not with the slow and even moment of a man working by the day, and I began to receive letters and messages every day telling me to be sure and let my friends know if I got hold of anything new that looked like being good, and that I need not always spend so much time *in severely testing* (my emphasis) before recommending anything new. They reminded me that they were willing to take risks…We are getting on, but I must ask you to still have patience as we have some distance further to go…'

The penultimate stage in the boom was associated with *Northern Star,* a maincrop variety brought out by Findlay in 1900. With difficulty Kime acquired twelve pounds of seed costing £6, and 'with carefully chitting this potato and utilising every eye'[13] it produced a crop worth close on £600. Disregarding the costs of production, this was equivalent to betting on the winner of a horse race at odds of 100:1! Up to a year or two before, only Lincolnshire had been involved in the mania, but now men came from as far away as Scotland to gaze on the magnificent one-sixteenth of an acre of *Northern Star* at Mareham. Other growers had been equally successful, so the demand for seed was breath-taking, and after news spread that Kime had paid Findlay £500 for a ton of *Northern Star*, prices quickly reached £1,000 a ton. This price was very similar to the £6 for twelve pounds of the year before – seed prices were holding steady instead of going down over time. In this climate, Kime recorded that many unscrupulous raisers and dealers got hold of untested new varieties, or gave old varieties new names and put them on the market where, such was the abandon of too many growers, and people who were not growers, but speculators, that silly prices were paid and the speed of the boom stepped up another gear.

Kime's narrative indicates that his judgement was based on a lot of travelling to shows and markets, and he became very well known in the 'potato world'. One of his regular visits was to the Cattle Show at Islington, held in December each year, but owing to illness he missed seeing Findlay at the 1902 show, when the latter introduced yet another new potato that:

> 'was to beat everything by a long way that had previously been placed on the market....growers whom he supplied with a few pounds each planted every eye, and more than that, the tubers were put into considerable warmth and small sprouts quickly grew, and these sprouts were promptly cut out of the potato and planted in flower pots. Even the sprouts, after growing a little, and showing some green leaf, were cut in half and planted, and quickly flourished and grew...Single tubers were sold for as much as £150 each and sprouts for as much as £5 each this first season...'

Prices of new seed for the 1904 season were between £3,000 and £5,000 a ton, or three to five times the price of *Northern Star* for the 1901 season. More speculators with no real knowledge of potatoes were rushing into the fray:

> 'Many grocers, drapers, bishops, parsons, schoolmasters, tailors, hawkers, bankers, doctors, and lawyers made up their minds to be in it...Fathers sacrificed their own savings and their children's; many sacrificed their insurance bonuses, and a good many who were able, mortgaged their life insurances to get hold of money to buy these wonderful potatoes...Farmer's daughters sold their poultry and ducks, and...gave something much more valued... in order to get hold of and grow this *Eldorado*...'

Those who know something about the Tulipomania in Holland which burst in 1637, will recognise some similarities in the wildness of behaviour in our potato boom of 1903 to 1904. The Lincolnshire public followed the story to the extent that Bernard Gilbert, a well-known dialect author, wrote a one-act play entitled *Eldorado*.

Owing to his illness, Kime was one year behind the vanguard, but already suspicious of *Eldorado*. According to family recollection, in the spring of 1904 Kime asked Harry Major to set a sample of seed potatoes, about which he was very secretive, in Harry's mother's cottage garden and to say nothing to anyone. One Sunday morning early in July Kime got Harry to dig up a few roots of the mysterious potatoes. I can imagine my grandfather wielding his potato fork with quick flicks of the wrist that would have been useful on a cricket field. Kime asked him to name the variety, his response being 'either *Northern Star* or *Evergood*'. When Kime revealed that he had bought the seed as *Eldorado,* the 'penny dropped'. Kime gave Harry

£20 for his part in the affair. For a labourer on about 17s a week, and soon to get married (to Kime's cook), this was a really marvellous stroke of luck. The money was spent on a substantial amount of second-hand furniture, including a dining armchair that I still have at my study desk.

Kime then (in July 1904) placed notices in three local newspapers stating that the '*Eldorado* is not a new potato', releasing all his customers from forward purchases of seed and returning their deposits. The version reproduced in Kime's booklet is as follows:

" E L D O R A D O. "

"**E**LDORADO" is not a new Potato. It was sent out by ———— amongst the "Evergood" some years ago, and therefore, because it is not new. it is not worth the exorbitant prices being charged for it, and I release all my customers from their purchases of this Potato and will return all deposits.

T. KIME, MAREHAM-LE-FEN, BOSTON, Lincolnshire.

Such notices continued to appear in the *Horncastle News* until at least 3 September 1904, by which date the wording had been altered. Now Kime was bold enough to name Findlay, but he had changed his mind about which variety to name, from *Evergood* to *Northern Star,* and was specific about which year the supposed new variety had been sent out among the latter. He also explicitly offered to cancel his customers' contracts.

These customers had bought 'forward', so that they could be supplied with seed from the 1904 crop, for planting in 1905. Kime had placed an order with some growers at Bardney (see below), and probably others with Findlay and elsewhere, worth £5,000, so that he could supply his customers. Deposits had been paid, but no potatoes had changed hands. The next week the *Horncastle News* carried an advertisement from Alfred Dunham, Riverdale, Horncastle, for a number of varieties of seed potatoes, including Findlay's *Eldorado*, with the rather pointed qualification: 'Before placing your orders...see them growing, and mind you get from true stock'. It is remarkable as late as 22 October the same newspaper reported the sensational amount of £161 12s being paid for 64 roots of *Eldorado* seed potatoes at Spalding, and

Dunham's advertisement continued to appear each week until 10 December.

So the *Eldorado* bubble did not burst immediately, but unsurprisingly, the *Horncastle News* of 12 November reported that Findlay had taken Kime before Mr Justice Warmington in his London Chambers. Findlay failed to get an injunction against him, which would have required the newspaper statements to be discontinued. A libel case, with damages claimed at £20,000, fell through. In the markets, farmers and others were buzzing with excitement, but now for different reasons. Some warned Kime to be on guard against bodily attack. Tremendous arguments between suppliers and customers went on about breaches of contract based on his advertisements, but since he had £5,000 of his own money at stake, he was eventually believed, and Findlay had to withdraw. It was generally accepted that the latter had misled customers by selling *Eldorado* mixed, either with *Northern Star*, or with *Evergood*.

By Cattle Show Week in London in December 1904 many parties had met to hammer out compromise agreements, so that losses could be spread and the general paralysis of trading in seed potatoes could be lifted. Generally the sellers made a reduction of one third in the price contracted for, and many of the buyers agreed to these terms, provided they were given a significant amount of time to find the money. Many buyers never paid, or if they did they ruined themselves, and it took the market several years to recover its normal rhythm. This was partly due to the failure of *Northern Star* to keep its vitality and yield. The many examples of forcing, as mentioned above, weakened the stock, its yields were often very poor, and its popularity disappeared. One sequel to the whole episode was the formation of the National Potato Society which was 'instituted …with the object of protecting the interests of raisers and growers alike'.[14]

Finally in this section, it is interesting to read the *Horncastle News* report of 19 November 1904 headed:

A Transaction in Potatoes. *Eldorado* Tubers at £200 per cwt.
Interesting Dispute at Lincoln County Court
'At the Lincoln County Court on Tuesday before His Honour Sir G Sherston Baker, Messrs Varlow and Blanshard, potato merchants, Bardney, sued Titus Kime of Mareham le Fen, potato grower and merchant for £50, balance claimed in respect of potatoes sold by the plaintiffs to the defendant under contract.
…the action arose out of a breach of contract, the defendant failing to accept and pay for one cwt of *Eldorado* potatoes at £200 per cwt, according to the terms and conditions of the contract note, dated 26 November 1903. The price of the potatoes was to be £200 and there was to be a deposit of £20 leaving £180. The defendant refused to

Fig. 7: Titus Kime in later life, from one of his self-published booklets, printed by W. K. Morton.

accept the potatoes and to pay for them and they sold at Boston market, and realised £130 leaving a difference of £50 which the plaintiffs claimed…

…When the contract was made both parties believed that *Eldorado* were only in the hands of Mr Findlay and three others, whereas that was not the case, for the defendant found *Eldorados* growing among some potatoes he had bought for *Northern Stars,* and the actual facts were that *Eldorados* had been sold two years previously with *Northern Stars* and there was a considerable quantity on the market…

Mr Titus Kime…stated that he had made a speciality of potato growing for 35 years. In the autumn of 1901 he bought from Mr Findlay a quantity of *Northern Star* potatoes – 22 pounds at 10s per lb, and he planted them in the spring of 1902, and he noticed some other varieties growing with the *Northern Stars*. They were not true *Northern Stars,* and he dug them out and gave them to the pigs, and preserved the *Northern Star* proper. In 1902 he bought *Northern Star* potatoes from Mr Findlay, one ton at £500. These were not true *Northern Stars,* but they contained other varieties. He planted some and sold some. He found two or three kinds with the *Northern Stars,* 1902, and he 'rogued' them out and gave some to the pigs. One which showed much character he preserved. In his view some of the potatoes which he bought in the autumn of 1902 as *Northern Stars* were *Eldorados.*'

This account is incomplete as the case was adjourned to the next sitting of the court, but it contains some useful points. First there is the manner in which Kime was buying 'forward', second the sharp observations made by Kime that must have caused him to suspect Findlay, third the confirmation of the price of £4,000 a ton that Kime was paying for *Eldorados*, and fourth the drop in that price by the time the consignment was sold at Boston – substantially below the agreed price (£130, compared with £200 per cwt), but still not a 'rock-bottom' price.

Kime in the community

In its obituary of Kime, the *Horncastle News* in December 1931 stated that he was a crack shot who had been among many Revesby Abbey shooting parties; he had played cricket at Revesby and was vice-president of Horncastle Cricket Club and the local Cricket League. He had 'held practically every public office in Mareham', had worked hard for the Revesby Show and had served as Mareham representative on Horncastle Rural District Council and the old Board of Guardians.

Looking through the same newspaper for 1905 to 1906 other similar information came to light, such as the fact that he presented *The Kime Tobacco Box* as a prize at the Volunteers' Shooting at Horncastle; a garden party for the Nurses' Fund was held at *The Lawns* (Kime's residence); and that he held a social evening for his employees on 1 July 1905. Kime was vice-chairman of the Mareham

Conservative Association, was one of the 'principals' attending the 1906 Foresters' (friendly club) dinner (listed third after the rector and Colonel Ellwood), and he had written notes on harvest prospects for the *Nottingham Guardian* in 1906. He is also known to have helped to get the village a second postal delivery and was involved in the campaign leading to the construction in 1913 of the branch railway line across the fens eastwards from Tattershall, with a station at Tumby Woodside to serve Mareham.

The most intensive record of his village activities which has come to light was found in the Church of England school log book.[15] Kime was one of the managers and his visits in the 1880s and 1890s and again in the early 1920s were recorded. Occasionally he left 2s 6d as a prize for 'some subject', but most notably he gave the school amounts of coal varying from one cwt to six cwt during all but three of the winters between 1892 to 1893 and 1911 to 1912. His wife was involved in some gifts, but she also visited to give instruction in sewing, an activity she had first taken up as the rector's daughter. Kime kindly provided the new playing field on 16 October 1922 and on 7 July 1923 he presented 'two bats for netball'! During 1892 and again in 1898, he checked the registers, an activity that sometimes seems to have been carried out in a tense atmosphere, judging by the Head's entry in the log for 16 February 1898:

> Mr Kime visited the school this morning. He took objection to my writing 'Checked by Mr Kime' in the registers after his last visit on the ground that he had not checked each individual register. All the registers are placed before him and he selects a sufficient number to test their accuracy and I conclude that all the attendance is considered checked. I make this entry as a protest against the idea of my behaving in any way dishonestly with regard to the registers.

So he was as careful with school attendance as he was with seed potato selection! He could be described as kind, but definitely strict in the Victorian mould. My grandfather would recall having to hurry to work for 6.00am, the figure of Kime standing by the yard-gate with his gold watch in his hand ready to unleash his disapproval at arrivals as much as a few seconds late. But it was Harry Major, the distant cousin with no father, who was selected as a teenager to ride in the gig with Kime to Horncastle on market days. Kime was fond of drink, so not only did Harry look after the pony's stabling and run errands, he was also an insurance against Kime's erratic driving which had once led to the gig being overturned.

Although twice married, Kime had no children to whom he could leave his business. About 1910 he sold the merchant side of this to William Sinclair and Co. Ltd., who already had several branches in the county, and in 1913 he retired from farming as well, probably to live on the rents from his own, and more particularly his wife's property. However, his influence continued to be felt in other ways. Walter Scrimshaw, one of his labourers, *walked* to Doncaster in the mid-1890s to work for a potato merchant, taking charge of a round at nearby Denaby. After a year he bought this round from his employer, with one horse and dray, selling potatoes to shops and fish fryers. Walter built up a very large potato and vegetable merchant's business in Doncaster and eventually also owned a cinema, two garages, several shops and Manor Farm, Braithwell, near Rotherham, with over 800 acres of land. Had he been imbued by Kime's get-up-and-go spirit?

Walter married Harry Major's sister and the two men kept in close contact. In 1920 Harry started out on his own account at Birkwood Cottage, Mareham, and eventually was to own a smallholding at Scothern and a 90 acre farm at Thurlby near Lincoln – not as successful a career as Walter's, but one in which he followed Kime's farming philosophy of not leaving anything to chance. More than that, it was Kime who put £100 in notes through the letter box at Birkwood, as an unsolicited loan. There are not many men who would today walk about with £10,000 on them so they could put it through a distant cousin's door without finding out whether the dog had got it!

Notes:

1. It is also appropriate that I should offer this topic to readers of David's *festschrift*, as Kime was the kind of village luminary in which David has taken an interest. Indeed, David has supplied me over the years with some of the information I have used, mainly typed-up copies of relevant advertisements and news items from local newspapers. I refer to my subject as 'Kime' throughout, except to avoid ambiguity, as that was how my family referred to him, although it would have been 'Mr Kime' to his face, and never 'Titus'. He was also known as 'Taatie' Kime.

2. Most of this account of Kime's youth comes from the third of his little books: *More Reminiscences* (n.d., c.1921). The other books are: *The Great Potato Boom 1903 to 1904: its rise, progress and fall* (n.d., c.1917); *Some Reminiscences of the Stanhopes of Revesby Abbey about 1855-1914* (n.d., c.1918-1921); and *Bits and Pieces* (n.d., c.1930). The books were printed by Mortons of Horncastle and distributed by the author. *The Great Potato Boom* I copied in Grimsby Public Library; the others were lent to me by Mrs Mary Daubney of Mareham. Other sources include the census enumerators' books, Mareham parish registers, numerous trade directories, family recollections, and those sources separately referenced.

3. 'The Work of the Railway Clearing House', *Railway Gazette* (1943): the main purpose of the RCH was to process used journey and parcel tickets, allocating receipts to the different companies.

4. Lincolnshire Archives Office (LAO), Chatterton 3/1.

5. LAO, CHAT 1/40. There are three items (1) an entry in the *London Gazette,* 16 December 1881; (2) Articles of Partnership, 16 May 1878 and (3) Deed of Dissolution of Partnership, 9 December 1881.

6. LAO, 6 TAX/1/Mareham le Fen. It is obvious that Kime, typically, challenged some of the assessments, since there are many small adjustments in the entries where he was owner or occupier.

7. S R Haresign, *Agricultural Change and Rural Society in the Lincolnshire Fenlands and the Isle of Axholme,* unpublished PhD thesis, University of East Anglia, 1981, tables I and VI.

8. Most of this section is based on an article in Mortons' *Horncastle Almanac* for 1907. E C Eagle, 'Some light on the beginnings of the Lincolnshire bulb industry', *Lincolnshire Historian*, 6 (Autumn 1950), pp. 220-29, makes the point that most early bulb growers in the Spalding area also had other occupations at this time.

9. Haresign, thesis, tables VIII and XVIII.

10. One hundredweight sacks were bundled in twenties, nineteen being folded and stuffed into the twentieth, so that each sack of sacks contained capacity for one ton of potatoes.

11. Auchtermuchty is about ten miles from Markinch and hereafter maintains itself in the records used.

12. The younger reader is perhaps beginning to feel dizzy at this arithmetic, but Kime would have done such sums in his head! There were twelve pennies (d) in a shilling (s) and twenty shillings in a pound (£). There were fourteen pounds (lbs) in a stone, eight stones in a hundredweight (cwt) and twenty hundredweights in a ton.

13. Chitting is the process of getting the tuber to put out shoots known as sprouts, often carried out in greenhouses or other places where the light is good. These sprouts come from 'eyes', of which a good tuber will have several. It is possible to cut the tuber into sections each with an eye, and to plant them separately.

14. *The Times,* 30 September 1907, when the Society was holding its first provincial show at Wye College, having been formed 'a few years ago, when fabulous prices were paid for new varieties'.

15. I am indebted to Mr R L Carter, then Head of the school, for the loan of this volume and to my late Mother for making extensive notes from it.

Jean Ingelow and Her Poetry

Roger Norburn

As early as 1850 Alfred Tennyson was thanking a Miss Hollway, of Spilsby, for sending him a copy of her cousin, Jean Ingelow's book of poems *A Rhyming Chronicle of Incidents and Feelings* which had just been published. The work was not a success, however. For that Jean Ingelow had to wait another thirteen years when her book simply entitled *Poems* was published. After that occurred the famous incident when Tennyson came across his fellow Lincolnshire-born poet and told her: 'Miss Ingleton, I do declare you do the trick better than I do'.[1] Both poets had many years of life and fame in front of them and, after Tennyson's death in 1892, there was a distinct possibility that Jean would succeed him as Poet Laureate. In particular her appointment was vigorously championed in the United States where she had been immensely popular for decades, some 200,000 copies of her books having been sold there. A petition arrived from the U.S., signed by leading writers, but this may have been counter-productive, turning Queen Victoria even more against the idea of a female Poet Laureate. In the event the banal Alfred Austin was eventually appointed in 1896. (Over a hundred years later we still await our first female Poet Laureate.) Supporters of Jean Ingelow may have been consoled by the thought that she probably would have turned down the offer, had it come her way.

Jean was born in Boston on 17 March 1820, the first-born of a large family. Her mother (also Jean, née Kilgour) was of Scottish stock and strongly evangelical. Her disciplined, even rigid outlook was to influence her daughter throughout her life. Jean's father, William Ingelow (the word is Norse, meaning a low-lying field), a Boston man, had gone into his father's own banking business and lived a few doors away from him in South Place. Sadly, when Jean was still an infant, their house burned down and the young family went to live with Grandfather Ingelow. The view from his large Georgian house, which overlooked the river, had a great effect on Jean's developing imagination. As she wrote some fifty years later:

> 'My father's house stood in a quiet country town through which a tidal river flowed. The banks of the river were flanked by wooden wharves, which were supported on timbers and projected over the water. They had granaries behind them, and one of my earliest pleasures was to watch the gangs of men, who, at high tide, towed vessels up the river where, being moored before these granaries,

Fig. 1: A little known engraving of Jean Ingelow used as the frontispiece of 'A Story of Doom' published by Roberts Brothers of Boston in 1867

> cargoes of corn were shot down from the upper stories into their holds through wooden troughs not unlike fire escapes. The back of my father's house was on a level with the wharves, and overlooked a long reach of the river. Our nursery was a low room in the roof, having a large bow-window, in the old fashioned seat of which, I spent many a happy hour with my mother, sometimes listening to the soft, hissing sound of the wheat in its descent, sometimes admiring the figureheads of the vessels, or laboriously spelling out the letters of their names.'[2]

This idyllic childhood was not to last. At the very end of 1825 the Ingelows' banking interests collapsed and the house in South Place was sold two months later. It is not known for certain where the Ingelows, with their now rapidly growing family, lived between 1826 and 1834. They may have moved to nearby Skirbeck, now a suburb of Boston, and stayed with William's unmarried sister, Rebecca. Jean certainly spent a lot of time there and began in her travels to delight in her own county. She would have heard about the devastating local floods of 1810. As the eldest child she would have helped with the family – by the end of 1831 there were seven children, four girls and three boys. All the children were educated at home.

In 1834 the Ingelows moved again, this time to Ipswich in Suffolk where William took up an appointment as manager of the East of England Bank. The Suffolk years, which lasted until 1845, are important for the development of Jean's poetic talent. She began to express her feelings in verse and undoubtedly pored over the poetry of Tennyson whose latest *Poems* had been published in December 1832. She must have felt a great kinship with the poet born just over ten years before her and only twenty miles, as the crow flies, from her birthplace. One revealing anecdote has her mother confiscating her writing paper so that she would help more with the ever-increasing members of the family. Jean promptly began to write on the white window shutters of her bedroom, folding them back against the wall when she had finished. Inevitably her mother discovered the ruse but, instead of punishing her daughter, wisely restored her writing materials.

Also in these years occurred the great tragedy of Jean's life. She fell in love with a sailor and there seems to have been some sort of agreement between them, although not a formal engagement, before he sailed away. He never returned. What his name was, what his ship was and what happened to him are unknown. What we have instead, throughout her poetry, are references, direct, oblique and symbolic, to her love and its tragic conclusion:

Oh, my lost love, and my own, own love,
  And my love that loved me so!
Is there never a chink in the world above
  Where they listen for words from below?
Nay, I spoke once, and I grieved thee sore,
  I remember all that I said,
And now thou wilt hear me no more - no more
  Till the sea gives up her dead.[3]

Her famous poem 'Divided', about an ever-widening 'beck' with the two lovers on either side, finds the perfect symbol for the hesitancy which ultimately caused their everlasting physical separation and what is her best known poem of all 'The High Tide on the Coast of Lincolnshire (1571)' but the story of the separation of Elizabeth, by drowning, from her husband, the narrator's son? These two poems will be discussed more fully later.

Poor William had no luck in banking. Towards the end of 1845 the Ipswich and Suffolk Banking Company (as it was now called) failed and the Ingelows had to leave their home. What happened to the family during the next five years is obscure. Jean certainly visited Filey with her mother but, more importantly, spent some time staying with the Reverend Edward Harston and his family in Tamworth. The Ingelows had become friendly with the Harstons when Edward was rector of a parish in Ipswich and now they encouraged Jean to write. The first result of this encouragement was her book *A Rhyming Chronicle*, edited by Edward, the publication of which coincided with the Ingelows' move to London in 1850.

Jean spent the rest of her life in London. After staying in lodgings the family moved to Kensington in 1855 where her father died, an exhausted man, in April of that year. Jean continued to live at 15 Holland Street until her mother died in 1876. By the late 1870s Jean, by now because of her writing a famous and wealthy woman, could afford to spend the winter in Cannes but her home was still in Kensington, although at a different address. Her last years were clouded by the deaths of favourite relatives and friends, including that of her brother, William Frederick, a bachelor with whom she had lived for over 30 years, in October 1886. Jean Ingelow herself died on 20 July 1897. John Ruskin, who was one of the many literary friends she had made over the years, attended her funeral. She is buried in Brompton Cemetery beside her parents.

Between *A Rhyming Chronicle* and the early 1890s, by which time her creativity seems to have dried up, perhaps because of all the bereavements she had recently suffered, Jean published over twenty books, an impressive body of work. Her writing can be divided into three main categories: novels, children's literature and poetry.

She wrote some half a dozen novels. The first, *Allerton and Dreux* (1851), published anonymously 'by the author of the *Rhyming Chronicle*', sank without trace, but the second, *Off the Skelligs* (1872), was extremely popular and, in part autobiographical, is generally regarded as the best of her novels. It was followed by a sequel, *Fated to be Free* (1875), and other novels in the 1870s and 1880s.

Jean contributed children's stories to *Youth Magazine* (which she also edited for a year) and in 1860 collected them in a volume published at her own expense entitled *Tales of Orris* (her pen name). Other collections of stories for children appeared throughout her writing life but her best, most lasting work for children was *Mopsa the Fairy*.

Lewis Carroll published *Alice in Wonderland* in 1865. *Mopsa the Fairy,* which begins with a little boy discovering a nest of fairies in a hollow hawthorn tree, was published only four years later and beautifully digests the influence of the earlier work.

It is on her poetry, however, that Jean Ingelow's fame chiefly rests. A decade after the failure of *A Rhyming Chronicle* she joined the Portfolio Society, which brought her into contact with other aspiring poets and also more established writers. Members were expected to write poems on set themes. The company she now kept and these exercises must have contributed to the runaway success of her 1863 collection, *Poems.* This book, which ultimately went through 30 editions, brought her wealth and fame on both sides of the Atlantic. She corresponded with Henry Longfellow and Oliver Wendell Holmes in the United States. In this country, besides Tennyson, whom she visited in 1870, she became friendly with John Ruskin, Robert Browning and members of the Pre-Raphaelite Brotherhood, which included the Rossettis. With Christina Rossetti she developed a friendship which was not untinged with professional envy, a relationship echoed by that between Virginia Woolf and Katherine Mansfield a generation or two later.

The 1863 volume contains 21 poems. If that sounds like the slim offering of a contemporary poet, the reader is mistaken. Indeed what is striking, besides her mastery of different metres and verse forms, is the length of many of the poems, several of which run to 700 or more lines. This in turn leads to a fault on which commentators often remark: there is in her poetry a diffuseness, a Victorian prolixity which does not always make for easy, even clear reading. The wit C S Calverley, another member of the Portfolio Society, seized on this in his parody of 'Divided', 'Lovers, and a Reflection' (the title, incidentally, must be a dig at the awkwardly titled 'Brothers, and a Sermon' also in the 1863 *Poems).* Calverley's poem begins:

In moss-prankt dells which the sunbeams flatter
  (And heaven it knoweth what that may mean;
Meaning, however, is no great matter)
  Where woods are a-tremble, with rifts atween....[4]

Of course to be parodied suggests you have arrived, you are a worthy target. Other victims of Calverley included Tennyson and Browning. Jean Ingelow, who became more and more a professional writer with each successive book, would surely not have minded being in such company.

Despite the attentions of Calverley 'Divided' is a fine poem displaying many of Jean's poetic virtues at their best. First of all there is her love of nature and careful description of it:

An empty sky, a world of heather,
  Purple of foxglove, yellow of broom;
We two among them wading together,
  Shaking out honey, treading perfume.

The poem is made up of 31 stanzas like this, rhyming abab with the 'a' line invariably ending on an unstressed and the 'b' nearly always on a stressed syllable. The rhythm is cleverly varied so that it does not become predictable.

The stanzas themselves are divided into eight roughly equal sections. The emotional climax occurs in sections III to V:

Sing on! we sing in the glorious weather
  Till one steps over the tiny strand,
So narrow, in sooth, that still together
  On either brink we go hand in hand.

The beck grows wider, the hands must sever.
  On either margin, our songs all done,
We move apart, while she singeth ever,
  Taking the course of the stooping sun.

He prays, 'Come over' – I may not follow;
  I cry, 'Return' – but he cannot come:
We speak, we laugh, but with voices hollow;
  Our hands are hanging, our hearts are numb.

And later:

No backward path; ah! no returning;
  No second crossing that ripple's flow:
'Come to me now, for the west is burning;
  Come ere it darkens;' – 'Ah, no! ah, no!'

Then cries of pain, and arms outreaching –
  The beck grows wider and swift and deep:
Passionate words as of one beseeching –
  The loud beck drowns them; we walk, and weep.

And later still, with nature nicely reflecting the mood of the lovers:

We two walk on in our grassy places
  On either marge of the moonlit flood,
With the moon's own sadness in our faces,
  Where joy is withered, blossom and bud.

The force of the lines of this middle section is such that it drowns the attempted upbeat conclusion of the poem.

If 'Divided' has its faults – the final section and section VI which nearly succeeds in dissipating the power of the immediately preceding sections – they are hardly apparent in the poem Jean Ingelow is mostly associated with today, 'The High Tide on the Coast of Lincolnshire (1571)'.

On 10 November 1810 a great tide struck the whole Boston area causing devastation and loss of life. There is the poignant story of the servant girl of a Mr Birkett who, whilst milking the cows at Fosdyke, south of Boston, was suddenly trapped by the tide which overflowed the bank. She was drowned within sight of the farmhouse. This tragedy is the central event of 'The High Tide'.

By transposing the setting to the disaster of the sixteenth century, however, Jean is able to use the style and spelling of the old folk ballads. Such ballads tell a simple story, as this poem does. They make use of repetition, as this poem does with repetition of sounds and words and frequent reference first to the tune the Boston bells were ringing as a warning to the surrounding countryside and secondly to 'my sonne's faire wife, Elizabeth'. The rhymes may be handled casually in the traditional ballad. Well, Jean is far too accomplished an artist to need that licence but the rhyme scheme does significantly alter during the poem. Having established a pattern, in her seven-line stanzas, of ababccb, the last three lines suddenly become a triplet with the introduction of Elizabeth into the poem.:

> I sat and spun within the doore,
>   My thread brake off, I raised myne eyes;
> The level sun, like ruddy ore,
>   Lay sinking in the barren skies;
> And dark against day's golden death
>   She moved where Lindis wandereth,
> My sonne's faire wife, Elizabeth.

Finally, such ballads often include a refrain. The refrain here is the cry of the milkmaid as she calls the cows for milking:

> 'Cusha! Cusha! Cusha!' calling,
>   Ere the early dews were falling,
> Farre away I heard her song…

These stanzas are repeated, with significant changes, at the very end of the poem:

> I shall never hear her more
> By the reedy Lindis shore,

Fig. 2: Jean Ingelow depicted in a window in the north aisle of St Botolph's Church, Boston

> 'Cusha, Cusha, Cusha!' calling,
> Ere the early dews be falling…

And so on.

The opening of the poem plunges dramatically *in medias res:*

The old mayor climbed the belfry tower,
  The ringers ran by two, by three;
'Pull, if ye never pulled before;
  Good ringers, pull your best,' quoth he.
'Play uppe, play uppe, O Boston bells!
  Ply all your changes, all your swells,
Play uppe "The Brides of Enderby".'

(There has been some speculation about "The Brides of Enderby". In fact no such chime existed when Jean Ingelow wrote the poem, let alone in the 1570s. It was her own invention. Since then a chime has been composed with that title: a good example of life imitating art.)

The opening stanzas effectively contrast the alarm of the mayor with the contentment, even complacency, of the narrator, the 'swannerds' (i.e. swanherds), 'shepherde lads' and indeed of Elizabeth herself. The pace of the poem dramatically alters with the arrival of the narrator's son who realises the danger they are all in and is frantically looking for his wife and children (an 'eygre' or eagre, is a tidal wave of great height);

With that he cried and beat his breast;
  For, lo! along the river's bed
A mighty eygre reared his crest,
  And uppe the Lindis raging sped.
It swept with thunderous noises loud;
  Shaped like a curling snow-white cloud,
Or like a demon in a shroud.

So farre, so fast the eygre drave,
  The heart had hardly time to beat,
Before a shallow seething wave
  Sobbed in the grasses at oure feet:
The feet had hardly time to flee
  Before it brake against the knee,
And all the world was in the sea.

How powerful that last line is in its simplicity.

The poem concludes with the aftermath of the tragedy. The lifeless bodies of Elizabeth and her children are delivered by the waters to her husband. Finally comes the refrain, Elizabeth's call to her charges, which will now echo only in the mind.

Jean Ingelow deserves to be better known today. A readily available edition of her poems which included 'Divided', 'The High Tide', 'Gladys and her Island', 'The Long White Seam', 'Perdita', 'Echo and the Ferry' and the charming 'Supper at the Mill' would be a start. She was respected by the London literary elite of the 1860s and 1870s, indeed John Ruskin went so far as to say she was one of the few people he had 'ever truly loved'. Nearer our own day W H Auden included her in an anthology of nineteenth century poetry which he edited. Any poet admired by Tennyson in the nineteenth century and anthologised by Auden in the twentieth should surely be still read in the twenty-first.

Notes:

1. quoted in *The Letters of Alfred Lord Tennyson, Vol I, 1821-1850* edited by Cecil Y. Lang and Edgar F. Shannon Jr. (1982).
2. from *Off the Skelligs* (1872).
3. from 'Supper at the Mill' in *Poems* (1863).
4. from *The Faber Book of Parodies* edited by Simon Brett (1984).

The Members of Parliament for Louth

Philip Norton

Introduction

The town of Louth has had its name attached to a parliamentary constituency for most of the period since 1885. The constituency of Louth existed from 1885 until 1983. Boundary redistribution in 1983 meant that the town became part of Lindsey East. In 1997, it had its name restored as part of the constituency of Louth and Horncastle. This paper treats the constituencies in which Louth has nestled since 1885.

In the first 40 years of its existence, the Louth constituency was noteworthy for forming part of the battleground between the Liberals and the Conservatives; since 1924, the town has been part of a constituency that has consistently returned a Conservative MP. Louth has also been notable for witnessing three by-elections. One of these saw the return of the second female MP to take her seat in the House of Commons and the last one was to see the election of a Tory MP who later went on to be a millionaire author and go to gaol. Three of the Members who have represented Louth have each sat for 21 or more years; one, having previously represented other seats in Parliament, had, by 2007, sat in the House of Commons for a total 46 years. The MPs to represent the town have included four knights, a Deputy Chairman of the Conservative Party, and may yet include a Father of the House of Commons, but the town has yet to be represented by a minister. What is most remarkable is not the positions held by the MPs but their characters: since 1945, none has gone unnoticed in the House of Commons.

The Constituency

Until 1885, MPs were returned in Lincolnshire from the boroughs of Lincoln (with two Members), Grantham (two Members), Great Grimsby, Boston (two Members), and Stamford (two Members until 1868 and one thereafter).[1] The county returned six other MPs, two each for North, Mid and South Lincolnshire. The Redistribution of Seats Act 1885 – the third major change of the century to the electoral map of the United Kingdom – saw these county seats transformed into seven single-member seats. One of these was the East Lindsey or Louth division. The seat returned its first MP in the General Election of November 1885 when, in a contest between Liberal Francis Otter

and the Conservative James Lowther, the Liberal emerged victorious by 4,801 votes to 3,594.[2]

The seat of Louth continued to exist for nearly another century. It grew in size and came to encompass a notable mix of industrial, coastal and agricultural interests. In 1906, the seat had an electorate of 10,075. The enlargement of the electorate in 1918, when women aged 30 or over were given the vote (as were males aged nineteen and over who had served in the war), created a major boost to the electoral roll and in the General Election of 1918 the seat had an electorate of 27,572. The enfranchisement of all women aged 21 and over in 1928 saw a further increase, the number of electors in 1929 standing at 38,624. By 1950 the electorate stood at just under 50,000. The lowering of the voting age to eighteen in 1969 resulted in the next substantial increase and in 1970 the seat had an electorate of 67,540.

The constituency was notable more for its geographic size and shape than for the number of electors. The seat spread from just south of Louth up to the River Humber, sweeping round the borough constituency of Grimsby. It encompassed the holiday resort of Cleethorpes as well as the industrial port of Immingham. There were boundary changes to the constituency in 1974, but these were minor; the Boundary Commission wanted seats of between 50,000 and 70,000 electors as the norm and the changes left the seat with an electorate of just over 70,000. A more substantial change took place in 1983, when another boundary review resulted in the constituency as such disappearing and the town becoming part of a new seat of Lindsey East. The northern part of the old constituency moved into the constituency of Brigg and Cleethorpes. Louth itself moved from being in the bottom half of a constituency to being in the top half, joining with two-thirds of the former Horncastle constituency. (The town of Horncastle was joined to Gainsborough to form the constituency of Gainsborough and Horncastle.) The main towns in Lindsey East were Louth and Skegness. The number of electors in the new seat stood at just under 70,000, though the number of people moving into the area grew over the next decade and by 1992 the electorate stood at 80,026. A further boundary review resulted in another substantial change in time for the General Election of 1997. The name of Lindsey East disappeared, with the bulk of the seat joining with the town of Horncastle to form the Louth and Horncastle constituency. (85% of the seat was drawn from East Lindsey.) The coastal town of Skegness was transferred to form part of the newly created seat of Boston and Skegness. The electorate in Louth and Horncastle was just under 70,000, though by 2005 the number had increased to 75,313.

The seat of Louth and Horncastle constitutes one of the most agricultural seats in England. It is also fairly prosperous, just over three-quarters of the adult population (on the 1991 census) being owner-occupiers of property. Just over half are in non-manual posts, nearly a third being professionals or in management.[3] The town of Louth is often singled out in constituency profiles for its aesthetic appeal: 'attractive' in the words of *The Times Guide to the House of Commons;*[4] 'elegant' according to *The Almanac of British Politics.*[5] The seat is also geographically large. The extent of the rural nature of the constituency was noted in a profile of the seat, carried by the *Sunday Times* during the 2005 General Election campaign, when it reported that there was not a dual carriageway anywhere in the constituency.

The Party Battle

The late nineteenth century was a time of conflict between Tories and Liberals. In Lincolnshire, there were significant landowners who supported the Liberal cause, but the biggest contribution to the electoral appeal of the Liberal party was religion. The link between nonconformism and Liberalism aided the party in the heartland of Methodism. The Tories in the county had leading figures such as Edward Stanhope (who owned land around Horncastle), Henry Chaplin and James Lowther. The party tended to attract support from the established church, the Church of England. The battle was most pronounced in the northern part of the county. In the 1870s and early 1880s, the Tories dominated in all three county divisions, though a Liberal – Robert Laycock – topped the poll in North Lincolnshire in 1880.

The results of the new constituency of Louth tended initially to reflect the position in the country but to deviate thereafter. In the first contest, when more Liberals were returned nationally than Tories, the seat returned a Liberal MP, Francis Otter. The following year (1886), when the Conservatives gained 316 seats to the Liberals' 200, a Tory, Arthur Heath, was returned unopposed, the only time in the history of the seat that there was no contest. In 1892,

when Gladstone was returned to office, the seat returned a Gladstone Liberal, Robert Perks. The Tories held office nationally from 1895, emerging with a notable triumph in 1900, but Louth continued to return Perks; he was re-elected in 1895 and 1900 as well as in 1906, the year of a Liberal landslide. In 1910, Liberal support declined and the seat returned a Conservative, Captain Henry Brackenbury, with a majority of 158. In the second General Election of that year, the tables were turned. Although it was largely a standstill election nationally, the Liberal candidate, Timothy Davies, who had been the unsuccessful candidate in January, was returned with a majority of 72.

The divide between the Liberals and the Conservatives reflected the religious influence of the period and also something of a clash between the town of Louth and the surrounding countryside. Robert Perks attributed his success to the fact that whereas there were 74 Anglican clergy in the constituency, there were some 300 lay preachers of one or other Wesleyan sect. (He also believed he had an Irish vote of about 500).[6] In 1910, the town of Louth was described by the *Grimsby News* as 'Tory almost to the backbone', with the nonconformists in the countryside providing the bulk of the Liberal support.[7] However, the 1906 election was seen as the first in which national issues played a dominant part and the influence of religion declined. Issues such as protection versus free trade came to the fore. There was also the emergence nationally of a Labour Party and the Liberals had to decide how to respond to this growing movement. However, according to Henry Pelling, the seat was seen, over the period up to 1910 as 'a safe Liberal seat'. The 'safeness' was not apparent as the religious impact on electoral behaviour declined and socio-economic background, or class, became more important.

The outbreak of war in 1914 resulted in the postponement of an election, so Davies sat for eight years until the 'coupon election' of 1918.[8] The Conservatives dominated the election – of 478 MPs elected as part of the Conservative and Coalition Liberal Government, 335 were Conservatives – and in Louth, where the two candidates were the same as in 1910, the Conservative, Captain Brackenbury – standing as a Coalition Unionist – was elected, defeating Davies by 9,055 votes to 7,559. However, Louth then witnessed a remarkable period of electoral history.

On 26 April 1920, Captain Brackenbury celebrated his 52nd birthday. Two days later he died. In the resulting by-election two months later, the Liberal candidate,

Thomas Wintringham (who had previously contested the Grimsby seat), was returned. He represented the seat for only fourteen months. He died on 8 August 1921 at the age of 54. His widow, Margaret Wintringham, was adopted to fight the by-election, which took place the following month when the Coalition government was not doing well in by-elections.[9] Out of respect for her late husband, Mrs Wintringham did not speak in public throughout the campaign.[10] Nonetheless, she was elected with a majority of 791, becoming only the second woman to take her seat in the House of Commons. She held on to the seat in 1922 with an increased majority (of 1,101), doing so despite a Conservative landslide nationally, but reflecting something of a brief Liberal revival in the county: Gainsborough, Grantham and Horncastle also returned Liberal Members.

The Liberal revival proved short-lived, including in Louth. In the General Election of 1924, despite Conservative support declining nationally, Mrs Wintringham lost to the Conservative candidate, Colonel Arthur Heneage: he won by 12,674 votes to 11,330. Heneage held on to the seat in 1929, in which for the first time a Labour candidate contested the seat. However, the contest remained primarily one between the Conservative and Liberal candidate, Heneage winning 13,999 votes to 13,560 for Mrs Wintringham and 4,027 votes for the Labour candidate. Heneage easily held the seat in the Conservative landslides of 1931 and 1935, facing only a Liberal challenger in 1931 and only a Labour challenger in 1935. Against the Labour challenger, he achieved a majority of 7,444.

Louth has been represented by a Conservative MP ever since. Heneage retired in 1945 and his successor, Cyril Osborne held the seat in 1945 in the Labour landslide of that year. He was returned with little difficulty in succeeding elections. Reflecting Liberal decline in the 1950s, he faced only a Labour challenger in the 1955 and 1959 General Elections. Osborne died suddenly in 1969 and in the by-election later that year Tory Jeffrey Archer was returned with a majority of 10,727 – the first time a candidate had been returned with a five-figure majority. Archer stood down in 1974 and was succeeded by Michael Brotherton. Following the boundary redistribution in 1983, Brotherton sought the candidature for the new Brigg and Cleethorpes constituency, losing it to the MP for the former Brigg and Scunthorpe seat, Michael Brown. Most electors from the former Horncastle constituency transferred to the new seat of Lindsey East, where the MP for Horncastle, Peter Tapsell, was selected as Conservative candidate.

He was elected with a majority of 7,517, being re-elected with little difficulty in subsequent elections. In 1992, he achieved a majority of 11,846. In 1997, with the seat renamed Louth and Horncastle, he was returned with a majority of 6,900, achieved in the face of the Conservative Party's worst General Election defeat since 1906. He was returned in 2001 with a majority of 7,554 and in 2005 with a majority of 9,896.

In its description of the seat in 2001, *The Times Guide to the House of Commons* commented 'The Tories are strong here and the opposition to them is evenly divided'.[11] Labour had succeeded the Liberal Party as the second main party nationally in 1922 and was the principal challenger in Louth from 1935 through to 1969. Labour came second in the 1969 by-election, but was run close by the Liberal candidate (Labour gained 5,590 votes to 5,003 for the Liberals). Labour restored its position in 1970, winning 34% of the votes to 13% for the Liberals. However, the Liberals enjoyed a revival in the 1970s. In the General Election in February 1974, Liberal candidate John Sellick just eased ahead of Labour candidate Alan Dowson by 15,440 votes (27.7%) to 15,148 (27.2%). In the October election of that year, he came the closest a Liberal has come to winning the seat since Mrs Wintringham in 1929. In what was a three-way contest, Michael Brotherton achieved 19,819 votes (38.5%) to 16,939 (32.9%) for Sellick and 14,747 (28.6%) for the Labour candidate Russell Mitchell. It was the highpoint of Liberal support. Sellick came second in the 1979 General Election with a higher share of the poll than in 1974, but Conservative support increased by a greater margin; Labour support fell. The situation was repeated in Lindsey East in 1983, Peter Tapsell achieving 53.3% of the poll, Sellick 38.5% and the Labour candidate Geoff Lowis only 8.3%. The situation was largely repeated in 1987. In 1992, with new Liberal and Labour candidates, Liberal support fell slightly (by almost 5%) while Labour support rose (by 4%); the Liberal Democrat Party, as the party had become, was still the principal challenger. However, in 1997 – with Labour winning a national landslide – the principal contest in Louth and Horncastle was between the Liberal Democrats and Labour for second place. The Labour candidate, John Hough, with 14,799 votes (29.6%), eased out the Liberal Democrat, Fiona Martin, who won 12,207 votes (24.4%). Labour remained in second place in 2001 – getting over 5,000 votes more than the Liberal Democrat – as well as in 2005, though by a narrower margin.

Until 1969, there were never more than three candidates in each contest. In the 1969 by-election, a Democrat candidate, Sir George Fitzgerald, stood, winning only 1,225 votes (4.3%) and losing his deposit. The first minor party candidate to contest the seat in a General Election was a National Front candidate in 1979: he won only 261 votes (0.5%). A Green candidate, Mrs Rosemary Robinson, stood in 1992 and 1997, winning just over 1,000 votes (1.6% of the poll in 1992, 2.5% in 1997). In 2005, a United Kingdom Independence Party (UKIP) candidate contested the seat. Standing against a noted Eurosceptic MP, the party nonetheless won 3,611 votes (7.7%), retaining its deposit. The occasional intervention of minor party candidates has not affected the outcome nor the nature of the contest.

The Members

Louth, as we have seen, has had different manifestations as a constituency since 1885. There have been twelve MPs who have represented the town (see Table 1). Of these, five have been Liberal and seven Conservative. They are noteworthy for the fact that very few have retired voluntarily and for none ever having become a Government minister. They nonetheless include several that have achieved national prominence.

Of the twelve, only three can be described as having retired at times of their choice (Otter, Perks, and Heneage). Three have died in office (Brackenbury, T Wintringham, Osborne). Two have gone at times not of their preference (Archer, Brotherton). Only three have ceased to be MPs

as a result of electoral defeat (Heath, Davies and M Wintringham). The twelfth, Sir Peter Tapsell, remains in the House.

During the twentieth century, Louth was one of only two seats in the county never to return a Member who became a senior minister or Government whip. (The other was Horncastle.) The closest the Louth constituency came to having such a Member was when it was first formed and the Conservative candidate in 1885 was James Lowther, previously MP for York and then North Lincolnshire. He had served in the Cabinet as Chief Secretary for Ireland. He lost the election to Francis Otter. Arthur Heneage did serve eleven years as a Parliamentary Private Secretary (PPS), that is, an unofficial and unpaid assistant to a minister, a position likened by Austin Mitchell to 'a kind of public school fag',[12] hovering in an unusual constitutional position between the back benches and ministerial office[13] and often seen as a stepping stone to office. Heneage, however, despite his long service, never progressed to a ministerial post.[14] (Most of his period was spent as a PPS to Sir Walter Womersley, the MP for Grimsby, who served as Assistant Postmaster-General and Minister of Pensions.) Peter Tapsell served two years on the Opposition front bench from 1976 to 1978, first as a spokesman on foreign affairs and then on treasury and economic affairs. He is the only one of the twelve MPs discussed here ever to sit on one of the front benches.

The MPs have generally been drawn from a professional, business or military background. The first four Members for the seat – Otter, Heath, Perks and Brackenbury – were

MPs FOR LOUTH 1885-2007			
MP	**Period of service**	**Background**	**Reason for ceasing to be MP**
Francis Otter (Lib)	1885-1886	Lawyer/academic	Retirement
Arthur R. Heath (Con)	1886-1892	Lawyer	Election defeat
(Sir) Robert W. Perks (Lib)	1892-1910	Lawyer	Retirement
Capt. Henry Brackenbury (Con)	Jan-Dec 1910, 1918-1920	Lawyer/army	Death
Timothy Davies (Lib)	1910-1918	Draper	Election defeat
Thomas Wintringham (Lib)	1920-1921	Timber inspector	Death
Margaret Wintringham (Lib)	1921-1924	Wife of former MP	Election defeat
Lt -Col (Sir) Arthur Heneage (Con)	1924-1945	Army	Retirement
(Sir) Cyril Osborne (Con)	1945-1969	Businessman	Death
Jeffrey Archer (Con)	1969-1974	Freelance journalist	Stood down
Michael Brotherton (Con)	1974-1983	Navy/advertising executive	Boundary changes
(Sir) Peter Tapsell (Con)	1983 -	Conservative Research Dept.	

Table 1: Members of Parliament for Louth, 1885 to 2007

all lawyers, though Otter was better known as a leading academic (he was a Fellow of Christ Church, Oxford), Perks had business interests and Brackenbury served as a Captain in the 3rd Battalion Lincolnshire Regiment. Otter had local connections, having been born in Gainsborough. He retired in 1886, at the age of 55, having served for only one year in Parliament. However, he subsequently contested unsuccessfully the Sleaford constituency in 1889 and Horncastle in 1892. Heath, who lived at Thorpe Hall, South Elkington, did not contest this or any other seat after his defeat in 1892 when he was aged only 38. (He lived to the age of 89.) Perks had particular business interests in the building of docks and railways, but had no obvious links with the area, his main affinity being religious. He was later to serve as First Vice-President of the Methodist Church (1932-33). He was made a baronet in 1908, two years before he retired from Parliament. Brackenbury, like Heath, also made his home at Thorpe Hall. He served as High Steward of Louth. He sat in the short 1910 Parliament before being elected again in 1918. As already detailed, his death in 1920 precipitated a by-election.

All those four MPs were University educated: Otter and Brackenbury at Oxford, Heath at Cambridge, and Perks at King's College London. Timothy Davies was the first who appears not to have had a University education: he is recorded as having been 'educated in Wales'. He set up in business, primarily as a draper in Fulham. He was active in local politics, serving as Mayor of Fulham and as a member of the London County Council. He sat in Parliament as the MP for Fulham from 1906 to 1910, when he transferred to Louth, losing in the first of the 1910 elections, but being returned in the December. He was 63 at the time of his defeat in 1918. He died in 1951 at the age of 94.

Thomas Wintringham was similar to Davies in that he lacked a University education. However, unlike Davies, he was a local man. He was born in Grimsby in 1867 and worked as a timber inspector. Active in Liberal politics, he contested the Grimsby seat in 1898. He was elected as Member for Louth in 1920, when he was aged 53. His death the following year propelled his wife into the history books. Being selected to succeed one's husband was the way in which women initially managed to get elected to the House of Commons, following passage of an Act in 1918 enabling women to sit in the House. The first woman to take her seat, Nancy Astor, succeeded her husband.[15] The third woman to take her seat, Mrs Hilton Philipson, did so as well. It has been argued that, given a perceived reluctance to elect women, succeeding the husband in a seat

gave some element of legitimacy to a female candidate. 'Their candidacy was the extension of their acceptable roles as wives, and in the case of Lady Astor and Mrs Hilton Philipson, mothers. Their husbands had, as it were, legitimised their political aspirations and this "halo effect" of male acceptability was perhaps at the time, essential'.[16] It is worth mentioning, in parenthesis, that when Sir Cyril Osborne died in 1969, the local Conservative association approached his wife, Lady Joy Osborne, to see if she would be willing to accept the candidature in succession to her husband; she declined on the grounds that it was a post best suited to a man.

Margaret Wintringham benefited from her local popularity. She was active in the county, undertaking voluntary activities, serving as a JP for Lindsey, and being a member of the County Agriculture Committee. She spoke in the House in support of bringing the voting age for women in line with that for men. After her defeat in 1924, she remained active in local politics and in 1929 again contested the seat. In 1933 she was elected to Lindsey County Council. In 1935 she unsuccessfully contested the Aylesbury seat in Buckinghamshire. She died in 1955.

Colonel Arthur Heneage was the first MP for Louth to serve for more than twenty years. Educated at Eton – the only Old Etonian to sit for the seat – and the Royal Military Academy, Woolwich, he served as a cavalry officer. He saw action in France in the First World War and was awarded the Distinguished Service Order in 1917. He served on the Inter-Allied Commission on Control in Berlin. After his election, he took an active interest in local government, serving for twenty years (1925 to 1945) as Vice-President of the Urban District Councils' Association and, from 1931 to 1945, of the Rural District Councils' Association. Three months before he retired in 1945, he was knighted. His interest in local government continued after his retirement and he was elected to Lindsey County Council. He was High Sheriff of Lincolnshire in 1947. He died in 1971 at the age of 90.

Cyril Osborne succeeded Heneage and, like him, was to serve for more than two decades in the House of Commons. The son of a miner, he had attended University College, Nottingham and was a self-made Leicester businessman; he continued to live at Rothley, Leicestershire, during his period as an MP. He was the first of Louth's MPs to achieve some prominence because of his political views. He attracted attention for espousing strong right-wing views on social issues: he was fiercely opposed to liberalising the law on such issues as homosexuality, while strongly espousing capital punishment and stricter controls on immigration. He was bitter that fellow MP Enoch Powell attracted national media attention for views on immigration which he had been advocating for years. (He did, though, take a different view to Powell on relations with the United States; when Powell in 1953 attacked America in the Commons, arguing that it had worked to weaken the British Empire, Osborne had shouted 'No'.)[17] Powell made the headlines for his views on immigration in 1968, but Osborne had raised the issue during the 1950s, both in the Commons and at a meeting of the 1922 Committee, the body comprising Conservative Private Members. At the latter, in 1958, 'he had broken down weeping at the end when no one seemed prepared to take any notice of the gravity of the problems the country would face'.[18] He was seen as being the leading figure in a small group of Tory MPs urging immigration controls.[19] In March 1965 he pressed a motion calling for 'precise' limits on immigration; he had initially tabled it calling for a complete ban except for those whose parents or grandparents were born in Britain. As a result of his toning down the motion, 162 Conservative MPs, including the Shadow Cabinet, voted for it.

He was, however, unusual for favouring stronger ties with Russia – he was chairman of the Anglo-Soviet parliamentary group – and held fairly liberal views on economics. He was also not afraid to attack his own party. In 1962, he told the Chief Whip that half the Tory Cabinet should be removed and replaced by younger men. The Chief Whip sent a minute to the Prime Minister, Harold Macmillan, saying he had only managed to persuade Osborne from publicly attacking the whole party structure by promising him a private word with Macmillan.[20] Although he had complained about superior social background being necessary to get on in the Tory party,[21] Osborne also appears to have been an early supporter of Alec Douglas-Home – then Earl of Home – for the party leadership in 1963.[22]

Osborne attended to the constituency from his Leicestershire office, assisted by a long-serving secretary who could usually draft appropriate letters on his behalf. He was knighted in 1961, after sixteen years in the House. He was aged 67 when he was elected for the seventh time in 1966 and was intent on carrying on as long as possible in Parliament. He collapsed and died in the Palace of Westminster on 31 August 1969.

The local Conservative association set about selecting a candidate to succeed him. They sifted through more than 200 applications before producing a shortlist and then narrowing it down to three, and then two, candidates. A freelance journalist, Jeffrey Archer, emerged successful over the presumed Central Office favourite, former Director General of the CBI, John Davies. The story of Archer's selection is recounted in Michael Crick's biography of Archer.[22a] Archer won because of some enthusiastic presentations and also because he wasn't John Davies; Davies gave a speech not geared to the needs of Louth and his wife failed to endear herself to party members.

Archer was an unusual choice. Though he had some political experience – he had been elected to the Greater London Council in 1966 – he had not previously fought a parliamentary seat (one of the prerequisites initially agreed by the selection committee) and was aged under 30. Though he had taken an education diploma at Oxford University, he had no degree. The only criteria initially set by the selection committee[23] that he fulfilled were that he was a male and married.

He was chosen because of image rather than because of his views. He stood in marked contrast to Osborne: he was more liberal and a supporter of membership of the European Community; he was an important fund-raiser for the European Movement. Like Osborne, though, he did attract attention. He excelled at self-promotion. He was also prone to exaggeration. He was 29 at the time of his election and billed himself as the youngest MP. He was not the youngest; he was not even the youngest Conservative MP. Four other MPs, including a Conservative elected at a by-election two months before Archer, were younger than he was when he entered the House.

He worked on achieving a high profile in the constituency, but was not among the most active of MPs in the chamber. When he did speak, it was often to criticise his own government. He opposed, in particular, the imposition of admission charges for museums. He also argued against the abolition of free school milk and, given his constituency, against local government reorganisation, under which part of the constituency would pass into the new and imposed county of Humberside. Crick recounts that Archer was delighted when his voting record was almost as disloyal as Enoch Powell's. He also cites this writer's work as showing 'Archer to have been amongst the most rebellious of all Conservative MPs'.[24] My work shows no such thing. Though Archer occasionally voiced his opposition to policies and would sometimes abstain from voting, his record of voting against the Government was in no way comparable to that of Enoch Powell or of the other leading Tory rebels of the Parliament, such as John Biffen and – from Lincolnshire – Richard Body.[25] Powell voted against the Heath Government on 113 occasions. Archer voted against it four times.[26] He was, at best, a rather minor rebel during the Parliament.

Archer employed researchers to assist with his duties – recruiting two that later went on to become MPs and serve as senior ministers (David Mellor and Richard Ryder) – while he devoted his energies to business enterprises. He invested heavily in a Canadian company that was fraudulently promoting a product and which, when its share price slumped, left Archer facing a lawsuit that could result in his bankruptcy. Shortly after his re-election in February 1974, the press picked up on the fact that he was facing court proceedings. Archer met with officers of the local party and, at their prompting, decided to stand down. In the October 1974 election, he was succeeded by Michael Brotherton, an advertising executive. Archer became famous and indeed infamous after stepping down. He reinvented himself as a novelist – producing several best-selling novels – and became a millionaire. He also became a leading fundraiser for the Conservative Party; Margaret Thatcher appointed him Deputy Chairman of the Party in 1985 and her successor, John Major – whom Archer had encouraged to seek the premiership in 1990[27] – elevated him to the peerage in 1992. However, he was never far from controversy. He resigned as Deputy Chairman of the Tory Party in 1986 following allegations he had given money to a prostitute. He fought and won a celebrated libel case over the affair, though with dramatic repercussions when it emerged several years later, in 1999, that he had tried to persuade a friend to give perjured evidence should he be questioned in the case. He was forced to abandon his campaign as Conservative candidate for Mayor of London and in 2000 he was charged with perjury and attempting to pervert the course of justice. He was convicted in July 2001 and sentenced to four years in gaol. During his imprisonment, he wrote about the experience. He was released on licence in July 2003. He announced that he had no plans of returning to politics and spent time in Spain writing.

His successor, Michael Brotherton, went to the Royal Naval Academy, Dartmouth, and had served sixteen years in the navy, reaching the rank of Lieutenant-Commander, before becoming an advertising executive with *The*

Times. He contested Deptford in 1970 before being adopted for Louth in 1974. He was a reversion to Cyril Osborne in terms of political attitudes. He was described in Andrew Roth's *Parliamentary Profiles* as a 'right-wing fundamentalist'[28] and became well known for his willingness to give his views an airing. He acquired the nickname of 'the mouth from Louth' for his enthusiasm in providing quotes to the media. Whereas Jeffrey Archer opposed capital punishment, Brotherton supported it. He was opposed to sanctions against South Africa – he voted against maintaining sanctions within days of entering Parliament – and also spoke out against computer 'mating madness'. He was far more of a rebel than Jeffrey Archer ever was. During the 1974 to 1979 Parliament, he voted against his own party on 56 occasions, putting him in the top five Tory rebels of the Parliament.[29] He rebelled on an eclectic range of issues. He opposed the Race Relations Bill and a directly elected European Assembly, voted in favour of enabling men to become midwives, opposed the requirement to use imperial units of measurement, voted against an attempt to restrict the scope of the Public Lendings Right Bill, and – perhaps not surprisingly given the seaside resorts in his constituency – opposed a measure designed to amend the law on the rating of caravans.

The son of a brewer, he also enjoyed social drinking and caused something of a local scandal after being banned from driving, as a result of a drink-driving conviction, and attempting to keep the fact hidden locally. Though active in the constituency – he liked to be seen about at weekends – he did not build up sufficient support to be adopted for the seat of Brigg and Cleethorpes when most of the northern part of the constituency was transferred to the new seat. He lost heavily in the adoption contest to Michael Brown.

Louth, as we have seen, became part of the new Lindsey East seat, drawing in most of the old Horncastle constituency, and the local Conservative association adopted the MP for Horncastle, Peter Tapsell, as the candidate. He was duly elected in 1983. Educated at Oxford, where he was a member of the Labour Club, Tapsell joined the Conservative Research Department in 1954 and served as political assistant to Prime Minister Sir Anthony Eden in the 1955 General Election. He went on to become a stockbroker (from 1957 to 1990) and a leading financial adviser; he was later to be described as one of the richest self-made men in the Commons. He was first elected to Parliament in 1959 as MP for the normally Labour seat of Nottingham West, winning by 164 votes.

He lost the seat in 1964. He succeeded Sir John Maitland as MP for Horncastle in 1966, before being adopted for Lindsey East and then Louth and Horncastle. By the time of the 2005 Parliament, he was the only MP to have been elected as early as 1959 and was the MP with the second longest period of continuous service in the House. Labour MP Alan Williams was first elected in 1964 and had unbroken service – the criterion for determining which MP has the courtesy title of Father of the House. Williams was expected to retire at the next election. If Tapsell were to continue in the House, he would assume the title.

Tapsell was an expert on finance, but held views that meant he was never to hold office. Though a friend of Edward Heath's, Heath as Prime Minister ignored him after he had been proved right on economic issues;[30] his anticipation of consequences of economic policy were often borne out in practice. He was appointed to the Opposition front bench when Margaret Thatcher became leader, but served only two years. His views were not those of Thatcher and he was a critic of the government's economic policies during her premiership. He was described by *The Spectator* as an 'unreconstructed Keynesian'. He was a friend and leading supporter of former Defence Secretary Michael Heseltine and seconded his nomination for the party leadership after Margaret Thatcher resigned in 1990.[31] His support of Heseltine led to criticisms in the constituency by supporters of Margaret Thatcher; an attempt to de-select him failed in 1991. He caused trouble for the Government of John Major by being a leading opponent of the Treaty on European Union (the Maastricht Treaty); he voted against it on more than thirty occasions.[32] He attacked the European Union as a vehicle for German domination. Although he was not afraid to voice his views and, if necessary, to vote against the party line,[33] he rebelled infrequently after the party returned to opposition in 1997. He was not the most frequent of speakers in the chamber, often preferring to make his views known in the privacy of the 1922 Committee.[34] When he did speak, though, his contributions had an effect.

Knighted in 1985, he was regarded by the time of the 2005 Parliament as one of the grandest of the 'knights of the shires'. Variously described by parliamentary sketch writers and colleagues as one of the most intelligent men in the House of Commons, aloof, grand, and speaking with a superior tone – 'a rich, patriarchal businessman' according to one Chief Whip[35] – his telling contributions in the House, often at the expense of ministers, including Prime Minister Tony Blair, attracted national media attention. A typical example of one of his interventions during Prime Minister's Question Time was on 13 December 2006, when he asked the Prime Minister: 'Since the Prime Minister is so fond of apologising to foreigners for the conduct of our long-dead ancestors, will he now, particularly in view of the accumulated turbulence, apologise to the British people for his own folly in leading us into the Iraq disaster?'[36]

He gradually acquired the status of a parliamentary celebrity, winning awards – he was voted the *Spectator's* 'Backbencher of the Year' in 1993 and 'Parliamentarian of the Year' in 2004 – and getting a cheer from Tory MPs whenever he got to his feet. By the time of the 2005 General Election he was 75 years of age, though his looks belied his age and he appeared fit and able, well in form to become the Father of the House.

Challengers

Parliamentary seats held by one party are often fought by candidates of other parties as a way of proving themselves and moving up the political ladder to a safe seat. On other occasions they may be fought by local candidates keen to engage in flag-waving on behalf of the party. Louth has tended to be marked by the former, especially in the period since the 1930s. In the first decades of the constituency, when there was a real contest between the Liberals and the Conservatives, the challenger was more often than not either a former or future MP for the seat (Heath, Davies, Brackenbury and Margaret Wintringham, both Davies and Wintringham being the losing candidate on two occasions each). Francis Lucas, who fought the seat for the Conservatives against Perks in 1895, went on to become MP for Lowestoft (1900 to 1906). In 1931, the Liberal candidate was a major figure in the party and a leading academic, Professor Ramsay Muir, who in total was to stand for Parliament eight times; he was successful only once, having been MP for Rochdale from 1923 to 1924.

Since the 1930s, local candidates have tended to be to the fore, especially as the principal challengers. In the 1950s and 1960s, Cyril Osborne faced opposition from a local headteacher (H J H Dyer, in 1950 and 1951), doctor (Dr Douglas Poirier in 1955) and farmer (Frank Macdonald in 1959 and 1964). In the 1970s and early 1980s, when the main challenge came from the Liberals (then the Liberal Alliance), the candidate was a company director with farming interests, John Sellick, who fought the seat five times.

Perhaps the most noteworthy feature of those who have fought the seat unsuccessfully in the past few decades is that two of them have gone on to become MPs, but they have not figured in the preceding discussion because neither was the principal challenger. The Liberal candidate who came third in the 1964 and 1966 General Elections was a university lecturer in mathematics, Dr Edmund Marshall. He joined the Labour Party in 1967 and was elected as MP for Goole in a by-election in 1971. He was to serve until the seat disappeared in 1983. The Labour candidate who came third in Louth in 1979 was Clive Betts, a local government economist. He was elected as Labour MP for Sheffield Attercliffe in 1992. He served as a Government Whip from 1997 to 2001. He remains in the House.

Conclusion

The town of Louth has been served by twelve MPs since the creation of single-member seats in the county in 1885. In the 39 years from 1885 to 1924, it had seven MPs. Of these, only one – Robert Perks – was to serve more than ten years in the House of Commons. In the period from 1924 to the Parliament elected in 2005, it has had five MPs. Of these, three have each served more than twenty years in the House. The first period reflected a contest between the Liberals and the Conservatives in the seat, the Liberals holding the seat for most of the period but variously losing it to the Conservatives (in 1886, January 1910 and 1918). The second period reflects a period of Conservative hegemony. Louth has been in a constituency that has returned a Tory MP even at times of Labour landslides nationally (1945, 1966, 1997, and 2001). This has affected the nature of the challenge mounted by opposition parties and enabled MPs to build up long periods of service. What is noteworthy about the four Tory MPs who sat prior to Sir Peter Tapsell is that only one (Heneage) ceased to be an MP at a time when he wished to retire. What is remarkable about the current MP is that by the time of the next election – assuming a General Election in 2009 or 2010 – he will have amassed nearly fifty years of service in the House of Commons.

Notes

1. On the history of Lincolnshire constituencies up to 1820, see the various volumes published by the History of Parliament. The volume covering the most recent period up to 1820 is R G Thorne, *The House of Commons 1790-1820,* Vol. II: Constituencies Secker & Warburg, (1986).

2. The election results for each constituency in the period 1832 to 1918 are to be found in (*McCalmont's Parliamentary Poll Book of All Elections 1832-1918),* 8th edn. edited by J Vincent and M Stenton The Harvester Press (Brighton, 1971).

3. Robert Waller and Byron Criddle, *The Almanac of British Politics,* 5th edn. Routledge, (1996), p. 551.

4. (*The Times Guide to the House of Commons June 2001*) edited by Tim Austin and Tim Hames,Times Books, (2001), p. 196.

5. Waller and Criddle, *The Almanac of British Politics,* 5th edn., p. 550.

6. The memoirs of Sir Robert Williams Perk, cited in Henry Pelling, *Social Geography of British Elections 1885-1910,* Macmillan, (1967), p. 224.

7. Pelling, *Social Geography of British Elections 1885-1910,* p. 224.

8. Coalition candidates received a letter from the two party leaders, Lloyd George and Bonar Law, endorsing their candidatures. Former Prime Minister Herbert Asquith contemptuously dubbed the letter 'a coupon', a term derived from war-time ration books.

9. Chris Cook and John Ramsden, *By-Elections in British Politics,* Macmillan, (1973), pp. 17-18.

10. Melanie Phillips, *The Divided House: Women at Westminster,* Sidgwick & Jackson, (1980), p. 44.

11. Austin and Hames, *The Times Guide to the House of Commons June 2001,* p. 196.

12. Austin Mitchell, *Westminster Man,* Thames Methuen, (1982), p. 89.

13. See Philip Norton, 'The Constitutional Position of Parliamentary Private Secretaries', *Public Law,* Summer 1989, pp. 232-6.

14. Biographical data for MPs are to be found in Michael Stenton and Stephen Lees, *Who's Who of British Members of Parliament* (Brighton: The Harvester Press), Vol. II: 1886-1918 (1978), Vol. III: 1918-1945 (1979), Vol. IV: 1945-1979 (1981), as well as in the various *Times' Guides to the House of Commons* and the annual *Dod's Parliamentary Companion.*

15. The first woman to be elected, Countess Markiewicz, in 1918, was a Sinn Fein candidate and refused to take her seat.

16. Elizabeth Vallance, *Women in the House,* The Athlone Press, (1979), p. 27.

17. Paul Foot, *The Rise of Enoch Powell,* Harmondsworth: Penguin, (1969), p. 23.

18. Simon Heffer, *Like the Roman: The Life of Enoch Powell,* Phoenix, (1999), p. 360.

19. Robert Shepherd, *Enoch Powell: A Biography,* Hutchinson, (1996), p. 192.

20. Robert Shepherd, *Iain Macleod,* Hutchinson, (1994), p. 274.

21. Andrew Roth, *Heath and the Heathmen,* Routledge & Kegan Paul, (1972), p. 72.

22. Shepherd, *Iain Macleod,* p. 310.

22a.Michael Crick, *Jeffrey Archer: Stranger than Fiction,* Hamish Hamilton, (1995), pp. 140-6. My own recollection, as a member of the selection committee, differs in some respect from what Crick recounts.

23. Based on the author's recollections as a member of the selection committee.

24. Crick, *Jeffrey Archer,* p. 168.

25. Philip Norton, *Conservative Dissidents: Dissent within the Conservative Parliamentary Party 1970-74* (Temple Smith,

1978).

26. Philip Norton, *Dissension in the House of Commons 1945-74,* Macmillan, (1975).

27. Anthony Seldon, *Major: A Political Life* (1997), p. 122.

28. Andrew Roth, *Parliamentary Profiles,* 1979 edn. Parliamentary Profiles, (1979), p. 17.

29. Philip Norton, *Dissension in the House of Commons 1974-1979,* Clarendon Press, (Oxford, 1980), *passim.*

30. Tapsell is the 'by-passed anti-Heath deflater' referred to in Norton, *Conservative Dissidents,* p. 234.

31. Philip Norton, 'The Conservative Party from Thatcher to Major', *Britain at the Polls 1992,* edited by Anthony King, Chatham NJ: Chatham House Publishers (1992), p. 54.

32. He was not, though, among the most rebellious Tory MPs on the treaty: six of them voted against it more than 50 times each. See

Philip Cowley and Philip Norton, *Are Conservative MPs Revolting?* Research Paper 2/96, Hull University: Centre for Legislative Studies, (1996).

33. Andrew Roth and Byron Criddle, *Parliamentary Profiles: S-Z, 1997-2002* Parliamentary Profiles, (2000), pp. 2136-2142.

34. Philip Norton, 'The Parliamentary Party and Party Committees', *Conservative Century,* edited by Anthony Seldon and Stuart Ball, Oxford University Press, (Oxford, 1994), p. 117.

35. Tim Renton, *Chief Whip* London: Politico's, (2004), p. 97. Renton was responding to Michael Heseltine in 1990, when Heseltine was promoting Tapsell's name as a potential minister. Heseltine rated him highly; Renton did not.

36. House of Commons: Official Report *(Hansard),* 13 December 2006, col. 866.

Navigation Wharf, Sleaford (Drawn by Hilary Healey)

The Lincolnshire Naturalists' Union and the Geological Work of David Robinson

Roger Parsons

'Any fool can appreciate mountain scenery. It takes a man of discernment to appreciate the Fens.'
(Harry Godwin - pollen analyst - c. 1932)

An understanding of biological communities is the foundation for understanding ecosystems and the science of conservation. To know which species are present, one must be able to identify them. Over the lifetime of the Lincolnshire Naturalists' Union, local naturalists have researched and recorded the natural history of the county. Taxonomists have wrestled with identifications, changes of nomenclature, the discovery of new species and the changes in species number and composition within communities. Ecologists have monitored changing ecosystems.

Plants are the foundation of most ecosystems. As the primary producers, the base of food webs, they determine the animal life that is found in association with them. Therefore, in order to understand animal communities, one must first understand the plants which provide their food and habitats. To appreciate the factors which determine the composition of a plant community, one must understand the (quite literally) underlying geology, which in turn affects which plant communities will be found. So it would be true to say that every zoologist also needs to be a botanist and every botanist a geologist. It is no accident, therefore, that the Geological Section of the Lincolnshire Naturalists' Union (LNU) has been a key part of the organisation since its foundation in 1893.

We all owe a great debt to the heroes who kindled our early interests. Many people have shared their enthusiasms with me, life-long enthusiasms which have engaged, entertained and (on some occasions) employed me. A geography teacher encouraged my early interest in palaeontology. He was one of those great educators who would heap pupils into his car and drive miles to look for fossils or minerals. A child of the tropical oilfields, I spent happy hours trudging about with company geologists. Two events stand out from that time - the discovery of a large glyptodon preserved in pitch and geologists setting fire to natural gas at a mud volcano, with startling consequences.

The child is the father of the man. I went on to study zoology and later trained as a teacher, knowing there are few greater gifts one can receive or give than a passion for a subject. I feel certain that every reader will be able to offer a similar tribute to their mentors but today we are risk-averse, over-regulated and litigious in our thinking. Many teachers now eschew school trips, let alone the kind of private educational jaunts that punctuated my childhood and teens. The task of countering this trend falls to the junior wings of organisations like the Wildlife Trusts and scholarly enthusiasts like the members of the LNU.

Read any review of regional geology or natural history and you will be reading the names of the scholarly and passionate. Many are gone, but their work 'continueth, deep beyond their knowing'. David Robinson is one in a long line of these local heroes, but there can be few Lincolnshire geologists who have influenced and inspired others as he has done and continues to do. Through his life he has championed the cause for the preservation and conservation of geological sites within Lincolnshire, for without actual geological sites what value is scholarship and passion?

Sites of Special Scientific Interest are a matter of public record and most people are aware that such a listing and legal protection exists. Natural England explains the classification: 'SSSIs are the country's very best wildlife and geological sites. They include some of our most spectacular and beautiful habitats...' and the Natural England website[1] goes on to set out the rules, procedures and benefits of the scheme for anyone to read. One can even search for SSSIs through their database, where some 92 can be found for Lincolnshire.

Search their website for 'Regionally Important Geological Sites' (RIGS) and you will find the few RIGS which are also geological SSSIs but not the complete list. RIGS are selected according to the following criteria:

  value of a site for educational purposes in life-long learning;

  value of a site for study by both amateur and professional Earth scientists;

  historical value of a site from an Earth science perspective;

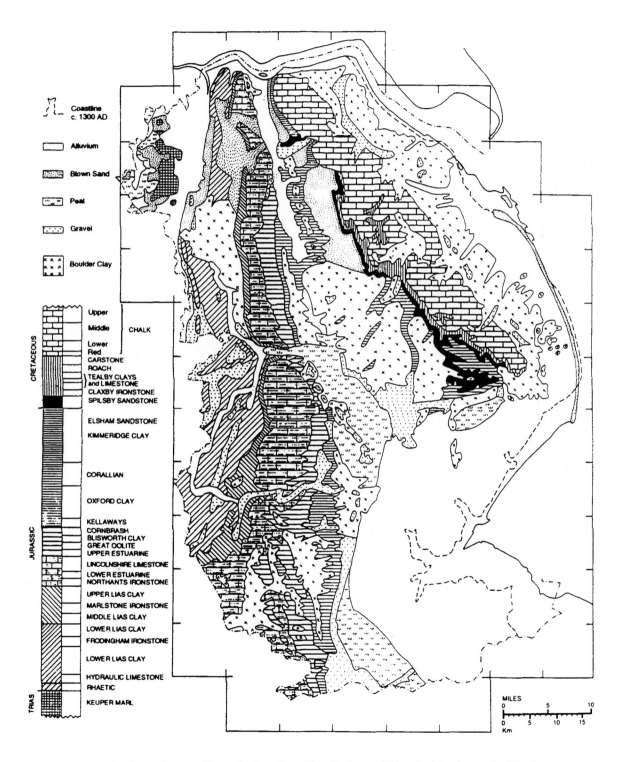

*Fig. 1: Geological map of Lincolnshire from The Geology of Lincolnshire (second edition)
by H H Swinnerton and P E Kent, published in 1976*

aesthetic value of a site from an Earth science perspective.

Natural England's introduction goes on to say: 'RIGS do not have formal statutory protection in the same way as SSSIs. However, the RIGS groups notify the local planning authorities of the RIGS which have been declared in their area and encourage the local authority to protect the RIGS through the planning process. For example, RIGS can be listed on local authorities' development plans.'

A working list of 91 candidate RIGS for Lincolnshire and South Humberside includes some well-known nature reserves belonging to the Lincolnshire Wildlife Trust (e.g. Red Hill near Goulceby and Ancaster Valley).[2] Other sites range from exposures such as cuttings and quarries to geomorphological sites such as valleys or dune systems. Details of the Lincolnshire Wildlife Trust's reserves are available on the World Wide Web.[3]

Whilst Lincolnshire is not as flat as reputation makes out, much of the county's geology is hidden underground. Exposures are a precious and endangered resource for research and education. Landforms can be adversely affected by unsympathetic treatment. Many important geological sites are privately owned and therefore inaccessible to the public, hence the sensitivity of any list. The sites are, nevertheless, a very important part of the county's heritage, one to be protected and conserved for future study. The work of David Robinson and his colleagues on the RIGS Steering Group of the Lincolnshire Wildlife Trust is a vital on-going process in the identification, protection and conservation of such sites, an endeavour we should all recognise, support and encourage.

The Lincolnshire Naturalists' Union was founded in 1893 and thus has over a hundred years' experience and information about Lincolnshire's wildlife and geology. In that time members have seen the county change almost beyond recognition. Those changes have affected our wildlife and over 600 field meetings all over the county have tracked and recorded this change.

The LNU is the only amateur Natural History Society covering the whole of the old county of Lincolnshire. Members study, record, hold meetings, supply information, publish books, exhibit, discuss and learn. Most LNU members also belong to organisations such as Wildlife Trusts or specialist natural history societies, so the Union is something of a hub for a much wider network. The majority of members are amateur in the sense that they may

Fig. 2: David Robinson with the late Jack Houghton on a geology field trip at the Lincolnshire Naturalists' Union Centenary meeting at Rimac. (Photo: C Rieser)

have little or no formal scientific training or qualifications. However, following the fine tradition of amateur scientific endeavour which is such an important part of British research, LNU members strive to achieve a professional standard of scholarship in their field. Most would take the view that reliable data is the only foundation on which to base decisions about conservation and environmental protection.

At the time of writing LNU membership numbers 140, with some 670 naturalists from the LNU and other organisations subscribing to a free weekly email bulletin detailing the observations and reports of the previous week. Information from the bulletin supplements more conventional reporting of biological records.

David Robinson served as Honorary Secretary to the LNU from 1966 – 1971 and was Editor of *Transactions* (the LNU Journal) from 1966 to 1976.

The key geological review of the county is the Lincolnshire Naturalists' Union publication 'The Geology

Field of Interest	Recorder
Freshwater Algae	Dr B Brierley
Fungi	Mr K Rowland
Geology	Mr D N Robinson
Lichens and Mosses	Prof. M Seaward
Plants	Mrs I Weston
Vertebrates	
Bats (mammals sub-section)	Mrs A Faulkner
Birds	Mr Steve Keightley
Mammals, Reptiles and Amphibians	Mr C Manning
Invertebrates	
Ants, Bees and Wasps	Dr M Archer
Beetles	Dr R Key
Butterflies	Mr A Binding
Dragonflies	Mr I Cappitt
Flies	Mr A Godfrey
Freshwater invertebrates	Mr R Chadd
Grasshoppers and Crickets	Mr B Redman
Hoverflies	Mrs J Mears
Moths	Mr C Smith
Plant Galls	Mr G Clayton
Sawflies	Dr D Sheppard
Shield Bugs	Mrs A Binding
Slugs and Snails	Mr E J Redshaw
Spiders	Mrs A Binding
Woodlice, Centipedes and Millipedes	Mr N Pike

Table 1: Lincolnshire Recorders with field of interest

of Lincolnshire'[4]. The second edition, which was edited by David Robinson, is still in print. The bibliography is extensive and revealing when read with Professor Mark Seaward's paper on the geologists of Lincolnshire[5].

David Robinson became Secretary of the Geological section in 1972 (still in office) and was LNU President from 1983 to1984. He identifies three landmark dates in Lincolnshire geological conservation.

1990 - The Nature Conservancy Council launched RIGS (Regionally Important Geological/ Geomorphological Sites) as the strategy for Earth Science Conservation in Great Britain

1991 - The Lincolnshire Wildlife Trust launched a RIGS steering group, convened by David himself, one of the first such groups to be established in the country. This has now evolved into a trust 'Team' with a volunteer RIGS officer.

1992 - 'Geological Conservation' published in the Trust's 'Conservation Management' set out an outline of the stratigraphical coverage of RIGS.

In his presidential address he spoke on The Theddlethorpe-Saltfleetby Coastline. Christine Rieser, current President of the LNU writes:

'[This was] a subject on which he has a wide knowledge. In the [LNU] centenary year he led a meeting here and gave a most interesting account of how this coastline was formed and how it has changed over the years.

Several years ago much damage was done to the sea bank off Huttoft, washing away the car terrace. To strengthen the sea defences, huge boulders were brought over from Norway in barges. These had to be carried in across the beach using giant tractors. In front of the car terrace is the ancient submerged forest. David realised that to cross this with tractors would destroy it and campaigned most strongly to save it. As a result artificial blocks were manufactured and put in from the landward side – the forest was thus saved.'

David Robinson's contribution to the understanding and conservation of Lincolnshire's geology is not limited to scholarship, but extends to his encouragement of public understanding and enjoyment of the geology and landforms of the county. Evidence for this is to be found in his prodigious output, a listing of which may be found in the Bibliography at the start of the volume.

For further information, the reader is referred to the LNU's publication: *The Geology of Lincolnshire*, which is still available. This can be obtained from the Publications Officer, Lincolnshire Naturalists' Union, via the LNU website.[6]

Notes:

1. Natural England website: www.naturalengland.org.uk
2. David Robinson. *pers. comm.*
3. Lincolnshire Wildlife Trust website: www.lincstrust.org.uk
4. H H Swinnerton and P E Kent, *The Geology of Lincolnshire – from the Humber to the Wash*. Second Edition Revised P E Kent. (edited by David N Robinson) Lincolnshire Naturalists' Union – Lincolnshire Natural History Bulletin No 7 (1949, second edition 1981)
5. Prof M R D Seaward, Geology in Lincolnshire: an account of the activities of the Lincolnshire Naturalists' Union Geological Section, in *The Mercian Geologist* vol. 1 No. 2, 1965.
6. Lincolnshire Naturalists' Union website: www.lnu.org

Thomas Linley: A Lost Lincolnshire Link

Valerie Purton

'Das Land ohne Musik' ('the land without music') is a scathing label for nineteenth century England. Had it not been for a disaster in Lincolnshire in the 1780s, we might well have had a very different reputation – in fact, we might have been celebrating in 2006 the 250th anniversary of the birth of an English composer ranked by the whole world alongside Mozart and Beethoven – Thomas Linley.

Born three months after Mozart, in May 1756 in Bath, Tom Linley, like Wolfgang Amadeus, was a child prodigy. He gave his first violin concert in Bristol at the age of seven; at ten he performed as Puck, singing, dancing and playing the violin at Covent Garden Theatre in London. Here he attracted the notice of the Duke and Duchess of Ancaster and it was their patronage which allowed him, at the age of twelve, to travel to Leghorn and on to Florence to study with the world-famous Italian violinist, Nardini. It was in Florence that he met the young Mozart and the two boys became bosom friends. Charles Burney records that 'The *Tommasino*, as he is called, and the Little Mozart, are talked of all over Italy as the most promising geniuses of this age.'[1] Returning to England, Tom threw himself into composition, producing many scores for soloists, chorus and orchestra, including the music for Sheridan's comic opera, *The Duenna*, the anthem 'Let God Arise', oratorios such as *The Shakespeare Ode* and *The Song of Moses*, a violin concerto and music for Sheridan's production of *The Tempest* at Drury Lane. Scholes's *Oxford Companion to Music* suggests that the song from that production, 'O bid your faithful Ariel fly', is perhaps his best-known work[2]. By the age of twenty two, in 1778, he had a substantial body of music behind him, surpassed only by that of the twenty two year old Mozart (though the latter had yet to write *any* of the operas, piano concertos, chamber music or sacred music for which we now acclaim him).

On the morning of Wednesday 5 August 1778, young Tom Linley was making his annual visit, with two of his sisters, to his loyal patrons, the Duke and Duchess of Ancaster, at their family seat, Grimsthorpe Castle, near Bourne. Obviously a lively, self-confident fellow, he insisted on going sailing on the Castle's boating lake, part of a magnificent Park which had been redesigned by Lancelot ('Capability') Brown seven years earlier. What followed was recorded vividly by the *Bath Chronicle*:

'Mr Linley…Mr Olivarez and another person agreed to go on the lake on a sailing boat, which Mr Linley said he could manage. But no sooner had they sailed into the middle of the lake than a sudden squall of wind sprung up and overset the boat; however they all hung by the masts and the rigging for some time until Mr Linley said he found it was vain to wait for assistance, and therefore, though he had his boots and greatcoat on, he was determined to swim to shore, for which purpose he quitted his hold, but had not swam above 100 yards before he sunk…. The Duchess…despatched several servants…to take another boat to their assistance, but which unfortunately came only in time enough to take up Mr Olivarez and his companion, not being able to find the body of Mr Linley for more than 40 minutes.'[3]

The shock was recorded across the country in the burgeoning national and provincial press, including the *Stamford Mercury*, which, stoutly ignoring the national reputation of the young victim, insisted instead on his Lincolnshire connection. To the *Mercury*, Linley is simply

Fig. 1: Portrait of Thomas Linley by Gainsborough
(by kind permission of the Trustees of Dulwich Picture Gallery)

'a Musician to his Grace the Duke of Ancaster'! Conscious perhaps of the potential damage to the Duke's reputation for hospitality, the *Mercury* does not mention the delay in finding the body and lays the blame for the accident squarely upon poor Tom himself for (by implication) acting imprudently. Seeking for what would now be called the 'human interest' angle, it also invents two destitute parents for him. The 'aged father', Thomas Linley the Elder, was in fact at the time of the tragedy at the height of his powers: forty-five years old, he had become the previous year Music Director of the Drury Lane Theatre in London. His three daughters, Maria, Mary and Elizabeth, were all celebrated professional singers. By setting the *Mercury*'s account against that of the national *Morning Chronicle* we can already see, at the very dawn of the British Press, that glaring contrast between provincial and metropolitan concerns which remains largely unchanged today. Here is the *Stamford Mercury*'s story:

'Yesterday a most unfortunate accident happened at Grimsthorpe: - Three persons were in a sailing vessel on the water in the park there, and it being apprehended the vessel would sink, one of the company (a Musician to his Grace the Duke of Ancaster) jumped into the water to endeavour to save himself, but was unfortunately drowned. His body was soon taken out of the water, and the methods usually tried to restore persons apparently drowned to life, were industriously used, but without effect. The death of the above person is much to be lamented, as he was the chief supporter of an aged father and

mother. – The other two persons prudently remained in the vessel, which gave time for others to come to their relief, and their lives were saved.'[4]

The *Morning Chronicle*, in contrast, reported on 11 August:

'On Wednesday last Mr. Thomas Linley…fell into a lake belonging to his Grace the Duke of Ancaster…and was unfortunately drowned; he remained under water full forty minutes, so that every effort made to restore him to life proved ineffectual. This accident has deprived the profession to which he belonged of one of its principal ornaments, and society of a very accomplished and valuable member.'[5]

The impact among the musical community was profound. King George III himself commissioned four memorial volumes of Linley's music. The drowning was seen as a sad, unnecessary and untimely end to a brilliant career. Thomas Linley had been the star of an exceptionally musical family. He had toured the length and breadth of Britain with his composer-father and three famous soprano sisters, and was a national favourite. It was during his apprenticeship to Dr William Boyce, Master of the King's Musick, that he had been sent to Italy to study and it was then, in Florence on 3 April 1770, that he had met Wolfgang Amadeus Mozart, also fourteen years old, and his father, Leopold. Leopold's letter to his wife records:

'In Florence we came upon a young Englishman…This boy plays most beautifully…The two boys performed one after the other throughout the evening, constantly embracing each other…On the

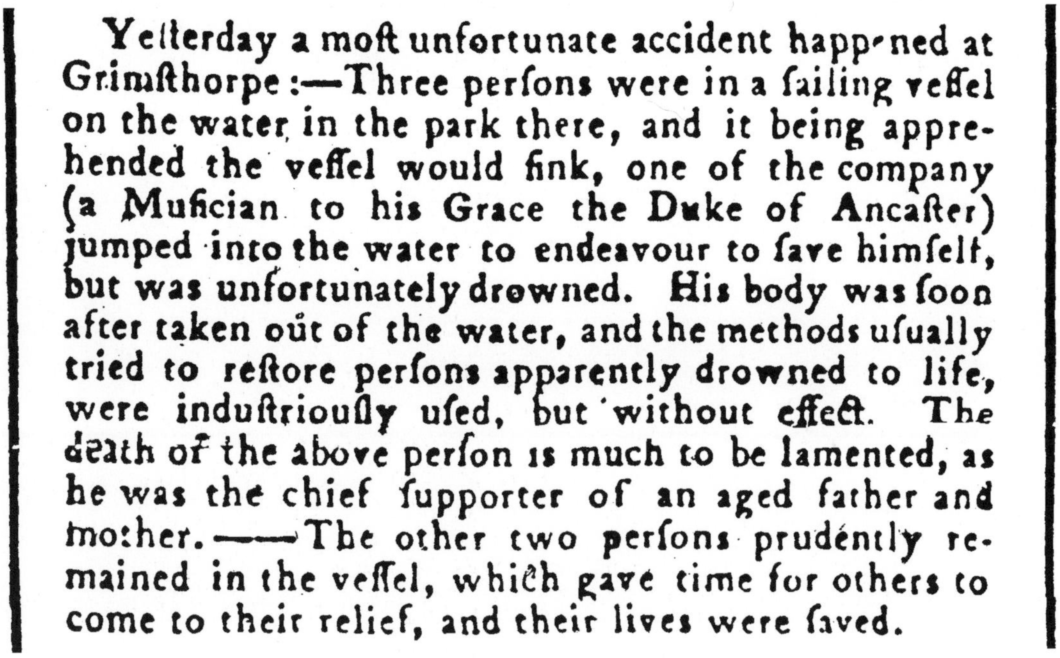

Yesterday a most unfortunate accident happened at Grimsthorpe:—Three persons were in a sailing vessel on the water in the park there, and it being apprehended the vessel would sink, one of the company (a Musician to his Grace the Duke of Ancaster) jumped into the water to endeavour to save himself, but was unfortunately drowned. His body was soon after taken out of the water, and the methods usually tried to restore persons apparently drowned to life, were industriously used, but without effect. The death of the above person is much to be lamented, as he was the chief supporter of an aged father and mother.——The other two persons prudently remained in the vessel, which gave time for others to come to their relief, and their lives were saved.

Fig. 2. The report of Linley's death, as it appeared in the Lincoln, Rutland and Stamford Mercury of 6 August 1778

following day, the …charming boy had his violin brought to our rooms and played the whole afternoon, Wolfgang accompanying him on his own…On the next day the two boys played in turn the whole afternoon, not like two boys but like men! Little Tommaso…wept bitter tears because we were leaving on the following day. But he called on us at nine o'clock in the morning and gave Wolfgang with many embraces the following poem which he had commissioned Signora Corilla to compose for him the previous evening. Then he accompanied the carriage as far as the city gate. I should like you to have witnessed the scene…'[6].

It was on an early visit to London, most probably when he played Puck in *The Fairy Favour*, a masque by Thomas Hull, at Covent Garden Theatre, that Tom had enchanted the music-loving Peregrine Bertie and his wife Mary (née Panton), the third Duke and Duchess of Ancaster, who were very much part of the Royal circle. The Duke was a Lord Great Chamberlain and the Duchess, Mistress of the Queen's Robes; the Royal Family (who are known to have been at the masque) were equally taken with Tom and with his beautiful sister Elizabeth (later Mrs Richard Brinsley Sheridan). It was the Ancasters' generous financial support that enabled him to travel in Italy; in return, he visited them every summer at Grimsthorpe.

Grimsthorpe Castle, on the southern edge of the great Lincolnshire forest, dates from the twelfth century and stands in a 3000 acre park. The manor was granted to the tenth Baron Willoughby de Eresby by Henry VIII in 1516. His successors were enthusiasts for the Reformation and were consequently persecuted by Queen Mary. His grandson, Robert Bertie, became the first Earl of Lindsey, having retired to Lincolnshire where he drained and reclaimed fens lying between Kyme Eau and the Glen. In 1626 he was made Lord Great Chamberlain and in 1636, Lord High Admiral of England. A Royalist, he died of his wounds after the Battle of Edgehill in 1642. The eighteenth century saw a further flowering of the family, with the ennoblement of the sixteenth Baron, another Robert Bertie, as the first Duke of Ancaster and Kesteven in 1715. To celebrate his ennoblement, he commissioned his friend, Sir John Vanbrugh, to build the magnificent North Front of the castle. (This was to be Vanbrugh's final work.) His grandson, Thomas Linley's patron, the third Duke of Ancaster, in or around 1745 employed the Spalding drainage engineer, John Grundy Jnr to turn a

Fig. 3. The 'great water' at Grimsthorpe Castle upon which Thomas Linley met his death
(by kind permission of Lady Willoughby de Eresby)

series of seventeenth century fishponds into a landscaped 'great water', grand enough to complement the Vanbrugh front. It was in that 'great water' (which still exists) that Thomas Linley met his death[7].

Quite apart from the mystery surrounding the tragedy, there is considerable mystery surrounding Thomas Linley's burial. His funeral service was in Lincolnshire on 11 August and local tradition has it that his distraught patrons insisted on his being buried in the Ancaster family vault in Edenham Church near Grimsthorpe. He is not, however, recorded in the Parish Register of Burials in Edenham Church and all the coffins in the vault have now been identified. His is not among them. There remains the possibility that, as the death took place in summer, Thomas Linley's coffin may have rested in the vault until a lead-lined coffin could be obtained and cooler weather came. It would, of course, have been impossible to bear the body any distance by horse and cart in midsummer. There is no other record of his burial, not even in his home city of Bath – and this for a young man who was, in his time, a national and even international celebrity[8].

In 2006, amid world-wide celebrations to mark the 250th anniversary of Mozart's birth, at least one festival took place in Europe to mark the Mozart/Linley connection and a Gala Concert was held at Dulwich Picture Gallery in west London, in the presence of his descendant Viscount Linley, to commemorate Thomas Linley himself. Contemporary comments were collected in the programme notes, including Mozart's own reaction to his friend's death, recorded several years after the event by the tenor Michael Kelly:

'[Mozart] conversed with me a good deal about Thomas Linley…with whom he was intimate at Florence, and spoke of him with great affection. He said that Linley was a true genius, and he felt that, had he lived, he would have been one of the greatest ornaments of the musical world.'[9]

The county of Lincolnshire has had more than its share of drowning tragedies but certainly never one which was to have such a profound impact on the future of English cultural life. There is a poignant and, as far as I know, previously unnoticed postscript which, for me, suggests something about the depth of Lincolnshire hospitality and the sense of absolute despair which must have been occasioned in the Ancaster family when, through no fault of their own, that hospitality resulted in tragedy. The *Annual Register*, set up in the early 1770s to record political and national events, in its summary of Notable Deaths of 1778, ignores the passing of young Thomas Linley. However, for 12 August, the day after Linley's funeral, it does record the death of '[t]he most noble Peregrine Bertie, Duke of Ancaster and Kesteven, Marquis and Earl of Lindsay [sic], Baron Willoughby de Eresby, and Hereditary Lord Great Chamberlain of England, in the 65th year of his age.' It is painful but logical to conclude that this noble and hospitable Duke's death must have been hastened by the unexpectedly tragic consequence of his generous patronage.

I would like to thank Lady Willoughby de Eresby and Jean Howard for their kind help in the preparation of this article.

Notes

1   P A Scholes ed., *Charles Burney: An 18C Musical Tour in France and Italy* (O.U.P. 1959) p184.
2   P A Scholes, *The Oxford Companion to Music* 9th edition (OUP 1965) p581.
3   quoted in Andrew Edwards, *Programme for the Gala Concert to celebrate the 250th anniversary of the birth of Thomas Linley the Younger* (Dulwich Picture Gallery, 22 May 2006), p13.
4   *Lincoln, Rutland and Stamford Mercury* Thursday 6 August 1778 p4/col 2.
5   quoted on http://www.rslade.co.uk/linley/index.html
6   Leopold Mozart, *Letters* quoted in Andrew Edwards pp11-12.
7   *pers. comm.* Lady Willoughby de Eresby.
8   *pers. comm.* Lady Willoughby de Eresby.
9   Michael Kelly, *Reminiscences,* ed. R Fiske, (1826) p112.

Some Brick Kilns and Brick Makers of East Lincolnshire

Ken Redmore

Introduction

The technology of brick making took a significant step forward in the middle years of the nineteenth century with the introduction of permanent kilns of a standard, reliable design.

This paper looks at four surviving kilns of this period in east Lincolnshire: at Baumber, Farlesthorpe, Stixwould and Sutton on Sea. These four east Lincolnshire examples, though closely related to the common Scotch kiln, are of a type rarely found outside the county. They are very similar in basic design to each other but also differ in one or two respects. It is not known who constructed these kilns or how many others of this type were built but have not survived.

The succession of men who worked at the four brickyards reflects changes in the occupation of brick making that occurred during the second half of the nineteenth century. Before that period the skilled brick maker still commonly travelled from site to site making bricks in clamps or in simple kilns on the building site. His labourers were usually employed on a part-time, seasonal basis. By the end of the century permanent brickyards with kilns supported resident brick makers who supplied bricks to the local area. Many brickworks were owned by builders or were bought as business investments.

The Process of Brick Making at the East Lincolnshire Sites

Clay was dug from the surrounding brick pits by hand in the winter and left in heaps to be tempered by weather and frost. In the spring it was passed through a pug or clay mill to create uniform plastic clay of the required consistency. Hand-made bricks were moulded by hand in wooden moulds (usually lined or edged in brass or iron) to create brick-shaped blocks. These 'green' bricks were then stacked in well-spaced rows in large open hacks or drying sheds (Fig. 1).

The main period of firing the kiln was in the summer between May and September. The kiln was loaded with approximately 30,000 bricks or maybe a combination of bricks in the lower part of the kiln, with roof tiles and drainage pipes higher up. The bricks were carefully laid in

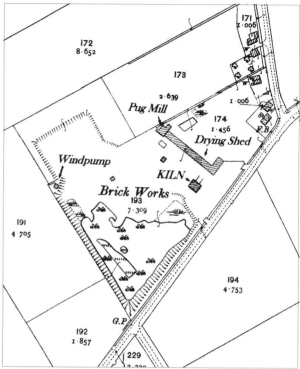

Fig. 1: Brick works at Sutton on Sea, 1906
(Photocopy from 25" OS map 1906, annotated)

a varied series of courses, a precise arrangement necessary to create a network of fire channels between the bricks, thus ensuring uniform firing. Coal, the preferred fuel, was burnt at the eight fire-holes along each side of the kiln. Most kilns had simple firing sheds which provided shelter for the coal and the stoker. These were lean-to structures, sometimes open-sided, approximately three metres wide and running the full length of each kiln side. The complex process of firing and cooling to control brick quality and colour took about eight days (five for heating, three for cooling).

The Kilns

Baumber

The Baumber kiln (TF 195752) was built *c*.1870, possibly to replace an earlier kiln, and is situated at the extreme western edge of the parish on land formerly owned by the Livesey family of Stourton Hall. As is the case for

Fig. 2: Baumber kiln: from the south, 2006 (K Redmore)

all four kilns, it is constructed in local brick (red, in this instance) with fire-brick used only to line the fire-holes. The kiln was operated until the mid 1890s. In 1986 and 1987 extensive restoration work created a new roof with an array of small vent chimneys, lean-to firing sheds and a pair of openings or wickets, one above the other, on the front (SW) elevation. These changes were designed by the foremost authority on historic kiln features at the time, but it is not clear to what extent they were speculative (Fig. 2).

Farlesthorpe

The kiln at Farlesthorpe (TF 480739), built in local yellow brick in about 1855, is coincidentally in one of the few villages where the Livesey family, minor gentry, owners of the Baumber site, also had an interest. The kiln was in use until about 1905, after which time it was probably used as a simple agricultural store almost up to the present day. At some point in the twentieth century a wide opening with sliding door was created on the south-

west end of the kiln and the firing sheds abutting either side were re-roofed and restored; they too have served some agricultural purpose. The internal structure of the kiln is currently quite sound; the external roof is covered in vegetation, including tree saplings. The earthen ramp to the wicket (opening) at the rear of the kiln (NE) was removed in 2006 (Figs. 3 and 4).

A row of red bricks along the sill of the wicket at the rear of the kiln stamped 'KINSLEY' is not part of the original structure. The kiln at Kinsley near Wakefield in West Yorkshire first operated in 1903 shortly before the Farlesthorpe kiln was last fired, so these bricks were presumably used to repair or modify this part of the structure.

Stixwould

The Stixwould kiln (TF 185664) was probably built in the late-1850s, and it was from here that red bricks were provided for building almost every house, farmstead and

Fig. 3: Farlesthorpe kiln: north-east elevation, 2006 (K Redmore)

other building in the village. (The Turnor family of Stoke Rochford and Panton owned the whole of Stixwould in the nineteenth century, as well as the kiln itself.) The last bricks were fired in the mid 1890s and the kiln and its associated buildings then became part of a farm small-holding. When the Turnor estate was sold in 1911, the tenant bought both the former kiln and the brickyard cottage alongside, which had been rented from the estate. During the course of the twentieth century the former ancillary buildings (drying shed, pug-mill) were removed from the site and one end of the kiln was modified to convert it into a store or workshop. The footprint of the building on the 1905 edition of the 25 inch O S map suggests that there were firing sheds on either side of the kiln. Like the Farlesthorpe kiln, the internal structure remains largely intact, though vegetation on the roof is becoming increasingly invasive (Fig. 5).

Sutton on Sea

The kiln at Sutton on Sea (TF 504808) was constructed at about the same time as the other three kilns but was in use for a much longer period, until just after 1930. At one point later in the twentieth century it served as a workshop for making firelighters; most recently it has become a simple store on a caravan park. This kiln, in bright red brick, is closest to its original condition; it has neither been restored

Fig. 4: Farlesthorpe kiln: interior, 2005 (K Redmore)

Fig. 5: Stixwould kiln: from the south, c.1975 (D N Robinson)

Fig. 6: Sutton on Sea kiln from the west, 2006 (K Redmore)

nor modified. The shape and size of the kiln on the 1906 O S map suggests that there were firing sheds here too, and there are brick paved areas on either side of the kiln today which indicate their extent. Some vegetation on the roof and over one end is beginning to threaten the building but the general condition of external brickwork appears to be sound (Fig. 6).

There is an additional feature of interest on the site at Sutton. A small wind pump was erected during the nineteenth century to drain water from the clay workings. Presumably the water table is relatively high at this location and the brick pit would have been prone to flooding.

The East Lincolnshire Kiln

The four kilns are correctly described as vaulted updraught intermittent kilns. The enclosed or vaulted roof is what differentiates them from the much more common Scotch kiln. Combustion of fuel occurs at the base of the kiln and hot gases pass through the bricks by updraught. The process of making bricks is intermittent rather than continuous; the kiln is operated on a loading/heating/cooling/unloading cycle.

The four east Lincolnshire kilns differ in a number of respects, apart from variations in brick colour and state of preservation. The Sutton and Stixwould kilns are constructed in English bond; the other two are in English garden wall bond. Only Farlesthorpe is without buttresses but is constructed with massive plain walls. Each kiln is extensively reinforced with tie-rods and timbers, though these vary between kilns. There is evidence that all four had attached firing sheds. The large difference in wickets between the kilns is discussed below.

The interior space of each kiln is very similar. Internal dimensions are as follows:

	Baumber	Farles-thorpe	Stixwould	Sutton on Sea
Length	8.05m	8.14m	8.00m	8.00m
Width (at floor level)	3.00m	3.00m	3.23m	2.88m
Height (to apex)	4.90m	4.59m	4.40m	4.95m

Firebricks have been used only to line the fire-holes and there are variations in the way they are incorporated in this element of the structure. (The source of the firebricks is unknown; they would not have been made locally.) The

vaulted roofs are each constructed in similar fashion using header bond, but the number and arrangement of vent holes in the roofs differ. The principal vents at the side of the kiln are immediately above fire-holes at Farlesthorpe, whereas, perhaps more logically, they are staggered between fire-holes at the other three kilns. There are eight central vent holes at Farlesthorpe, nine at Baumber and Stixwould, and eighteen at Sutton on Sea (Fig. 7)[1].

The Wickets

Loading and unloading the kiln was a lengthy process. Bricks were brought from the drying sheds in hack barrows (sturdy open-sided wheelbarrows) and wheeled into the kiln through the wickets (openings) at the ends of the kiln. In order to fill the kiln to the top, each kiln had two wickets, one at ground level and one in a higher position. When the lower part of the kiln had been filled, access was made through the higher wicket either via a permanent earthen ramp where the wicket was at the opposite end of the kiln, or along a makeshift ramp of planks where the wicket was immediately above the lower one. Prior to firing, a temporary infill of bricks and clay would be used to seal the wickets.

The positioning or design of the wickets is markedly different in each of the four kilns. At Baumber the wickets are one above the other on the SW end of the kiln; they were reconstructed in the 1986 to 1987 restoration of the kiln. The other three kilns each have wickets at opposite ends, though the shape of the wicket is different in each case. Both wickets at Sutton on Sea survive, but the earthen ramp to the higher wicket on the NE end has been removed. The ground level wicket at Farlesthorpe was lost when the SW end of the kiln was converted into a large door opening. The other wicket remains at this kiln but the ramp was removed in 2006. At Stixwould the ground level wicket in the NW end was bricked up when the kiln was converted into an agricultural building – perhaps because of the opening's awkward shape and size. The second wicket at a higher position in the opposite end of this kiln was completely destroyed together with any external ramp when a conventional door and window were inserted (Figs 8 to 12).

The Brick Makers

The story of the brick makers is most simply told at Stixwould, where for about 45 years the kiln on the north-east edge of the village produced red bricks, tiles

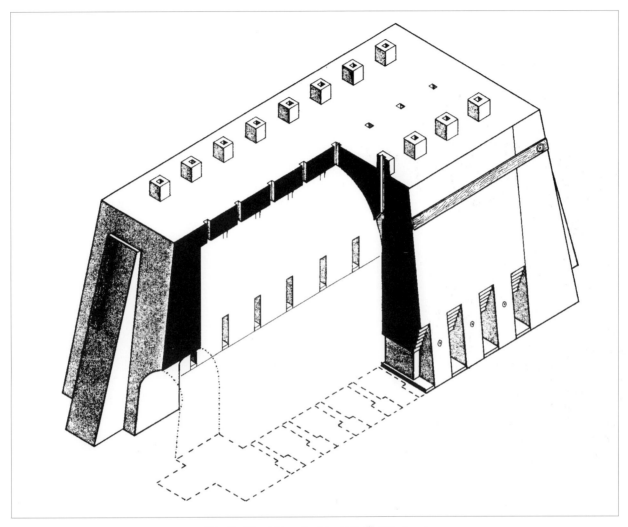

Fig. 7: 'East Lincolnshire' kiln[1] *(K Redmore)*

and drain pipes for the Turnor estate. Not a single brick maker was recorded here in the 1841 census; ten years later there were no fewer than eight brick and tile makers plus two labourers. This coincided with the beginning of the rebuilding of the village over a thirty year period from about 1845, as indicated by the dated plaques on houses and farmsteads. It is tempting to assume that the new kiln was built at this time, i.e. 1845 to 1850, but a date close to 1860 is much more likely. (Regrettably, apart from the rent books, which give limited information, the Turnor estate records for this period have not survived.)

From 1859 William Parker was the principal brick maker in Stixwould, having previously worked at Langworth for a short period. He remained at the Stixwould kiln until his death in 1893 at the age of 77, from which time the kiln was no longer fired. Parker was born at Fenny Stratford in the Buckinghamshire brick making area, which intriguingly is also close to his landlord Turnor's ancestral home. When he first moved to Stixwould, he was joined for a short time by his younger brother James (who was later brick maker at Edlington Moor, South Reston and Baumber); later William's own sons John and James worked with him.

The names of Hutchinson and Jordan are associated with brick making at the Baumber kiln during the forty or so years of its operation. Richard Hutchinson was the brick maker on site in 1841, thirty years before the new kiln is thought to have been built. Ten years later Crispin Hutchinson, son of Richard, was the only brickyard worker

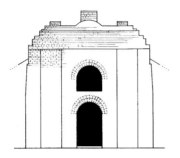

Fig. 8: Baumber kiln:
SW elevation (K Redmore)

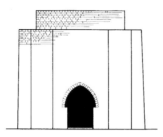

Fig. 9: Stixwould kiln:
NW elevation (K Redmore)

Fig. 10: Sutton on Sea kiln:
SW elevation (K Redmore)

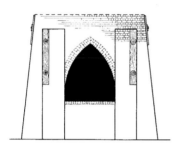

Fig. 11: Sutton on Sea kiln:
NE elevation (K Redmore)

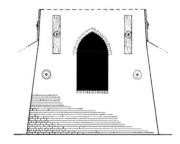

Fig. 12: Farlesthorpe kiln:
NE elevation (K Redmore)

recorded at Baumber, whilst Richard's wife, Charlotte, was one of the eight brick makers listed at nearby Stixwould. None of the directories for the period 1850 to 1870 mentions a brick maker and most unfortunately the 1861 census record for the parish is lost. By the 1871 census, the next available record, the brickyard provided occupation for three brick makers: Richard Hutchinson, James Parker (brother of William Parker of Stixwould), and George Bourn (one of four Bourns who had been making bricks at Stixwould in 1851). This is probably about the time when the kiln was built. Richard Hutchinson continued as brick maker in Baumber for a short time longer; his son Crispin meantime had become brick maker first at South Reston and then at neighbouring Great Carlton in the 1860s and 1870s.

In the mid 1870s William Jordan and his two sons, William and Thomas, took over the Baumber kiln. They had previously worked in brickyards in Prospect Street, Horncastle, but the move to Baumber was not a lasting success for the family. William senior died within ten years and for a while his widow and William junior continued

with brick making alongside farming. The 1891 census does not record their brick making activity at all, though it is probable that the kiln was still occasionally fired until the middle of the decade before finally closing.

The excellent brick making clay at Farlesthorpe, close to the town of Alford, was known and exploited long before the census returns in 1851 recorded a brick maker, William Evison, assisted by his two sons and his son-in-law. The potential of this site was fully realised *c*.1855 when William Spalding, master brick maker, took over the site. This is very likely the date of the building of the new kiln. Spalding retained ownership until about 1871, but with his interests from time to time in at least three other brickyards (Sutton on Sea, Hogsthorpe, South Reston), he exercised probably no more than a supervisory role. At the time of the 1871 census, when he was living at the South Reston brickyard, William Spalding employed ten men and three boys, of whom three of the brick makers and one of the boys were at Farlesthorpe.

In the following year the Farlesthorpe kiln was taken over by Edward Hasnip, builder and joiner of Alford, and it was to remain with the Hasnip family until about 1900. The Hasnips had an office in West Street, Alford, and used the distinctive yellow Farlesthorpe bricks in many building projects in the town. They employed a foreman to run the brick making operation at Farlesthorpe, and the census records indicate that there was usually at least one other brick maker employed at the kiln. For the last five years of the brickyard's operation until its closure in about 1905, Walter Forman, local farmer and Alford RDC dike-reeve, ran the kiln as part of a brick and tile business.

The brickyard at Sutton on Sea was the largest of the four and, as noted above, it operated until the 1930s. It is not known when brick making started here but the first detailed UK census of 1841 records two brick makers: William Spalding and William Barton. Spalding stayed at the Sutton site until the 1860s, i.e. until about the time the new kiln was built. It was his son, William, recorded as a tile maker journeyman at Sutton in 1851, who later became master brick maker at Farlesthorpe, South Reston and Hogsthorpe. (Thomas Spalding, from another branch of the Spalding family and, like the William Spaldings, originating in north Lincolnshire, had been making bricks at Hogsthorpe in the 1850s.)

In a similar way to Farlesthorpe, the Sutton brickyard was taken on as a business venture in about 1870. Each of a succession of owner/investors employed master brick makers to manage the day to day work of the brickyard. First Schofield Dauber took ownership, to be followed a decade later by John Motson Thompson, builder and brick maker of Grays Road, Louth, whose business employed a total of sixteen men and three boys. After his death two of Thompson's sons continued running the brickyard before selling out in about 1896 to William Haddon Owen of Little Grimsby Hall, later Louth. Owen was a Louth solicitor and the Superintendent Registrar of Births, Deaths and Marriages, but also a businessman. For the final few years of its life, from 1922 to about 1930, the brickworks became the Sutton on Sea Brick & Tile Company, with Arthur Cox as manager. Its heyday was 1880 to 1914, when the small coastal village, with its new railway, grew to become a significant seaside resort. Today, rows of red brick villas in Sutton on Sea are a fine tribute to the local kiln and its brick makers.

Conclusions

It is not known for certain how the 'East Lincolnshire' kiln originated and why it is mainly confined to Lincolnshire.

Probably it was developed from the Scotch kiln in order to achieve better control of combustion and hence more uniform brick quality.

The four surviving examples suggest that each kiln was based on an accepted standard layout and was constructed using local bricks with some features (e.g. vents, wickets) modified to suit the preferences of the local brick maker.

It is known that a large number of kilns were built in Lincolnshire in the second half of the nineteenth century; perhaps many of these were of the 'East Lincolnshire' type. For example, the movements of the master brick makers to South Reston and Hogsthorpe, mentioned in the account above, suggest that such kilns were located in those two villages. Other 'East Lincolnshire' kilns have been positively recorded at the Humber Bank brickyards around Barton and South Ferriby, although they have not survived. (There were also several conventional Scotch kilns, i.e. 'open topped' kilns, operating at the same time in that area, though they were probably constructed at an earlier date.) There is also a record of an 'East Lincolnshire' kiln at Swanage in Dorset.

Brick making was traditionally a peripatetic occupation and this pattern continued to be followed up to the twentieth century at the four east Lincolnshire sites, where, apart from Stixwould, there were frequent changes in brick makers recorded at successive censuses. The master brick makers (the Parkers, Spaldings, Hutchinsons) also moved between sites, possibly as the new kilns were introduced and first fired. Maybe it was the role of men such as these to spread expertise to other brick makers who later ran the kilns.

The kilns at Stixwould and Baumber were sited in villages where the local need for bricks was much reduced in the 1890s. By contrast the kilns at Farlesthorpe and more particularly at Sutton served communities that were still growing at the end of the century. Thus firms of builders or business men considered it a good investment to buy the kilns at these locations and employ brick makers to work for them.

Notes:

1. The drawing of the 'East Lincolnshire' kiln (Fig. 7) combines actual measurements of the kilns at Farlesthorpe and Sutton on Sea together with an impression of the vents as originally proposed by Martin Hammond for the restoration of the Baumber kiln in 1986.

Making their Mark:
First World War Scout Graffiti at Gibraltar Point

Chris Robinson

The subject of graffiti is a contentious one. We naturally perceive it to be disfiguring, a blight on the environment and perhaps also physically damaging to surfaces and structures. This article does not attempt to explore the psychology of past graffiti artists or to address the question of precisely at what point their work may achieve historic importance. The use of this Lincolnshire example will however demonstrate that graffiti can, given a little luck and rather more research, help illuminate the period of history in which it was made - in this case a period of history and events that have been almost forgotten.

If you look closely you will see, carved into the wall of the old Coast Guard Station (now the Wash Study Centre) at Gibraltar Point National Nature Reserve, numerous initials, names, dates, signs and symbols. Now eroded, worn by the elements and partially obscured by lichens, they are testament to a little known period in the history of the Lincolnshire coast.

The graffiti was recorded both photographically and by taking rubbings between the years 2000 and 2003; the bricks being numbered 'anti-clockwise' in sections from the remaining part of the west wall to the northern end of the east wall. See Fig. 1.

Where legible, the dates all fall between May and August 1915. Initially thought to be soldiers' graffiti (an army presence on this part of the coast is evidenced by several WW1 pill boxes and trench lines on the reserve), research has shown that the inscriptions have a very different origin.

The early years of the war saw vast numbers of men volunteering for, and being conscripted into, the armed forces. These included many Coastguards, themselves mostly ex-Merchant and Royal Navy men, either rejoining or being recalled from the reserve. This left the stations seriously undermanned and it was decided to supplement and expand the force using Scouts, and in particular Sea Scouts. The Sea Scouts had been founded in 1908 (one of

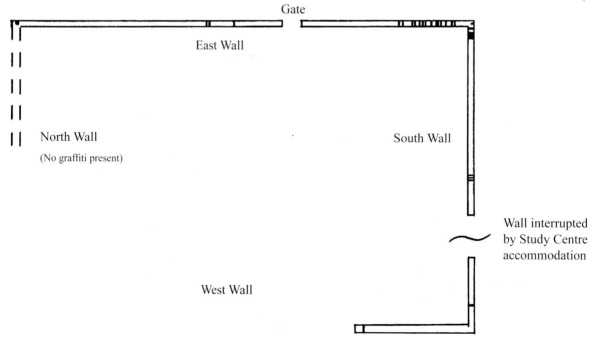

Fig. 1: Schematic diagram showing existing wall. Graffiti marked as ▮▮▮

the first troops of existing scouts to specialise being the 1st Cleethorpes) and by the outbreak of the First World War they were already well established – according to their founder Baden-Powell, theirs was to be an essential function in light of the growing threat of war with Germany. In 1911 he had written to the Admiralty requesting that Sea Scouts be established as Seamen and Coast Watchers with a view that they would then progress to the Royal Navy when old enough. This was agreed and their Coastguard duties were organised by the regional and county commissioners of the Scouting Movement, who wrote to the various troops asking for patrols and their accompanying Scout Masters to be available to cover particular areas of the coast. In September 1914 there were already 1,300 Scouts on Coast Watching duties and by the end of the war 25,000 had served in this capacity.[1]

Of all the graffiti, Northampton and Eydon are the only place names present. One name and place in particular – 'L. Golby, Eydon' - proved to be the key to the mystery. See Fig. 2.

It was not only Sea Scouts that were engaged in the coast watching duties; due to the numbers required, they were supplemented by Scouts from inland towns and villages.

Eydon is a small village to the south west of Northampton and, coincidentally, has somewhat of a tradition in graffiti. Numerous examples exist in the village, carved into the soft local stone and in some cases these date back to the late seventeenth century.

Enquiries through the Eydon Historical Research Group revealed that 'Golby' was an old established local surname and led to a remarkable discovery. The 'L Golby' in question was, in fact, one Leonard Golby – in 1915 a friend of the uncle of a current member of the Group, David Kench.

David Kench's uncle, Fred Kench was a Scout during the early years of WW1 and a diary of his survives which details his experiences during an earlier two-month period of coastguard duty undertaken from January 23 to March 20 1915 at Gedney Drove End when he was 19 or 20 years old. In this diary he makes frequent mention of one of his patrol colleagues, Leonard Golby.

The make-up of this Patrol consisted of seven Scouts, all over fourteen years of age, with their Scout Master, Mr Morrison, in accordance with the regulations of the time.[2] All bar one were from villages and towns near Eydon; Chipping Warden, Byfield, Wardington and Middleton.

The diary tells us how, at 11.00pm on Saturday 23 January 1915, after a journey of some seventeen hours, the Scouts arrived at their destination. Attached to the Coast Guard Station at Gedney Drove End, their accommodation appears to have been a fairly substantial wooden hut (or huts) situated on the landward side of the outer sea bank (OS map ref. TF 477 293) about a mile east of the village (Fig. 3).

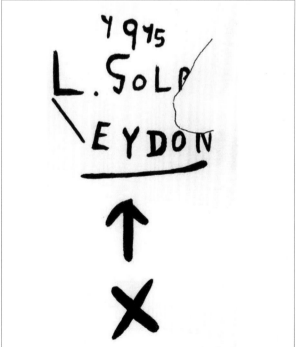

Right: '1915. L. Golb Eydon' + tracking signs for 'This way' and 'Not this way' East wall SE corner to gate.
Brick 90

Fig. 2: above: 'L. Golby'. East wall. SE corner to gate.
Brick 43

Patrol duties were carried out in pairs and shifts were of two or three hours duration, including night duty, totalling up to nine hours per day. The shifts would have been organised in consultation with the resident Coast Guard officer who was a frequent visitor. Only one officer is mentioned though earlier census records indicate that two men and their families had been resident in the village.

It is not known where the lookout post was, but considering the time of year there must have been some form of shelter, probably on the bank above the hut . The building of a 'sentry box' is mentioned in the diary (though this may also have been a euphemism for the latrine!) Fred describes the often appalling weather conditions endured while on duty, stoically recording it, rather than complaining about it. Regulations also required that pairs of Scouts patrolled the coast on foot – two in each direction for a distance of up to three miles. The northern and southern limits of these patrols seem to have been 'Poplar Tree Hole' and Guy's Head respectively. The

former appears to be what is now called Popple Tree Hall, the sluice on Dawsmere Creek. In addition to bad weather these patrols carried the associated risk of becoming stuck in mud (as once happened at the mouth of the Nene) or of inadvertently walking into one of the numerous dykes at night.

That their duties also included being on the lookout for suspicious activity is illustrated by an entry for 7 February and shows how the national paranoia concerning potential spies and invasion scares had reached even these remote parts:

> 'Day off. At dinner time a suspicious character appeared on the bank (supposed German) 3 or 4 Scouts ran about a mile after him. Turned out to be a poor innocent man from Holbeach. Very disappointed at failure of enterprise.'

The reaction of the suspect to this incident is not recorded.

In the same vein, on the night of 13 March on hearing sounds from within a tramp's covered cart:

Fig. 3: A mixed group of Northamptonshire and local Scouts outside their hut at Gedney Drove End. Standing, L – R: Unknown. Leonard Golby, Eydon. Frederick Davy, Gainsborough. Sid Hartley, Holbeach. Frederick Kench, Eydon. Sitting, L – R: Unknown. Unknown. Jack Almey, Gedney Drove End (?). (Photo. courtesy David Kench)

'I said "alright guvnor" and passed on – quite exciting. Think Davy [a Scout from Gainsborough] thought it was Kaiser Bill himself!'

Any direct impact of the war is mentioned only rarely in the diary most dramatically two days after Fred Kench's arrival:

'Monday 25th January: On duty 8 to 10 and 2 to 4. Heavy firing heard at sea. Went up to Gedney Drove End. Night on duty 12 to 3.'

No explanation has been found for this; however it occurred on the day after the Battle of Dogger Bank, a major naval engagement between the Royal Navy and the German Fleet and may or may not be related. Gunfire was also heard on the morning of Tuesday 9 March and is, again, unexplained.

There are also several references to the searchlights at King's Lynn being visible at night. These would have been newly installed after the air raid of the 19/20 January. Zeppelin L4 had bombed the town after becoming lost, in the belief that it was a 'fortified place between the Humber and the Tyne' in the process receiving 'heavy artillery fire from a big city'. King's Lynn had no anti-aircraft guns at the time and the raid killed two people.[3]

The Scouts duties also included helping out on local farms and, being a country lad, Fred Kench took a keen interest in the agriculture of the area, comparing it to that of his part of the country. Recording his observations in a few short sentences, he gives us a vivid picture of farm life and the appearance of the fenland countryside at that time:

'Monday 15th. February. I was surprised on my walk this morning to notice the difference in farming here from Northants. Much more ploughing, large number of corn ricks, mustard and turnip, seed potatoes, hardly any grass, no sheep. Windmills at work, one 7 or 8 storeys and 6 sails. Absence of hedges, all dykes, straight roads, level country…great number of men at work, tidiness of farms, good condition of most of the buildings.'

He also seems to have taken every opportunity to inspect threshing machines and other equipment, noting power output and manufacturers in a way typical of boys of his age:

'Tuesday 2nd. March ..went to the threshing machine at Hutchinson's. The engine of this set is a very old type, big governors, about 10 horse power, single cylinder…. ancient but runs well… The corn is very different to what I generally see. Straw about 4 to 6 feet long, very heavy corned, too heavy to be tied by machine but by hand with straw.'

'Thursday 25th. March. Have been to see threshing tackle today. Traction engine 6 h.p. by Marshall in very good condition…Clayton and Shuttleworth box.'

In noting the local wildlife such as hares, partridge, rats and mice (the latter being hunted amongst the corn ricks), a somewhat pragmatic approach is obvious:

'Tuesday 16th. February. Davy brought in a wounded seagull, beautiful bird. Wrung its neck and S.M. [Scout Master] is going to cure it.'

When not on patrol duty or helping out with farm work, time was spent undertaking orderly duties, cooking, writing home, fetching supplies from the village and studying for badges. Fred travelled the two miles or so to Guy's Head to examine for his Signallers' badge. Guy's Head at that time had a wooden church and a Scout camp, described as 'a poor place and dirty', and was the limit of a southerly foot patrol, often being mentioned in entries for night duty. (Both buildings have since been demolished). He also studied for his Cook and Pioneer badges; the latter involved the making of model rope bridges with a view to spanning a nearby dyke – one model being strong enough to bear the weight of the Scout Master! Other work included making a latrine, an incinerator for camp waste and surveying the sea bank – possibly for yet another badge.

The diary also mentions visits from and to local scouts which would suggest that they were attached due to their Sea Scout training and knowledge of the area. At one point they are visited by a Scout from Anderby to the north, where a number of Scouts from Byfield (a neighbouring village to Eydon) were stationed. This would suggest that the Lincolnshire coast was a major destination for many Northamptonshire Scouts. That there may have been a certain level of aspiration to Sea Scout status by the inland Scouts, is indicated by the following diary entry:

'Wednesday 10th. March. Received parcel from Hd. Qrs. Len [Golby] and Lowery swanking in Sea Scouts hats after this.'

Each Scout received one shilling a day from the Admiralty in lieu of food and it seems to have been common practice for this money to be pooled and supplies bought from the fund. (It should be remembered that, being over fourteen and thus above school age, many Scouts would have been absent from their jobs in order to fulfil their Coastguard duties. This loss of income would have placed some families in considerable hardship).

'Messing allowance is 1s. per day. Housing, fire and light provided: also railway passes when joining or leaving…. Warm clothing, blankets and cooking utensils are required: also good thick boots, and a complete change of clothes. Oilskins or waterproofs should be taken if possible.'[4]

Parcels were sent from home and collected from the local post office. On one occasion a parcel of 'shirts, socks, gloves and mufflers' was received from the Daily Graphic, indicating the national level of recognition that their duties attracted. Local residents also provided an important support network for the visiting Scouts. The diary makes

Fig. 4: The Coast Guard Station at Gibraltar Point in the 1930s, from the south east corner. Before alteration and much as it would have appeared in 1915 (Photo. courtesy Barry Wilkinson)

frequent reference to meeting with local residents and to meals being taken – Fred visiting the Hutchinsons, a local farming family. It seems even closer relationships were formed with some residents:

> 'Sunday 28th February. ….Stalking L. Golby courting. Went into a hovel to shelter from the rain and the two came in. Had to stand in one position for 1 hour. Didn't we hear something.'

Fred Kench had a strict Methodist upbringing and even if a day off fell on a Sunday, church was nearly always attended, either at Gedney or Guy's Head. Spare time seems to have been spent in exploring the local area. This included salvaging useful materials from the shore and even going swimming in the sea in early March. On Thursday 18 March, obviously keen to experience as much as possible of the local way of life, Fred and a colleague took a trip on a shrimp boat, owned by a Mr Smith from Sutton Bridge. Putting the nets out in a snow storm and catching 'about a peck' of shrimps, the boat was blown onto a mudbank on the falling tide and stuck fast for two hours. The time was spent cooking the shrimps on board and sheltering in

the foc'sle before they 'sailed back in a favourable wind at a very good speed'.

Two days later, their period of duty finished, the Scouts set off for the station at Gedney at 5.50 in the morning. After changing trains at Spalding, Boston, Grantham, Nottingham and Leicester they arrived at Woodford, the nearest station to home, at 5.25 p.m.

Some months later the graffiti record shows the presence of Leonard Golby at Gibraltar Point as he undertook a second period of Coastguard duty. The station, built in 1859, and situated on the southern tip of the 300 year old west dunes was, by 1915, separated from the foreshore by a wide stretch of salt marsh and a recently formed outer ridge of dunes (Fig. 4).

Access to the beach was complicated by the development of what is now the Main Creek, running south along the western edge of the salt marsh at the foot of the west dunes and into the Steeping estuary. A photograph taken in 1915 (Fig. 5) shows a group of young Scouts standing on a newly

Fig. 5: Scouts on the new bridge across the Main Creek at Gibraltar Point, 1915 (Photo. courtesy Barry Wilkinson)

Fig. 6: The remains of the 1915 bridge in 2004
(Photo. Chris Robinson)

constructed bridge over the creek and it is thought that they may well have been involved in building it.

That a new bridge was needed points to the probability that the lookout position was on the outer dune ridge rather than at the Station itself. (Access to the Station's tower roof was made during the Second World War, before this only the four small first floor windows were available). This bridge, itself a replacement for one shown on earlier OS maps just to the south, was in use until the construction of the present structure built by the Army during the Second World War. The remains of the 1915 bridge are still visible in the creek bed on the northern side (Fig. 6).

That Scouts were involved in this sort of work is highlighted by Fred Kench's diary entries which refer to the surveying of the sea bank at Gedney Drove End and the construction of model bridges. It may be that older Scouts with the relevant training, including Leonard Golby, were sent to Gibraltar Point in the summer of 1915 to help in the construction.

Gibraltar Point in 1915 was, in one sense, perhaps an even more remote posting than Gedney Drove End. It is

Fig. 7: 'PL A.W. Wickes July 1915' -
'PL G Tarry Aug 1915' -
'HY' - East wall. SE corner to gate

J. PEARCE CPT JAMES TROOP NORTHAMPTON

Fig. 8: 'J. Pearce Cpt James Troop Northampton'
- East wall. SE corner to gate. Brick 65

three miles from the amenities of Skegness, though there were at least a few neighbours. The Gibraltar Inn stood on the sea bank to the east of the road and the haven was, at that time, still in limited use by commercial shipping. Local farms would also have been available for supplies.

It may be that the visiting Scouts stayed in the Station itself, though there were probably a number of huts and sheds associated with both the haven and the Coast Guard Station that may have served as accommodation.

So far as is known, the full circuit of the original rectangular perimeter wall existed in 1915. At present only approximately 60% remains. A substantial amount of the north-west corner was removed during WW2 to make way for army buildings; most of the west wall and a central section of the south wall disappeared in the 1960s and early 1970s during the development of the Study Centre accommodation.

The remaining stretches of the brick wall bear some 48 identifiable individual inscriptions, though more may have been lost through demolition, reconstruction or

erosion. All of them are carved into the half-round coping on top of the wall. The distribution map shows that the majority of the graffiti is clustered around the south-east corner of the wall. (Fig. 1). This could indicate either a muster point or one of the look-out positions; however the fact that nearly all of the inscriptions have been made by people standing outside the wall (and thus facing away from the sea) would seem to discount the latter. It is perhaps more likely that this was the area in which their activities were least likely to be observed - the existing portion of the north wall, which could be seen from the access road, bears no graffiti at all. This would also explain the presence of the largest and most deeply cut graffiti on the outer part of the wall at the south-east corner. One can only imagine the number of Scout knives that were blunted in the execution.

There is not space here to list all of the inscriptions; a representative selection of the clearest and most interesting will be illustrated below.

Fred Kench's diary[5] refers to the fact that both he and Leonard Golby were Patrol Leaders. The prefix 'PL' to many of the names shows that quite a number of such Scouts were among those that added their names to the wall (Fig 7). If we assume from the dates that most of the graffiti was carved between May and August 1915, and each patrol of seven included two Patrol Leaders, then this would mean a minimum of 45 Scouts visiting during this period. However some, such as Leonard Golby, did not include their rank and others visiting before or after, did not include the date.

Tracking signs were an obvious favourite for the Scouts to engrave, some like Leonard Golby, including them with their names and initials (Fig. 2). In all there are five other instances of the 'This way' arrow engraved on the wall.

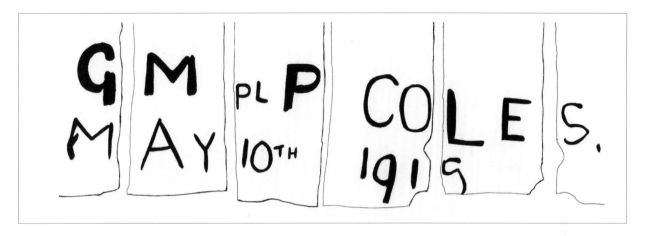

Fig. 9: 'GM' 'PL P Coles. May 10th 1915' Study Centre to SE corner. Bricks 219 – 224 inc.

Fig. 10: 'T. W.' Study Centre to SE corner. Bricks 233 & 234. This is just visible in the photo, Fig. 4

One of the clearest Northampton inscriptions is shown in Fig. 8. Scout Troops were often commanded by ex-military personnel.

As mentioned above, some of the inscriptions are large, deeply cut and must have taken a considerable amount of time to complete.

One inscription records the badges and service stars awarded to a particular Scout; possibly the 'WS' whose initials appear on the same brick.

Some of the more enigmatic graffiti remains unidentifiable but may have some symbolic meaning, or alternatively may just be complicated 'doodles'.

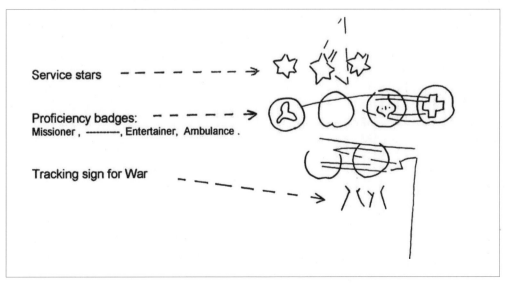

Fig. 11: East wall. SE corner to gate. Brick 46

Fig. 12: Two of the unidentified engravings. - Left: East wall.SE corner to gate. Brick 213. - Right: South wall. Study Centre to SE corner. Brick 43.

To conclude, this graffiti, now with a firm provenance, has undoubted historical value. Given the nature of its exposed position, however, its future survival and preservation is a moot point. It is to be hoped that, in the event of future developments at the site or repairs to the wall, the engraved bricks can be saved and either relocated, or kept for future display. Removal of lichens may be problematic as they are now protected by their being on a nature reserve, though their continued presence will further damage the brick surface. From a conservation perspective it should be recognised that an accurate record of existing evidence is the minimum though perhaps, in this case, most important initial step that can be achieved.

Of course, were anyone to add their name to the wall today it would instantly be condemned as an act of vandalism; in a hundred years time could it be a valuable social document?

Postscript.

Shortly after his period of duty at Gedney Drove End, Fred Kench rejoined the family building business, which explains why he did not go to Gibraltar Point. He then enlisted and served with the Royal Artillery during the war. He died in 1978.

Leonard Golby later joined the Machine Gun Corps, becoming a painter and decorator after the war. He died in 1980. They both lived all their lives in Eydon.

Acknowledgements

David Kench and Kevin Lodge, Eydon Historical Research Group; Mrs Pat Styles The Scout Association Archives; Barry Wilkinson; Mr. G. Golby

Notes:

1. *The Early History of Sea Scouting.* Johnny Walker's Scouting Milestones Pages, www.scouting.milestones.btinternet.co.uk/seascouts.htm
2. *Headquarters Gazette,* Scout Association, (Feb 1915) p.33.
3. C Cole and E F Cheesman, *The Air Defence of Great Britain 1914-1918* (1984) p.25.
4. *Headquarters Gazette, op. cit.*
5. F Kench, *Diary for Scouts Duty carried out on behalf of the Coast Guard at HMCG Station Gedney Drove End. January 23rd 1915 to March 20th 1915.* Unpublished.

David Robinson and Horncastle College

The starting point for this book involved two lists: one of people who should/might like to contribute, the other of subjects which ought to be covered. One 'must be' included was Horncastle College with which David has been involved for many years. However, as with a significant number of such subject areas, potential writers have insisted on their inadequacy for the task and that the only person to write it is David himself!

Therefore, the editors crave the reader's indulgence and offer the following piece written in 1989 by David for the publication to celebrate the college's first twenty years. David joined the College as a Governor at its inception in 1969 and later served as Chairman of Governors until the governing body was dissolved in 2005.

Fig. 1: David Robinson's long association with Horncastle College was celebrated in March 2006 when the main lecture theatre was named in his honour

The Setting Of Horncastle College

David N Robinson

The College is bounded to the east by open farmland sloping down to the Thunker Beck. On the other side of the road to Mareham on the Hill are interwar Council houses, and to the west the early nineteenth century terraced labourers' houses of Foundry Street. Behind the College is the former Union Workhouse, now regrettably minus the gatehouse buildings.

The diminutive Thunker Beck rises near Scrafield. After heavy rain on 7 October 1960 it was a raging torrent, discharging four times its normal flow, as was the River Waring which it joins by the Spilsby Road. They were the major cause of serious flooding in the town, when many premises were flooded to a depth of six feet. From the 1840s to the 1890s the Beck had been harnessed to power a waterwheel for an iron and brass foundry and bonemill

near Holt Lane. Other floods in 1900, 1920 and 1981 were the result of the River Bain overflowing its banks.

The residential houses of the College were built in 1934 and 1937 as the Holmeleigh Children's Homes. This followed the bold move of Lindsey County Council in 1930 when they took over from the Board of Guardians and moved all 'workhouse' children, 104 of them, to Horncastle. For the first few years the boys and girls were accommodated in the main block of the old workhouse, and the infants in the infirmary block. The Horncastle Poor Law Union of 68 parishes had been formed in 1836, and the Workhouse, built to the design of George Gilbert Scott, opened two years later. Looking rather like a prison and with separate wings for men and women, it could have accommodated up to 260 paupers.

Foundry Street was aptly named. Outside the entrance to the Workhouse was the Gas Works of 1833. At the corner of Cross Street the factory building was the Horncastle and Woodhall Spa Steam Laundry and before that the Wesleyan Day School (1859 to 1907), but it started in the l830s as the Union Iron Foundry making agricultural implements and steam engines, and with nail, tin and braziery departments. The hollow iron posts in the shape of a cannon at the entrances to St. Mary's churchyard were made in that foundry. At 45 Foundry Street were a wheelwright and agricultural implement maker, and at the corner of Albert Street was a feather factory, formerly a brass and iron foundry.

Queen Street is nearly parallel with Foundry Street but of pleasant middle class villas. In the 1870s it was favoured by the leather 'barons', four of them living there, the town being important for tanning and the manufacture of boots and shoes. The name of the Street had been changed to 'Queen' from 'Union' in 1867 by the Local Board of Health, the forerunner of the Urban District Council. Building in Foundry Street was particularly rapid in the 1840s, when 76 new houses appeared bringing the total to 92; in the same period only eight new houses were built in Union Street, to give a total of 31.

The streets had been laid out from the 1820s by Robert Clitherow on land allotted to his father Richard under the Enclosure Act of 1803. At that time what is now Queen Street above the chapel, Foundry Street above Paradise Place and all the land where the College now stands were part of Becks Field, one of six fields totalling just over 1,000 acres, in the town's open field farming system. Becks Field was divided from South Field by the Long Hedge; this is the hedge on the College side of the road to Mareham on the Hill. It is at least 400 years old, as can be seen in the section beyond the farm on the left where the hedge is made up of a wide variety of shrubs including unusually barberry, dogwood and crab apple. North of the College and the Workhouse, the Vicarage stands on land allotted to the Vicar for glebe at enclosure.

The process of enclosure not only changed the farming system of the parish, but opened up new building land, and the town also expanded along Prospect Street and the Louth, Spilsby and Boston Roads. The brick and tile yards off Southwell Lane rapidly expanded to meet the demands for building materials, and a new pit opened along Elmhirst Lane; both were adjacent to the River Bain on the north side of the town. The rapid growth of industries in the first half of the nineteenth century - tanning, boot and shoe making, iron works and agricultural implement manufacturers - and a population increase from 2,000 to nearly 5,000 required cheap terrace housing for workers - in Foundry Street, Albert Street, Stonewell and Waring Rows, Cagthorpe and Stourton Place.

Horncastle no longer has a railway. The line from Kirkstead Junction through Woodhall Spa closed for passengers in September 1954 but remained open for goods for a further seventeen years. The occasion of the opening in August 1855 had been a cause for great rejoicing - shops and schools closed, church bells pealed, there was an enormous procession with two brass bands from the Bull Ring to the railway station, and 2,500 lbs of beef were distributed to the poor.

It was one of the high points of the nineteenth century, when Horncastle was a boom town, but soon the population would begin to decline, a trend which would continue until after the Second World War. Inevitably the arrival of the railway heralded the decline of the canal which had opened in 1802 with two branch basins in the town - the Bain and the Waring. Wool and grain warehouses, tanneries and soap works, maltings and agricultural machinery by the canal have been replaced by light industry on greenfield sites on the edge of the town, for example Linpac just along Mareham Road from the College.

An unexpected effect of the railway was to shorten the Great August Horse Fair which, during the nineteenth century, was the largest in the world, attracting buyers from the Continent, America, Africa, Australia and New Zealand. The Fair had been established for at least 600 years, and had extended from the statutory eight days to nearly three weeks, but the ease of railway transport meant quicker deals and by the beginning of the twentieth century the Fair was all over in a couple of days. Continental wars increased the demand for cavalry remounts: horses from Horncastle Fair were in the Charge of the Light Brigade, and served the Lincolnshire Yeomanry in Egypt and Palestine in the Great War; and future Grand National winners passed through the Fair. George Borrow - the Romany Rye - was in Horncastle for the 1825 Fair.

At the height of the Fair, horses were on show in the streets from the Black Swan through the Bull Ring to the top end of North Street. Along the centre of that axis were the major inns of the town - Ship, Bull, Red Lion, New and Rodney - all with extensive stabling. In fact the town could stable over 1,000 horses. The requirement to accommodate dealers and horses for the August and other fairs was the major reason for the very large number of inns and taverns - a maximum of 48 licensed establishments in 1860, one for every 100 of the population, having grown from a mere fourteen at the end of the eighteenth century.

Horncastle grew to be, and still is, a classic small market town serving an agricultural hinterland where the horse was the source of tractive power. Before fenland drainage and enclosure, the Lincolnshire Black, the progenitor of the shire horse, was bred around Boston; the Wildmore Tit pony supplied the coalmines of Nottinghamshire and the leadmines of Derbyshire; the Lincolnshire Trotter was supplied as a coach horse; and hunters were bred widely on the Wolds. Horses pulled the carriers' carts to market from surrounding villages, over fifty of them once or twice a week for around seventy years.

Two centuries earlier in the Civil Wars, horses were required for the cavalry when Horncastle was involved with the decisive skirmish which won the county for Parliament. That took place on 11 October 1643 on a ridge of the sandstone Wolds near Winceby, three miles east of Horncastle, where the townspeople had barricaded the entrances with carts and timber. The Roundheads under Cromwell and Fairfax - 1,850 mounted cavalry and dragoons - were gathered on high ground above Kirkby and Bolingbroke, while the Royalist Forces under Henderson, Hopton and Saville - 3,700 cavalry and 5,000 foot soldiers - advanced from Horncastle through High Toynton and Scrafield. When they came over the brow of the hill at Winceby they found the Parliamentary cavalry drawn up on the open ridge between the ravine of Snipe Dales and the slope to the Fens.

In the close fighting Cromwell was unhorsed but remounted and Hopton, who had tried to capture him, was killed. After half an hour the Royalist retreat under pressure became a disorderly rout. In the hollow west of Winceby they were trapped against the big parish boundary hedge and many were cut to pieces; it became known as Slash Lane. Cromwell is supposed to have stayed the night in Horncastle, where he arranged for the burial with honours of Sir Ingram Hopton. Hopton Street and Ingram Row are named after him.

Just over a century earlier, in 1536 and also in October, there had been other troublesome times in Horncastle. Local abbeys were in the process of dissolution, Dr Raynes, the Bishop of Lincoln's Chancellor, was beginning his inquisition of clergy, rumours were rife about closure

of parish churches and seizure of church jewels, and townspeople feared for the statues, vestments and plate of St Mary's church with its magnificent new roof.

The mood became ugly when local agitators tried to enlist the gentry to their cause and in a mob lynching, probably on The Wong, Dr Raynes and Thomas Wolsey, one of Thomas Cromwell's servants, were killed. Many men of Horncastle formed part of the 30,000 who mustered at Lincoln. Their demands of Henry VIII were summarily rejected in that famous reply to the 'rude commons' of Lincolnshire, 'and that one of the most brute and beastly of the whole realm'. The Lincolnshire Rising dissolved and retribution followed. The Abbot and three monks of Kirkstead Abbey who had supported the rebels were executed with others, some of the hangings taking place in the town the following March. The prominent ringleaders - Nicholas and Robert Leach, Philip Trotter, Robert Sotheby, Roger New - were hanged, drawn and quartered at Tyburn.

In medieval times St. Mary's church would almost certainly have been the only stone building in the town, and much of that robbed from Roman walls. All others were of timber, mud, stud and thatch, including the rectory. The Bishops of Carlisle were both lords of the manor and patrons of the benefice from 1229; one of the rectors, Simon de Islip, became Archbishop of Canterbury in 1349, the year when the pestilence of the Black Death decimated some surrounding villages and seriously affected the growing market status of Horncastle. When the Bishop had bought the manor he was Treasurer to Henry II, and he used the position to obtain Royal charters including a weekly market and annual fair.

Two centuries earlier, at the time of the Domesday Survey, the town's open field farming system operated with 100 acres of meadow and two watermills. Narrow burgage plots had wooden buildings facing a central open market place and a main street within what remained of the Roman fort walls, with a north-south street outside the east wall and a Danish out-settlement or shack suburb - Cagthorpe - on the edge of the open field south of the Waring. The Saxons had given the place its name - Hyrnecastre (fortress in the corner).

The nameless Roman fort, built for military purposes and enclosing five acres, was on a tongue of gravel between the rivers Bain and Waring. The civilian settlement, including some buildings with sandstone walls and chalk floors, covered an area of about 50 acres on higher ground to the south, from the Wong to the Workhouse and the College.

Not only was Horncastle strategically placed for military control of this Lincolnshire part of the Roman empire, but the subsequent market town occupied a key position between the Wolds and the Fens. Most of the land immediately adjacent to Horncastle owes its form to moulding by ice and water during the last two stages of the Ice Age over the last 200,000 years. The curious course of the River Bain, rising in the central Wolds and breaking through the escarpment to flow in a broad valley south to the Witham, is due to glacial diversion of melt waters. These left the string of gravel terraces, exploited for aggregate and now water recreation at Hemingby. South of Horncastle a huge delta fan of sand and gravel spread from Woodhall to Tattershall and into the Fen edge.

The Fens in Roman times looked very different from today: a shallow coastline much further inland than now, with a fringe of marshy islands specialising in the production of salt. The later rise of sea level swept masses of silt into the fenland basin, rivers meandered towards broad estuaries where salt was still made, villages became established on the silt bank from Wainfleet to Boston and beyond, and accumulating saltmarsh was reclaimed apace from the seventeenth century. Vast acres of summer grazing were intercommoned by the fringing villages. Horncastle had its own grazing rights in Wildmore Fen. The Lindsey Fens - 40,000 acres of East, West and Wildmore Fens - were not finally and effectively drained until the completion of John Rennie's scheme, with the backing of Sir Joseph Banks, in 1814. The pattern of drains, locks and pumps, duck decoys, new churches, and new settlements like New York and New Bolingbroke provide historical interest in what might appear to be a featureless agricultural landscape.

There is still woodland along the gravelly northern edge of Lindsey Fens. Here also is Revesby Park, established by the Banks family in the early eighteenth century and the Lincolnshire home of Sir Joseph, the great botanist, President of the Royal Society for 42 years, and the 'Father of Australia', who also had a town house in the High Street at Horncastle.

Kirkby and Roughton Moors were once extensive heathlands until enclosure and the exploitation of mineral waters early in the nineteenth century to create Woodhall Spa, and the opening in 1855 of the branch railway line from Kirkstead to Horncastle. Today only fragments of the heathland remain on Woodhall golf course and the two nature reserves of the Lincolnshire and South Humberside Trust for Nature Conservation [now the Lincolnshire Wildlife Trust] at Kirkby Moor and Moor Farm.

Westwards from Horncastle the land is largely of heavy glacial clays, with the group of woodlands between Bardney and Wragby still retaining ancient woods such as Gosling's Corner nature reserve and the stands of small-leaved lime in Hatton Wood, as well as the Forestry Commission plantations. In contrast the land east of Horncastle is a platform of Spilsby Sandstone much dissected by tributaries of the River Lymn (Tennyson's Brook) which cut through to the Kimmeridge Clay in Snipe Dales, a nature reserve and country park near Winceby, and the spectacular New England gorge near Somersby. Higher ridges at Fulletby and Harrington are capped by Roach Stone, as is the distinctive flat-topped Hoe Hill near Fulletby.

Beyond, the scalloped escarpment of the chalk Wolds rises to nearly 500 feet, the narrow crest followed by the lonely Bluestone Heath Road. There are extensive views eastwards into the deep cut valleys of the Calceby Beck system and across to the spire of St James in Louth nestling at the east foot of the Wolds, and westwards across the central clay vale of Lincolnshire to the towers of Lincoln Cathedral. There is a labelled viewpoint on the Bluestone Heath Road above Belchford. The other panoramic view is from the Red Hill nature reserve above Goulceby where the splash of red chalk on the hillside is itself a landmark. On Good Friday every year it is a place of pilgrimage when three crosses are erected on the hilltop and a service held on the old grassy chalk quarry which will bloom with cowslips and lime-loving orchids in the summer.

The setting of the College has much to offer in townscape and landscape, an area as well as a place for study. As Horncastle has been called the 'Gateway to the Wolds', so the College can be the gateway to learning.

Reprinted from *Horncastle Residential College 1969-1989: Foundation and Success*

Wildlife in a Changing Landscape
The Work of the Lincolnshire Wildlife Trust

Ted Smith

Lincolnshire's diverse landscapes are shaped by rocks and soils and physical features and by the vegetation which covers them and which supports other forms of wildlife. That vegetation may be entirely natural; it may have 'come by itself' but in conditions determined by human agency in which case we call it semi-natural in contrast to sown crops and plantations. Lincolnshire landscapes have undergone vast changes over the centuries, largely as a result of human activity. It was the first Neolithic farmers who began the long process of destroying the wilderness and converting the land and its resources to human use, a process accelerated by the Anglian and Danish invaders with their permanent settlements. By the Middle Ages most of the woodland had gone or had been reduced to scrub, but there were still vast areas of semi-natural heath, downland and fen, all of it put to some human use but retaining a great variety of habitat and wildlife. Until the first half of the eighteenth century in fact this was still a half-wild county, remote and sparsely populated.

Within the next hundred years the agricultural revolution had converted Lincolnshire into the most intensely cultivated county in England. Of the sheep-grazed downs of the chalk and limestone hills and of the meres and reedbeds and wet heaths of the old fenland scarcely a vestige remained. Only the acid heathlands in the northwest and around the Fen edge escaped, but their turn came later in the twentieth century with afforestation and a new agricultural revolution. Meantime the process of enclosing the centuries old open fields was accelerated and largely completed by 1830. The sand dunes and saltmarshes of Lincolnshire's long coastline remained the only natural or near natural habitats, but they too were affected in later years by increased reclamation and by sea defence works within the last fifty years.

Enclosures had destroyed much of the special habitats, but there was compensation for wildlife in the hedges and trees, copses and field ponds of the new landscapes. In the second half of the twentieth century, however, these landscapes and the remaining semi-natural habitats suffered further changes when intensive arable cultivation converted large swathes of the countryside into bleak,

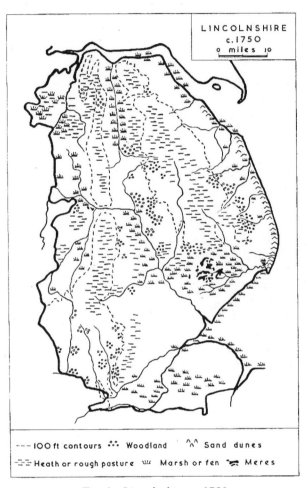

Fig. 1: Lincolnshire c. 1750

treeless arable prairies. In the process old pastures in the Lindsey Outmarsh and elsewhere were ploughed and only a handful of the once abundant flower-rich meadows survived. Rivers and streams were drastically deepened and straightened in the interests of land drainage and lost many of their semi-natural features.

Coastlands

Lincolnshire has a long coastline, 103 miles of it from Trent Falls to Wingland beyond the Nene estuary. The bulge of the coast bordered by the great estuaries of the

Fig. 2: The residential Wash Study Centre which incorporates the old Coastguard House

Wash and the Humber has been subject to severe erosion by the sea for the last seven centuries, and following the 1953 floods much of it is now protected by concrete walls. In the more sheltered conditions at either end of the bulge, however, extensive sand dune areas have survived at Gibraltar Point south of Skegness and to the north of Mablethorpe, whilst in the estuaries, in the Wash in particular, some of the most extensive saltmarshes in Britain have developed and are of major international importance for migratory and wintering waders and wildfowl. Periodic reclamations, intensified in the twentieth century, have almost halved the area of Wash saltmarsh, but the recognition prompted by conservation bodies that the rate of loss of saltmarsh and inter-tidal mudflats was unsustainable has halted further reclamation. A large amount of the Wash shore is now included in nature reserves managed by Natural England, the RSPB and the Lincolnshire Wildlife Trust.

Much of the sandy coastline has been developed to holiday-making. Railways in the 1870s promoted the growth of Skegness and Mablethorpe, whilst the advent of the motor car in the 1920s helped to spread development along the intermediate stretches of coast.

Sand dune areas at Gibraltar Point and Saltfleetby-Theddlethorpe and at Donna Nook, however, have survived and are recognised as of national importance for wildlife and are protected in National Nature Reserves. Gibraltar Point was threatened by development in the 1930s and again in 1953, but was saved by the acquisition of land by the former Lindsey County Council which had secured the unique Sandhills Act in 1932 to protect the coastal sandhills. Gibraltar Point became a nature reserve in

1948 by agreement between the County Council and the Wildlife Trust, and in 1953 was the first statutory Local Nature Reserve to be designated in England. It was a pioneering reserve of national significance for reconciling conservation of its outstanding wildlife and natural features with use for education, research and public enjoyment of nature. The reserve has been expanded in recent years by the acquisition of former arable land on Croftmarsh and its conversion into pasture and wetland. The gradual development of facilities for education and interpretation have culminated in the residential Wash Study Centre and the recently expanded Visitor Centre.

The Saltfleetby-Theddlethorpe stretch of coast has older sand dunes and a freshwater 'slack', a kind of maritime fen, an unusual coastal feature in eastern England. There too holiday huts and chalets had been built on the dunes in the 1930s, but were removed after the area was taken over by the Air Ministry as a firing range. Established as a reserve in the 1950s by the Wildlife Trust, it was threatened again in the 1960s by caravan camp development which – as at Gibraltar Point – was fended off only by hard fought public inquiries. At the instigation of the Trust and the County Council the then Nature Conservancy declared the area a National Nature Reserve in 1984.

Further north the Trust established a reserve on the sand dunes and saltmarshes at Donna Nook by lease from the Ministry of Defence, and that too is now a National Nature Reserve, especially notable for one of the largest and most accessible breeding colonies of grey seals in the country. These reserves have protected many of the dynamic features and diverse wildlife of Lincolnshire's coastline including rare and endangered species like the natterjack toad and the little tern.

Heathlands

Inland, Lincolnshire's once extensive heathlands are found on the Fen edge sands and gravels, on the Trent valley deposits to the west and south-west of Lincoln, and on the Coversands in the north-west which overlay the limestone ridge in places from the vicinity of Market Rasen northwards to Scunthorpe. Acid grassland predominated on these heaths, but there were substantial tracts of heather, and bogs and pools were formed in wet areas. A rich flora was also matched by an equally diverse fauna. Until well into the nineteenth century and in some cases even later, breeding birds included hen harrier, dunlin, ruff, stone curlew, black grouse and wheatear. There were widespread colonies of silver-studded blue, grayling and large heath butterflies, and notable calcifuge plants such as sundews, common butterwort, marsh gentian and bog asphodel. In spite of destruction by ironstone mining and the growth of Scunthorpe, more than 5,000 hectares of heath survived up to 1920. In the next thirty years, however, most of it disappeared under a blanket of conifers as the Forestry Commission acquired cheap land for plantation to fulfil its production target. In the middle years of the century agricultural intensification and mineral extraction made further inroads, so that by 1995 little more than 600 hectares remained mainly at Risby, Manton, Messingham and Scotton in the north-west, and at Kirkby on Bain and Roughton on the Fen edge. There are no significant remains of the habitat on the Trent valley gravels, although some elements of flora and fauna survive in the worked-out gravel pits at Whisby. More of this heathland habitat would almost certainly have disappeared had it not been for the action of the Wildlife Trust in acquiring notable examples at Linwood Warren, Scotton Common, Kirkby Moor and Moor Farm. The Trust, however, could not prevent the destruction of other notable examples at Messingham Heath and Waddingham Common both destroyed in the 1960s in spite of their designation by the Nature Conservancy as Sites of Special Scientific Interest. Publicity given to the destruction of the latter site was an important contributory factor in persuading the Government to give more meaningful protection to SSSIs. The relatively small remnants of heathland that have been saved in the reserves have been vulnerable to external changes. In particular a falling water table due to the growth of neighbouring conifer plantations and more intensive land drainage encouraged the spread of trees and scrub at the expense of open and wet habitats. Enlargement of the reserves where feasible and the resumption of traditional grazing of sheep and cattle has helped to restore the situation.

Fens, marshes and wetlands

Until the eighteenth century much of south-east Lincolnshire was still un-drained or only partially drained fenland. In fact the most extensive area, the East Fen, remained 'in a state of nature' – as Gough described it in his 1806 edition of Camden's *Britannia* – until after 1800. 'A vast tract of morass' Gough called it, 'a specimen of what the country was before the introduction of drainage'. Its meres and vast reedbeds with tussocky pastures and moorland around the higher margins supported a wealth

of wildlife unimaginable today. There were vast flocks of wildfowl – the East Fen decoys sent more than 36,000 ducks a year to the London markets – there were bitterns and bearded tits, ruffs and black-tailed godwits and harriers, and almost certainly swallowtail and large copper butterflies. By 1830 it had all gone; nothing of the great wetland remained. Some of the plant and animal species adapted to living in the fenland drains and in the washlands, the embanked flood relief channels on the lower reaches of some of the rivers. The principal washes in Lincolnshire, however, at Crowland and Cowbit on the Welland went out of use when a new relief channel was constructed around Spalding in the 1950s. Only one example of a wash now remains – in the Trust's reserve at Baston Fen on the River Glen. The Trust, however, has plans for the re-creation of a substantial area of fen based on its Baston Fen and Thurlby Fen reserves.

Drainage of Lincolnshire's other fenland and bog in the Isle of Axholme was almost equally complete, but a few remnants survive there in the form of turbaries, peat bog areas – possibly the sites of former meres – allotted at Enclosure for turf digging to the inhabitants of several of the parishes. Only two of these now survive, Epworth Big Turbary and part of Haxey, both owned by the Trust. These retain a range of fen and wet heath conditions including areas of sphagnum bog, reed swamp and mixed fen vegetation in which occurs the fen sedge *cladium mariscus* once abundant in the southern fens and now confined in Lincolnshire virtually to these two reserves. Further north in the Isle the Trust owns a larger reserve on Crowle Moors, another area extensively dug for peat in the past. The interest of these Axholme reserves is enhanced by the northern elements in their flora and fauna, exemplified by bog rosemary, cranberry and the large heath butterfly both found here at the south-eastern limit of their range in Britain. Crowle Moors is now part of an extensive National Nature Reserve which includes the adjoining Thorne and Hatfield Moors.

There has been some compensation for the loss of fen and marsh in the worked-out pits dug largely for clay and in more recent years for sand and gravel. Many of the older brickyard claypits are small, but the series of pits along the Humber Bank, the legacy of the brick and tile making industry there, have extensive reedbeds of national importance for breeding bitterns, bearded tits, marsh harriers and other reedbed birds. The Trust has acquired more than a hundred hectares of reedbed and open water in these pits, with a Visitor Centre and wardens' base

Fig. 3: Crowle Moors Nature Reserve showing the pattern of long narrow 'ribbons' of individual ownerships
(G Trinder 1995)

at Far Ings at Barton-upon-Humber in converted farm buildings. As part of a new South Humber Wildlife and People Project, the Trust is also converting a former County Council pursuit centre into an education and information centre.

Sand and gravel excavation has created extensive wetlands in all the major areas of deposition in the county, including the lower Bain valley where the Trust owns a large pit at Kirkby on Bain; and at Deeping St James where a large nineteenth century ballast pit together with more recent gravel pits now form an extensive reserve. Another major wetland reserve which is the result of gravel excavation is at Whisby south of Lincoln where visitor and education centres are managed by the Trust in association with the County and District Councils. All these wetland reserves support a wide variety of aquatic and waterside plants and animals including scarce species like the greater water parsnip, the water vole and water shrew, the kingfisher and great crested newt. They are also places which offer special opportunities for people to see and study wildlife.

Chalk and limestone grasslands

Like the old fenland, the downs of Lincolnshire's chalk and limestone hills are a vanished landscape. Until the middle of the eighteenth century these hills carried extensive tracts of semi-natural grassland. Their extent and condition may have varied somewhat over the centuries according to the fluctuating fortunes of sheep farming, but they were rich in plants and animals adapted to the open habitat and to sheep and rabbit grazing. We can reconstruct the composition of their flora from their present day relics, and there is historical evidence for the existence until the early nineteenth century of downland birds such as great bustard, stone curlew and wheatear.

From the mid eighteenth century onwards these grasslands were systematically destroyed and converted to an arable system within an enclosed landscape. When Arthur Young came to Lincolnshire in 1799 to make his report for the Board of Agriculture he saw great changes in the Wolds since his previous visit 30 years earlier, but even so there were still extensive tracts of open sheep walks and rabbit warrens. Yet by 1830 William Cobbett saw only 'a very fine corn country' with fenced fields, and 'the hills not Downs as in Wiltshire were cultivated all over'. A similar picture was painted by J A Clarke in *The Journal of the Royal Agricultural Society* in 1851: 'All the open fields have disappeared, a great part having been enclosed in the last 30 years'. ...... 'No portion of the ground has been allowed to remain (as on the Downs of southern England) a tract of sheep walks in its primitive vegetation of heath and fern, but the highest parts are all in tillage and the whole length of the Wolds is intersected by neat whitethorn hedges, the solitary firs bush appearing only where a roadside or plantation border offers an uncultivated space'. One of the improving Wold farmers who effected these improvements was Tennyson's Northern Farmer who proudly remembered on his death-bed his achievement in cultivating 'Thurnaby Waste' (Thorganby Warren). The same process was taking place on the limestone heath where even by 1800 Arthur Young found little further reclamation to be done.

The great bustard, stone curlew and wheatear were banished, but remnants of the flora survived here and there on hillsides too steep to plough, in disused quarries and on road verges. Agricultural intensification in the second half of the twentieth century inflicted further losses, and some remaining sites deteriorated into scrub owing to the cessation of grazing. Nearly 60% of the remaining chalk and 40% of the limestone grasslands were lost between 1940 and 1995. There are a few relatively larger sites which have survived, and it was a high priority for the Wildlife Trust at the outset to seek protection and appropriate management for them. One such site at Red Hill near Goulceby on the Wolds was a small patch of species-rich grassland above a well-known exposure of the red chalk – the scene was painted by Lincoln artist Peter DeWint in the early nineteenth century. Complexities of ownership were overcome and the site came into Trust management. More recently the reserve has been expanded by acquisition of sixty acres of adjoining arable land which has been converted into sheep and cattle grazed grassland, already colonised by the chalk plants from the original reserve. A similar but more complex restoration has been carried out at Robert's Field at Holywell in the south of Lincolnshire, a ten acre patch of limestone grassland which was the richest butterfly site in the county. In spite of the

Fig. 4: The Red Hill Local Nature Reserve and Site of Special Scientific Interest at Goulceby, showing famous fossil-rich exposure of Red Chalk with underlying Carstone and thin capping of white Lower Chalk

Trust's efforts to save it and the fact that it was part of a proposed national nature reserve, all but one acre of it was planted with conifers in the 1960s. When the Trust was at last able to acquire it 30 years later the conifers were felled and uprooted and the grassland successfully restored. The largest and floristically richest limestone grassland in Lincolnshire is the narrow, steep-sided Ancaster Valley. Plants there include fragrant and bee orchids and the beautiful pasqueflower in what is now its only site in Lincolnshire. Scrub and lime-loving shrubs on the hillside add to its interest.

Disused quarries provide a variety of habitats – cliff faces, screes and the quarry floor – for re-colonisation by plants and animals. The Trust has acquired a number of such quarries including Mill Hill at Claxby St Andrew, Candlesby and Little Cawthorpe on the Wolds and Clapgate Pits on the northern limestone.

Because of the scarcity of calcareous grassland, road verges, which occur on all soils, are of special conservation importance. In 1960 the Lindsey and Kesteven County Councils and the Wildlife Trust concluded an agreement for the protection and management of verges which were considered by the Trust to be of special interest. These verges, some 64 of them, are marked by special posts, and the Trust receives a grant now from Lincolnshire County Council to manage them by cutting for hay or other appropriate means. The scheme was the first of its kind in the country and was subsequently adopted by most other county councils and Wildlife Trusts in England.

Meadow and pasture

Grassland as meadow and pasture was formerly abundant on all clay soils in Lincolnshire. Pasture was the predominant use in certain areas, notably in river valleys and in the coastal Marshland where Wold and Middlemarsh farms owned or rented land for summer grazing. The pastures were important for breeding birds like lapwing and snipe and for the golden plover flocks in winter. The reedy dykes which served as field boundaries and which are rich in aquatic plants and animals were an important wildlife feature of the Outmarsh. In many river valleys there were damp rushy pastures which often flooded in winter. In all mixed farming areas – like the Lindsey Middlemarsh – small meadows were an essential feature of mixed husbandry farming. They were managed on traditional lines by cropping for hay with aftermath grazing where necessary, the only fertiliser being animal dung. The flora was invariably rich and varied with many flowers familiar to country people for their herbal or medicinal qualities. Butterflies, grasshoppers, bees and other insects abounded, and the generous hawthorn hedges were home to yellow hammer, whitethroat, turtle dove and other hedgerow birds.

In the agricultural revolution which followed the Second World War the concentration on arable cultivation soon diminished the area of both pasture and meadow. In 1938 there were 41,000 hectares of meadow and nearly 190,000 hectares of pasture in the county; by 1995 they had been reduced to 142 and 48,000 hectares respectively, and were still disappearing. The Trust mounted surveys to discover and acquire the best remaining old meadows, and over a few years some fifteen of them were acquired in various parts of the county. They support a representative range of meadow flora including species which have become rare such as the green-winged orchid, and the meadow saxifrage.

The loss of pasture was particularly severe in the Lindsey Outmarsh where only isolated patches remained by the end of the century, mainly to the west of Skegness and in the Saltfleetby-Theddlethorpe area. Lowering of the water table in the interests of arable cultivation made it impractical to retain small areas of grass, and in any case most of the Wold and Middlemarsh farms no longer had cattle. Now a Coastal Grazing Marsh Project, funded by Natural England with involvement of the Wildlife Trust and other bodies, is investigating the economic and practical feasibility of restoring grazing marsh over wider areas.

This would also restore something of the historic landscape and benefit a wide variety of birds and other wildlife.

Woodlands

Woodland of all kinds in Lincolnshire covers some 22,500 hectares which is little more than 3% of the total area of the county. Of that only 6,300 hectares or 28% of the total is considered to be ancient in origin. The rest consists largely of conifer plantations established by the Forestry Commission mainly on acid heathland soils between 1920 and 1960, as at Laughton and Willingham Forests. These dense coniferous plantations are of limited wildlife interest, although this improves as thinning and felling takes place. Heathland flora and fauna sometimes persist in rides and marginal areas, and in places the Commission is now leaving felled areas to revert to heath. Other woodlands not of ancient origin comprise small woods, coverts and shelter belts planted in the eighteenth and nineteenth centuries on large estates and newly enclosed land. Planting on a larger scale took place on the Brocklesby Estate where some 3,000 acres of mixed woodland was planted between 1750 and 1850.

The main areas of ancient deciduous woodland in the county lie on the boulder clays of the Middlemarsh, on the Kesteven uplands and in the central clay Vale. Many of the scattered woods in these areas were traditionally managed on a coppice-with-standards system, the standards for larger timber requirements, the coppice felled at regular intervals for small wood for farm and estate purposes and for mud and stud buildings. Oak and ash were the usual standard trees with birch, alder and field maple commonly occurring. In the central Vale woods small-leaved lime occurs with oak and ash as standards, a combination which makes these woods of national significance. The layered structure and the coppice management of all these ancient woods supported a rich and varied flora and fauna from the primroses, wood anemones and bluebells on the woodland floor to the insect and birds of the shrub and tree layer, all familiar sights, sounds and scents of English woodland.

By the mid nineteenth century these woods had begun to lose their economic value. Large areas were felled for conversion to arable in the mid century years of Victorian high farming, and by the early twentieth century other materials were beginning to replace coppiced wood. After the Second World War many of these broad-leaved woods were felled and re-planted with conifers. In others the coppice was neglected, became outgrown and was replaced by dense bramble cover which suppressed the ground flora. Overall there was a marked decline in plant and animal variety, butterflies being particularly affected.

The Trust has acquired woods in all three of the main areas described: Dole, Tortoiseshell and Lawn Woods in Kesteven; Goslings Corner a fine example of central vale oak-lime woods, and Hoplands, Rigsby and Muckton in the Middlemarsh. All these are being restored to traditional types of management with large areas of hazel coppice. The magnificent displays of bluebells at Dole and Rigsby – enjoyed by many hundreds of people on open days in the spring – are testimony to the success of such management. In the last few years relaxation of the Forestry Commission's production targets and requirements has resulted in the restoration of more broad-leaved deciduous woodland.

Nature reserves: their value and their future

The establishment of nature reserves in Lincolnshire has saved specialised habitats and rare species from further decline and extinction. 32% of the county's remaining heathland, for example, is found in six reserves; 40% of the hay meadows, and no less than 87% of peatland and bog. Reserves are not only sanctuaries, they also act as 'reservoirs' from which plants and animals with special requirements can spread more widely once suitable habitat becomes available, as is happening at Red Hill and Robert's Field. Reserves may become even more vital as plants and

Fig. 5: Mill Hill Quarry Nature Reserve and Site of Special Scientific Interest, Claxby St Andrew, showing exposure of the Middle and Lower Chalk with floristically rich chalk grassland in the foreground. The Bronze Age round barrow is to the right of the picture

animals seek to adapt to climate change conditions. The Trust is therefore enlarging existing reserves wherever possible by re-creating habitats like grassland, heathland and wetland.

Nature reserves are an indispensable means of conserving nature. Many of them also represent landscapes and land usages which have otherwise largely disappeared. Some have geological, archaeological and historic interest and remains. The little Mill Hill chalk pit at Claxby, for example, shows a fine exposure of the Middle and Lower chalk; it has a Bronze Age burial mound on which once stood a post mill overlooking the Marshland; two mid nineteenth century lime kilns; the remains of a blacksmith's forge, and all that in addition to being a place of great natural interest and beauty. The Trust's reserves are indeed an essential part of the county's heritage.

The Trust's reserves also serve their other main purposes: to enable people to appreciate and enjoy nature and to provide opportunities for field study and research. Special facilities are provided by the Visitor Centre and Residential Wash Study Centre at Gibraltar Point; by the Visitor Centre and Study Centre at Far Ings on the Humber; by the Education Centre at Whisby Nature Park and Reserve, and at Snipe Dales. There are interpretation leaflets and boards on site and viewing hides at many other reserves. Management in all the most popular reserves is designed to reconcile access and use with the conservation of wildlife and natural features. A programme of special events on reserves and elsewhere is published each year and is made widely available. It is estimated that at least 500,000 people visit the reserves and attend events each year.

For more than forty-five years David Robinson has been at the forefront of the administration and management of the Lincolnshire Wildlife Trust. His first contact with the Trust came through survey work in 1950 whilst an undergraduate in the Geography Department of Nottingham University. Later, in 1956, when he was already a teacher, he undertook survey work on the north-east coast of Lincolnshire for his MSc thesis. Meantime he had become a member of the Trust's East Lindsey Regional Committee. Then in 1963 he was appointed Chairman of a new Publicity Committee.

Following the untimely death of the Trust's Chairman Dick Cornwallis in 1969, David became Honorary Secretary, a post which he has occupied with dedication and distinction to the present day, almost certainly the longest service in the same senior post of any Wildlife Trust Officer. With the appointment of the Trust's first Administrative

Fig. 6: HRH The Prince of Wales on an informal visit to Gibraltar Point in 1971 with David Robinson, Ted Smith and Walter Lane

Officer in 1969 followed three years later by a Conservation Officer, David exercised an important co-ordinating managerial role until the appointment of a Director in 1976. He also played a leading role in those years in negotiation for the acquisition of new nature reserves as, for example, at Crowle Moors. Later, in addition to the Honorary Secretary's basic responsibilities, he was able to concentrate on the development of the Trust's educational and promotional work and communication with its growing membership. Outstanding in that connection has been his editorship of the Trust magazine *Lapwings* to which he has devoted all his skill and experience as writer and editor. *Lapwings* is widely regarded as one of the best Wildlife Trusts' magazines. His skill and experience as geographer and teacher has also been invaluable to the Trust in nature reserve selection and management and in the development of educational work at Gibraltar Point and elsewhere. In his professional capacity as the University of Nottingham's Resident Tutor in North Lincolnshire, he organised and conducted many weekend and summer courses at the Gibraltar Point Study Centre.

Through the Trust David became closely involved in the affairs of the Trusts' national body, now the Royal Society of Wildlife Trusts, as a long serving member of the Executive Committee and of the Editorial Board of *Natural World*, the Trusts' national magazine, and as Chairman of the Education and Promotions Committee. He also served for several years as the Honorary Secretary of the Watch Trust for Environmental Education, the organisation for young naturalists. There are few people who have given such outstanding service for so many years throughout the Wildlife Trusts' movement locally and nationally.

The Underground Mines of Lincolnshire

Stewart Squires

The mineral most extensively mined within Lincolnshire was ironstone. Deposits of ore were worked following the line of the Lincoln Edge from West Halton to Scunthorpe in the north; from Lincoln to Honington; and on to Harlaxton and Denton. To the south of Grantham, the ore was found in the Colsterworth and South Witham area. In addition there were mines on the western scarp of the Lincolnshire Wolds at Claxby and Nettleton. Most workings were by opencast methods but there were no less than sixteen locations where the ironstone was mined underground. The first underground mine went into production in 1868 and the last closed in 1981 and so underground mining was part of the county's industrial history for 113 years.

For the purposes of this paper a mine is defined as one that went into production. What is not included are a number of exploratory shafts sunk over the years as part of the continual exercise of proving the extent of workable deposits of ore.

The history of some of this industry has already been written, most notably by Eric Tonks[1] and by Neil Wright.[2] However, apart from a gazetteer of mines listed by I J Brown[3] much about the industry solely on a county basis has yet to be written. Inevitably, some of the information included within this essay has appeared in print before but, in the interests of breaking some new ground, pardon the pun, this takes the form of a chronological history together with what the various methods of working can tell us about some of the changes in the technology of underground mining over the period.

From the beginnings through to the late 1930s mining production depended largely on the muscles of men and horses. From the late 1920s, after a short overlap period, mechanisation was very much the watchword and increasingly, machinery operated by the miners took over. Mining remained, however, a dirty and dangerous job, its workers inhabiting a subterranean world lit and ventilated by artificial means.

The first mine was opened in 1868, the Acre House Mine at Claxby, between Market Rasen and Caistor (TF 114 967).[4] The West Yorkshire Iron and Coal Co. leased land from the Yarborough Estate and opened a mine notable for the appalling rates of industrial accidents resulting in the death and injury of the miners. The technology was typical of the time. Adits were driven into the hillside, to the foot of which a railway ran from a point south of Holton le Moor station. Railway wagons were drawn up to the mine on a self acting incline where a small number of loaded wagons would drop down the hill balanced by the same number of empty wagons going up. The two sets of wagons were connected by a rope passing around a braked drum at the head of the incline and the drum here was a prominent sight on the exposed hillside.

In any mine a through-flow of air has to be maintained to the working faces and this was done by creating a circulation of air, the route directed by the closure of doors to side passages and worked out areas. From the centre of the mine a vertical shaft was driven up to the field above and a fire lit at its foot would force air to be drawn in through the adits. This was known as 'furnace ventilation'.

Mining was new to the county and so experienced miners brought their skills from traditional mining areas such as Cornwall, Derbyshire, Durham, Gloucestershire, Nottinghamshire, Staffordshire and Yorkshire. Up to 250 men were employed and there can be no doubt that local men, used to hard physical labour and long hours on farms, found the mine an alternative source of employment. However, accidents were frequent even, on one occasion in 1871, involving the death of a man who had worked at the mine for 'only a day or two'. His name was not known and resulted in the manager introducing a policy of registering the name, age and belongings of every man, the latter, presumably, so that his body could be identified following an accident. In 1872 the curate at Nettleton, M H Sumner, felt the situation so awful that he wrote to the Stamford Mercury about 'that gloomy cavern of disaster, the Claxby iron ore mine'.

The mine was worked by the 'pillar and stall' method. From the working galleries, side chambers, or stalls, would be excavated and the stone removed. These were around six metres wide and up to 30 metres long, or around half the distance to the next parallel roadway. The next chamber was excavated about twelve metres away leaving a pillar of stone to support the ground above between the two chambers.

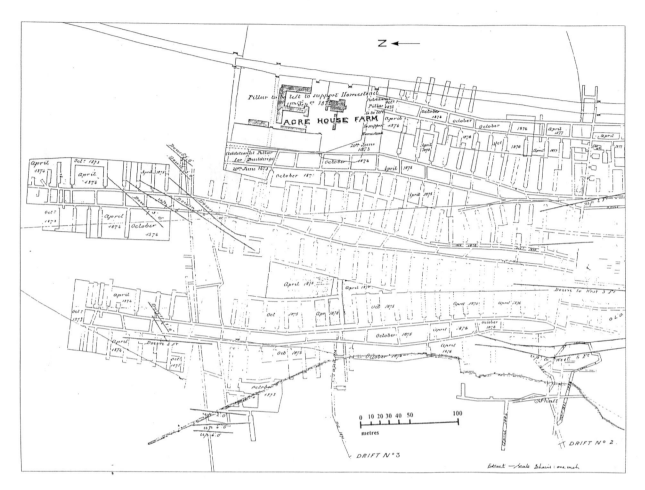

Fig 1: Claxby Mine, Pillar and Stall working. This is an extract from the Abandonment Plan deposited with the British Geological Society. The plan shows a series of parallel roadways. These provided access from the mine entrances to the working faces and they are paired to enable a circulation of air. Depending on where miners were working the cross passages and the links to other parts of the mine would be opened or closed to ensure air flowed in along one passage and out through the other. The chambers at right angles to the roadways are the stalls from which the stone was extracted. Between them the unworked stone forms the pillars that support the land above.

Drift No 2 and Drift No 3 are two of the mine entrances, ending on the hillside where they came out into the open air. (Author's collection)

The mine closed in 1885 after almost 500,000 tons of ironstone had been taken out. Investigation into the extent of the workable ore reserves in this area during the Second World War, revealed that the quality of the stone was very poor and suggested that it was for this reason that the Claxby mine workings never proceeded.[5]

In 1874 a small mine is said to have opened at Coleby, south of Lincoln (SK 977602). This was at the top of the scarp of the Lincoln Edge and the first edition of the six inch Ordnance Survey map does show a tramway running down the hillside to the Lincoln to Grantham railway line. It is not clear if this ever went into production or whether it was an underground mine. Given that ironstone quarries in a similar location were worked in Waddington to the north and Leadenham to the south, it may be that this was not intended to be an underground mine.[6]

The next mine to open was the Appleby Ironstone Mine (TF 949135), about 500 metres north of the former Appleby railway station, to which it was connected by a railway siding.[7] It was one of only two shaft mines in

Lincolnshire. All the others were drift mines, that is, they utilised horizontal entrance shafts. Here, two vertical shafts were sunk between 1870 and 1875 to reach the bed of the Frodingham ironstone located at a depth of 97 metres. The buildings at the head included an engine house and a chimney about 36.5 metres in height. Evidence within the former indicated that the mine used a large, probably two cylinder, horizontal steam engine driving a centrally positioned winding drum.

This was a short-lived ironstone mine, there being no ore produced after, it is thought, 1881. It probably closed because of drainage problems and because extraction by opencast methods was far less expensive; most ore was to be gained by this method in the Scunthorpe area for the next 100 years. It was not until 1939 that ore would be mined underground again here.

A pumphouse was built at the top of the shaft in 1920 and it provided a water supply until the shaft collapsed and was sealed in the late 1940s. The buildings remained until demolished in 1971. The author of this article was responsible for this as part of a small team who were charged with restoring derelict land and the sites of redundant buildings to agricultural use. The work resulted in the loss of many sites and buildings of industrial archaeological interest; a sin for which he has tried to atone ever since.

In 1878 the Mid Lincolnshire Ironstone Company opened the first of their seven mines on the eastern outskirts of Lincoln. Here, around Greetwell Hollow, underground mining was to take place for over 60 years, the longest lived in the county. The Monks Abbey Mine was the first, to the north of Monks Road (SK 991717) under land that was then allotments but subsequently the site of the new County Hospital. The entrance adits were from the north side of Monks Road, straight into the hillside. Monks Abbey Mine was worked up to about 1900 and, when it was worked out, production moved to a new mine, Rudgards Mine. This had an entrance at the north end of Greetwell Hollow (SK 999725) and the mine ran eastwards parallel with Wragby Road. South of this, around 1904, the East Drift Mine opened (SK 004724) and the Long Harry Mine, between the latter two, probably in the 1920s.

In 1923 what was to become the largest mine, Wilsons, opened. Access to this was originally in the west side of Greetwell Hollow (SK 998724) and it grew to take in what was then farmland and allotments right up to Lincoln Prison in the west. Once again this lay between Wragby

Road and Greetwell Road. A second entrance was opened up at about SK 991723. Finally, two small mines, one on either side of Greetwell Road as it leaves the City, were opened, Grundy's No 1 (TF 003716) to the south side and Grundy's No 2 to the north (TF 003719).

The ore began to run out in the 1930s with the closure of East Drift in about 1930, Wilsons, Long Harry and the two Grundy's in the mid 1930s and, finally, Rudgards in 1938. Over the preceding 60 years something like four million tons of ironstone had been removed.

The work was done by men wielding picks and shovels. They loaded narrow gauge railway wagons, pulled by horses. Locomotives were tried out, a small steam engine from 1911 to 1916 and, in 1934, a new Ruston diesel loco.

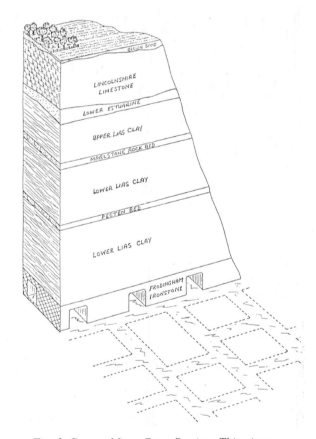

Fig. 2: Santon Mine, Cross Section. This gives an indication of the depth of the mine. Extraction here was by the Room and Pillar method. Parallel workings are linked with staggered cross passages between which unworked pillars are left. About 30% of the stone is taken out. (David Elford)

This was sent to the same owners' new Nettleton Mine in 1935, probably because the ore in Lincoln was about worked out. The Lincoln mines were some of the last in Britain to use horses for all their haulage needs, both under and above ground.

Almost every trace of the mines on the east side of Greetwell Hollow disappeared as the limestone quarry here developed and spread from the time of the Second World War. The best remains are to be found in Greetwell Hollow itself. Here the rough ground is not only the product of nature but also years of mining and quarrying. The routes of the tramways can be found as well as the sites of adits into Rudgards and Wilsons Mines.

If the closure of the Greetwell Mines saw the end of the era for the reliance on muscle power in Lincolnshire mines, it was the opening of the Nettleton Top Mine in 1934 (TF 112981) that saw the first major introduction of new technology. Work on driving the first adit into the

Fig. 3: Nettleton Top Mine. A horse at work underground. The steel hoops over the roadway have baulks of timber behind them to support the sides and roof. This was in one of the mine roadways and, as these provided access around the mine, they were more permanent than the stalls where the roof would be collapsed when the stone had been taken out. This photograph is believed to have been taken in about 1938 when the mine was still lit by acetylene lamps. One can be seen hanging on the right.

Horses were used for 'tramming', that is, keeping the miners supplied with empty wagons and taking away filled ones. This was very important work as miners were paid by the amount of stone they dug and would lose time if they had to wait for the wagons to be changed. (Author's collection)

hillside of this part of the Lincolnshire Wolds had started in 1928 but, due in part to roof problems, there were delays in getting the mine into production.[8]

The owners were the Mid Lincolnshire Ironstone Company and, in contrast to their Lincoln mines, they determined to mechanise. So, for example, this mine is believed to be the first in England to use diesel locomotives underground.[9] Horses were to be used to haul wagons from the working faces to the main roadways where the diesels took over. Gas was not a problem here and, sited as it was on the top of a hill and cut into by a valley of a subsidiary stream to the Nettleton Beck, there was plenty of hillside to push out a 'daylight hole'. This was a hole dug to the outside to enable a flow of fresh air within the mine.

A second innovation was the use of pneumatic picks driven by compressed air.[10] The mine was having a problem recruiting and retaining suitable labour and it was felt that the picks would improve the output and decrease the need for skilled labour. The use of explosives would not be required and, as a side benefit, the compressed air released by the process would help to ventilate the mine.

Here the mine also made use of an aerial ropeway. The nearest railway, at Holton le Moor station, was a mile and a half away. Sidings were laid here and linked to the mine by a line of eighteen pylons supporting a cable from which 72 buckets were suspended. Each bucket was filled from a hopper at the mine and discharged into another hopper at the sidings. Despite all this new technology the mine was the last in the county to use horses underground and this continued until closure at which time they were given an honourable retirement, grazing in the field above the mine workings.

Nettleton Top Mine closed in 1959 with the opening of the Nettleton Bottom Mine but, in the meantime, underground mining was starting again in the Scunthorpe area. It was in 1939 that the Santon Mine opened. The depth of the ore bed in the Scunthorpe area is an average of 7.6m and a maximum of 10m. This had been exploited on a large scale by open cast working to the south and north of the town. As extraction moved eastwards the seam fell below the rising scarp of the Lincoln Edge putting it out of reach for surface working. In 1935 work had begun on a vertical shaft to the north of Dawes Lane, reaching a depth of 61m. In 1938 an adit was driven to the foot of this shaft from the south of Dawes Lane, near to the North Ironworks (SE 926115). The junction between the two was made in 1939 although, perhaps surprisingly because of the demand for

home grown raw materials during the Second World War, it was not until 1948 that it went into production.[11]

Production methods were very similar to those at the Dragonby Mine, see below. However, before the introduction of conveyor belts in May 1958 to carry mined ore from the workings to the shaft, a 2 feet 6 inch narrow gauge railway was used with a fleet of five diesel engined locomotives. Three of these were from Ruston and Hornsby of Lincoln. These pulled rakes of loaded wagons to the foot of the shaft where the ore was tipped into a skip, hauled to the surface and again tipped, into railway wagons.

Work on opening up the Dragonby Mine (SE 904147) began in 1947. A large basin was excavated, involving the removal of some 250,000 tons of clay, to expose the ore bed into which the mine entrance was formed. From here five parallel headings were driven, later increased to seven, to form the main roadways underground. Each of these was 6m wide at floor level, tapering to 4.6m at the roof level and 5.4m high.

Production began in 1950, using equipment mainly of American manufacture. Shot holes were driven in the face and

Fig. 4: Dragonby Mine. This photograph shows the relatively large chambers within this mine. To the right the stone has been brought down using explosives. In the centre the loader is pushing its nose into the heap, gathering the stone and bringing it onto the elevator at the rear of the machine. The elevator is discharging into a shuttle. The shuttle was battery powered and took the ore to the end of the conveyor belt that carried it out of the mine. The loader is electrically powered and the cable carrying its supply can be clearly seen.

(Bryan Longbone)

Fig. 5: Nettleton Bottom Mine. Here in 1965 miners are using compressed air picks to loosen stone. They stand on removable platforms cantilevered out from the side of a wagon. Below them the stone falls into the wagon, helped at the sides by sloping panels of timber. These were detached when the wagon was full but their use reduced the amount of fallen stone to be loaded by hand. (Author's collection)

charged with gelignite to bring down about 200 tons of stone. This was done in the early hours of the morning so that the smoke would clear before the morning shift began loading stone into battery driven shuttle cars that 'shuttled' between the face and the end of a 1.2m wide conveyor that, in turn, took it to the surface. Here it discharged ore direct into railway wagons.[12]

The Santon and Dragonby Mines were connected underground in 1969. Access for workers was by the shaft while vehicles used the adits. Loading of the conveyors was by forward loading shovels. Working was by 'room and pillar'. Parallel 6m wide headings were driven, connected by cross cuts of the same size, leaving pillars of stone 15m square unworked to support the ground above. There was confidence that the mines would be in operation for many years after surface quarrying ceased in the Scunthorpe area but this optimism went unrewarded when both mines closed in 1981.

At South Witham a thick bed of limestone was revealed during the building of the railway line between Bourne and Saxby, opened in 1894. In 1907 the Holwell Iron Company opened a quarry to exploit this stone. The stone was taken out using a hoist which lifted it directly into the South Witham station yard.

It was in 1944 that the Stanton Ironworks Company, who by then were the operators, decided to exploit the ironstone bed that lay beneath the limestone. They opened up an adit in the north side of the quarry face, (SK 920190) from where a roadway ran down into the ironstone, curving through a half circle as it did so to face south. The quarry had a narrow gauge railway of the unusual gauge of 2 feet 8½ inches and this was extended to serve the mine. Two small locomotives were brought in to haul the ore out to the foot of the hoist which was now used for both limestone and ironstone.

The mine proved that there were substantial workable ore reserves and, to exploit them, a new mine, the Thistleton Mine of Stewarts and Lloyds Minerals Ltd was proposed in 1951. This entirely new mine complex, with a new entrance adit, to the north of the limestone quarry, opened in 1958 (SK 916193) although in Lincolnshire the area to be worked lay largely below the adjacent county of Rutland. The earlier adit was retained for ventilation purposes but the hoist was closed. The mine was served by its own railway line, running eastwards from the line between Buckminster Sidings to Stainby which served many of the opencast ironstone quarries in the area.

From the outset it was envisaged that underground haulage would be by electric locomotives, drawing their current from an overhead wire and running on the three foot six inch gauge. However, only the first of six planned were delivered and two diesel locomotives made up the shortfall. In practice, the ore was loaded into shuttle cars underground for transfer to the mine railway. Here, the diesel locos took the train to the adit from where it was drawn out by the electric loco to a tippler for transfer to standard gauge wagons.

The mine suffered from geological problems and the ingress of water. It proved to be more costly to work than the opencast quarries and it closed in 1964, only a small part of the ore field having been removed.

In 1958 the United Steel Company began work on their Easton Mine, alongside the railway line from High

Fig. 6: Thistleton Mine. Unique in Lincolnshire was the use of an electric locomotive taking current from an overhead wire. Here it is framed by the mine entrance. Built by English Electric it was delivered new to the site in 1957. The building in the left background is the crusher, to which the stone was taken by this locomotive and where it was crushed and loaded into standard gauge railway wagons. (Bob Darvill and the NGRS)

Dyke, about one mile north of Colsterworth (SK 940268). The owners considered this to be an experimental mine, although it was expected to produce up to one million tons a year. Here too, stone was brought out of the mine by a conveyor belt discharging into railway wagons on the surface. The success of the American shuttle cars at Santon Mine encouraged British manufacturers to produce their own designs and three Barnsley made shuttles were supplied. But Easton was another short lived mine that never lived up to its original expectations; it closed in 1967 following the contraction of the UK ironstone industry.

It was in 1959 that the last of the Lincolnshire mines was opened, at Nettleton Bottom, back in the Lincolnshire Wolds (TF 123983). The owner was John Lysaghts Scunthorpe Works, also owners of Top Mine from 1944. Development work here started as the Nettleton Top Mine was becoming exhausted. New tunnels were driven through the Top Mine to the Nettleton Bottom valley, across the Nettleton Beck on an embankment and into the new mine. The demand for ore at that time was such that while the Bottom Mine was being opened up, the valley sides were quarried for outcropping stone and the pillars of stone left in Top Mine were 'robbed'. That is, they were removed causing many pitfalls on the hillside above. The Top Mines yard was modernised to serve the new mine

and the improvements included the replacement of the aerial ropeway with a road along which large dump lorries travelled to the sidings at Holton le Moor.

Inside the mine a fleet of battery electric locomotives worked underground to bring stone from the working faces to the main roadways where a new fleet of diesel locos took over for the one and a quarter mile journey to the hopper at the mine's yard.

Bottom Mine was expected to have a 40 year life but this was another mine that fell victim to the changing demands for ironstone and it closed in 1968.

Closure of the later mines came about because the iron content of the Lincolnshire stone varies from 25% to 35%. Foreign ores have to be imported but they can contain up to 70% iron. Nevertheless, this does mean that if the demand for home ores ever were to arise in future there are extensive workable deposits underneath the county's landscapes.

Acknowledgements

The author is grateful to Bryan Longbone of Scunthorpe, Bob Darvill of the Narrow Gauge Railway Society and David Elford of Corus, Scunthorpe, for their help in providing background material for this article and to David Robinson, for the article in Lincolnshire Life, April 1971, which sparked his interest in mining in the county.

Notes:

1. Eric S Tonks, *The Ironstone Quarries of the Midlands, History, Operation and Railways, Part VIII, South Lincolnshire*, 1991, and *Part IX, Leicestershire*, 1992, Amadeus Press.
2. Neil Wright, *Lincolnshire Towns and Industry, 1700 to 1914*, History of Lincolnshire Committee, vol. XI, (Lincoln, 1982).
3. I J Brown, Gazetteer of Ironstone Mines in the East Midlands, Lincolnshire Section, *Lincolnshire Industrial Archaeology*, vol. 6, nos 2 and 3 (1971)
4. S Squires and R Russell, Claxby Ironstone Mine, Lincolnshire, *Lincolnshire History and Archaeology*, 34 (1999) and S Squires, Claxby Ironstone Mine, Lincolnshire, Industrial Archaeology Notes, *Lincolnshire History and Archaeology*, 38 (2003).
5. Lord Yarborough Estate in the Nettleton and Normanby Parishes of the Caistor Rural District Council, Lincoln. A report on exploration

of the possibilities of the Claxby Iron Ore bed to the south and east of the old Claxby Mine workings. February 1943. Copy in possession of the author.
6. S Squires, *The Lincoln to Grantham Line*, Oakwood Press (1996)
7. M J G Upton, The Appleby Ironstone Mine, *Lincolnshire Industrial Archaeology*, 6, no. 4 (1971).
8. S Squires, Visit to Nettleton Mines, Sunday 17 September 1995, *Lincolnshire Past and Present*, 23 (Spring 1996).
9. Letter from the Mid Lincolnshire Iron Co Ltd dated 3 June 1937. Copy in the possession of the author.
10. Letter from the Mid Lincolnshire Iron Co Ltd dated 14 September 1937. Copy in the possession of the author.
11. *Appleby Frodingham News*, 12, no. 2 (summer 1959).
12 *Appleby Frodingham News*, 8, no. 4, (autumn 1954).

Linwood Warren – A Journey of Discovery

Catherine and Peter Wilson

Foreword

Linwood Warren is a small patch of land near Market Rasen which has been a nature reserve in the care of the Lincolnshire Wildlife Trust (LWT) (previously the Lincolnshire Trust for Nature Conservation) since 1957. Peter Wilson was the Honorary Warden of the Reserve for a number of years from the late 1960s until 1980. Catherine (née Bowyer), who was then Museum Assistant at the City & County Museum, Lincoln, was invited by him to visit the Reserve to see the Roman pottery kilns there. That was the start of a 'beautiful friendship', and we have now been married for 40 years! We have also both known David Robinson, for almost as many years through our respective interests of natural history and local history. We knew that Linwood Warren had strong historical as well as natural history interest, but that this had not been fully investigated or written up. This seemed an ideal opportunity to redress that. What seemed initially like a fairly straightforward task has led us into many unexpected avenues of enquiry and has proved to be a fascinating exercise though there are still a number of unanswered questions. However, we hope what follows explains our fascination and does justice to the importance of this special place.

N.B. The area we are concentrating on is that of the nature reserve, which is the only surviving part of what was once the much larger Linwood Warren. For clarity we will use the term 'Warren' when referring to the whole area, and 'Reserve' when talking about the current nature reserve site.

Where and what is Linwood Warren?

The nature reserve known as Linwood Warren is an area of lowland heath some 26 hectares (64 acres) in extent lying about 2.5 km (1.5 miles) east of Market Rasen, centred on Grid Ref. TF133874. The site lies on the eastern extreme of the parish of Linwood, with the parish boundary forming the south and east sides of the Reserve. It adjoins Forestry Commission woodland to the south and east; the Market Rasen to Legsby road and the Market Rasen Golf Course to the north; and farmland to the west (Fig. 1).

North Wood (confusingly situated to the south of the Reserve) at this point forms the watershed between the Witham and Ancholme river systems. Rain water from North Wood drains down the hill into the boundary ditch which then runs through the Reserve and eventually flows into a tributary of the River Rase.

Fig. 1: Aerial photograph of Linwood Warren Nature Reserve from the south
(From flights flown in 1999, copyright Lincolnshire County Council and Getmapping plc. Reproduced courtesy of Lincolnshire County Council)

The Reserve is part of a natural area identified by English Nature (now Natural England) as the Lincolnshire Coversands and Clay Vales.[1] Lowland heath is a nationally important habitat and, in Lincolnshire, is found on the windblown post-glacial sands deposited particularly around Scunthorpe and Market Rasen, which includes Linwood Warren. 'The light Coversands soils are generally dry and nutrient poor. Until the general introduction of cheap fertilisers and irrigation, the land was unprofitable to farm except as extensive sheep walks and warrens.'[2] The Reserve was designated as a Site of Special Scientific Interest (SSSI) in 1966 and is listed in the above report as a key habitat, together with four other SSSIs in the Scunthorpe area.

The blown sand at Linwood Warren overlays Upper Jurassic clays, and it is this feature that has determined some of its land-use history.

The Domesday Book of 1086 records the name of this area as *Lindude*, spelt *Lindwda* in the Lindsey Survey of c.1115. Both mean 'the lime-tree wood' from the Old English words *lind* and *wudu*.[3] The small-leaved lime tree is a native of Britain and is an indicator species of ancient woodland. It is very significant in Lincolnshire, a fact that has been recognised by the National Nature Reserve status given to the Lincolnshire Limewoods in the Bardney area, which has the highest concentration of small-leaved lime in the country.[4] Although there are no lime trees on the Reserve, other woodlands in the parish of Linwood, such as North Wood and Eleanor Wood, do contain some lime, so have been there for a very long time, even back to the days of the 'wild wood'.

The name of Linwood has been spelt in various ways over the years – Lynwode, Lynwoud, Lynwod, Lyndwood, Lynwood, Linwodde, Lindwoode, for example.[5] Although the village has generally been spelt Linwood for some 200 years, the Warren and Warren House have been spelt Lynwode on maps more recently. However we use the now accepted Linwood spelling throughout.

The area denoted as Linwood Warren on the first edition of the Ordnance Survey (OS) map in 1824 was four times larger than the present nature reserve, but the land to the west of the Reserve has been ploughed for many years whilst that to the north has been used as a golf course since 1921, so that the Reserve is all that is left of the apparently once extensive warren.

Since 1957 the site has been a nature reserve, owned by the Lincolnshire Trust for Nature Conservation, now known as the Lincolnshire Wildlife Trust (LWT), but it is far from being a natural landscape, having been utilised by man in a variety of ways over at least the last 5,000 years, as we shall explain.

The wildlife interest of the area was recognised as long ago as 1876 when it was visited by botanist F Arnold Lees[6] and the Lincolnshire Naturalists' Union held a number of field meetings there before 1957, when its main interest was considered to be its botany and its entomology. In view of this known interest it is perhaps surprising that it is not mentioned in the selection of biological sites of national importance to nature conservation in Britain as published in '*A Nature Conservation Review, 1977*'.[7] Although it is mainly known as a sandy heath, in fact there are a number of distinct zones all with different habitat types which make it such an interesting place today. Several areas are quite wet, and the soil quality is generally poor which is probably why it has survived as a wildlife area, rather than succumbing to the plough.

A brief description of the different zones may be helpful. Starting from the west, which is the end nearest Market Rasen, Crab Apple Lane marks the start of the Reserve. Then there is the West End Field, a very damp area with coarse grass, rushes and sedges. It has very different characteristics to the rest of the Reserve, and shows evidence of ridge and furrow cultivation at some time.

East of the field is the line of old Willingham Lane, marked by banks, with several mature oaks and pines. East again is the dry heath. This area is slightly higher

Fig. 2: The dry heath showing the dominant Wavy Hair Grass Deschampsia flexuosa (Photo. Peter Wilson)

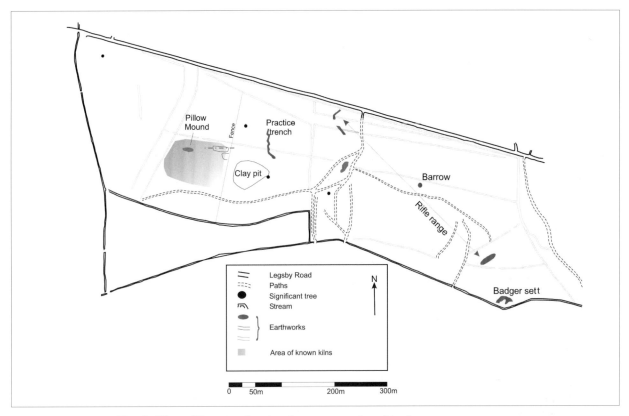

Fig. 3: Plan of Reserve showing features mentioned in the text (Ian Rowlandson)

and drier than the rest of the Reserve and is where Roman pottery kilns have been found. It is characterised by patches of heather but is dominated by the grass *Deschampsia flexuosa.* (Fig. 2)

Along the north side of the Reserve, adjacent to the Legsby Road, is a belt of mature Scots pine trees, originally planted about 1900, as evidenced by tree rings of specimens blown down in the gales of 1976 which showed them to be about 80 years old. This area was the final stronghold for Red Squirrel on the Reserve, last seen by us in 1972.

The main entrance to the Reserve is roughly in the centre of its north side, just inside which is a memorial to Richard (Dick) Cornwallis, a farmer at Legsby, who was a founder member of the LWT and to whose memory the Reserve is dedicated.

To the east of the entrance is the wet heath, characterised by Ling *Calluna vulgaris*, Cross-leaved heath *Erica tetralix,* and Bell heather *Erica cinerea.* The wetter parts have a thin layer of peat and semi-permanent pools. The area was formerly covered in pine woodland, cleared in the

1950s, and it has recently been cleared again of birch and pine scrub. Some areas are dominated by Purple Moorgrass *Molinia caerulea.*

To the south, where the Reserve adjoins Forestry Commission land, are the remnants of mature oak woodland with its associated flora including Bluebell, Lily of the Valley and Early Purple Orchid. There is an area of bracken and larch trees where a large badger sett is situated (Fig. 3).

The first evidence of human activity

The earliest artefacts found on the Reserve itself are chance finds of a few worked flints from the Neolithic period, which have been recovered over the years from rabbit scrapes and other areas of bare soil. There are three 'waste' flakes, struck from flint cores but not worked into tools, one of honey coloured flint, one grey and one almost white. The tools found are: a honey coloured graver (Fig. 4D); a scraper-knife on a hinge flake (Fig. 4B); a flake from thermal flint worked into a micro-denticulate; and a fine

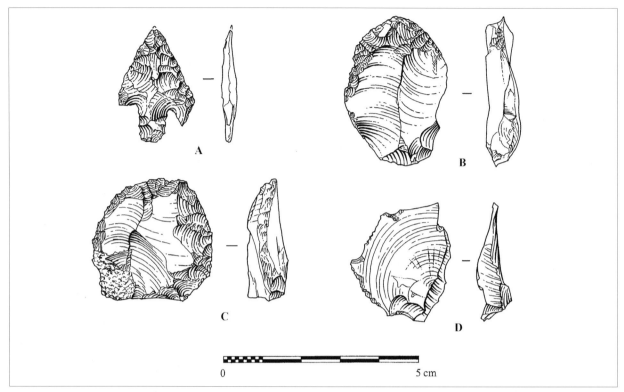

Fig. 4: Flints found on the Reserve: A. barbed and tanged arrowhead; B. flint scraper-knife on a hinge flake; C. fine scraper of black flint; D. honey coloured flint graver (Drawn by David Hopkins, Heritage Lincolnshire)

scraper of black flint (Fig. 4C).[8] All these appear to be of Neolithic date, so they are at least 4,500 years old. They are not necessarily evidence of people living on the site, but they do show that people were using the area.

But of course the present boundaries of the Reserve would not have existed at that time so it is reasonable to look at what has been found close by, to gain a fuller picture of the area at this period. The county Historic Environment Record (HER) records part of a Neolithic polished axe of black flint found at Linwood Warren in 1905 (HER No.50552). The grid reference given shows that this was actually found just to the north of the Legsby Road, the area that is now the golf course. This axe was found by Arthur Smith, the first Curator of the City and County Museum in Lincoln, and was published in *Lincolnshire Notes and Queries*.[9] Another flint axe head of partly polished honey coloured flint was found slightly to the south of the Warren adjacent to College Farm (HER No.53362), though the date of this may be open to some doubt. Both axes are now in the collection of the City and County Museum at Lincoln (Accession Nos. 1003.06 & 178.77). Perhaps more

interestingly, a short distance to the west of the Reserve, the HER notes two areas of cropmarks, interpreted as prehistoric enclosures and boundaries, discovered by aerial photography in 1979 (HER Nos.53368 & 53371). No investigation of these crop marks has taken place so their date within the prehistoric period cannot be determined.

The HER also records a scatter of worked flints from the early Bronze Age found 'in quantity' in the early 1960s (HER No.50706). Unfortunately, this material can no longer be traced and as the area now forms part of the golf course, further investigation has not been possible.

Other Bronze Age material though can be firmly located on the Reserve itself. Len Watkinson was the first warden of the nature reserve and, with his wife Betty, he also had a strong interest in archaeology and local history. Together they undertook a huge amount of survey work on the reserve, producing a contour map, and a very detailed plan of the flora of the reserve. The original colour plan, dated 1960 to 1962, is still in the LWT archives. Presumably as part of his detailed survey work, Len discovered a Bronze

*Fig. 5: Catherine Wilson and Ian Rowlandson
measuring the round barrow, 2006 (Photo. Peter Wilson)*

Age round barrow in the wet heath area. The barrow is still clearly visible today and is approximately 12 metres (39ft 6in) in overall diameter, with the mound itself measuring 8.6 metres (28ft 3in) (Fig. 5).

Len undertook a modest excavation in about 1962, opening a narrow trench on the east side and towards the centre of the mound. Unfortunately no written records of the work survive, but the finds do. In the centre of the mound was a plain burial urn which probably contained the remains of a cremation. The vessel was of poorly fired pottery which was very crumbly and riddled with fine tree roots. Only the lower half of the pot survived, but most of this was so crumbly that it could not be saved. The thicker base of the pot though was rescued and it has recently been conserved by Claire Chope, a student on the conservation-restoration course at the University of Lincoln, under the guidance of Lincolnshire County Council Heritage Service's Conservation Department (Fig 6). Most interesting is the fact that a barbed and tanged arrowhead was found underneath the pot in the centre of the mound (Figs 4A and 7). The arrowhead is made of grey flint and is finely worked. It is not quite symmetrical, the tang is longer than the barbs and one of the barbs is shorter and more pointed than the other. At first glance the shorter barb looks as if it were broken off, but examination under a microscope suggests this is not the case and that the shape was deliberate, or that it might have broken as it was being made and was reworked.

The mound itself is now quite shallow being only about 0.5 metres (1ft 6in) high, with a ditch surviving right round it. This initially gives the impression that the mound has been reduced in height either by erosion or by human action. However, this is not necessarily the case, at least not to any great extent. For example, a round barrow cemetery at Broughton Common near Scunthorpe was excavated in 1850. Before the excavation, the 'barrows were visible as low flat-topped mounds, 0.7 to 1.5 metres high',[10] so the Linwood barrow may not have been much higher than it is now. Landscape archaeologist Paul Everson, on a visit to the site in 2006, remarked that 'there has not been much change here for the last 4,000 years or so'.[11] Barrows are more usually found in groups than as single monuments, but there do not appear to be any more in the immediate vicinity. However, an RAF vertical photograph from 1947 shows an area of Forestry Commission woodland to the north of the Reserve, at TF138877, without its current tree

*Fig. 6: Base of Bronze Age pot from the round barrow.
(Lincolnshire County Council – Heritage Services Conservation Department)*

Fig. 7: Barbed and tanged arrowhead from the barrow. The scale is in mm

cover. Traces of what appear to be two or more barrows can be seen, so the one on the Reserve may well have been part of a group in the area.[12]

Lincolnshire was once noted for its round barrows and there are a number of early references to the quantity of them. For example the *Eastern Counties Herald* for 1852 speaks of 'a chain of tumuli or barrows stretching from the Humber to the interior of the county'. These were not all on the high ground, as is usually imagined, but were quite common in lower lying areas as well.[13] However, the vast majority of those that once existed have been destroyed by ploughing in the last 100-150 years, so that they can now be identified only by soil marks and aerial photography.

The HER shows that there are only about 25 sites in Lincolnshire where Bronze Age barrows survive as earthwork monuments. Most of these lie on the high ground of the Wolds, or on the limestone ridge in South Kesteven. The survival of lowland barrows is much rarer. An example at Barlings, part of the otherwise ploughed out Barlings/Stainfield group, still exists,[14] but there are very few others, so the Linwood barrow has a particular importance.

Industrial activity
Iron Working

The Reserve today is a quiet and peaceful place, but it was not always so. From the Late Iron Age to the end of the Roman period, it seems to have been an industrial site where the natural resources were exploited to provide some of the necessities of a civilised life. This activity may not have been continuous, and there is no evidence of people actually living there, but the timber, clay and water were certainly used to produce both iron and pottery.

In the south east corner of the Reserve, abutting the Forestry Commission fence, is a large badger sett which has been active for as long as we can remember. It is covered in bracken, so it is difficult to measure but it is about 28.5 metres (94ft) in one direction and 20.5 metres (67ft 6in) in the other, making it the largest feature on the Reserve (Fig. 8). It is about 2 metres (6ft) high. Where exposed in the badger holes the soil is sandy but dark in colour. Whilst the badgers have been burrowing there for many years, it is unlikely that a mound of this size could result purely from their activity and there is evidence that something else was going on there. A few years ago we found a large lump of iron slag weighing 2.5kg (5lb) (Fig. 9) which had been pushed to the edge of a burrow by the badgers (an indication of just how powerful they are). The lump has been identified as tap slag from iron smelting. The shape of the piece suggests that it came directly from a tapping pit. 'The slag lump is fairly fresh and has a projecting sprue or run of slag and, clearly, would not have been moved far from the original point of deposition'.[15] We had assumed that this was of Roman date but we sought the expert opinion of Jane Cowgill, archaeological metal-

Fig. 8: Site of the badger sett and Late Iron Age iron smelting activity from the west (Photo. Peter Wilson)

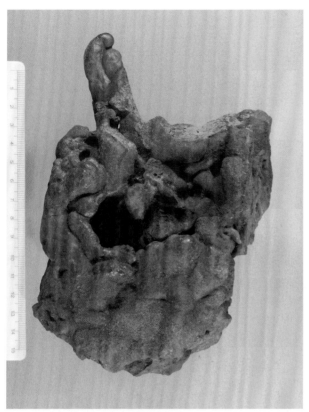

Fig. 9: Piece of iron slag from the badger sett.
(Scale in cms)

working specialist, who is firmly of the opinion that it is not typical of Roman slag deposits, and is most likely to be Late Iron Age in date.[16]

This is not the first piece of slag to come from that area. Another large piece weighing 1.8kg (4lb) and several smaller pieces have been found over the years. In fact two small pieces of slag were found in 1969 and we were able to have them analysed by staff at the then Appleby Frodingham Steel Co. at Scunthorpe. These are now in the City & County Museum (Acc.No.203.76). The analysis noted an iron content of over 40%, which is fairly typical of the inefficient smelting process used.

But this discovery is nothing new. An earlier reference to iron-working activity at Linwood Warren occurs in an article in *The Naturalist* for 1900. In June of that year, members of the Grimsby Natural History Society and the Louth Antiquarian and Naturalists' Society visited Linwood Warren, 'leave of access having been kindly granted by Col Conway-Gordon', who was the Lord of the Manor of Linwood. The Revd Edward Adrian Woodruffe-Peacock,

secretary of the Lincolnshire Naturalists' Union, wrote an account of the visit with lists of the birds and insects found. At the end he said 'We came across the *scoriae* (slag) of ancient British iron-smeltings on the Warren' and proceeded to describe the process whereby ironstone is produced in sandy areas such as Linwood. The report splendidly concluded that at the end of the meeting 'A high tea was provided for the visitors at Market Rasen … , the Mayor of Louth (Mr. S. Gresswell), senior vice-president of the Louth Society, presiding with his usual felicitous kindness'.[17]

Woodruffe-Peacock described how iron particles passed through sandy soils in solution and were precipitated when a non-porous surface was reached at which point the iron-rich sand was cemented together and ironstone was formed. To extract the iron for smelting, this ironstone had to be crushed to a small particle size then washed to remove impurities. The resulting iron ore was placed with alternate layers of charcoal for fuel in a furnace constructed of clay, and heated until the iron (known as 'bloom') was molten and could be separated from the impurities (slag). The relatively pure iron was then taken away for conversion into tools, weapons, utensils, or whatever was needed, whilst the slag and residue from the crushing and smelting process would be left behind. Vast quantities of good quality charcoal were needed, so the proximity of woodland was important. Several generations of such activity could result in a large mound of waste, including slag. No evidence of the furnaces themselves has been found, but unlike pottery kilns, the process does not bake hard the clay of which they are made, so the remains are difficult to recognise, even in full excavations.

There is also other evidence of iron working in the area. The HER records the existence of a 'bloomery hearth' (SMR No.50553) consisting of a low mound of 15m diameter and 0.5m high with evidence of clinker and possibly forge slag at a site west of College Farm and some 500 metres from the badger sett, though no date is given for this feature. Additionally, evidence of iron smelting was found during the recent excavations of the pottery kilns in Market Rasen.[18]

Pottery

Rabbits are an active part of the fauna of the Reserve and their burrows exist in many areas, but in particular on the central dry heath. There is a slightly raised area of short grass here and walking across this over many years, we have picked up a number of sherds (broken fragments) of pottery kicked out by the rabbits. These fragments are Roman and appear to be third and fourth century in date. Most are of the very common coarse greyware fabric, though a few are of other fabrics.

Roman pottery kilns have been known about on the Reserve for many years and a number were excavated on the central heath in the mid twentieth century. Unfortunately the record of these excavations is not as complete as it might be, and some material is only now, 50 years later, being considered by a Roman pottery specialist, but we summarise here the information that is currently available, which has not previously been brought together.

During the late 1930s and 1940s the nearby De Aston School in Market Rasen ran a Scientific Society, the Chairman of which was T H Court. Tommy Court was a keen naturalist as well as being interested in archaeology and was also the editor of the school magazine, *The De Astonian*. It was widely known that Roman pottery could be found at Linwood Warren and under his leadership, members of the Society started investigating the site. The first reference appeared in *The De Astonian* No. 102 of June 1939,[19] when there was a report of an excavation on Linwood Warren. This produced a quantity of greyware 'wasters' (pots broken or damaged during the firing process that were thrown away on site) including fragments of a bowl and a jar. A vessel of thin red clay was also found, but no actual kiln. The City and County Museum has two boxes of pottery (Acc.No. 45.97) labelled as being from 'Linwood kiln, 1939'. One box contains sherds of a fairly thin reddish shelly fabric cooking pot, which could be the one mentioned in the report. This vesicular or pitted pottery appears to result from the leaching away of fossil shell inclusions in the pottery due to the acidic soil conditions. The other box has more standard greyware bowls and dishes in fairly large pieces, which again accords with the description. The site was visited by F T (Tom) Baker, then curator of the Lincoln Museum, who suggested that the investigations continue to try to find the kiln.

In 1941 an excavation was carried out probably on this same site, again under the leadership of Tommy Court, and under the supervision of Tom Baker. The site had been identified by a large number of potsherds on the surface, including many 'wasters'. Tom Baker published a brief summary of the excavation in the *Journal of Roman Studies* for 1942,[20] which is worth quoting here in full:

'A round kiln was found, the combustion chamber of which measured 4 ft diameter, the clay walls being 12 inches thick. The

unusual flue and oven floor support consisted, at the centre, of two blocks of limestone (2ft 3 inches by 1ft 6 inches) set 7 inches apart, across which gap were five baked-clay bars (12 by 4 ft by 3½ in) *[12 x 4 x 3 ½ inches? Ed]* the three centre being arched and perforated with two 1-in holes, the others flat with a slight central depression. The once existing oven floor had been supported by this central structure and a flange in the kiln wall, the bars projecting into the oven above its floor level. The kiln wall was damaged at the stoke hole, but much charred material showed its position, and the combustion chamber floor sloped down towards it. The pottery was all greyware of the third century A.D. and included a variety of forms.'

A slightly fuller report appeared in *The De Astonian* for September 1941,[21] including a photograph and a drawing of the kiln by Tom Baker (Fig. 10). So far, no finds from this excavation have been traced so no reassessment has been possible.

This kiln, kiln 1, is of considerable interest to archaeologists as it has given its name to a small but distinctive group of kilns in the north Lincolnshire and south Yorkshire area, called 'Linwood-type' kilns, as

Fig. 10: The 1941 Roman pottery kiln excavation.
(Reproduced by permission of Lincolnshire County Council – Lincolnshire Archives and De Aston School)

identified by V Swan in her scholarly work on the pottery kilns of Roman Britain. The characteristic features of these kilns are the two rectangular blocks in the centre of the firing chamber and the rectangular clay bars spanning them. Swan dates kiln 1 to the late third to early fourth centuries but records that one Linwood-type kiln, presumably kiln 2, 'was apparently in use until after the middle of the fourth century'.[22]

The Easter 1943 edition, No. 109, of *The De Astonian* reported that 'A piece of burnt clay containing clear fingerprints from the pottery kiln site was exhibited' (at the Scientific Society meeting), and in the following issue, October 1943, there was a report of a further excavation at Linwood Warren but on a fresh site. 'Evidence of the probable existence of another kiln upon this site was found in the form of broken pottery, charcoal and quantities of burnt earth and clay, but the actual kiln was not found'.[23]

Another kiln was excavated in 1950, again by De Aston School with supervision by Tom Baker. The *Journal of Roman Studies* for 1951 merely noted that another kiln was excavated, but gives no details. Material from this kiln does survive in the City and County Museum. It is currently being assessed by Ian Rowlandson, Community Archaeologist with North Lincolnshire Museums, and will hopefully be prepared for publication at a later date. Ian has kindly drawn a selection of pottery for this article and he has contributed this preliminary assessment:

'The pottery in the Lincoln Museum stores from the 1951 excavation consists mostly of large jar and bowl rims. The assemblage suggests that excavators were selective and retained mostly rims with few body sherds. The pottery from the kiln has similarities with late Roman assemblages from Lincoln and Horncastle. Dating of the kiln products is dependant upon comparison with other published pottery from the region as no coins are recorded from the excavations. The boxes relating to the 1951 excavations contained a body sherd from a Swanpool/Cantley tradition *mortarium* or mixing bowl, which was probably not made on the site but helps to date the kiln products to the late third to fourth century, and a bowl with an inturned bead and flange rim which suggests that the kiln was last fired in the second half of the fourth century. Although these vessels suggest a late fourth century date for the final firing, the boxes also contain a number of completely wheelmade 'dales type' jars in a grey sandy fabric which suggests that there was also pottery production at the site from the middle of the third century. As large quantities of pottery waste litter production sites it is not surprising that material from earlier firings is present in the assemblages retrieved by the school boys. Three jars from the 1951 kiln site are illustrated:

an unusually large narrow-necked jar in a sandy grey fabric; (Fig. 11, 1)

another jar in a coarse sandy, pebbly and vesicular grey fabric which was obviously misfired and must have been made on the site. The rim of the jar had cracking or *dunting* along the edge of the rim as a result of rapid cooling during the firing process.

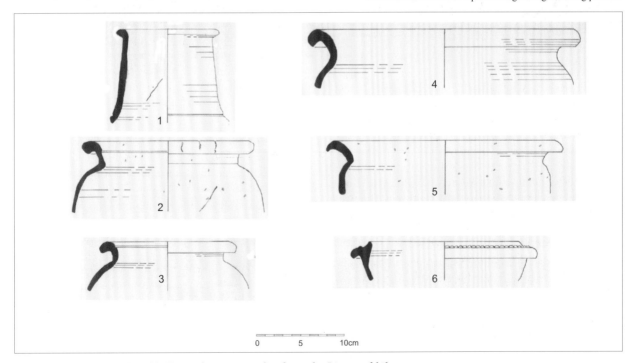

Fig. 11: Typical pottery styles from the Linwood kilns (drawn by Ian Rowlandson)

This jar is similar to a vessel found at The Park, Lincoln;[24] (Fig. 11, 2); a lid seated jar in a grey sandy and pebbly fabric which has similarities to a 'Huntcliff' form, similar to a vessel found in the late Roman assemblage from 27 High Street, Horncastle[25] (Fig. 11, 3).'

In 1955 there was a partial excavation of a further kiln in which well-known local archaeologist Mrs J Mostyn Lewis was involved. We have not traced any information on the type of kiln found, but there is a box of sherds at the museum (Acc.No. 202.76). There is one cooking pot of which the lower third survives, which is clearly a 'waster'. Otherwise the pieces are quite small and of varying fabric.

Following work by the LWT to install a water trough on the heath in 2000, we found sizeable lumps of kiln fabric and pottery sherds which had been disturbed during the pipe laying, which indicate the presence of another kiln, in an area where we had not previously found surface pottery. This material consisted of a variety of jar and bowl fragments mostly similar to the material recovered from the other kilns Two wide-mouthed bowls are illustrated, one in a dark grey sandy fabric with burnished surfaces which is similar to examples from the kilns at Swanpool, Lincoln (Fig. 11,4)[26] and another is shown which occurs in the sandy and vesicular fabric common in the kiln material (Fig. 11,5). A bowl with an inturned bead and flange with a frilled decoration and a grey sandy fabric was also collected (Fig. 11,6). This bowl is similar to an example from Horncastle and must date to the second half of the fourth century.[27]

In addition to the above, the HER records pottery scatters and dark soil, evidence of further kilns, from other locations on the western half of the Reserve, although some of the grid references given may not be completely accurate. In addition, a number of sherds from the Reserve have been accessioned into the North Lincolnshire Museum at Scunthorpe, along with two small fragments of a non-ferrous slag which may be fuel ash slag from a kiln firing (NLM S 2006.056, OS grid ref. TF 130 875). The pottery includes a small fragment of a carinated bowl, probably dating to the second century, and a bowl with a triangular rim probably dating from the mid second to early third centuries. This suggests that there was some activity on the site in the second century A.D. probably prior to the development of pottery production which may have been active from the mid third century. No definite sherds of Iron Age pottery forms have been seen during the quick assessment of the material in both museums.

In short, there is evidence for five or six kilns on the Reserve, but there may well have been more. Without a detailed survey it is not possible to delineate the full extent of the 'kiln field', but it would not be an exaggeration to say that there was an extensive industry on the Reserve for 100-150 years towards the end of the Roman period.

Further evidence of the size of the industry comes from what is quite likely to have been the clay pit from which the raw material was extracted. This lies immediately east of the main 'kiln field' and shows very clearly as a large, oval depression, roughly 50metres (166ft) across its longest dimension. The speculative identification of this depression as a clay pit has been confirmed by Ian Rowlandson, who excavated similar features adjacent to pottery kilns during recent work in Market Rasen, and he has calculated the volume of clay produced.[28] If the Linwood pit was as deep as those at Market Rasen, to which it is similar in size, it would have produced at least 76m³ of raw clay for pottery production and kiln construction.

Pottery production needed ready and convenient supplies of three commodities – clay, water and timber for the firing process. Linwood Warren had all three in close proximity. The blown sand on the surface of the site is quite shallow in places and immediately overlays the Kimmeridge clay which is a good material for pottery making. There is water close by, and the area is still well wooded, providing a good source of timber. Heather growing in the area, could also have been used as a fuel, as was the case with the Market Rasen kilns.[29] It is likely that all elements of the process – the digging and preparing of the clay, the wheel throwing of the pots and the kiln firing – took place within the same field.

The products of the Linwood kilns were coarse grey kitchen wares, such as cooking pots of various sizes, bowls and jars, of a general type common throughout Roman Britain (Fig. 11). The grey fabric was produced by excluding oxygen when firing the kilns. Some sherds of red or oxidised fabric have been found, but these may be the result of oxygen getting into the kiln during firing by mistake. The pots are generally plain but some have burnished lines on them by way of decoration. A range of coarseware pottery was also produced in an area to the south of Market Rasen from the second to the fourth centuries, another site which was investigated by the De Aston Scientific Society in the 1960s and which has been more thoroughly excavated in recent years.[30] The generally utilitarian nature of this pottery suggests that it was produced largely for the local market and would not have been transported over large distances. Other kilns existed in the Lincoln area, in the Trent Valley near Gainsborough and in North Lincolnshire, all producing coarse grey pottery. So we can assume that the Linwood products would have been used quite close to where they were made.

The assembled evidence from the site suggests that the Roman pottery industry was active from the middle of the third century until the end of the Roman period, but there was probably some activity on the Reserve throughout the Roman period.

Roads

One other aspect of the Roman period, which would have affected the industries on the Warren, is transport links. In his book *Roman Lincolnshire*, Ben Whitwell noted that there is a possible Roman road running from Ermine Street in the parish of Spridlington east through Toft Newton to Linwood Warren.[31] He gave no further detail of the conjectured line of this road. However, there is a letter in the Lincolnshire Archives Office (LAO) from Miss Joan Gibbons to Mr Swalwell of Linwood dated April, 1937, as part of the information collected for a history of the parish of Linwood.[32] In this she states 'Mr. Phillips (CW Phillips, who undertook much work in Lincolnshire during the 1930s to identify and record archaeological sites and features) has followed up a Roman road from Wood Hill Farm westwards to Ermine Street near Spridlington. The road along Gibbet Hill between Middle Rasen and Faldingworth is part of it, but he couldn't trace it east of Wood Hill Farm.' Examination of the 1:25,000 OS map shows a series of remarkably straight parish boundaries running east from Ermine Street, of which Gibbet Lane is a part, to Wood Hill Farm, where the parish boundary between Linwood and Market Rasen takes a sharp turn to the north. The present boundary of the Reserve is only about 400 metres east of Wood Hill Farm and there is, or was until recently, a straight field boundary between the two. This possible road also passes a similar distance to the south of the Market Rasen kiln field. So it seems likely that the people running the industry in the area had access to a good road for the transport of their produce, at least to the west.

At some time after the Roman period this road ceased to be used as a through route, and survived only in parts. From Linwood village today there is a lane known as Willingham Lane which runs in an easterly direction towards the Warren. It lies south of the supposed line of the Roman road and is now a public byway.

Running diagonally across the west end of the Reserve, are two parallel banks with ditches and a flat area in between. The banks are roughly 18.5 metres (60ft) apart and on top of the western bank are mature oaks which could be more than 200 years old. The strip of land around the banks has considerable tree cover, and is quite distinct from the areas on either side of it, the West End Field to the west and the dry heath to the east. At the north end of the Reserve, the banks run up to the Legsby Road, whilst at the southern end they just peter out at the edge of the Reserve where it meets Crab Apple Lane, which gives access to College Farm. On the opposite side of this lane is Willingham Lane. Though now little used, Willingham Lane must once have been a main access to the Warren area and its name would suggest that it continued northwards towards Willingham village.

The first edition of the OS map was published in 1824. This clearly shows that, at that date, Willingham Lane continued across the Reserve on a line that coincides with the parallel banks. Interestingly, it did not carry straight on, on the other side of Legsby Road, but there was a track slightly to the west which continued north to join the Willingham Road roughly where the racecourse now ends. The lane is also shown to cross the Reserve on the 1842 tithe map. By the time of the 1891 25 inch OS map, it is no longer there, but its course is marked with a line of trees, a number of which are still there. So at some time in the second half of the nineteenth century that part of Willingham Lane went out of use though there is no indication as to why, or exactly when. The area is quite wet, so perhaps it just became too boggy for continued use. It was replaced by Crab Apple Lane, which follows an old field boundary and now has the re-routed stream running alongside it.

Where the Willingham Lane banks approach Legsby Road they join further banks running at right angles to them. These banks continue eastwards right through the Reserve roughly parallel to Legsby Road but slightly to the south of it. It can be seen from the 1824 map that this was the original line of the Legsby Road, which has been straightened to its present course, probably at the end of the nineteenth century, but leaving the traces of its former line clearly visible today.

Fig. 12: The bank across the dry heath (Photo. Peter Wilson)

Why is it called Linwood Warren?

There are other earthworks on the Reserve as well as these old road banks. There is a significant bank, which runs in a straight line across the dry heath from Willingham Lane to the centre of the Reserve, and then continues on a slightly different course almost to the eastern boundary. (Fig. 12) Len Watkinson and Peter Wilson dug a section through this bank which confirmed that it was built of turves. In LWT literature this is described as a medieval field boundary, but its western end overlays the eastern bank of Willingham Lane, which was in use until at least the mid nineteenth century, so the bank must be later than this. Close to the Roman pottery kilns is a long low mound which is barely noticeable when the grass is high, but can be seen distinctly in winter, and there are other, less regular mounds in the area. They do not have the appearance of 'waster heaps' associated with the pottery industry and are too regular to be the spoil heaps from excavations.

There is also reference in the LWT literature to a 'medieval' or 'Elizabethan' house. We have found no evidence of any structure resembling a house, but there is a strange sub-rectangular earthwork, with a flat area inside and no apparent entrances, which is situated approximately in the centre of the Reserve. This has been referred to as the 'warrener's cottage' but it does not appear on any map, nor have we found any reference to a warrener in Linwood parish. It also appears to be built of turves and to be contemporaneous with the bank.

When we started this project we knew that the area had 'always' been called Linwood Warren, and that a warren was an area where rabbits were kept, but then we started wondering and questioning. There are certainly rabbits on the Reserve today, though fewer now than there were, but is there any evidence apart from the name that it was a warren? For how long was it a warren? Was it a managed warren, or simply an area where rabbits lived? How large was it? What follows addresses some of these questions.

The earliest map which marks the warren is Armstrong's map of 1778.[33] Despite being at a scale of one inch to two miles, the detail does not appear to be very accurate. For example, the road from Lissington to Linwood is shown as straight, omitting the many sharp bends, but just to the north of Linwood village, a property called 'Warrenhouse' (*sic*) is marked. This must have been a place of some significance for it to be noted, but there is no further detail, nor an indication of the size of any warren.

The first edition of the OS one inch to one mile map for Lincolnshire was surveyed in 1818 and published in 1824. This is the first really accurately surveyed map to a scale large enough to show detail for a small patch of land such as the Reserve. It shows an area marked 'Linwood Warren', extending from the stream north of the present golf course at the northern end, to the Linwood parish boundary in the south, and from that parish boundary at the eastern end of the Reserve westwards to Wood Hill, which still exists as Wood Hill Farm.

A few years later (1825 to 1827) Bryant's map for the county was published.[34] This is also to a large scale and shows additional detail. For example Warren House is marked in the position it still is (though now used as the Golf Club House). Linwood Warren covers the whole area indicated on the OS map, except for a small area that equates to the West End Field of the Reserve, indicating that this area was farmed at that period.

Then we come to the most important surviving document about Linwood and the Warren - the Tithe Award Map of 1842.[35] This identifies every field in the parish, and gives the name of the occupier, the acreage and the land use. It is a wonderful source of information. (Fig. 13) It shows three fields about 500 metres east of Linwood village along Willingham Lane, two of which are named Coney Garth and one Coney Garth Hill. These fields lie a short distance north of the earthworks of the medieval manor, adjacent to Linwood church. Rabbits are not native to Britain but were introduced by the Normans soon after the Conquest. They were not hardy animals and were valuable so they were kept in enclosures to protect them and so that they could be fed to keep them through the winter.[36] In the early Middle Ages, rabbit meat became a 'fashionable delicacy of the wealthy' and was four or five times more expensive than chicken in the thirteenth century.[37] Setting up warrens was a manorial privilege, and rabbits were kept in small enclosures or *coneygarths,* a corruption of the two words coney and earth, which were located close to the monastery or manor house which owned them.[38] So it seems highly probable that the *Coney Garth* fields marked on the Tithe map were indeed used for keeping

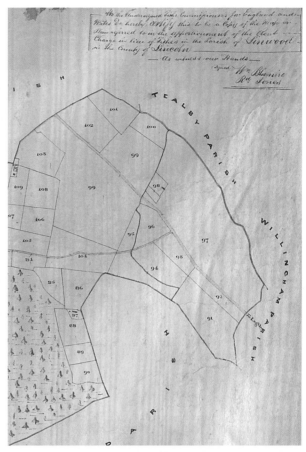

Fig. 13: Part of the Linwood Tithe Award Map, 1842.
Fields 91 to 96 are now the Reserve.
(LAO, F.309 Reproduced by permission of Lincolnshire County Council – Lincolnshire Archives, and the Diocese of Lincoln)

rabbits in the medieval period, and were associated with the nearby manor house. In this period the adult animals were known as *coneys* or *conys*, the word rabbit being used for young animals only. The terminology changed gradually, so that by the eighteenth century the terms rabbit and rabbit warren came into common use, but the word *coneygarth* can survive as a place name long after its original function has ceased.[39] The Linwood Coney Garth fields lie south of the area described as 'warren' on the OS map and are some 500 metres from the Reserve. These three fields are all described as in arable use at the time of the Tithe map.

The area covered by the present Reserve incorporates fields 91 to 96 on the Tithe map, all of which were in the ownership of Sir Arthur Ingram Aston, who was the Lord of the Manor and owner of the whole parish, and in the

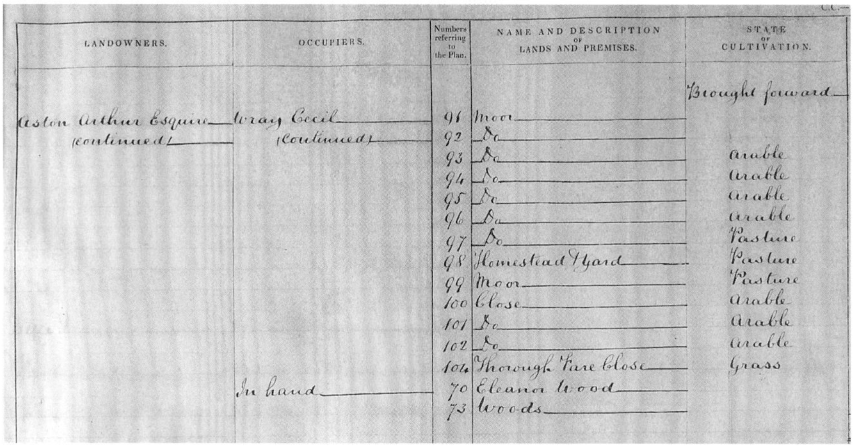

LANDOWNERS.	OCCUPIERS.	Numbers referring to the Plan.	NAME AND DESCRIPTION OF LANDS AND PREMISES.	STATE OF CULTIVATION.
				Brought forward
Aston Arthur Esquire (continued)	Wray Cecil (continued)	91	Moor	
		92	Do	
		93	Do	arable
		94	Do	arable
		95	Do	arable
		96	Do	arable
		97	Do	Pasture
		98	Homestead & yard	Pasture
		99	Moor	Pasture
		100	Close	arable
		101	Do	arable
		102	Do	arable
		104	Thorough Fare Close	Grass
	In hand	70	Eleanor Wood	
		73	Woods	

Fig. 14: Ownership and usage of the fields which now form the Reserve (LAO, F.309 Reproduced by permission of Lincolnshire County Council – Lincolnshire Archives, and the Diocese of Lincoln)

occupation of Cecil Wray. These fields are all described as 'moor', with no other description for Fields 91 and 92, but the four fields 93 to 96 are said to be in arable use. (Fig. 14) Field 97, the area which is now the golf course, is in the same ownership and described as 'pasture'. There is no mention of a warren anywhere.

Fields 95 and 96 lie to the north-west of Willingham Lane and now form the West End Field of the Reserve. Although wet, the area is flat and in Field 95 we have noted parallel ridges running roughly north south, with the ridges some 7.5 metres (24ft 6 in) apart, which may be evidence of former ploughing. Field 96 is now very wet and it is hard to imagine it being very productive as arable land but, as noted above, Bryant's map depicts this area differently, so perhaps, for some period at least, this area may have been cultivated. Fields 93 and 94 are the pottery kiln area. In certain lights when the grass is short we have noted faint parallel lines across the heath. These were also seen by Len Watkinson who interpreted them as lines of ploughing, but they could possibly be the results of mole-draining which was certainly taking place in Lincolnshire from the late eighteenth century. The fact that pottery kilns survive in fairly complete condition suggests that it cannot have been subjected to much ploughing and certainly not over an extended period. This is also the driest and sandiest part of the Reserve, and so most suitable for rabbits. Fields 91 and 92 are generally much wetter and must always have been fairly unsuitable for rabbits, as for other forms of farming, which must be why the round barrow has survived.

There are straight lines on the Tithe map marking the divisions between Fields 91, 92, 93 and 94, and the line which runs east-west is about on the line of the extant turf bank across the Reserve. So there was a boundary there in 1842, though as noted above, the bank itself seems to be later than that. Such a bank would have taken some effort to construct; it would not have been needed if the fields were in arable cultivation, but would form a suitable barrier, with gorse on top, for fields used by animals.

The next evidence chronologically comes from White's Trade Directory for 1856. Under the introduction for the parish of Linwood it states that the parish is '2,410 acres, including a rabbit warren of 250 acres and an extensive wood'. At this date the parish had 232 'souls', Sir Arthur Ingram Aston was Lord of the Manor, and farmer George Belton was living at Warren House. We accept that the information in trade directories cannot always be relied upon, but it seems unlikely that this information was simply invented. White's Directory for 1872 is slightly different. The parish is given as 2,316 acres in extent 'including a rabbit warren of 300 acres'. By this date Capt. Conway-Gordon was Lord of the Manor, but George Belton was still at Warren House. Exactly the same information is given in the 1882 edition of the Directory, so this could have been a direct copy, without checking the current accuracy of the information, but it does suggest that not only did a rabbit warren exist at least into the 1870s, but that it actually increased in size between 1856 and 1872. The directories do not give a precise location for the warren, but we must assume that it is the area marked as such on the maps.

Linwood Warren continued to be marked on maps. The first large scale survey, at 25 inches to the mile, was undertaken in the late 1880s and the OS map was printed in 1891. This shows 'Lynwode Warren' covering only the area of the Reserve and the golf course, with Lynwode Warren House where the Golf Club House now is. The same information was given on the 1905 edition of the map.

Evidence from census records is not very helpful. In 1841 Cecil Wray, the occupier of Warren House, and the land around it, was described as a farmer, aged 40 with a wife and three children. By 1851 he had been succeeded by George Belton, aged 60, with a wife and seven children, who is described as a farmer of 250 acres employing one labourer. His eldest son, another George, was also employed on the farm. This second George continued in tenancy of the farm until at least 1905, with other members of the family. At no point is there a mention of a warren or of a warrener living at Warren House, or elsewhere in Linwood parish.

So despite the name of the place, the maps, and the trade directories, other evidence does not fully support the existence of a warren, at least not in the eighteenth and nineteenth centuries. But is there any physical evidence on the site itself which might give more clues?

The Black Death in the mid fourteenth century caused a shortage of labour and this led to an increase in the amount of land used for warrens which required less manpower than regular farming. This in turn led to rabbit meat becoming more plentiful, and thus less of a luxury. As warrens became larger, poaching became easier so that even the poor acquired a taste for rabbit meat.[40] On some warrens, buildings were erected for the warrener to live on the site to deter poachers and to make managing the rabbits easier.

Many warrens continued in existence through the later middle ages and into the post-medieval period, particularly in areas of poor soil where other types of farming were not profitable, such as the Norfolk Breckland, and there was renewed interest in warrens as a source of income between 1650 and 1750 when some new ones were created.[41] But by the mid eighteenth century agricultural improvements were under way and many warrens were turned to more profitable uses such as cereal production. In Lincolnshire, there had been extensive rabbit warrens, particularly on the Heath south of Lincoln and on the Wolds. At the end of the eighteenth century this began to change. Arthur Young in his *General View of the Agriculture of Lincolnshire,* 1800, noted that along the south western side of the Wolds, thirty miles of warrens had been replaced by sheep and turnips,

although on the eastern side of the Wolds there were still too many warrens.[42] By the mid nineteenth century most of the upland areas of the county had been improved and were under the plough. There was still money to be made from rabbits, though, as the meat continued to be popular and the fur also had a value. Most rabbits were grey in colour, like the wild rabbit of today, but black rabbits were favoured in some medieval warrens, and a speciality of Lincolnshire during the eighteenth and nineteenth centuries was the silver-grey. This had fur of outstanding quality which was much sought after, the skins fetching one shilling each in the 1790s.[43]

Brigg was one of the most important centres in the country specialising in producing felt for hats from rabbit fur. Each rabbit could produce an ounce of 'wool' and in 1800 this was worth 20 shillings a pound.[44] The dressing of rabbit skins provided employment for most women and girls in Brigg at this time, but the ploughing up of the warrens quickly brought an end to the industry. By 1856 only two furriers remained in business, and they had both gone by 1872.[45] Thus it would be logical to suppose that if there were warrening activity at Linwood, it would have ceased by the mid nineteenth century. But some warrens did continue up to the end of the nineteenth century and beyond, particularly in areas of very poor soil such as the Norfolk Breckland[46] and this is probably what happened at Linwood.

A full explanation of the features to be found on rabbit warrens is given by Dr Tom Williamson in his recently published Shire book *The Archaeology of Rabbit Warrens.*[47] Warrens were often enclosed by banks topped with stakes and furze to keep the rabbits in. As the rabbits tried to burrow through the banks, the holes would be filled up by the warrener, although inevitably some would escape. The book has an illustration of a bank running across High Lodge Warren in Suffolk (p. 46) which looks very similar to that running across the Reserve.

A physical feature of many managed warrens was the 'pillow mound', an earthwork raised a few feet above the ground surface that was usually a long, thin rectangle, but could also be circular. These mounds were constructed of light or sandy soil to provide easy burrowing for the rabbits. They were particularly used in wet areas to keep the burrows above ground and therefore dry, and they concentrated the rabbits in one area making them easier to catch when they were ready for market. Pillow mounds often occur in groups over a wide area, but in areas that

Fig. 15: The possible pillow mound on the dry heath (Photo. Peter Wilson)

are naturally dry single mounds are sometimes found that were used specifically for the does and young animals. They continued to be constructed right up to the end of the nineteenth century.

We sent Dr Williamson a photograph of the long mound near the bank and he replied that 'it looks like a pillow mound to me', and he has seen hundreds of them[48] (Fig. 15). Paul Everson, a leading landscape archaeologist, also suggested it could be a pillow mound, so we feel some confidence suggesting this. Its proximity to the bank, to which it runs parallel, strengthens the possibility that this was a bank of the warren. The east bank of Willingham Lane could have provided another side, with the stream on the south side providing an effective barrier there. Eight other possible pillow mounds in Lincolnshire are noted on the HER, three of which are definitely associated with medieval moated or monastic sites, and one with the place-name 'coneygarth'. The others are of less certain date, but probably post medieval.

So a possible scenario is that the whole area marked on the 1824 OS map was a rabbit warren in the eighteenth century. In common with what was happening elsewhere, attempts may have been made to drain and improve the land in the early nineteenth century, and even some cultivation was perhaps attempted, leading to the description of the fields on the Reserve as 'arable' in 1842, but that soon proved unprofitable so the area reverted to warren. There is definite evidence of its unsuitability for crop growing in the story that the farmer tried to grow potatoes there in the 1920s but did not get back the cost of his seed.[49] Later in the nineteenth century further attempts at improvement seem to have been made, but this time directed towards improving the efficiency of the warren by building, or rebuilding, the banks to enclose the rabbits and possibly constructing at least one pillow mound. As no 'warrener' is mentioned in the census records, we can perhaps assume that managing the site was not a full-time occupation but was undertaken by George Belton and other family members from Warren House as part of their other more regular farming activities.

from otherwise unprofitable land. However, this is only one interpretation of the evidence, and there may well be others. The features are not easy to see under the long grass cover, and even less easy to photograph (Fig. 16). A full archaeological landscape survey of the Reserve is really needed to clarify these earthworks and their relationship to one another.

There remains the enigmatic earthwork in the centre of the Reserve. As noted above, it is roughly rectangular, being some 18 metres (nearly 60ft) long by 5 metres (16ft) wide, with rounded corners. It is hollow in the middle, this hollow being about 2.5 metres (8ft) across, but there are no obvious entrances and the interior seems to be full of sand. This feature does not appear on any maps, even the very detailed 25" OS map of 1905 which clearly marks the details of the agricultural buildings at Warren House nearby. It could possibly have been some kind of cattle shelter, or perhaps it was used in connection with the rabbit warren, or it could be associated with the military use of

Fig. 16: Peter Wilson photographing the features on the heath (Photo. Catherine Wilson)

Certainly there would always have been a market for rabbit meat, even if it did not command the high prices of medieval times, and this would have produced some return

Fig. 17: The shooting butt from the south (Photo. Peter Wilson)

the area – perhaps in connection with the Volunteers using the rifle range.

Rifle range

Near the eastern edge of the reserve is a substantial oval mound, approximately 24 metres (79ft) long, 12.8 metres (42ft) wide, and 1.52 metres (5ft) high (Fig. 17). It is made of sand and now has some tree cover but is clearly a man-made feature. Over the years, four bullets have been found at the site, where rabbits have disturbed the surface, suggesting its purpose as a shooting butt for rifle practice. This is confirmed by the OS map for 1891 which shows a rifle range running through the Reserve, across Legsby Road and on to the golf course to the north. The map marks intermediate distances of 250, 500, 600, 700, and 800 yards, with the 500 yard mark being where the range crosses the Legsby road. The map also marks a flagstaff at the shooting butt. Eight hundred yards must have been its fullest extent as a further 200 yards would take it right to the buildings of Warren House, now the Golf Club House. The orientation of the rifle range is almost exactly north to south, with the butt running at right angles to it. A detailed description for the construction of shooting butts is given in *The Book of Field Sports* about 1860, as well as instructions for their use.[50] It is interesting to compare the professional instructions given with the Linwood example, which is shorter and lower than is recommended, and without traces

of the recommended brick walls, though it may well have been protected with much cheaper faggots instead.

The four bullets found in the mound are all of the same type. They are made of lead with a clay plug in the base and three sawtooth ridges or cannelures around the circumference. They are cylindro-conoidal in shape, though the hollow 'nose' in each case has been flattened on impact. The casing for the cartridge, which would have enclosed the gunpowder, was extremely thin brass and would not have been projected, so no trace has been found (Fig.18). These bullets can be precisely identified and dated. They are Mark IX type bullets, introduced in August 1871, for the Snider breech-loading rifle. The Snider was standard issue to the military between 1864 and 1874 and was the first breech-loading rifle to enter common use, replacing the muzzle loading types. In 1874 the Snider was replaced as the standard issue rifle by the Martini-Henry,[51] but these new guns were not available in Market Rasen until 1885. So, we can say with certainty that these bullets were deposited between 1871 and 1885.

But why was a rifle range needed, who used it and for how long was it in use?

There had been militia forces in Britain since the sixteenth century, and they played a key role during the Napoleonic wars, but they were little needed during the early nineteenth century and fell into abeyance. However, renewed threats from France in 1853, led to a revival of the militia, which

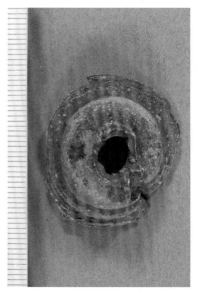

Fig. 18: Snider rifle bullets found in the shooting butt. Scales in mm. (Photo. Peter Wilson)

Fig. 19: Part of practice trench, 1975
(Photo. Peter Wilson)

were organised on a county by county basis. These militia were served by newly-constructed barracks such as the Old Barracks in Lincoln, now housing the Museum of Lincolnshire Life, which was built in 1856 as the base for the Royal North Lincolnshire Militia. The *Market Rasen Mail* for 25 October 1856 records the visit of a recruiting party from Lincoln *en route* to Louth which paraded through the town expecting to 'obtain several recruits to make up the required number of about 400 men to serve in the corps'.[52] A more immediate threat of invasion from France in 1859 led to the authorisation of a large expansion of the volunteer force, and their operation was put on a more regular footing. The concept of volunteer soldiers proved popular so that by 1861 there were 614 rifle corps and 63 regiments of artillery country-wide.[53] Lincolnshire was not slow to respond to this need for local defence, and within a few months rifle corps had been formed in most of Lincolnshire's market towns.[54] Market Rasen was no exception as the Market Rasen Rifle Volunteer Corps was formed in the town in January 1860, following a meeting in

the Corn Exchange chaired by H H Boucherette of nearby Willingham Hall. A meeting was held the following week to 'receive names of anyone anxious to take part in the protection from invaders of their own shores'.[55] Finance was raised by subscription, and by June of 1860 there were 30 to 40 'effective' members, the style and colour (scarlet) of the uniform had been chosen, and a band appointed.[56] In fact the Market Rasen Volunteers really deserve an article to themselves, as the *Market Rasen Mail* gives regular details of their activities, including instructions for their week-long camps at Thornton Abbey when they were told, amongst other things, that they could take a small amount of personal belongings on the train, but no barrels of beer![57] We can only summarise the main relevant points of this interesting story here.

Hambleton Hill, to the north east of Market Rasen, was initially chosen as the practice ground, the first 'ball practice' being held there in December 1860[58] but in 1863 this location was 'pronounced dangerous' by a government inspector and 'the butt was moved to Linwood Warren' where William Conway-Gordon had presented the Corps with 'an eligible range'.[59] 'The Rifle Range was used daily at 9.00 am'[60] on some occasions but the term 'ball practice' was used, suggesting that they were using the old muzzle loading Enfield rifles at this time. The times and frequency of practice varied considerably through the years, but it seems that the range was well used. It is perhaps surprising that no lead bullets from this period have been found at the butt, but there may well have been a system for recovering the considerable quantities of lead that were expended.

The first mention of the Snider rifle is at the end of 1870, when the *MRM* records an accident with the 'new' breech loading rifle during shooting practice.[61] During the 1870s the Volunteers appear to have had monthly shooting competitions against corps from Caistor and Hainton, over different distances – 200, 300 or 500 yards. Occasionally the competition was over 600 yards, but longer distances are not mentioned. Six hundred yards would have involved shooting across the Legsby Road and this may be one reason why the shorter distances were preferred. The competitions would have meant the expenditure of 28 to 30 pounds of lead in each of the six shoot-offs, in addition to that used in normal practice firing.

In 1881 there was a national reorganisation as part of which the Rifle Volunteers became K Company, First Battalion of the Lincolnshire Regiment[62]; the following year they are recorded as having 90 members, the Captain being A A Padley, Esq.[63] In 1885, the Volunteers were issued with Martini Henry rifles to replace the Sniders.[64] Later that same year it was reported that 'class firing' had been prohibited on the Linwood range and had to be performed at the Caistor range instead.[65] No reason is given, but thereafter mentions of K Company at Market Rasen diminish and disappear altogether by 1890. The Range however must still have been sufficiently visible to be marked in detail on the 1891 OS map, which was surveyed in the late 1880s. It is not shown on the 1906 edition of the map so had obviously ceased to be of any importance by then. The Rifle Range is the one feature on the Reserve that can be securely dated and for which significant documentary information exists.

But this was not the end of the Reserve's use for military training. In the north-eastern part of the dry heath are the visible remains of a zig-zag trench. It is approximately 16 metres (50ft) long, with 7 changes of direction in its length. It has an average width of 3.7 metres (12ft) and current depth of about 0.6 metres (2ft). The area is now covered with coarse grass *Deschampsia flexuosa* and has been for many years so the trench looks quite shallow but a photograph from 1975 shows its outline quite clearly (Fig. 19). This was thought to be a First World War practice trench, although there was no independent documentary or dating evidence. However, we sent photographs and drawings to Graham Brown of English Heritage, who has surveyed the extensive complex of practice trenches on Salisbury Plain, and also more modest examples on Lincoln's South Common. He confirmed that the Linwood trench is certainly of WWI design, and is likely to date from that period or immediately afterwards.[66] Its form shows it to have been a communication trench, as there are no crenellations to denote firing bays. It was almost certainly constructed by a local unit for their own practice. Such practice trenches were used extensively during WWI, but their importance to the archaeological record is only now being realised and their remains recorded. The extensive remains on the large military estates such as Salisbury Plain, were designed to give recruits a realistic idea of what the war zone was like. Smaller trenches, such as that at Linwood, would give the merest familiarisation with trench life.[67]

Nature Reserve

The land which now comprises Linwood Warren Nature Reserve was acquired by the LWT from A T Padley, a local solicitor, and D F Torrens, a retired doctor. These two were part of a consortium of local businessmen who had purchased the land on both sides of the Legsby Road on behalf of the Golf Club. The Club then raised the money to buy from them the land to the north of the road to use as a nine-hole golf course, but decided not to purchase the area to the south, leaving this available for preservation as a nature reserve.[68] The conveyance was dated 28 June 1957 and was signed by Ted Smith, now the President of LWT, F T Baker and Sir Francis Hill. The area was initially intended to form a further nine holes of the golf course, but the present Golf Club has managed to construct eighteen holes on their original site, thankfully leaving the Reserve area untouched. It is pleasing to note that the Golf Club is aware of the conservation importance of the site and the course is being managed to leave 'wild' areas, specifically to retain as much of its wildlife interest as possible.[69]

Its acquisition as a nature reserve did not, however, mean the end of human intervention on the Reserve, though now the priority is to retain and enhance what is there, rather than to exploit its resources as in the past. Len Watkinson was appointed the first warden; he gathered round him a keen group of volunteers including Peter Wilson, Charlie Brumpton, John East, Vic Knight, Ken Herrick, and Roger Winslow; and the complex job of managing the area began. It was soon recognised that due to a variety of factors, the Reserve was drying out, threatening some of the damp-loving plants.

Some of this drying out was caused by a general lowering of the water table, but also by drainage works which had taken place over the years, presumably to improve its usefulness as grazing land. Originally the water falling on North Wood ran straight down on to the Reserve, ensuring that it was a very wet area. The 1824 OS map shows a watercourse meandering across the Reserve and through the West End Field, presumably an early attempt at drainage. By 1891 the watercourse had been straightened and, at the west end, diverted into a new course running under and then to the west of Crab Apple Lane, the western boundary of the Reserve. Near the mid way point of the Reserve, the stream seems, at some time, to have run from south to north to exit at the Legsby Road, as this course can still be traced on the ground. At some time between the two maps of 1824 and 1842 the stream was diverted, forming an unnatural right angled bend, to run on its present course. The bank which runs east to west across the heath has subsided where it crosses the old course of the stream, so it cannot have been constructed/reconstructed before this change took place.

When the botanist F A Lees visited the Warren in 1879 he described it as 'a wet, peaty tract, water-logged sand on Kimmeridge Clay (producing) several rare Sedges'. He visited again in the late 1880s when he found that 'some water cuts had been made'. Ten years later again he found 'the ground .... heather and ling clad ... I daresay some drainage had been effected by Colonel Conway-Gordon ..... but the old bog had vanished'[70]

This and other evidence suggests that considerable changes took place during the second half of the nineteenth century, possibly related to its use as rough grazing or as a rabbit warren, which were intended to improve the land for farming purposes. Some effort went into trying to drain the land, as we have found land drainage tiles, both U-shaped ones, with a separate flat base, and the later D-shaped ones, in the south-west area of the wet heath with mature birch trees.

One of the aims of the new management was to make the Reserve wetter again. Len and his team dammed the stream which runs through the Reserve and formed a pond with a sluice towards the western end which could direct water on to the Reserve. This pond has since been enlarged and modified so that the water now runs down its original course across the West End Field. Similar activity took place at the eastern end of the site which also has since been modified. But this has not prevented changes to the flora, including the loss of some damp-loving species.

Len Watkinson and his wife Betty did much detailed survey work, including producing a contour map and a detailed map of the vegetation communities. They also encouraged Peter to undertake population studies on water bugs, grasshoppers, crickets and tiger beetles as well as birds.

Water Boatmen

As noted, the amount of water on the Reserve has varied considerably over the years. At least one pond in the south west corner of the reserve is permanently dried up, but there are now two other areas of open water as a result of recent human intervention. These are: a pond near the western end of the Reserve, previously referred to; and an area of open water on the layer of peat to the eastern end of the Reserve which dries out in some summers. In 1967 Peter took up the challenge to survey the Greater and Lesser

Water Boatmen families, and has resurveyed the area more recently. However, direct comparisons cannot be made as there have been a number of management changes to the habitat in the intervening years. Because the species within this group of invertebrates are very similar, varying mainly in size and depth of the general dark brown colouration, they do not have common names and so they have to be identified by their Latin ones.

Water boatmen are small bugs that have specific habitat needs and preferences so that they are good indicators of the water type where they are found. There are two main families: big ones, or Greater Water Boatmen, called *Notanecta,* which swim 'up side down' on their backs; and small ones, Lesser Water Boatmen, called *Corixidae,* which swim legs downwards. Both families have the stabbing and suckering mouth parts typical of bugs. *Notanecta* are about 15mm long and are predators which readily eat Lesser Water Boatmen and even prey larger than themselves such as large tadpoles or small fish. They have a powerful stabbing rostrum (mouth parts) and toxic saliva, which is very painful to man. There are four species of *Notanecta* in the British Isles, but the *N. glauca* is the only one found breeding on the Reserve. The *Corixidae* are between 4 and 9 mm long and are either predators or feed on detritus and algae, though recent studies have shown that their diet can be a mixture of the two, and that there is a food preference between the sexes.[71] Some species will even feed on other, smaller *corixids* and their nymphs.

Although they live in water, water boatmen do migrate by flying from pond to pond. In fact they sometimes mistake shiny surfaces for ponds and on occasion we have found our car roof covered in the little creatures, recovering from the shock of hitting a hard surface instead of water. It has been calculated that some of the smaller *corixids* can fly for between 2.5 and 3.5 hours, giving a range of 9.5 to 14.5 kilometres before they become too desiccated.[72] They will also fly at night, and are often recorded in moth traps.

The survey was done using a triangular net, rather than the more conventional circular, pond net because most water boatmen prefer the warmer, shallow bottom of the sloping margins of a pond. The flat bottom of the net was used to skim the bottom of the pond from about two metres out to the pond edge. This sweep was repeated five times round the edge of the pond, to give some consistency to the results. The sampling took place from the end of October to the end of December, when the water boatmen are over-wintering as adults. Mating and egg-laying occur from

February, and we have observed, on a cold but bright and sunny day, *Hesperocorixa sahlbergi* mating under a thin layer of ice in the western pool. In an attempt to record actual numbers of bugs, a capture-recapture programme, was tried on the *N. glauca* using a different coloured paint to mark the thorax each week. However, whilst this was interesting to do, the results were inconclusive due to several factors such as the unsuitability of the marking paint, migration into and out of the pond, and variations in water temperature on the sampling days. The insects were identified using the Freshwater Biological Association's keys by T T Macan[73] and A A Savage.[74]

The stream near the southern edge of the Reserve is shaded along most of its length and also clogged with *phragmites* reeds, but the pool is an important site for water boatmen, containing eight species out of a British total of approximately 30.[75] The group of species here is typical of permanent acid pools, and similar to that found in pools in Willingham Forest about a mile to the north. But the number and type of species found depends on the state of the pool at any given time. So in years when it is shaded and has a lot of weed (*potamogeton*), and particularly *phragmites* reeds, the water boatman *Hesperocorixa linnei* is dominant. When the pool has been cleared of weed, which must be done on a regular basis to keep the open water, *H. sahlbergi* is the dominant species, almost to the exclusion of other species. It seems that this pool at times, depending on the management regime, is the near perfect habitat for these two species.

The other species recorded are:

Sigara dorsalis (Fig. 20) – a very common water bug which can be present in very large numbers along the edges of slow moving rivers and drains. A migrant tending to occur in high numbers, but not breeding.

S. distincta – prefers cleaner water with less sediment than *H. sahlbergi* and *H. linnei*.

S. nigrolineata – a common species and known migrant but much darker than *S. lateralis* with which it often shares cattle ponds and other small bodies of water.

S. lateralis – a small, light coloured species but one of the most frequent migrants, mainly because its preferred habitat is organically polluted field ponds, which tend to dry up in summer.

S. falleni – there seems to be a progression of species from *S. dorsalis, S. falleni, S. distincta* to *H. sahlbergi* as the water contains more suspended organic detritus and

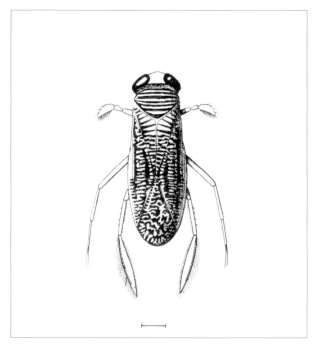

Fig. 20: A typical water boatman, Sigara dorsalis
(Reproduced with permission of the Freshwater Biological Association from their publication: A A Savage, Adults of the British Aquatic Hemiptera Heteroptera: a key with ecological notes. Scient. Publs. Freshwater Biol. Assoc., No. 50, p.23)

the bottom has more organic sediment.[76]

Corixa punctata – one of the larger species with a greater flying range which is found in a wide variety of habitats.

At the eastern end of the Reserve, the pool, which is in an open area with no overhanging vegetation, sometimes dries out in summer, but most autumns has an overwintering breeding population of four species and two others that are probably migrants.

The dominant species here is *Callicorixa praeusta*, a species which likes rather less organic detritus and a more open moorland type of habitat than *H. sahlbergi*. It contains some of the same species as the west end pool but not *S. distincta, S. lateralis* or *H. sahlbergi*. Occasionally *Corixa panzeri* has been found, a species which is more associated with the coast and deeper water than other *corixid* species but is a known migrant.[77]

This pool also attracts dragonflies and of the five species seen laying eggs in the water the most interesting is the Black Darter, *Sympetrum danea*, a typical species of northern bogs and moorland, which is also very common on the LWT Crowle Waste Reserve.

There are three cattle troughs on the reserve. These might seem unlikely habitats, but the trough in the north west corner was for some time, in the late 1960s, home to a population of *Sigara nigrolineata*, a species that likes small open habitats.

Other insects

There is a wealth of insect species on the Reserve, but we have selected a few which are associated with past or present human activity. The plants on the heathland track include *Juncus squarrosus* which is the food plant of an interesting micro-moth of the *Coleophora alticolella* species group. The larva feeds on the *J. squarrosus* seed heads, but only needs 2½ seeds to complete its life cycle.[78] The moth is present on almost all the seed heads especially those on the dry heath track. The track is of course man-made and has received considerable wheeled traffic in the past.

This track, together with rabbit activity, has provided a sandy habitat with short grass where we have noted a small but persistent colony of Green Tiger Beetle *Cicindela campestris*. As part of the surveys instigated by Len Watkinson, Peter tried to estimate the numbers and area of this colony, by systematic catching, marking and releasing individuals. There were never more than five individuals in any one year. All were associated with the track. Recent management activity has cleared tussocks of Wavy Hair Grass *Deschampsia flexuosa*, leaving bare sandy patches to encourage growth of Heather *Calluna vulgaris*, which has also benefited the Tiger Beetle.

Another invertebrate associated with warm sandy areas is the black and yellow spider *Steatoda* (formerly *Asagena*) *phalerata*. We first recorded this in 1962 on the eroded sandy walls of the practice trench. The spider was found among the nest holes of the fly-catching black and yellow digger wasp *Crabro sp.*, which the spider was thought to mimic, though the spider is a specialist feeder on ants.[79] It was found again the following year and the record was passed on to the then county recorder, G W Whatmough. It was subsequently published in the LNU transactions.[80] We have since found this spider in exactly the same place in 2004 and 2006.

In 2005 we recorded for the first time the rare Longhorn Beetle *Leptura rubra,* which we had previously known only

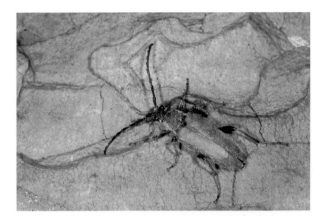

Fig. 21: Longhorn beetle Leptura rubra
(Photo. Peter Wilson)

from Weeting Heath and one other Norfolk site. (Fig. 21) It is known to be extending its range northwards and there is an earlier record from the Scunthorpe area. Its larva feeds in dead pine trunks. The adults are usually found feeding on umbellifer flower heads but we have also seen it on bramble flowers.[81]

One of the losses to the Linwood lepidoptera list is the attractive day-flying Forester moth *Adscita statices* which we last saw on the heather in the mid 1980s. It was recorded by R E M Pilcher in 1990 but has not been seen since.[82] There is no obvious reason for its extinction as its food plant, sorrel, is still common in the more open area of the dry heath.

Reptiles and Amphibia

We have seen both frog and toad spawn in the west pool. The frog spawn was certainly introduced and the toad spawn is also suspected as an introduction. During more than thirty years of sampling for water boatmen in this pool, we only encountered smooth newt *Triturus vulgaris* but in 2006 we found a palmate newt *T. helveticus* so this too may have been introduced.

Common lizard *Lacerta vivipara* (Fig. 22) has been found in several areas of the Reserve, such as the bracken area around the badger sett, on the stumps of felled pines in the drier parts of the wet heath, and around the west end pool. Those from the eastern wet heath are markedly darker than those in the west of the Reserve. Lizards used to be seen on every visit to the Reserve, weather and season permitting, but now they are seldom seen, even when a special search is made.

Fig. 22: Common Lizard (Photo. Peter Wilson)

Slow Worm *Anguis fragilis* used to be seen along the southern edge of the Reserve and occasionally on the dry heath and pine wood/heath edge in the late 1960s, but we have no record for at least the last ten years despite searching for it. It is now thought to be extinct on the Reserve.

When we first knew the Reserve, we regularly saw adders *Vipera berus* basking on sandy patches near the base of mature birch trees which were probably their over-wintering sites, in the north-east part of the Reserve. During summer they could be seen almost anywhere on the Reserve, but particularly the pine/heathland edge and the central cross bank and particularly on the east side of the central earthwork. We have not seen any for about ten years now, perhaps because of the removal of the mature birch on the wet heath, and the rising water table. Although they may no longer be on the Reserve, there is still a small population in the dry pine and heather area of the golf course.[83]

Grass snakes *Natrix natrix* are still present and in most years it is possible to find their cast skins, particularly in the marshy area of the West End Field.

Flora

The Reserve has an interesting, complex and important flora about which much could be written. But here we are concentrating just on the changes we have noticed over the last 40 years, during which time at least seven species have disappeared. As noted above, the gradual drying out of the Reserve has been taking place for at least 150 years and this has affected the plant species. Despite management efforts, a number of wet heath species have been lost in recent years. These include Sundews *Drosera rotundifolia* and *D. intermedia*, Marsh Cinquefoil *Potentilla palustris* and Heath Spotted Orchid *Dactylorriza maculata*.

Some Sundew and a few plants of Butterwort *Pinguicula vulgaris* were introduced into this area in 1957 from Scotton Common by local naturalists A D Townsend and Tom Beverley, to supplement the existing well-established population, but did not survive more than two to three years.[84] In 1976 the Reserve had a flourishing population of 207 Sundew plants, 57 of them flowering in the eastern wet heath area. Sometime shortly after 1980 both species of Sundew became extinct in the localities where we had known them.

Marsh Cinquefoil existed in a wet area, where the previous water course ran out, in the northern pine wood near the Legsby Road, but this area is now dry and being invaded by bramble, though there is one straggly bush of Alder Buckthorn *Frangula alnus* as a reminder of its previously water-logged state. Its extinction was always a possibility following the changes in drainage.

There is a record of Heath Spotted Orchid being seen in a wet area near to the southern boundary of the Reserve. This was churned up probably by timber hauling when the North Wood was felled in about 1950. At that time timber from the Forestry woodland was extracted over the Reserve across a brick-arched culvert over the stream. This work churned up the land to such an extent that the access had to be moved about 60 metres (200 ft) to the west. However, it was in this disturbed area that Ted Smith had recorded Heath Spotted Orchid.[85] We last saw Heath Spotted Orchid in a wet patch at the northern end of the West End Field in 1976.

Plants of the dry heath area are being affected by the encroachment of the invasive grass *Deschampsia flexuosa*. We have seen Harebell *Campanula rotundifolia*, Bird's Foot *Ornithopus perpusillus*, Heath Milkwort *Polygala serpyllifolia* and the grass *Danthonia recumbens* all flowering along the track and dry banks, but with the exception of Bird's Foot, they have not been seen since 1998.[86] Petty Whin, *Genista anglica*, has not been seen since 1972. Both Bird's Foot and Petty Whin were specifically mentioned as having been seen by the party of naturalists who visited the area in 1900 so these are plants which have a long history of growing at Linwood Warren.[87] The grass *Nardus stricta* is still to be found along the track across the dry heath but it is limited to about 40 tussocks and in danger of being crowded out by *D. flexuosa*. The rush *Juncus squarrosus* occurs in similar numbers along the track and is also in danger of overcrowding by *D. flexuosa* (Fig. 23). Fortunately, the clumps of both species are long lived and some have been known to us for more than twenty years. The *Juncus* may have a better chance of long-term survival as it is doing well in the areas managed for heather regeneration. Both

the *Juncus* and the *Nardus* are good examples of upland moorland species growing in a low level habitat, which is one of the characteristics of the Reserve. Another species, for which the Reserve is especially known but which is more usually found in upland areas, is the lichen Iceland Moss *Cetraria islandica*. This used to grow in two relatively large distinct areas on the wet eastern half of the Reserve, one of which was close to the shooting butt where it must have been subject to considerable disturbance if indeed it was there in the 1870s. It is now restricted to two or three small patches in one area and seems to be declining towards extinction.

There was a sizeable colony of Twayblade Orchid *Listera ovata* along the road verge adjoining the Reserve. We recorded more than 400 plants in the early 1970s, but it is now reduced to only two plants.[88]

The third orchid species is the Early Purple Orchid *Orchis mascula* of which there is a small group growing on a narrow ridge of clay on the south-eastern boundary, the number of flowering spikes varying from one to seven. This site is increasingly being smothered by bramble which seems to be responding to the increase in light following the blowing over of the Larch trees and the felling of trees on Forest Enterprise land nearby.

There are now two alien plants growing near the main entrance gate – daffodil, and an iris species - probably introduced with garden rubbish dumped there. Two other potentially invasive plants are also present – sycamore *Acer pseudoplantanus* on the south-eastern boundary near the badger sett and dandelion *Taraxacum officinale* in the drier area towards the east end where it is establishing on ground recently cleared of birch.

Some plants though are doing well. About fifteen years ago Skull Cap *Scutellaria galericulata*, was seen only around the edge of the western pool, but in 2006 was growing well along the recently re-established stream through the West End Field. Here too the Square-stemmed St John's Wort *Hypericum tetrapterum* is growing well in the boggy edges to this stream.[89]

So there are real management challenges to maintain the species variety whilst also achieving priorities for the Reserve set by Natural England and others.

The Scots pines on the Reserve are an interesting feature. The severe gales of 1976 blew over a number of trees in the plantation at the northern edge, alongside Legsby Road, and to the west of the Reserve entrance. They

Fig. 23: Rush Juncus Squarrosus growing on the track across the heath (Photo. Peter Wilson)

could not have been planted before the Legsby Road was straightened, as they lie on top of its old course.

Counting the growth rings of the fallen trees suggested an approximate planting date of 1900, so the road straightening must have taken place before then. On the 1905 25 inch OS map, the whole of the eastern half of the Reserve was mixed broadleaf and pine woodland, but on the aerial photograph of 1947[90] the area is low scrub, so the trees were probably felled shortly before that date. This area has recently been cleared of birch trees and scrub again, as shown on the aerial photograph of 1999 (see Fig. 1). However there are at least six old Scots pine on the Reserve which are shown as single trees on the 1905 map. They must have been sizeable trees at that date to be shown in this way, and they can still be seen in the same positions today. Three of these are on the dry heath, two on the edge of the pine wood, and one near the disused Willingham Lane. These trees must have been present when Lees visited the site in 1876.

There are a good number of mature oak trees on the Reserve. The oldest, which appear to be in the region of 200 years old, are to be found on the western bank of Willingham Lane, and on the southern edge of the Reserve where they may be a remnant of the old North Wood before it was replanted with conifers. A number of younger but still substantial trees, perhaps 100 years old, are to be found mainly on the banks of the water courses through the Reserve, and in the hedgerow alongside Crab Apple Lane.

Birds

There is a woodland fringe around the Reserve of varying age, composition and width, all abutting on to other habitats that influence the bird population, such as arable fields, golf course grassland, Forestry Commission short-term scrub due to felling and replanting, and mature oak woodland. The three main types of woodland on the Reserve are: mature Scots pine plantation, alongside the Legsby Road; mature oak and birch on the southern edge; and mature birch woodland. There is a graduation between all three with a varied ground flora from *sphagnum* bog, honeysuckle and bramble, to dry bracken. In the pines, the canopy can be completely closed, with little or no ground flora, while some of the birch wood has features of wood pasture with a restricted ground flora. Other habitats include both wet and dry heath, marsh and hedgerow, an old arable field and two ponds. These habitats are not extensive but their contact with the neighbouring habitats increases the number and variety of species that can breed on the Reserve.

Since 1960, sixty-one species have been recorded as breeding, or holding most of their territory, on the Reserve. We give here a short summary of some of the more interesting information gathered from the surveys that Peter has undertaken. The purpose of the surveys was to make a complete census of all the birds breeding on the Reserve each year, with the intention of relating breeding numbers and territories to the Reserve management activities, and of seeing if any of the changes there might be the result of national trends. We know of few other sites in Lincolnshire capable of supporting this number of species.

The survey started with a pilot scheme in 1960 and continued for fifteen years until 1975. It was restarted in 2000, continuing until 2006. In both these periods, some birds only bred once or twice, whilst others, breeding in good numbers during the first period, had ceased to breed by the second survey period. Some species maintained a low population of one or two pairs in all years, though others showed a slow decline and three species showed a slight increase. Sadly no less than fifteen species had dropped from the breeding list by the time the second survey period started.

At the start of the survey, there were no absolute guidelines on breeding bird census methods but by 1962 the British Trust for Ornithology (BTO) established a method based on a hierarchy of certainty of breeding, from mere presence in the breeding season through to

Fig. 24: Great Tit (Photo. Peter Wilson)

confirmed breeding by seeing birds feeding nestlings, nest building or other confirmation of breeding criteria. Much of the BTO census method relies on the presence of singing males or other territorial behaviour. In the field, the activity of all birds of all species was recorded on a site map for later analysis, which involved making a site map for each species for each year where groups of adjacent records on different dates were taken to define individual territories. The site maps were produced by Len Watkinson and provided in the early days by the Cleethorpes and District Field Club. The method recommends that at least ten site visits are made, timed to cover early breeding birds and the later breeding migrants.[91] In some years it was impossible to meet this criterion due to poor weather. On some occasions, the weather cut short a visit with only part of the Reserve covered. Wherever possible we returned the next day to complete it. During the early period, Reserve volunteers Ken Herrick and Brian Chapman sometimes helped with the surveys.

The full results of both survey periods have yet to be published but the following discussion will give an insight into the work. The table shows the situation for four consecutive years from 1967 to 1970, compared to six consecutive years from 2001 to 2006. The woodlark is known as a specialist bird of dry grassland and heathland, but has recently been shown to breed in young forestry plantations and arable fields. We found woodlark breeding on the Reserve in the 1950s but by 1961 it had ceased to breed. It was however breeding again in 2001. Whilst its main feeding area and territory was on the central dry heath, in 2005 and 2006 the actual nest was on the arable land to the west of the Reserve. The resurgence of this bird, and its nesting in arable fields is in line with the national picture.[92]

Great Tit (Fig. 24) and Blue Tit (Fig. 25) are familiar birds to most people and both species seem to be maintaining their breeding levels, with slight variations from year to year possibly due to adverse weather conditions. As part of the management of the Reserve, a nestbox scheme for the tits has been in operation since 1985, even though there appears to be plenty of natural nesting sites.

Wren is another familiar bird and is the only one to show a slight increase in numbers in the later period.

Redstart is a bird of mature woodland habitat but will also breed at low densities in scrub.[93] Although present in the early period, it had ceased to breed by 1976[94] but returned in 1999 and by 2003 there were possibly two singing males on the Reserve. There are problems counting this species. The study referred to above showed that one pair needed 1.1 miles of linear scrub along a deserted railway line for

Fig. 25: Blue Tit (Photo. Peter Wilson)

Species	1967	1968	1969	1970	2001	2002	2003	2004	2005	2006
Woodlark	0	0	0	0	1 pr	1 pr	1 pr	2 prs	1 pr	1 pr
Great Tit	9	8	9	9	11	13	13	11	13	9
Blue Tit	13	12	13	12	14	14	14	13	11	11
Wren	18	16	16	11	18	18	23	18	22	18
Redstart	2	2	0	1	1	1	2	2	2	2
Robin	17	18	16	14	13	15	17	15	12	12
Willow Warbler	34	26	26	26	14	10	14	12	12	10
Starling	13	16	16	14	0	0	0	0	0	0

successful breeding, but other research has found four nests within twenty yards of one another, with a fifth only 60 yards away.[95] So the widely distributed song posts on the Reserve could be taken to represent just one male, but the finding of two concurrently used nests confirmed at least two territories in 2004.

Robin, (Fig. 26) like the wren, is a very common bird on the Reserve, in similar but slightly more open habitats. There is some indication in the results for 2005 and 2006 that numbers are declining, though reasons for this are unclear.

Willow Warbler is closely associated with mature birch scrub and, in the 1960s was the most common breeding bird on the Reserve, with as many as 34 singing males, but the second period of the survey shows a loss of about 75% from that peak. This is in line with national trends which show a greater than 50% loss of nest survival.[96]

Starling reached peak breeding numbers in the early 1960s with twenty two occupied nest holes. They mainly fed off the Reserve and in the breeding season there was a continuous passage of birds from the arable land to the west and the golf course grassland to the north. By the late 1960s, numbers were down to the upper teens, and by the second survey period, there were no breeding Starlings on the Reserve at all. This is a striking loss but one that again reflects the national position. All the Starlings were nesting in old Woodpecker holes, of which there is no shortage. A range of other species nest in old complete or part-complete Woodpecker holes of the two species – Green (one pair) and Great Spotted Woodpecker (two pairs) (Fig. 27) – which

Fig. 26: Robin (Photo. Peter Wilson)

Fig. 27: Great Spotted Woodpecker
(Photo. Peter Wilson)

nest on the Reserve, thus providing at least three new holes annually. Species using these holes have included Great Tit, Blue Tit, Coal Tit, Redstart and Starling.

Other interesting results show that the following have all ceased to breed on the Reserve since the survey started: Snipe, Turtle Dove, Nightjar, Skylark, Marsh Tit, Willow Tit, Grasshopper Warbler, Lesser Whitethroat, Meadow Pipit, Yellow Hammer, Reed Bunting and Tree Sparrow. This list needs some qualification. Nightjar, which had song posts in the North Wood, used the Reserve for feeding, and its last recorded nest on the Reserve was 1976.[97] Skylark, Reed Bunting and Yellow Hammer now nest on the arable fields to the west of the Reserve and have, in the last two years, started to include the Reserve in their territories, so this is a welcome return. Lesser Whitethroat did not actually nest on the Reserve, but in the adjacent tall hedgerows close to Crab Apple Lane, but gathered much of the food for their young from the Reserve.

The areas with the highest density of breeding birds are the scrubby areas in the north-west and south-west, where, amongst other species, no less than six finch species have bred, and where Bullfinch has occupied a territory for the last forty years or more, emphasising the importance of managing scrub as a breeding habitat for birds.[98]

Afterword

When we started this article, we thought we knew Linwood Warren. However, thinking about all its many features and searching for answers has shown that the site is far more complex than we imagined. It has also shown just how important the site is. It represents a nationally scarce habitat; it has a rich flora; it has a high number of breeding birds; and a wealth of important insect species. But in addition there is a full record of its use by man from the Neolithic period onwards. Individually perhaps the remains are not important, and there are many other sites that demonstrate the same longevity of use. But those sites have mainly been discovered by excavation, and so are now destroyed, or by aerial photography, surviving only as crop marks. What is different and special about this Reserve is that a considerable amount of evidence survives as standing earthworks, from a Bronze Age barrow to a nineteenth century shooting butt. This is real tangible history and the survival of so much in a relatively small area makes it very special – we hesitate to use the word 'unique'. We do not claim that this account is definitive – there is much more to study and to learn about this site. There are other features we have not discussed, and a professional landscape survey is really needed to understand fully those that we have discussed. We hope such a survey may happen in the near future, perhaps with other non-invasive surveys. Meanwhile we hope that the information we have found will be useful for the future management, understanding and enjoyment of this fascinating place.

Acknowledgements

We have received considerable help and information from a number of people in the preparation of this article. In particular we would like to thank Ian Rowlandson, Community Archaeologist for North Lincolnshire Museums, for his input into the section on the pottery kilns, for the pottery drawings, and the Reserve map. His help has been invaluable. Thanks are also due to: Bill Bee, flint specialist; Dave Bromwich, Assistant Director – reserves, LWT; Graham Brown, English Heritage; Claire Chope, conservation student at Lincoln University; Jane Cowgill, independent archaeological metal-working specialist; Mark Bennet and his colleagues, Historic Environment Record, *Lincs. County Council*; Adam Daubney, portable antiquities officer, *Lincs. County Council*; Maggie Darling, Roman pottery specialist; Paul Everson, landscape archaeologist; Paul Kirby, botanist; Anthony Lee, Heritage Services, *Lincs. County Council*; Peter Smithurst, Senior Curator – firearms, Royal Armouries; Rob White, Head of Conservation, Heritage Services, *Lincs. County Council*; Dr Tom Williamson, Reader in Landscape Archaeology, University of East Anglia; Susan Paine and staff at the Lincolnshire Archives Office, *Lincs. County Council*; Staff at Market Rasen Library, *Lincs. County Council*. Finally, we wish to acknowledge and pay tribute to the excellent detailed work of Len and Betty Watkinson of Cleethorpes, first wardens of the Reserve who freely passed on their knowledge and enthusiasm to us and to others, and on whose work we have been able to build for this article.

Notes:

1.   Andrew Windrum, *Lincolnshire Coversands and Clay Vales,* report for English Nature (1997).
2.   Windrum, *op.cit.*
3.   Kenneth Cameron, *A Dictionary of Lincolnshire Place-Names*, English Place Name Society (1998) p.81.
4.   Woodland Trust promotional leaflet (2006).
5.   G Swalwell, *History of the Parish of Linwood,* Vol. 1, (1931) (Lincolnshire Archives Office (LAO), MISC DON 1021/1&2).
6.   F Arnold Lees, *The Naturalist,* (1900) p.233.

7.   *A Nature Conservation Review,* edited by D Radcliffe, Nature Conservancy Council (1977).
8.   Flints kindly identified by Bill Bee.
9.   *Lincolnshire Notes & Queries,* Vol. XIII, p.99.
10. Jeffrey May, *Prehistoric Lincolnshire,* History of Lincolnshire, I, (Lincoln, 1978) p.73.
11. Paul Everson, *pers. comm.,* (2006).
12. Aerial photograph reference: UK.2012.16 April.47.FL.20, no. 3049, 58 Squadron
13. May, *op. cit.,* p.71.

14. Naomi Field, *pers. comm.,* (2006).

15. Gary Taylor, Archaeological Project Services (2006).

16. Jane Cowgill, *pers. comm.,* (2006).

17. E A Woodruffe-Peacock, 'Lincolnshire Naturalists at Linwood Warren', in *The Naturalist* (1900) pp.273-276.

18. Ian Rowlandson, 'Raising Rasen's Roman Potters', *Lincolnshire Unearthed* No. 4, Autumn 2005, p.10-14.

19. *The De Astonian,* No. 102, (1939) (LAO, MARKET RASEN GS 17/13)

20. F T Baker, *Journal of Roman Studies,* Vol. 32. p. 110.

21. *The De Astonian,* Vol. viii, p. 26,(LAO, *op. cit.* 17/15).

22. V G Swan, *The Pottery Kilns of Roman Britain,* RCHM Suppl. Ser, 5, HMSO (1984).

23. *The De Astonian,* No. 110, Oct. 1943 (LAO, *op. cit.*)

24. M J Darling, 'A group of late Roman pottery from Lincoln' in *The Archaeology of Lincoln,* 16/1 (1977) Fig. 7, p.138.

25. F N Field and H Hurst, 'Roman Horncastle' in *Lincolnshire History and Archaeology,* 18 (1983) Fig. 29, p.79.

26. N Booth and G Webster, 'The excavation of a Romano-British pottery kiln at Swanpool, Lincoln', *Antiquaries Journal,* Vol. 27 (1947) Fig. 4; D41.

27. Field and Hurst, *op. cit.,* Fig. 29, p.133.

28. Ian Rowlandson, *pers. com.,* (2006).

29. Rowlandson, *op. cit.*

30. Darling *forthcoming,* and Rowlandson, *op. cit.*

31. Ben Whitwell, *Roman Lincolnshire,* History of Lincolnshire II, (1970) p.54.

32. G Swalwell, *op.cit.*

33. Armstrong's map of Lincolnshire, 1778, Lincoln City Library, no. 879.

34. Bryant's map of Lincolnshire, 1825-6, Lincoln Central Library, 843.

35. Linwood Tithe Award, 1842, LAO F/309.

36. John Sheail, *Rabbits and their History,* David & Charles (1971) p.9.

37. Joan Thirsk, *Alternative Agriculture,* OUP (1997) p.10.

38. Tom Williamson, *The Archaeology of Rabbit Warrens,* Shire Publications (2006) p.6.

39. Sheail, *op. cit.,* p.18.

40. Thirsk, *op. cit.,* p.1.

41. Thirsk, *op. cit.,* p.53.

42. quoted in J Thirsk, *English Peasant Farming,* Routledge & Kegan Paul (1957) p.261.

43. Sheail, *op. cit.,* p.26.

44. Sheail, *op. cit.,* p.75.

45. Neil Wright, *Lincolnshire Towns and Industry,* History of Lincolnshire, XI, (1982) p.75.

46. Tom Williamson, *pers. comm.,* (2006).

47. Williamson, *op. cit.*

48. Williamson, *pers. comm.,* (2006).

49. Mr Rands, Legsby, *pers. comm.,* (1967).

50. H D Miles, *The Book of Field Sports,* Henry Lea, (c.1860) p.63.

51. Peter Smithurst, Senior Curator-Firearms, Royal Armouries, *pers. comm.,* (2006).

52. *Market Rasen Mail,* 25 October 1856.

53. Exhibition information from Royal Armouries, (2006).

54. R J Olney, *Rural Society and County Government in Nineteenth Century Lincolnshire,* History of Lincolnshire, X (1979) p.97.

55. *Market Rasen Mail, (MRM)* 7 Jan 1860.

56. *MRM,* 9 June 1860.

57. *MRM,* 20 June 1885.

58. *MRM,* 1 December 1860.

59. *MRM,* 29 August 1863.

60. *MRM,* 21 November 1863.

61. *MRM,* 31 December 1870.

62. Steve Rowan, *pers. comm.,* (2006).

63. White's Directory (1882).

64. *MRM,* 3 January 1885.

65. *MRM,* 25 July 1885.

66. Graham Brown, English Heritage, *pers.comm.,* (2006).

67. G Brown and D Field, 'Training trenches on Salisbury Plain: archaeological evidence for battle training in the Great War', *Wiltshire Archaeological Journal,* (forthcoming)

68. Chris Padley, *pers. comm.,* (2006).

69. Les Brumpton, Chairman of the Greens, *pers. comm.,* (2006).

70. Lees, *op.cit.*

71. A A Savage, *Adults of the British Aquatic Hemiptera Heteroptera, a key with ecological notes,* (1989).

72. E J Popham, 'A study of the changes of the water bug fauna of North Surrey with special reference to the migration of Corixids' in *J of the Society for British Entomology,* Vol 3 (1951).

73. T T Macan, *A revised key to the British Water Bugs with notes on their ecology,* (1965)

74. Savage, (1989), *op. cit.*

75. Savage, (1989), *op. cit.*

76. T T Macan, 'A contribution to the study of the ecology of Corixidae' in *J of Animal Ecology,* Vol. 23, No. 1 (1954) pp.115-141.

77. Macan, (1954), *op. cit.*

78. A M Jordan, 'Coleophora alticolella Zell' in *J of Animal Ecology,* Vol. 31., No. 2, (July 1962) Colin Smith, county moth recorder, confirmed the identification, *pers. comm.,* (2006)

79. Locket and Milledge, *British Spiders,* Ray Society, (1951 and 1981); M J Roberts, *Spiders of Britain and Northern Europe,* Collins (1995).

80. *Lincolnshire Naturalists' Union Transactions,* Vol. XV, No. 4 (1963).

81. Identification confirmed by R. Key, county recorder, *pers. comm.,* (2005).

82. Colin Smith, *pers. comm.,*(2006).

83. Les Brumpton, *pers. comm.,* (2006).

84. A D Townsend, *pers. comm.*

85. A E Smith, *pers. comm.,* (1966).

86. Paul Kirby, *pers. comm.,* (2006).

87. Woodruffe-Peacock (1900) *op. cit.*

88. Paul Kirby, *pers. comm.,* (2006).

89. I D Weston, *pers. comm.,* (2006)

90. Aerial photograph, (1947), *op. cit.*

91. R J Bibby et al, *Bird Census Techniques,* Academic Press (1992).

92. S R Wotton & S Gillings, *The status of breeding woodlarks Lullula arborea in Britain in 1997,* Bird Study, Vol. 47, part 2, July 2000.

93. K Williamson, *The Importance of Managing Scrub as a Breeding Habitat for Birds,* County Trusts' Conference (1968).

94. Peter Wilson notebooks.

95. J Buxton, *The Redstart,* New Naturalist No. 2 (1950).

96. BTO News, Sept/Oct, 2006.

97. LWT archives.

98. K Williamson, *op. cit.*

'Exquisitely Beautiful Articles':
Goss Heraldic Porcelain and Toynton All Saints Earthenware

Jane Young and Anne Boyle

A rural medieval pottery industry based in Lincolnshire and the early-modern manufacturer of Goss pottery in Stoke-on-Trent may, on initial consideration, appear to have little in common. Indeed, there are differences in the character of the medieval and early-modern pottery industries. Medieval potting was located in both urban and rural environments, but usually took the form of small cottage industry with a family unit occupying themselves with the craft at certain times of the year. Potters may have worked alone within a community or been part of a wider network of potters working within a village or group of villages. Medieval pots are often viewed as naïve, the result of small scale, low key activity which resulted in a hotchpotch of products that display a limited range of forms and reflect a diverse scope of skill and execution. Medieval pots tended to be sold in local markets and responded to the needs of those in the immediate vicinity. The pottery industries of the modern era are perceived as producers of uniform products on a mass scale; their output was achieved through the employment of many hands, both men and women, young and old, and they were established in large industrial centres of manufacturing. These were often urban or suburban in their location. Their output was market sensitive, widely distributed and often included a range of utilitarian and specialist pottery.

However, though separated by some five hundred years, these pottery industries of the medieval and modern eras shared the same core value: their primary aim was to produce marketable, saleable pots. In some cases the similarities run deeper, with the technology they utilised, the fashions they responded to, the raw products they sourced and the way in which they operated being comparable. The connections between the two are interwoven in a tale of how an 'ancient ewer' from Louth was subject to the pioneering ideas of an antiquarian-cum-potter, who encapsulated it in miniature and created a phenomenon.

The Toynton potteries were concentrated in a cluster of villages in Lincolnshire. These villages, Toynton All Saints, Toynton St Peter's and Old Bolingbroke were involved in potting from the thirteenth to the mid eighteenth century (Figure 1). The earliest industry occurred at Toynton All

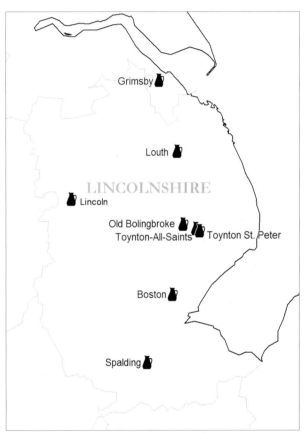

Fig. 1: Map of Lincolnshire showing the location of the Toynton potteries

Saints, with coin and documentary evidence for potting dating to the fourteenth century[1], though it is generally accepted that pottery was produced at Toynton from the late thirteenth century onwards. In time, the potteries shifted and the post-medieval manufacturers were based at Old Bolingbroke. Recent archaeological excavations have uncovered pottery wasters in a Toynton-type fabric from sites located on the Lincolnshire coast: this suggests at least one other pottery was operating in the vicinity[2].

At Toynton All Saints and Toynton St. Peter's three kilns have been excavated and numerous dumps of pottery waste are known throughout the villages[3]. Toynton pots occur in archaeological ceramic assemblages from across

Lincolnshire, and regularly travelled into surrounding counties. The ware is a major medieval type across eastern Lincolnshire, probably being sold in great numbers at the local markets and fairs at Alford, Boston, Horncastle and Spilsby, as well as finding its way in lesser amounts to sites throughout Lincolnshire, parts of Cambridgeshire, Norfolk, Nottinghamshire and Yorkshire and also across the North Sea to sites on the continent. Stocks are known to have been held at Spalding[4] and no doubt the large number of ecclesiastical establishments within the south of the county placed large orders, as the size of Toynton ware assemblages from sites at religious houses such as Partney, Skendleby and Haverholme attest. The potters are known to have used carts to transport their wares but must also have made use of packs, carried either by horse or human. The numerous small waterways in Lincolnshire would have made water transport easy, especially before the enclosure of the fens when water access across the pools and deeps between the clay islands was probably safer than by road. Rural sites tend to produce assemblages with a higher jar and bowl content than urban ones that are predominately formed of varying sized jugs.

The wide distribution of the Toynton products is not to say they were special, as they consisted, in the main, of the three most common pottery forms produced in the medieval period: jugs, jars and bowls. Their quality ranges from fine to quite crude, with the earliest products (from 'The Roses' kiln) being more consistently well potted and attractively decorated. The standard of the pottery declines over the centuries, deteriorating to crude and poorly potted vessels in the post-medieval period. Despite their declining quality, competition from other locally and regionally produced wares and a somewhat limited repertoire, the distances these wares were traded and the longevity of the Toynton and Bolingbroke industries is testimony to their success.

Toynton vessels can be identified by a number of characteristics. The most prominent feature is their surface finish which, if unglazed, is covered with a salt 'skin' (a thin creamy-yellow coating) and when covered with a lead glaze is an olive green colour through which a pocked body is visible. The jars and bowls were usually plain vessels as they were intended for utilitarian culinary and domestic tasks. The jugs were more likely to be used at the table for serving drink: this is reflected in the fact that decoration is common on the larger jug forms which were possibly on display during meal times. As a result, the potters employed a range of decorative motifs on jugs.

These most commonly take the form of applied strips of clay which were sometimes iron-rich, resulting in a brown design on a green glazed body. These strips could be embellished with thumb presses or stamping (using a die or roller stamp). The designs were composed of applied linear strips and pellet decoration, sometimes in the form of scrolls, crosses, fleurs-de-lys, horseshoes, ladders and brooch/buckle designs[5]. The horseshoe motif is one of the most common medieval decorative motifs found on medieval pottery in the East Midlands, the fleur-de-lys is common on Lincoln ware jugs of thirteenth to mid fifteenth century date. Several Toynton-type jugs have been found with a combination of these two designs, adapted to fit different sized jugs, and these may represent an individual potter's signature design or may be just part of a mix and match element.

The most impressive designs came from 'The Roses' kiln. This kiln, excavated in the 1960s, was dated by archaeo-magnetic analysis of clay kiln structure to have last been fired c. 1300[6] and a coin found in one of the flues was of Edward I, evidence used to date the activity of the kiln between 1275 and 1300[7]. This fits with evidence from other potting industries, where thirteenth century vessels tend to be well made and highly decorated. At 'The Roses' the most highly decorated jugs tend to be the larger ones, with the decorative elements applied to the upper half of the body. Wasted finds of other similarly decorated jugs have been found away from the Roses site suggesting that it was not the only kiln to be producing such wares, but to date it appears to have been the most prolific. The lack of variance in form shape, manufacturing techniques and decorative elements over nearly two hundred and fifty years suggests little change in organisation within the industry, unlike at the nearby urban centre of Lincoln where shapes and decorative elements changed rapidly. The traits which combine to form an industry show only a slow progression at Toynton suggesting perhaps that the Toynton potters were not open to new innovations, certainly they never developed a well fitting fritted glaze as used at the major nearby urban centres, instead using a slip with coarsely ground lead lumps in and neither did they use copper colourant to enhance the lustre of the glaze. Despite a widespread distribution area their market was perhaps not large enough to warrant investment in new ideas, or their customers (mainly rural) were content with a familiar product.

A complete Roses-style vessel was excavated at Upgate in Louth in the nineteenth century. Known as the 'Louth

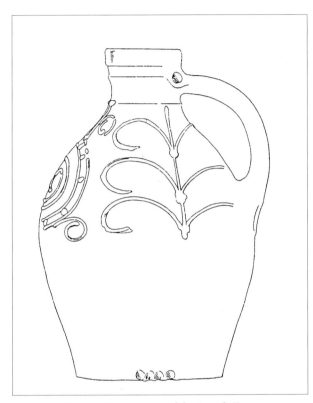

Fig. 2: Illustration of the Louth Ewer

responded to the demand for vessels associated with newly introduced drinks, foods and styles of dining. The basic methods of pottery production in Staffordshire and across the country remained relatively unchanged from the medieval period until the mid eighteenth century, with only limited developments in domestic manufacturing processes during this time[8]. The domestic post-medieval pottery industry in England was a continuation of the medieval lead glazed earthenware tradition, though often (as in the case of Bolingbroke) these wares were quite crudely made. Eighteenth century dealers of utilitarian wares complained they were coarsely made, did not respond to new fashions and were often more expensive than pottery imported from the continent[9]. Such comments suggest that although pottery was a cheap commodity, it was still expected to respond to the trends of the time. Tin and lead glazed earthenwares and stonewares were imported in vast amounts through the ports of the east coast and were increasingly available to a wide range of people. Therefore, imported ceramics began to have a great influence on domestic production, with technological leaps in English pottery often taking place through following foreign precedents.

Ewer', this jug was at first identified as a Toynton product, though subtle differences in decoration and form suggest it may have originated not from Toynton itself, but from a place producing Toynton-type vessels. The jug, currently on display at Louth Museum, is large, standing some 52cm tall. The jug has a wide strap handle springing from between two sharp neck cordons which ends in a foliate pressed join at the belly. The body is decorated with a central horseshoe motif with a scroll beneath and two flanking three-branched fleurs-de-lys (Figures 2 and 3). What marks it out is the relative body thinness and marked girth grooves, especially around the lower body. The basal angle is pinched, which may have been decorative but also helped to stabilise jugs that had slightly sagging bases. This fine example of medieval pottery would, some five hundred years after it was made, be resurrected in miniature form by the Falcon Factory in Stoke-on-Trent.

The Falcon Factory, owned and run by the Goss family, was founded *c.* 1860. By this time, potting had evolved through the use of machinery and new techniques to allow the production of a great range of utilitarian earthenwares and finewares (often in imitation of porcelain) which

Fig. 3: Detail of the horseshoe decoration on the Louth Ewer

Fig. 4: The Goss Louth Ewer decorated with the Coat of Arms for the City of Canterbury

In the 1880s the Goss family introduced a line of souvenir pottery in a fine china. This was somewhat unusual in that these vessels were not intrinsically useful; their appeal lay in an appreciation of them as objects with a symbolic rather than actual function. The introduction of 'Heraldic ware' to the Goss repertoire is attributed to Adolphus Goss, who aimed to capture in miniature porcelain copies of antiquities and items of social, political or religious interest from across the country. A part of the range concentrated on reproducing prehistoric, Roman and medieval vessels. One of the antiquities used by Adolphus as a model for his heraldic range was the 'Louth Ewer' (Figure 4). The discipline of studying ancient ceramics was in its infancy at this time, and the identification and interpretation of these vessels was pioneering work. The driving force behind this idea appears to be Adolphus's interest in antiquities and the ancient world. His father William, and friend Llewellyn Jewitt, were also intrigued by history and archaeology; they travelled across the country to view new antiquarian discoveries and participated in the excavation

of historic sites. Llewellynn published the *Ceramic Art of Great Britain* in 1876 and was a great supporter of the Goss pottery; it was he who described the heraldic range as containing 'exquisitely beautiful articles'[10]. Goss heraldic porcelain strongly reflects the interests of all three men, and was made possible by Adolphus's talents and business acumen: Adolphus toured the country making sketches of the original vessels and managed to persuade his father the range would be popular[11].

The Goss factory produced utilitarian earthenwares using the same types of clay as the Toynton potters. Earthenwares in both periods were made from secondary clays, so called as they have been affected by glacial action and contain impurities (such as iron) that produce sandy orange and red bodied pots. Medieval potters would initially exhaust the clay supplies which lay within their croft, removing deposits from common land or roads once this was used up. Numerous documents record the nuisance potters made by digging up clay: at Toynton All Saints in 1409, Alice Attwell appeared before the manorial court for 'diggin clay at claypittes in Colngar to the detriment of the road'[12]. The specific clays used in the later potteries could also be difficult to source; Wedgwood was interested in shipping clays from the New World to his Etruria pottery[13]. Clay stocks mentioned in inventories indicate potters bought clay in large batches, which then had to be exposed to sour before being thrown into pots[14]. This could prove problematic for modern potteries which had a large output requiring the processing of large amounts of clay. The modern pottery at Longton Hall was bankrupt by 1760 due to high production costs; their clay stock required three years of weathering before it could be used to make a return on their investment[15].

However, the Goss factory also produced vessels in a type of hard paste china. This 'Parian slip' consisted of primary clay (various known as kaolin, china or pipe clay and unlike secondary clay, not contaminated with impurities), feldspar, white glass and flint[16]. In terms of appearance, these ingredients (which were finely ground and added to water) produced a very fine body that was ideal for producing delicate moulded pieces of pottery. The addition of feldspar produced a translucent body giving a porcelain type appearance. Primary clays can be hard to source and medieval potting traditions often used white clays sparingly; they were reserved for slips (a white slip covering a red clay body produced the same finish as making the entire pot from white clay) or for decorative elements in a contrasting colour to the main body of the pot.

The glaze used on Heraldic ware is composed of flint, china clay or carbonate of lime, Cornish stone, boracic acid, borax, carbonate or oxide of lead, carbonate of soda, potash and feldspar. These had to be ground to a fine powder and mixed with water. This mixture is heated, fused into a glass, ground down and then added to water to create a thin glaze[17]. The medieval production of glaze was simpler, though followed the same idea. Two types of glaze are known: splashed glazes were created by taking raw lead ore or white lead, beating it to a fine powder and mixing it with sand or clay to make a paste[18]. This was then brushed onto the body of the pot as a semi-dry application. This type of glaze produced patchy coverage and left the body with distinctive pock marks on its surface. The Toynton potters employed a type of liquid (suspension) glaze. This is evident from the good internal and external coverage often achieved on the pots. After the pot had been dipped in the liquid glaze, which was also produced from a lead glass frit ground and added to water and clay, the excess was allowed to drain off. A feature of the Toynton products is that, despite using a suspension glaze, it must have contained lead lumps as the body beneath the glaze is pocked.

Both the Toynton and Heraldic wares would have been allowed to air dry before firing. This creates a 'leather-hard' pot which has shrunk as the water evaporates from the clay body. The Goss pots underwent an initial 'biscuit' firing. The heraldic wares, being small and delicate, were placed in large coarse earthenware vessels known as saggars. The saggars were placed in the kiln's oven with ground flint powder sprinkled on them to stop the pots from sticking to one another[19]. Similar techniques were used in some medieval and post-medieval kilns; in the late medieval period saggars were employed to protect more delicate vessels from the intensity of heat or from being crushed beneath the stack of pots in the kiln. The base of each saggar and the kiln floor was covered with a light sprinkling of sand to prevent the wares from adhering to them.

There are differences in the types of kiln in which these wares were fired. A bottle kiln was used for firing at the Goss pottery, so called because its outer shell resembles a tall brick bottle shaped hovel. The filled saggars were placed within the oven (or firing) chamber. The bottle kiln used at the Falcon works had a diameter of twenty feet and held two thousand saggars. It took over twenty tons of coal to fire it, over a period of 50 hours (during which it was constantly attended to) reaching temperatures of 1200 degrees Celsius. The kiln and its contents cooled slowly over three to four days before removal[20]. The pieces were fired a further two times: once after the Goss crescent was added and the pieces were glazed, then again after the heraldic designs had been applied by transfer printing, and these filled out with colour enamels. The second firing took place in a smaller kiln holding just 500 saggars, which took only five tons of coal to fire over twenty four hours[21]. The final firing was in an enamel oven for between five and nine hours at a temperature between 700-800 degrees[22].

Most medieval pottery kilns are 'multi-flued kilns' and were built out of a variety of materials. They have no standard shape, size or internal structure and appear to vary widely in how they were constructed and in their design. The number of flues a kiln had was important as more flues resulted in an increase in the amount of oxygenated air and hot gases passing through. The even spacing of flues theoretically allows the even heating of the kiln. These kilns had a semi-permanent nature, and it is likely that a 'dome' of broken sherds was constructed over the stack of pots inside the kiln oven for each firing. The amount of pottery fired in a single load would depend very much on the size of the kiln, the size of pots and the skill of the potter in successfully packing it. At Toynton, the thirteenth century multi-flued kilns were 8ft in diameter and in the early fifteenth century, two spoilt kiln loads were valued at 10s. It seems a maximum of around five hundred pots could be contained in the larger multi-flued kilns such as those found at Potterton and Cowick[23]. A major drawback in estimating the capacity of a kiln is in not knowing its height. However, experimental firings have shown the height of the kiln cannot exceed one and a half times the width of the oven, as the pots in the top of the kiln would go unfired[24]. Medieval potters used a variety of fuels for firing, and coal, wood and peat were all utilised. The fuel used depended on geographical location. At Toynton All Saints in 1399, Nicholas Potter paid 5s. 8d. for turves of peat (around 6,000) and 9d. for their carriage[25]. Such large amounts of peat, turves or bundles of firewood would be needed in order that each flue could be stoked with its own fire over several hours. For those potters using peat, turbaries were common and peat was relatively cheap, costing in the fourteenth century between 8d. and 11d. for one thousand turves.

The Goss and Toynton potters employed a range of people to carry out different tasks during the potting process. The Goss pottery employed men, women and children within the factory. There were 120 employees between 1900 and 1914, but by the 1920s this had dropped to 80 people[26]. Women did much of the sorting and finishing work within the manufacturing process, such as sorting the fired pots into grades (best, second and lump) and in the decoration of the pots by cutting the transfers to shape, applying the design to the pot and in painting the enamels[27]. Medieval potting was a household activity and required many hands to help prepare the clay, throw the pots, stack them for drying, apply finishing touches and tend the firing. Child sized finger impressions are common on medieval pots, and children could have been put to work adding handles and decoration to the semi-dried vessels before firing. Documentary evidence records that the Toynton potters also took on apprentices to work with them, though these relationships were not always happy: in 1368, a potter's wife from Toynton sued for arrears in wages of 3s. 4d. which she had earned working at the clay pits and for a piece of work. She also requested a hundred pots (possibly

a kiln load) so she could set herself up in business. A few years earlier Agnes Porrel sued her employer for 3s. 3d., her stipendium (wages) for the previous year[28]. A later potter sued for arrears saying he was owed 13s. 4d. 'pro labore suo in arte figuli' [for his work as a potter][29]. As these examples show, potting was not just a male concern and there is evidence that women ran their own production sites; Susannah Ward of Heath End (South Derbyshire) employed Richard Knifton to pot for her. He was paid between 3 and 5s. a week, but this was not sufficient and he began work for someone else[30]. However, a woman could not be seen as working in a craft in a professional (guild) capacity. This can be seen at Siegburg, where a woman could run a potting workshop if her husband was ill or deceased, but once she remarried her new husband oversaw the production[31].

Both the Goss miniatures and Toynton pottery were decorated with heraldic devices. Heraldry was a popular mode of decoration because of its connotations of aristocracy and status. The production of pottery containing such devices has a long history and the incorporation of these symbols on a medium like pottery (which is affordable by the majority of people regardless of class) suggests an interest in and a desire to be associated with 'high' society and culture. The pots from Toynton sometimes incorporated elements which were associated with powerful institutions and local families. The fleur-de-lys was a symbol of the diocese of Lincoln and features on the coat of arms of the Welby family and the Bernards of Hagnaby; the ladder was used in the Willoughby coat of arms and three buckles appear on the 'armorial bearings' of Sir Thomas Roseline who married the daughter of Sir John Willoughby in the early fourteenth century[32]. The Louth Ewer has fleurs-de-lys and a large central horseshoe design. The horseshoe is well known as a symbol of good luck. Horseshoes also offered protection from witches who could pass by them[33]. The horseshoe shown right way up, with the points facing down (folklore has it the inverted horseshoe keeps luck inside it) is found on the badge of the Derbyshire de Ferrers family[34]. The de Ferrers family had connections with Lincolnshire through marriage; the wife of William de Ferrers (fifth Earl of Derby) was Margaret de Quincy. Her uncle (Robert II de Quincy) was married to Hawise of Chester. Hawise became Countess of Lincoln on 27 October 1232, but already had links with the area after she inherited the Castle and Manor of Bolingbroke after her father's death in 1153. Hawise and Robert's great-great-great granddaughter, Alice de Lacy married

Thomas Plantagenet (second Earl of Lancaster) in 1294; he became Earl Ferrers of Derby in 1301[35].

The use of ancient vessels and heraldic devices as the basis of Goss ware is reflective of the interest in the past that was held by many in the late nineteenth and early twentieth centuries. The 'medieval revival' seen in the literature and architecture of the Victorian age is part of a wider and older tradition of reviving the material culture and social ideals of the past. Often these revivalist ideas had a romantic view of the past and reveal more about the period during which they were popular than that which they exalted. However, these ideas were incorporated into material culture and the domestic sphere during that time. In the same way, Wedgwood was keen to incorporate Greek and Roman ideas into his wares as he quite adroitly noted that the Grand Tours of the aristocracy had prompted an intellectual and artistic interest in the architecture and material culture of these periods. Wedgwood's Basalt and Jasper ware designs were inspired by classical and Renaissance pottery, and often incorporated elements from several ancient vessels into a single piece[36]. Wedgwood, in a similar vein to Goss making faithful illustrations of the antique pots of Britain, had artists installed in Rome to copy designs of antique and Renaissance works which were sent back to his factory[37].

The use of local antique pieces as the basis of the Goss heraldic range also combined a piece of local interest into a small, collectable item that could be purchased at low price and taken home. This not only served as 'proof' that a place had been visited and a trip taken but also responded to the Victorian love of collecting. This is most typified, perhaps, by the creation of cabinets of curiosities, but also in terms of interest in geological and natural history which were themselves subject of collections. The age of tourism allowed the masses to indulge in these interests for themselves, as places became more accessible (both in terms of time and finance) with the extensions of first the canal and then the rail network in the eighteenth and nineteenth centuries. The 1871 Bank Holiday Act provided bank employees with a day off on Boxing Day; this was extended in 1875 to include most government offices; in a short period of time *'much of the population happily followed suit'*[38]. Days off work and an accessible transport network allowed many to travel, with the seaside becoming the *'destination choice of many'*[39]. This tourism initiated an interest in souvenirs and the Goss heraldic wares were attractive reminders of places visited; their popularity is attested to be the commonly quoted statistic that by the early twentieth century around ninety percent of homes owned a piece of Goss china. Whether this is a true reflection of the popularity of Goss is difficult to determine, though the products of their pottery obviously sold well as the Falcon Pottery had to treble in size to meet demand.

The Toynton potters, like the Goss family, responded to the desires of their customers to create a highly sought-after type of pottery. The use of the Louth ewer as a basis for one of the Goss models and the shared interest these vessels show in heraldic devices demonstrate how pervasive this iconography has been through the ages. The potteries of Toynton and Goss used the technology of their day to create popular wares and though there are variations in how the two operated, it is perhaps surprising that there are as many similarities as there are between these two pottery producers.

Acknowledgements

Many thanks to Hilary Healey for allowing use of her illustration of the Louth jug and decoration.

Notes:

1. E H Rudkin, *Notes on the history of Toynton All Saints and Toynton St Peter*, Old Chapel Books, (Burgh le Marsh, 1992) p.6.
2. J Young, 'The Post Roman Pottery (SIP04)' in *Skegness to Ingoldmells Water Reinforcement Scheme 2004: Assessment Report on the Evaluations, Excavations and Watching Brief* edited by R Moore (Network Archaeology, Forthcoming).
3. H Healey and E Rudkin in P C D Brears, *An English Country Pottery, Its History and Techniques*, David and Charles, (Newton Abbot, 1971) p.195.
4. H E J Le Patourel, 'Documentary Evidence and the Medieval Pottery Industry', *Medieval Archaeology* 12 (1968) p.119.
5. H Healey, 'Toynton All Saints: Decorated jugs from the Roses Kiln' in *A Prospect of Lincolnshire* edited by N. Field and A. White (Lincoln, 1984) p.76.
6. Rudkin *op. cit.* p.6.
7. Healey *op. cit.* p.75.
8. L Scammell, *The Beginnings of Industrialisation in the English Pottery Industry: 1660 to 1760* (Internet, 2000). Available from http://www.campus.ncl.ac.uk/databases/history/pottery/ba.html
9. B Dolan, *Josiah Wedgwood: Entrepreneur to the Enlightenment*, Harper Perennial (2005) pp.27-28.
10. L Pine and N Pine, *William Henry Goss, the story of the Staffordshire family of potters who invented Heraldic Porcelain*, Milestone (Portsmouth, 1987) p.183.
11. Pine and Pine *op. cit.* pp.179-183.
12. Rudkin *op. cit.* p.6.

13. Dolan *op. cit.* pp.186-187.

14. J Spavold and S Brown, *Ticknall Pots and Potters from the Late Fifteenth Century to 1888*, Landmark (Ashbourne, 2005) p.27.

15. J Flanders, *Consuming Passions: Leisure and Pleasure in Victorian Britain*, Harper Press (2006) p.62.

16. Pine and Pine *op. cit.* p.218.

17. Pine and Pine *op. cit.* p.233.

18. P C D Brears, 'The Continuing Tradition, the Eighth Gerald Dunning Memorial Lecture', *Medieval Ceramics* 13: (1989) p.7.

19. Pine and Pine *op. cit.* pp.228 & 229.

20. Pine and Pine *op. cit.* pp.228-231.

21. Pine and Pine *op. cit.* p.233.

22. Pine and Pine *op. cit.* p.238.

23. Le Patourel *op. cit.* p.116.

24. R Coleman-Smith, 'Excavations in the Donyatt Potteries: Site 13', *Post-Medieval Archaeology* 36: (2002) p.139.

25. Le Patourel *op. cit.* LRO Anc. I, 18/50, p118.

26. Pine and Pine *op. cit.* p.239.

27. Pine and Pine *op. cit.* pp.236-238.

28. Le Patourel *op. cit.* p.115.

29. Le Patourel *op. cit.* LRO Anc. I, 18/33, 18/27, 18/59, p.115.

30. Spavold and Brown *op. cit.* p.30.

31. D Gaimster, 'Stoneware Production in Medieval and Early Modern Germany' in *Pottery in the Making, World Ceramic Traditions*, edited by I Freestone and D Gaimster, British Museum Press (1997) p.127.

32. Healey *op. cit.* p.76.

33. C K Bayliss, 'Witchcraft', *The Journal of American Folklore*, Vol. 21, no.82 (1908) p.363.

34. D Townsend, 'Horseshoes', *Folklore* 31 (1920): pp.233-234.

35. J Cardinal, *A genealogical survey of the peerage of Britain as well as the royal families of Europe.* (n/d) [Internet, accessed April 2007] Available from http://www.thepeerage.com.

36. J Montagu, 'A Renaissance Work copied by Wedgwood', *Journal of the Warburg and Courtauld Institutes*, Vol. 17, No. 3/4 (1954) pp.380-381.

37. Montagu *op. cit.* pp.380-381.

38. Flanders *op. cit.* p.470.

39. Flanders *op. cit.* p.241.

Heckington Mill (Drawn by Hilary Healey)

'I Cannot Sing The Old Songs' - Claribel's Musical Milieu

Kate Witney

Charlotte Alington Barnard (née Pye), under her pen name of Claribel, became one of the foremost songwriters of the mid nineteenth century. Her songs were sung across the English speaking world, in the bars of the Wild West, on sheep stations in the Australian outback and, of course, in parlours and drawing rooms throughout Britain. What influenced her? What music did she hear as a girl growing up in Louth? Have her songs stood the test of time?

Charlotte was the daughter of Henry Pye, a solicitor and prominent citizen in Louth. She received the genteel lady's education typical of her class, being a pupil at Miss Elizabeth Leak's Ladies' Academy at The Sycamores where 'the careful instruction [is] united with every elegant accomplishment requisite for the completion of a superior education'. And music was, naturally, an 'elegant accomplishment'. Charlotte was only seventeen when her mother died after a long illness. Margaret Loft acted

as chaperon to Charlotte during her mother's illness and after her death and, in 1845, wrote 'Charlotte played a great many Scotch Airs for me and two polkas of her own composition'. Two years later she wrote 'Charlotte has a most sweet voice and great taste and is altogether a most loveable girl'. After two broken engagements Charlotte married The Revd Charles Cary Barnard in 1824 and within days her father remarried, his bride being Lady Albinia Frances Hobart, the daughter of the Earl of Buckingham. In 1857 Charlotte and Charles moved to London. One of their neighbours was Michael Costa, the musical director of the Royal Opera House, Covent Garden. Charlotte attended many performances there and took singing lessons from the tenor Guiseppe Mario.

Charlotte's first published song, a setting of Tennyson's 'The Brook', appeared in 1859 and it was at this point that she adopted her pen name of Claribel. Just three years later she was successful enough for her publisher John Boosey to pay her a £300 retainer and for dance music arrangements of her most popular songs to have appeared (The Claribel Quadrille, The Janet's Choice Waltz, for example). Charlotte divided her time between London and Lincolnshire. In London she hob-nobbed with Charles Dickens and renewed her acquaintance with Jean Ingelow; in Lincolnshire she arranged concerts, hunted and, on one visit, won an archery contest at South Elkington! In 1863 Charles accepted the living of Kirmington and Brocklesby, but Charlotte continued her highly successful musical career and, despite a period of what we might now recognise as depression, was happy in her double life.

In 1868, however, disaster struck. Henry Pye, who had in 1855 begun an ambitious scheme of land reclamation in North Somercotes and had built himself a grand house there, Pye Hall, was exposed as an embezzler of his clients' funds. 'The £5 note of the trusting servant and the £15,000 of the confiding friend were alike swallowed up in the maelstrom of his miserable pride and extravagance' reported *The Louth Gazette* on 31 July 1868. Henry made an abortive attempt at flight in an open boat into the North Sea, but was picked up by a passing fishing vessel. Charlotte, Charles, Albinia, Henry and their young daughter fled to the continent.

Fig. 1: Watercolour sketch of Claribel from the frontispiece of The Story of Claribel by Phyllis Smith and Margaret Godsmark (Lincoln 1965)

Like so many market towns across England in the late Georgian period, the Louth into which Charlotte was born in 1830 was the social and commercial centre for the countryside for miles around. It was the hub of entertainment and culture, too. In common with other towns of a similar size it boasted a professional theatre. Certainly from the late 1760s there was a theatre at the north west corner of what is now the Cornmarket (known as the Beast Market until the cattle market moved to Newmarket). In the early 1800s the theatre was demolished to make way for the new Guildhall, but theatrical performances continued in the premises to the rear of that building at least until the 1830s (later the site of the Corn Exchange and now the Halifax Building Society). There is no evidence that Charlotte ever attended the theatre in Louth, but nonetheless the posters for the performances give a fascinating insight into what formed and reflected public taste of the time. As a matter of fact one suspects that the theatre would not have been considered a suitable place for a child of Charlotte's very tender years and delicate upbringing. Theatrical performances in the late Georgian and early Victorian period were robust affairs, which brought together all classes and ages. The beautifully restored Georgian Theatre at Richmond in Yorkshire, surely similar to the demolished Louth theatre, is now a delightful and elegant venue. One sits comfortably and quietly on cushions, claps politely and enjoys a civilised drink and trip to the modern facilities in the interval. It was not always like this. In the early nineteenth century the theatre offered the only real entertainment and was available to a wide public, many of whom had been drinking all market day long. Doors opened at around 5.30 for a performance which started at 6.30 and must have lasted until nearly midnight. There will have been scene changes, if not intervals but, as seats were unreserved, people tended to stay where they were and bring food with them. Audiences were by no means silent. The gentry sat in the stalls with the cheaper seats being in the tiers above. The stalls offered a clear view of the stage and a chance to be seen, but these were their only selling points; the patrons in these more expensive seats were also sitting targets for those in the 'gods', who could take the opportunity, for example, to throw food at their 'betters'. It is even reported that there were worse affronts. How can I put this delicately? It may be that some in the stalls felt the occasional drop of water on their heads. They may have assumed that the roof was leaking and that it was raining. If so, they were mistaken. Remember that many of the audience had been drinking for hours. There were no facilities. It was dark and no one could see what

Fig. 2: Poster for Louth Theatre
for 29 January 1830

Fig. 3: Poster for Louth Theatre for 6 February 1829, featuring Monsieur Gouffe with 'Surprising feats never attempted by any man in the Kingdom but himself...'

they were doing. Enough said. I should stress that there is no evidence that anything so shocking ever occurred in the Louth Theatre. Is it significant, though, that posters for theatrical performances in Louth as late as January and March 1853 stress that 'police will be present'?

At the Louth Theatre the performances followed a predictable pattern: a play would be followed by a comic song or a dance and the evening rounded off with a farce or musical comedy. The bill for 19 March 1819 is a typical example:

> *Hamlet*
> [in its entirety? – surely not!]
> *Comic song – 'Chit Chat for the Ladies' by Mr. Northhouse*
> *'The Sailor's Return' recited by Mr. Dickens*
> *'A Broad Sword Hornpipe' by Miss. Stoker*
> *'Bucks have at ye all' by Mr. Chiswell*
> *The whole to conclude with the laughable farce (never acted here) called Animal Magnetism or The Power of Love*
> *Doors open at 5.30 to begin at 6.30.*

The names of the actors turn up time and again, of course, and it is interesting to note that many of them must have been able to sing well beyond the demands of the odd comic song because the meat of the programme on 24 December 1834 was Weber's opera 'Die Freischutz'. By 1831 several of the actors may have been approaching retirement age as there were a number of benefit concerts, for example for Mrs. Huggins Senior and Mr. Kean.

What is so striking about the performances at the Louth Theatre are the length of the programmes and the breadth of material. These were to be features of concerts throughout the nineteenth century.

By the end of the 1830s though, the Mansion House in Upgate had become the preferred venue for concerts. Here are the programmes for two:

18 July 1838
A Musical Soiree by Infant Trumpeter Master Phillips
[we do not know his age, but he was perhaps only a little older than Charlotte, who was then eight]
and Gentleman Amateurs.
Popular Airs of the present day with difficult variations composed by himself.
To give additional effect to the concertos he has engaged
Mr. G. Leng, Leader of the Hull Choral Society
and
Mr. J. Gleadow, Principal 2ⁿᵈ violinist from
the Hull Philharmonic and Choral Societies
[Children were admitted half price to this concert, so let's hope Charlotte went!]

Wednesday 24, Thursday 25 and Friday 26 July 1839
[A great many concerts at The Mansion House were performed on more than one day, or twice in a day, at this period. The venue

is not huge but, none the less, this indicates that large audiences were expected]

A Vocal and Miscellaneous Entertainment
An Exordium on Modern Improvements, Rail Roads and Steam Boats.
Song: The Wondrous Power of Steam
Sketches of Life and Character
Daniel O'Rourke's Dream
The Popular Irish Melody of Rory O'More
Law Trial or Slack v. Broadwood by Mr. Donaldson
In the course of the evening Miss. Bolton, whose vocal abilities have met with the most unqualified approbation in the chief fashionable Towns in England, and lately at Leicester and Grantham, will sing the
following admired and popular songs:
The Rose of Allandale
John Anderson
The Irish Melody of Savourneen Deelish
Young Susan Had Lovers
The Light of Other Days
Jock O'Hazledean
Black-Eyed Susan
Come dwell with me
Bright are the beams
Kate Kearney
Grace Darling, or the Wreck of the Forfarshire Steamer
Mr. Donaldson will give his imitation of [various actors in different roles]
A Negro Song: Sitch a getting up stairs
A Mono-Polylogue, in which Miss. Bolton will personate various characters in sketches of Irish Scenery, portraying the humour and peculiarities of the Green Isle…
The whole to conclude with God Save the Queen.
Children half price. Begin 8.30.

This particular concert is mentioned in their biography of Claribel in 1965 by Mrs Smith and Mrs Godsmark. They credit it with being the inspiration for Charlotte in her ambition to become a composer and performer.

There were non-musical entertainments as well, though. The date is uncertain, but around this time there was a visit by The Royal National Menagerie, amongst which were:

Lions, Tigers, Leopards, Hyaenas, Wolves, Racoons, Civet, Mancranco, Ant Eater, Sledge Dog, Great Ursine Baboon, Zebet Cat, The Great Girsley or Russian Monster of Siberia, several large serpents…one of them having swallowed six fowls at one meal, the Rhinorceros or Unicorn of Scripture and… a Gnu!

And on 24 September 1847 *Cooke's Equestrians* appeared in Louth:

In his new Char'-a'-bon (made in Paris) containing his brass band, followed by the Superb Dragon Carriage containing the huge monster St. George and the Dragon

There seem to have been three main threads of influence on popular song composers in the Victorian period: Scottish and Irish songs, the works of Handel and opera, Italian opera in particular. One might think that Louth was rather off the

beaten track when it comes to opera and certainly, that performance of Der Freischutz in 1834 notwithstanding, complete performances must have been few and far between. Performances of arias, even if in instrumental arrangements, were not so rare, however. These influences come together in one concert at The Mansion House in 1845, which is particularly interesting:

Evening and Morning Concert
Friday evening 8.00 p.m., January 31ˢᵗ and
Saturday morning February 1ˢᵗ at 2.00 p.m.
Includes Richardson's Rock Band
[Yes, that really does say 'Rock Band'. A pamphlet, 'to explain', was advertised as being available. It was a sort of xylophone which had a brief vogue at this period made of, well, a sort of rock.]

Rossini:	*Overture to L'Italiana in Algieri*
Strauss:	*Waltzes*
Donizetti:	*Fra poco*
	To che die spiegarvi
	Finale (Lucia di Lammermoor)
Muzard:	*Le Danoir Quadrille*
Messrs. Richardson: Medley on favourite Scotch and Welch Airs	
Haydn:	*God Preserve the Emperor*
Barnett:	*Original Irish Quadrilles*
Jullien:	*Original Polka*
Interval	
Rossini:	*Overture to Il Barbiere di Siviglia*
Jullien:	*Real Scottish Quadrilles*
Handel and Moore: The Harmonious Blacksmith, Sound the Loud Timbrel, Hark the Vesper Hymn	
Rossini:	*Zitti, Zitti, Piano, Piano (Il Barbiere di Siviglia)*
Jullien:	*Royal Irish Quadrilles*
Bellini:	*Ah, non giunge (La Sonnambula)*
	God Save the Queen

So what effect did all this have on Charlotte's ballads? It might be worth, first of all, thinking a little about the Victorian use of the word 'ballad'. Its traditional meaning is, of course, a song which tells a story, usually in four line stanzas (in present day folk clubs it usually has the added connotation of at least 30 verses and several corpses). In the seventeenth and eighteenth century broadside ballads were sold in markets to disseminate a political viewpoint or simply to publicise news stories. The words were printed on cheap paper and a tune suggested. During the nineteenth and twentieth centuries the meaning of the word very slowly changed and nowadays, in popular music at least, it means a sentimental song, usually slow. This change in meaning has been gradual, however. In 1915 the term still clearly had the rousing overtones of the broadside. Winston Churchill (then First Lord of the Admiralty) called on the Poet Laureate, Robert Bridges to write some 'patriotic ballads' to inspire the populace.

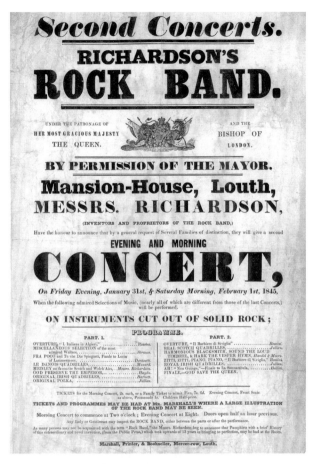

Fig. 4: Poster advertising Richardson's Rock Band at the Mansion House, Louth on 31 January and 1 February 1845

When Bridges refused Churchill suggested to Parliament that the Laureate's pension be axed and his remuneration revert to the traditional hogshead of sack in hopes that 'We may yet loosen his tongue'!

Many of Charlotte's, or should I say Claribel's most successful songs fall into the category of faux Scottish or Irish ballads. It is often assumed that the fashion for all things Scottish mirrored Queen Victoria's obsession with Scotland after her self imposed banishment to Balmoral following the death of Prince Albert in 1861. However, English interest in Scottish song dates at least from the late eighteenth century. Robert Burns was for many years engaged in collecting Scottish fiddle tunes and writing his own verses to them and these were always hugely popular south of the border. A generation later James Hogg, 'The Ettrick Shepherd', was doing the same thing. Indeed,

Charlotte Stainton Dolby, a friend of Claribel, who set a number of her poems, set one of Hogg's most famous verses, 'Come O'er the Stream, Charlie'. The Edinburgh publisher George Thomson commissioned Scottish folk song arrangements from composers such as Beethoven, Haydn and Hummel, although it is said that Beethoven hated doing them and only accepted the commission for the money! Those long evenings at the theatre in Louth in the 1830s also seem to have been incomplete without a 'Scotch Ballad': Kate Kearney (described as a 'favourite air' and performed on 5 January 1835), 'My heart is sair for somebody' (12 January 1835), Auld Robin Gray' and 'Last May a braw wooer' (14 January 1835)… and so on.

Irish songs had also been popular much earlier than the nineteenth century. The poet Thomas Moore achieved enormous success with his Selection of Irish Melodies, a huge collection which included such favourites as 'The Harp That Once Through Tara's Halls' and 'Oft in the Stilly Night', published between 1808 and 1834 with piano accompaniments by John Stevenson. The tunes were traditional with Moore writing new words. Welsh folk songs, though, seem to have been much less popular and interest in English folk music appears to have been negligible.

For two days in December 1852 The Mansion House (formerly known as the Assembly Rooms but in the middle and latter years of the twentieth century better known as the old public library) was the venue for

'George Barker's English Ballad Entertainment'
Lectures and songs, including Moore's Melodies.

Moore:	*Last Rose of Summer*
Rich and Rare were the Gems she Wore	
The Meeting of the Waters	
The Minstrel Boy	
Oft in the Stilly Night	
Through Erin's Isle	
Shakespeare's songs:	
Haydn:	*She never told her love*
Barker:	*Come live with me and be my love*
Barker:	*Blow, blow thou winter wind*
Arne:	*Under the greenwood tree*
Barker:	*Shall I compare thee to a summer's day?*
Barker:	*Sigh no more, ladies*

That was Tuesday. Wednesday's lecture covered:

The Ballad Music of England
Introduction: The musical characteristics of different Nations.
Distinguished Monarchs, Astronomers, Theologians etc. who have been composers. Opinion of Addison – Shakespere [sic] – Influence of music over the human heart.
Barker: The Dream of Life
The Poets of the East – Persia and its melodies – An Imitative

Example:
Barker: *The Rose of Cashmere*
Ireland and its minstrelsy – A Story of Emigration – The Pangs
of Parting
Barker: *The Irish Emigrant*
A Starry Night and its associations – The Music of the Spheres
– A Dream of the poets
Barker: *Beautiful Stars*
Ethiopian melodies – Peculiarities of this style of composition
– Their simple and affecting Character – Negro Pathos
– Popularity of the songs
Barker: *Mary Blane*
The Old Writers – Contrast between the Ancient and Modern
School of Song Writing
Barker: *Shall I wastynge in despair*
Part 2
The 'Lays of the Forest' or songs of Robin Hood
Mr. Barker will accompany himself on the pianoforte.
Between the first and second parts on each Evening Mr. Barker
will sing (by desire) his own celebrated song, 'The White Squall'
and his last new ballads, 'Lucy, the Slave Mother' and 'The
Lament for Eva' from 'Uncle Tom's Cabin'.

Schools admitted to the unreserved seats at half price.

Given that Mr Barker's lectures seem to have been illustrated entirely with his own compositions it is, perhaps, no surprise to learn that: ***Books of words of songs are available at 3d each.***

As a matter of fact, this is not the only example of what might now be called 'tie-in marketing'. It was advertised on the posters for a performance by Henry Russell, the 'Celebrated American Composer', at The Mansion House, which included 'anecdotes of Negro life and Character' that the Kirkman and Sons' 'newly invented Grand Fonda Piano [no, I'm afraid I don't know what a 'Fonda Piano' is either], bought expressly from London, will be used on this occasion and will be FOR SALE after the concert'.

Incidentally, the educational aspect of Mr Barker's performance seems to have become more and more a feature of concerts in Louth at this period partly, one suspects, because of the rise of the temperance movement. The Town Hall, opened in 1855, amongst other venues, hosted a great many temperance meetings and entertainments. It is interesting to note that Charlotte's father, Henry Pye, in *The Louth and North Lincolnshire Advertiser* of 12 November 1859, is listed as a subscriber to the Temperance Society in a report of its packed annual meeting at the Corn Exchange, although it must be said that his is not amongst the most generous of the donations listed.

Two typical evenings' entertainments with an educational flavour were:

The Mansion House May 30th to June 4th 1853

Gompertz's Panorama of the Invasion of British India
by the Sikh army of the Punjaub.
Accompanied by a splendid Sax-horn band, leader Mr. A. Young
A descriptive lecture by Mr. C.G. Bell
Diorama of The Great Fire of London and
The Crypt of the Holy Sepulchre at Jerusalem.

Both lectures begin at 8. Carriages at 10.

A concert presented at the Town Hall in October 1859 by the newly formed Louth Musical Union did not just involve music. Fifty stereoscopes were on display, exhibiting 200 views, as well as microscopes and 'philosophical apparatus' (thinking caps, perhaps?). It was, however, not well attended, according to *The Louth and North Lincolnshire Advertiser.*

During this period Louth was well provided for in the way of entertainment, musical and otherwise, with some big names appearing. In 1857 General Tom Thumb appeared at Louth Town Hall and several prominent musicians performed in the town. Also in 1857, for example, Sig. Alberto Randeggar, conductor of the opera houses of Turin and Brescia appeared at Louth Town Hall on 26 March. His name may not ring many bells now, but he is still familiar amongst singing teachers as he published a volume of singing exercises. A year earlier Michael Balfe, well known singer and composer of 'The Bohemian Girl', an opera phenomenally popular at the time and from which the aria 'I dreamt that I dwelt in marble halls' comes, had given a ballad concert in aid of the St James's organ. Many of these performers appeared in the town thanks to the efforts of a Mr Willey. *The Louth and North Lincolnshire Advertiser* of 23 April 1859, after lamenting that one of Mr Willey's concerts was, unusually, poorly attended, goes on to say 'we trust that one comparative failure will not damp the zeal of Mr Willey, considering his many brilliant successes, but he will continue to keep his eye upon the movements of the celebrities of the day, when they are in the humour to take a provincial tour, so that Louth may continue to maintain the honourable position in which this talented young tradesman has placed it, of being second to scarcely any town of its size for the number of first-class concerts, with which its first-class inhabitants are indulged, by first-class performers.' I assume that this Mr Willey is the C F Willey to whose Musical Warehouse audience members were directed, for example, by Henry Russell when he appeared 'for one night only' at the Corn Exchange in 1854:

All the … songs are published in the Musical Bouquet which may be had at C.F. Willey's Musical Warehouse. Books of the words 6d each.

Louth clearly had favourite performers who returned time and again during this period. Sam Cowell 'That Prince of Comic Song' *[Davidson's Musical Miracles, 120 comic songs sung by Sam Cowell, price 6d, or with music 1s, may be had with the Tickets]* made more than one appearance in the town, as did the sisters Sophia and Annie, who were clearly versatile performers. Their *Mimic and Musical Entertainment entitled Sketches from nature* presented sixteen characters in full costume over two hours, without a break. The songs ranged from 'O luce di quest anima' by Donizetti to 'I'm so troubled with the Rheumatiz'!

Claribel herself had been a frequent performer in Louth during her teens and early twenties, often in fund raising concerts in aid of the Mechanics Institute. After she moved to the capital she made return visits to the town and used her influence on the London musical scene to persuade some big names to perform. In 1862 two of the most famous singers of the day, Jenny Lind and Sims Reeve

gave a concert in Louth. Arias by Bellini and Donizetti featured in the programme as well as 'John Anderson, My Jo' by Robert Burns.

A composer whose works appear frequently in concerts of the period is, of course, Handel. Mr Braham's Farewell Concert at The Mansion House on 4 December 1846 is one example. The baritone Mr Braham had had the foresight to beget two sons, a tenor and a bass, which made for a balanced programme. The evening consisted of songs, arias and duets by Pergolesi, Rossini, Balfe, Lindley, Donizetti and H R Bishop, as well as selections from Wallace's 'Maritana' but the heart of the programme was works by Handel. Looking at volumes of music published for home music-making it is interesting to see how many Handel arias, from his operas as well as his oratorios, feature, as well as songs from earlier periods, such as by Purcell and Morley. Am I being fanciful in seeing reflections of Handel's 'Lascia ch'io piango' in Claribel's song 'Yes, we must part'?

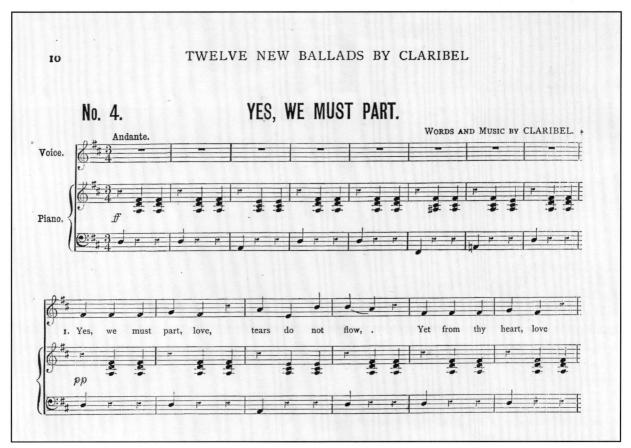

Fig. 5: The opening phrases of Claribel's ballad – 'Yes, We Must Part'

Fig. 6: Claribel's ballad 'Janet's Choice' was first published in 1859 and proved to be very popular and profitable

In the days well before recordings, the market for popular music was for sheet music but no one would buy the sheet music for a song unless they had heard it. One of Claribel's mock folk songs is a jaunty 6/8 ballad in folk song style, 'Five O'Clock in the Morning,' which talks of flirtation amongst rustics as they begin work – the 'old, old story'. This was one of Claribel's most successful songs, financially speaking, thanks to the efforts of the royalties system. Prominent singers were given a royalty on a song in return for which they would sing it in order to 'bring it before the public'. 'Five O'Clock in the Morning' was the royalty song of an opera singer named Euphrosene Parepa, who sang it to great effect in concerts hard on the heels of a Bellini aria. Such juxtapositions may seem strange to our sensibility, but Victorian audiences were used to them, just as the Georgian audience had been. 'Janet's Choice' is one of my favourite Claribel songs. It is a bouncy tune, again in a folky 6/8 time, with a distinct Scottish flavour, which tells the story of a girl who refuses to marry the laird, preferring to wed Donald, 'my own love', despite

the lure of jewels and status. This song spawned a reply from another composer, a practice typical of the period, which enabled Claribel to respond with 'Janet's Answer'. Such a money spinner was 'Janet's Choice' that Charlotte Stainton Dolby, a singer as well as a composer, bought outright the rights to the royalties on it.

The royalties system was not without critics, though. Even in Lincolnshire Charlotte was well aware of the debates raging in the London periodicals.

'The habit of giving singers a pecuniary interest in the music they sing is making it easier to cram some inane ballad into the ears of all and sundry and is keeping the popular taste low. The publisher suggests a song and pays him a royalty to sing some wishy-washy production. I have in mind a certain lady who since the royalty system gets ridiculous tunes sent by a non musical lady from the country. Publisher gives her 6d a copy for it. She sings it everywhere and everybody buys it.'
From *The Orchestra* 3 May 1868

Charlotte had her champions, though. Tom Hood wrote:

'it has been the fashion to sneer at Claribel and talk of her being

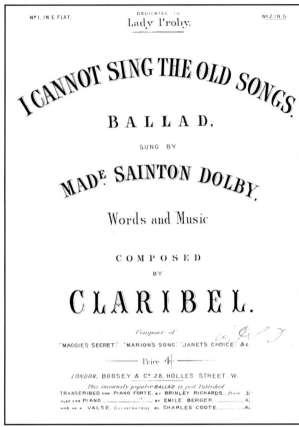

NO I. IN E FLAT.   DEDICATED TO   No 2. IN G
                                    Lady Proby.

I CANNOT SING THE OLD SONGS.

BALLAD,

SUNG BY

MADE SAINTON DOLBY.

Words and Music

COMPOSED

BY

CLARIBEL.

Composer of
"MAGGIE'S SECRET." "MARION'S SONG." "JANETS CHOICE" &c.

——— Price 4/ ———

LONDON, BOOSEY & C° 28, HOLLES STREET. W.

This immensly popular BALLAD is just Published
TRANSCRIBED FOR PIANO FORTE, BY BRINLEY RICHARDS... Price 3/-
ALSO FOR PIANO ————— BY EMILE BERGER ————— 4/
AND AS A VALSE. (ILLUSTRATED) BY CHARLES COOTE. ————— 4/

*Fig. 7:   Claribel's ballad 'I Cannot Sing The Old Songs'
was published in 1865 by Boosey & Co*

forced upon the public by the singers… The public cannot guess what a song is like until it is sung…it is absurd to talk of a singer being able to force a composer as a reviewer to force an author upon the public'.

Another writer, under the pseudonym Fairplay, also spoke up for Charlotte, although there was an element of damning with faint praise:

> 'Again, I maintain that Claribel's songs are not half so bad as you make them…after all, the public are judges of what they like…'

What Claribel's critics forgot, though, was that for amateur music makers at home her songs had a great deal to recommend them. They are not demanding to sing and even *I* can play the piano accompaniments!

This was 1868, however, and the blow of Henry Pye's disgrace was about to fall. After the family's flight to Europe they settled in Ostend, where Charlotte lost no time in enrolling in composition classes. Her songs provided an income for them all, but Charlotte was distraught at being exiled from home and hugely concerned for her father. In January 1869 she journeyed to England but on 8 February

The Louth and North Lincolnshire Advertiser, in amongst the advertisements for Holloway's Ointment and Pills, the Corn Market reports and the railway timetable, carried the following terse announcement:

> Deaths
> At Waterloo Crescent, Dover, on 30th ultimo
> Charlotte Alington,
> wife of Rev Charles Cary Barnard, Rector of Kirmington.

Charlotte had succumbed to typhoid fever. She was 38.

Have Charlotte's songs survived? Do they deserve to do so? Well, like many another Victorian ballad, some of Claribel's songs do not accord with modern tastes, being too whimsical, too sentimental or too maudlin. One such is 'The Passing Bell', a song about a child's deathbed which it is almost impossible to imagine singing now. Many of the others have real melodic flair and charm, however, and what they lack in harmonic sophistication is made up for with memorable and graceful tunes. The only song which is generally known, though, is 'Come Back to Erin', which was a great favourite of John MacCormack's. There is one delicious irony about this song. Claribel strove to write a convincing Irish folk ballad and she succeeded too well for her own good. Do an internet search on the title or look it up in a volume of songs and you are very likely to be assured that it is genuine traditional Irish song – no mention of Claribel at all!

Bibliography

Margaret Godsmark and Phyllis Smith, *The Story of Claribel*, Lincoln (1965).
Martin Loft, More about Claribel, *Lincolnshire History and Archaeology* Vol. 32 (1997).
David N Robinson, *The Book of Louth*, Barracuda Books (1979).

Acknowledgements

To Louth Museum for access to posters and handbills for concerts and theatrical performances and to Louth Library for access to microfilm copies of *The Louth and North Lincolnshire Advertiser* for the period.

Subscribers

The publication of *All Things Lincolnshire* has been made possible by the generosity of many individuals and organisations who have subscribed to the book. Our grateful thanks go to all of those listed below:

Mark Acton	Lincoln
P H Albone	Kirton-in-Lindsey
Margaret Anderson	Louth
Hilary & Jim Ashman	Louth
Geoff Atkin	Sleaford
Roger & Christine Audis	Bardney
Mr M E & Mrs H J Bailey	South Thoresby
Mr Iain Banks	Spilsby
Belinda Barnard	Lincoln
Edna & Raymond Barnard	Alkborough
Jeanne & Bob Bates	Scartho
Pauline & Tony Batten	Tillingham, Essex
Mr D Baxter	Grimoldby
Alexander Beeby M.A	Metheringham
Barry Beeby	Fiskerton
J W Belsham	Holbeach
Mark Bennet	Lincoln
Eleanor Bennett	Louth
Paul & Flora Bennett	Brackenborough Hall
M & P Berry	Middlemarsh, Burgh-le-Marsh
David & Hilary Beverley	Scunthorpe
Francesca & Paul Billings	Louth
Laurence & Jennifer Blanshard	
D G Boulton	Kirkby-on-Bain
Neil & Mary Boulton	Burgh-le-Marsh
Mrs L A Brabben BSc	
Miss Teressa Broddle	Louth
Derek Broughton	Lincoln
Ron & Marjorie Brown	Cleethorpes
Rodge Brownlow	Sturton-by-Stow
S Brumpton	Louth
Mr & Mrs J D T Butterworth	Horncastle
P G D Byllam-Barnes	Ashtead, Surrey
Rodney & Janet Callow	Lincoln
Mr F A Cawthorpe MA(Oxon)	Skegness
Dorothy Chadburn	Lincs Wildlife Trust
Reg & Margaret Chalkley	Spalding
Martin A Chapman	Saltfleetby
Mrs Jean M Childs	Nettleton
Lynne Clarke	Lincs Wildlife Trust
Peter & Jane Conner	Louth
Diane Conrad-Daubrah	Switzerland
Steve & Marion Cooney	Scamblesby

David Cotton	
Brenda Coulson	Lincoln
Mr & Mrs David Cressey	Saltfleet
Rex Critchlow	
Stuart E Crooks	Lincs Wildlife Trust
Mr & Mrs John Crozier	Marston
Joyce Cunliffe	Kenilworth
Steve & Helen Czornyj	South Thoresby
Mr Michael Davenport	Cote Hill Farm, Osgodby
Peter & Betty Davis	Tetford
Anthony John Dent	North Hykeham
Anthony Dixon	Wensleydale (formerly Louth)
Alan & Pam Drewell	Leeds
Ken & Mary Drinkel	Louth
Bruce Duncan	
Mrs G Dyson	Scunthorpe
Mr P & Mrs A E Ellershaw	Deeping St James
J W & E Ellis	Nettleham
Simon & Dilly Erskine Crum	Wellingore
Geoff & Gwen Espin	Colsterworth
Mr & Mrs D H Evans	Boston
Paul & Elizabeth Everson	Nantwich, Cheshire
Anne-Marie & Frederick Fearn	Tetney
Helen Fenning	Boston
Mrs E M Fenton	Scunthorpe
Helen Fenwick	Hull University
B H Ferrier	Cleethorpes
Douglas & Nancy Ford	Whaplode
Geoff & Jackie Freeman	Walesby
Donovan N Fry	Skegness
Andrew Gallop	Woolsthorpe by Belvoir
Dora & Tony Garner	Nottingham
Eddie & Joan Gaunt	Scunthorpe
Mrs Maureen Geeson	Louth
John & Pauline Ghest	Friskney
Stuart & Joan Gill	Kirkby-on-Bain
Robin Goodyear	Woodhall Spa
Cyril & Stella Gray	Market Rasen
John Joseph Green	Alford
Miss Angela Green	Scawby
Heather Grierson	Louth
Sue & Ken Griffin	Claxby
Robert & Margaret Gwynne	Louth
Brian Hall	Frieston
Mr G Hall	Grimsby
Mr J W & Mrs E Hall	Boston
Chris Hallgarth	Cleethorpes
M G Hammond	Middle Rasen
Michael Hanna	Lincoln
G Hardwick	Lincoln

Richard & Linda Hardwick — Louth
Peter & Joan Hargreaves — Radclive, Buckingham
Mr & Mrs J R Harrison — Legbourne
Mrs J M Harrison — Skegness
Jane Hawkes — Woodhall Spa
Michael & Janet Hawson — Louth
Joan Haxby — Louth
Josephine Hay — Glasgow
Miss Susan Hector — Muswell Hill, London
W B Herbert — Grimsby
Heritage Trust of Lincolnshire
Enid Hill — Woodhall Spa
Margaret & Geoff Hill — Louth
Mr & Mrs R Hillier — Peterborough
Geoff & Liz Hilton — Legbourne
Val Hinkins — High Wycombe
Mr & Mrs R J Hirst — Grantham
Ken Hollamby — Lincoln
Martin & Mary Hollingsworth — Kirton-in-Lindsey
David Hopkins — Heckington
Horncastle Civic Society
Jean Howard — Tathwell
Robert Hoyes — Stixwould
R L Hudson — East Ravendale
Rosemary & Douglas Huke — Louth
Mick & Ruth Hutson — Sleaford
R C & T M Isherwood — Laceby
Michael J Jackson — Mansfield
Mr & Mrs Ken James — Louth
Ian Jebbett — Sleaford
Dr Richard Jefferson — Bourne
Mary & Michael Jenkin — Lincs Wildlife Trust
K D Johnson — Lincoln
Ruth Johnson — Ashbourne, Derbyshire
David S Jones — North Carlton
Rhys & Laura Jones — Metheringham
David Kaye — Mayor of Louth 1998/9
Kenney George
John R Ketteringham — Lincoln
Winston Kime — Skegness
Paul King — Seal Sanctuary, Mablethorpe
Nigel & Sue Kirkman — Malmesbury
Drs J L & S M Knight — Collingham
Lawrie & Ann Lambert — Wragby
Roselle Lamle (née Cade) — Grimsby
Mrs E Lancaster — Sleaford
Susan Lane — Burton-by-Lincoln
Mark Richard Leggott — Holland Fen
Chris Lester — Newark
Mr & Mrs K Liddle — Grasby
Lincolnshire Archives — Lincoln
Lincolnshire Library Service
Mr & Mrs G Lindsay — Louth

Stephen Lorand — North Somercotes
Louth Naturalists', Antiquarian & Literary Society
K E Lowis — Lincs Wildlife Trust
Joan Lubin — Lincoln
Mrs P & Mr L Lyon — Scunthorpe
Simon & Sue Makinson-Sanders
Mr G & Mrs D Malkinson — Cherry Willingham
Frank W Marston
Michael May — Skegness
Teresa Maybury — Louth
Dr & Mrs M Mcgregor — Bourne
Janet Mckee — Grimoldby
Caroline Mckenna — London
Tony Merriman — Marrow, Middx.
Peter & Betty Middleton — Alford
Mid-Lincs Methodist Circuit
Revd J C Moon — Moulton
Dr & Mrs Michael Morgan — Great Steeping
J C Morgan — London
Cliff Morrison — Theddlethorpe
Stephen & Beryl Mugglestone — Mumby
Peter & Deborah Mullins — Grimsby
James Munton — Ruskington
Sally Munton — Osbournby
Miss Flora Murray — Lincoln
John & Margaret Needham — Louth Ants & Nats
Joan Newcomb — North Thoresby W.E.A.
Mr C Newton — Cleethorpes
Roger Norburn — South Elkington
J L & P Norman — Theddlethorpe
Deborah Normandale — Grimsby
North East Lincolnshire Council
Lord Norton of Louth — University of Hull/ House of Lords
Dr Richard Oliver — University of Exeter
John H Osgerby — Alford
Joan Osterfield — Burton-by-Lincoln
Jane Ostler — Woolsthorpe-by-Colsterworth
Arthur Owen
Angela Packer — Thorney Green, Suffolk
Revd Bill Page — Sibsey
Nigel Panting — Ruskington
Patricia A Parker — Lincoln
Ken & Jean Patience — Little Cawthorpe
Mrs Phyllis Peddie — Scunthorpe
Robert Pendell — Horncastle
Mrs J B Phillips — Louth
D W J Price Esq. — Harrington
Mrs Lesley T Raines — Louth
G Patrick Ranyell — Kirton-in-Lindsey
Brian Redman — Lincs Wildlife Trust

Ken Redmore — Nettleham
Jennifer Redpath — Grimsby, Lincs Wildlife Trust

R H K & Mrs J M Richards — Horncastle
Christine Rieser — Louth (LNU member)
Mrs E A Rogers — Louth
John Roper — Sheffield
Revd David & Vivienne Rowett — Barton on Humber
Mr & Mrs P D Rowett — Sibsey
Mrs E Rubery — Louth
Brian & Rosalind Ruffell-Ward — Irby-upon-Humber
Colin & Norma Rushby — New Waltham
Rex Russell — Barton on Humber W.E.A.

Tim Sands — Scothern
Joan Sanger — Beckingham
Sandra M A Sardeson — Heckington
C L & S Scott — Fiskerton
Janet & Graham Searston — Lincoln
L E & M P Sewards — Spilsby
E M Sharpe — Alford
Norah Sharpley — Louth
Mr J K Shaw — Wragby
Margaret Shuttleworth — Langton-by-Wragby
Bishop Grosseteste Univ College — Lincoln
Professor I G Simmons — Univ of Durham
Ann Simpson — Boston
Jack & Phyl Simpson — Horncastle
Janet Simpson — Gainsborough
Frank & Patricia Singleton — Waltham
Ellaline Sivil — C.P.R.E.
Mr & Mrs P Sizer — Louth
Mick Skipworth & Nicky Marshall — Benniworth
Diane Slater — West Torrington
Ian S Smart — Market Rasen
Christopher Smith — Louth Ants & Nats
Dr. Richard & Mrs. Rachel Smith — Little Staughton, Bedfordshire

Monica Smith — Horncastle
Mr Renny Smith — Goxhill
Miss W M Spilman — Lincoln
Mrs Queenie Spink — Tealby
Mr & Mrs P Sproston — Utterby
Richard & Anne Stamp —
David Start — Lincoln
Alan & Sue Stennett — Woodhall Spa
Keith J Stephenson — Langton-by-Wragby
David Stocker — Thorpe-on-the-Hill
Peter Stopp — Bishop Norton
Professor Allan Straw — Exeter
E H & Ian A Stubbs —
Donald Sutherland — Sutton Bridge River Trail Group

Mrs J Sutton — Middle Rasen

Heather Sykes — Lincoln
David J Symonds — Maltby-le-Marsh
Roger & Anna Tagg — Spilsby
Enid Tate — North Hykeham
Edward Taylor — Willoughton Local History Soc
Josie Taylor — Barton on Humber
Mr K W & Mrs C R Taylor — Lincoln
Peter J Taylor — Welton-le-Wold
Sarah Taylor — Willoughton Local History Soc
Ruth Tinley — North Hykeham
Michael Turland — Sleaford
Eileen & Dennis Turner — Horncastle
John Turner — Dunholme
Mark & Dinah Tyszka — Keelby
D van Baaren — Louth Ants & Nats
Mrs Elys Varney — Lincoln
M J Vickers — Lea
Mrs M Vincent — Horncastle
Stephen Vogt — Grantham
Ralph Wadsworth — Potterhanworth
Miss E T Wagstaffe — North Hykeham
Mrs Jean Waite — Waddingham
Andrew Walker — Univ of Lincoln
John & Helen Wall — Tetford
Jane Ward — Washingborough
Mr Barry Ward — Full Throttle
Thelma Warren — Weston Hills
Susan Watkin — Lincoln
Derek Wattam — Humberston
Graham Weaver — Louth
David & Joan Webb — Louth
David J Wedd — Framfield, E Sussex
Hazel & Phil West — Crowle
Richard T Westland —
Mr G Wheatley — East Keal
Pearl Wheatley — North Greetwell
F G White — Alford
Roy & Doreen Whitehall — Skegness, Burgh History Group

Anne Whittern — Louth
Justine Whittern — Louth
Norvel & Christine Willerton — Alford
H B Williams — Louth
R & M Willoughby — Tothby, Alford
Catherine & Peter Wilson — Reepham
Cynthia & Bob Wilson — Manby
Kate Witney —
David & Pat Wood — Alford
David Wright — Swineshead
Mrs Nora Wright — Sleaford Wildlife Trust
Neil & Sarah Wright — Lincoln

Index of Placenames and Personal Names